A Forest on the Sea

A Forest on the Sea

Environmental Expertise in Renaissance Venice

KARL APPUHN

The Johns Hopkins University Press

Baltimore

This book was brought to publication with the generous assistance of the Gladys Krieble Delmas Foundation.

The Johns Hopkins University Press
2715 North Charles Street
Baltimore, Maryland 21218-4363
www.press.jhu.edu

Library of Congress Cataloging-in-Publication Data
Appuhn, Karl Richard.
    A forest on the sea : environmental expertise in Renaissance Venice / Karl Appuhn.
       p. cm.
    Includes bibliographical references and index.
    ISBN-13: 978-0-8018-9261-5 (hardcover : alk. paper)
    ISBN-10: 0-8018-9261-9 (hardcover : alk. paper)
    1. Forest policy—Italy—Venice (Municipalità provvisoria : 1797)—History. 2. Forest management—Italy—Venice (Municipalità provvisoria : 1797)—History. I. Title.
    SD624.V37A67 2009
    333.750945'311—dc22

A catalog record for this book is available from the British Library.

Title page illustration: "View of Venice," from Bernard von Breydenbach, *Journey to the Holy Land* (Mainz, 1482). Courtesy of the Walters Art Museum, Baltimore, Maryland.

Special discounts are available for bulk purchases of this book. For more information, please contact Special Sales at 410-516-6936 or specialsales@press.jhu.edu.

CONTENTS

TABLES AND FIGURES

Tables

Figures

ACKNOWLEDGMENTS

I would like to thank the following institutions and grant agencies for their generous financial assistance during the decade I have spent researching and writing this book: USIA Fulbright, the Gladys Krieble Delmas Foundation, the American Academy in Rome, the Institute for Advanced Study, the Renaissance Society of America, the American Philosophical Society, the University of Oregon History Department's Meihoff Fund, the University of Oregon Junior Faculty Research Fund, and New York University's Goddard Fund. The Gladys Krieble Delmas Foundation also helped defray the costs of publication.

I would also like to thank the following archives and libraries. In Venice I used the collections of the Archivio di Stato, the Biblioteca Nazionale Marciana, and the Museo Civico Correr. In Belluno I used the collections of the Archivio di Stato, the Archivio Curiale Vescovile, and the Biblioteca Civica. And I would be remiss if I did not thank the staff at the Archivio di Stato di Venezia, in particular the indefatigable Renata, Antonio, and Marco, who retrieved countless boxes on my behalf and were always ready with a good word and a smile despite the constant staff reductions in their department. Unless otherwise noted, all translations are my own.

I have been fortunate to have had wonderful colleagues throughout my career. I would be remiss if I did not mention those who kept me going. At the Columbia Society of Fellows, Jordanna Bailkin, Greg Downey, Jonathan Gilmore, John Tresch, and Andrew Zimmerman all kept me sane at a difficult time. Steven Epstein, though technically not a colleague, also deserves special mention in this regard. At the University of Oregon, Matt Dennis, Jeff Hanes, Ellen Herman, Julie Hessler, David Luebke, Ian McNeeley, Jim Mohr, John Nicols, Jeff Ostler, Dan Pope, Martin Summers, Lisa Wolverton, and most of all Alex Dracobly were the very best colleagues anyone could wish for. At New York University,

Zvi Ben-Dor, Laurie Benton, Katy Fleming, Fiona Griffiths, Yannis Kotsonis, Karen Kupperman, Michele Mitchell, Molly Nolan, Leslie Peirce, Jeff Sammons, Joanna Waley-Cohen, and Larry Wolff still are.

Special thanks go to Ed Muir, who has been my most important intellectual and professional mentor. John Marino, Ken Alder, Rolf Strøm-Olsen, Alfredo Viggiano, Guido Candiani, Jason Moore, Giovanni Caniato, Michela Dal Borgo, and John Shovlin all provided advice and encouragement at crucial moments in the development of the project. Angelo Bassani passed on several references and hosted me in Venice when funds ran low. My father, Richard Appuhn, steadfastly read every one of the numerous drafts of the manuscript, including the several chapters that I wound up omitting altogether. All of these individuals contributed far more than I can say. All errors and omissions are, of course, mine alone.

My most heartfelt thanks go out to Maria Farland, who has been a true intellectual and emotional companion. It is no exaggeration to say that without her occasionally rough-edged advice, criticism, and encouragement, I could not have written this book. She pored over every draft, tirelessly hammered at my worst habits as a writer, made invaluable suggestions about the flow of the argument, and mercilessly pointed out the places where cuts could and should be made. Most of all, she believed in the project even when I feared that I might never finish it. I owe her a debt that cannot possibly be repaid.

NOTE ON DATES

Before 1797, the Venetian calendar year began on March first. For the purposes of clarity for the modern reader, I have converted the dates in the main body of the text so that all years begin on January first. In the notes I have indicated the equivalent dates in the Venetian style, to make the documents easier to locate in the archives. January and February dates that are in the Venetian style (*more veneto*) are followed by the abbreviation m.v.

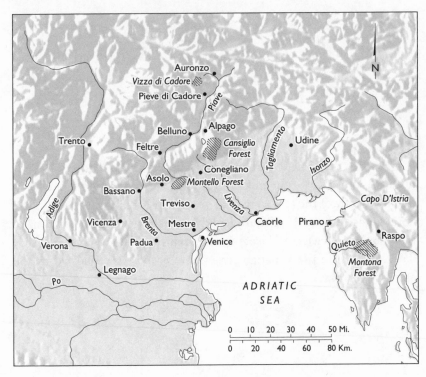

The Venetian *terraferma* and Istria, with major timber reserves
SOURCE: Adapted from Lane, *Venice*, 227.

A Forest on the Sea

Introduction

And thus oak that nature had toiled so long to
grow, and firewood too, were wantonly destroyed
by reckless harvesting and pasturing of animals,
so that forests are no longer worthy of the name,
but have become mere wilderness.

I N A REPORT DELIVERED before the Venetian Senate at the beginning of
the eighteenth century, the Venetian patrician Leonardo Mocenigo
decried the condition of the forests under the control of the Republic,
which at that time included northeastern Italy, the western half of the
Istrian peninsula, and much of the Dalmatian coast. Mocenigo had been
assigned to inspect Venice's forest resources and make recommendations
for improving their management. Mocenigo was outraged at what he
had discovered. He claimed to have seen forests stripped of the best
poles, animals pasturing in timber reserves, and local residents helping
themselves to firewood and other forest resources, apparently without
any regard for the many laws governing such activities. The problem
facing the Republic was not, he argued, simply a lack of forests. Instead,
the problem was that the unrestricted activities of local residents had
depleted the region's forests to the point where they no longer contained
the large oak and beech poles the Venetians needed to build ships and
maintain the critical system of levees and breakwaters that regulated the
influx of the tides into the lagoon and the city.

Mocenigo reckoned that Venice faced a critical shortage of high-
quality timber, especially oak, and his opinion has been echoed by later
generations—to the point that it has been taken for granted by nearly
everyone who has written about the history of the Republic. Conventional wisdom holds that at some point in the late seventeenth or early

eighteenth century, Venice simply ran out of the timber resources it needed to support a modern fleet, thus cementing the Republic's long, steady decline into provincial backwardness.

In the eighteenth century, the fear of crippling timber shortages plagued every European maritime power, but Venice was especially vulnerable, and, therefore, especially self-conscious about the prospect. Without access to the Baltic trade, and without suitable overseas colonies to exploit, the Venetians were forced to make do with what was available within the boundaries of their own relatively small territorial state.

In 1704, when Mocenigo composed his report, the importance of high-grade timber should have been on the mind of every Venetian senator. The Republic was about to embark on what would be its last major war against the Ottoman Empire, which meant the Arsenal needed to produce powerful heavy frigates to defend Venice's Peloponnesian possessions against the enemy fleet. Naval-grade timber was not a luxury in 1704; it was a necessity if the Venetians were to hold on to the last major piece of their once-extensive Mediterranean empire. As it turned out, the Venetians put between twenty and twenty-five new first- and second-rate warships into service, more than enough to hold off the weaker Ottoman fleet, but to no avail. Betrayed by the Austrians, who had designs of their own on Ottoman territory on the far side of Danube, the Venetians were forced to accept the permanent loss of their hard-won Peloponnesian territories in the peace negotiations at Passarowitz. The end of their Mediterranean empire did not signal the end of Venetian maritime power, however. The Republic continued to build mercantile and military vessels; continued to trade actively in the eastern Mediterranean despite aggressive competition from Atlantic fleets; and even fought one final naval war outside the Adriatic against Tunisian corsairs (1784–92). The Republic retained a presence on the sea throughout the eighteenth century, even if the idea of reclaiming its lost Mediterranean empire had become mere fantasy.

In an age in which the Republic retreated from active participation in the international scene into a safe condition of political neutrality, the Venetians still managed to build ships, maintain the complex lagoon infrastructure, and supply a city of around 150,000 inhabitants that was entirely surrounded by water with firewood and other low-grade forest products. The Republic's success in these endeavors points to one of the major problems with the assertion that the Venetian timber supply was in a state of acute crisis by the turn of the eighteenth century. The Venetians clearly continued to enjoy access to important sources of timber, despite the dire warnings of Leonardo Mocenigo and other patricians concerned about the imminent destruction of the region's forests.

That Mocenigo believed deforestation represented a serious threat to the Republic is entirely understandable. On his tour he would have seen evidence of a good deal of recent harvesting in mainland forests. Over the previous half century both the Republic and private parties had purchased large quantities of naval-grade timber from private suppliers, stripping many mainland forests of their best oak trees. Private suppliers had been less scrupulous about how they harvested than Mocenigo would have liked. They preferred to clear-cut rather than selectively thin because the cleared land could be converted to more profitable uses such as cereal production, pasture, or viticulture. Consequently, many areas harvested by private suppliers on behalf of both the Republic and private shipbuilders no longer supported the durmast oak the Venetians needed to build and maintain ships and breakwaters. Nevertheless, the total stock of oak on the mainland was not so very different from what it had been two centuries earlier. It was distributed differently, to be sure. A much smaller proportion of it was found on privately held lands, and a good deal more stood in large public reserves that had been established over the course of the fifteenth and sixteenth centuries. Moreover, while in the middle of the seventeenth century the age distribution of oak in mainland forests had been tilted towards larger poles, by the beginning of the eighteenth century younger growth dominated. The stock was there, but until hundreds of thousands of immature poles reached a suitable size it was, in practical terms, far less useful than it would later become. In this sense, the crisis of which Mocenigo spoke was not nearly as evident as he claimed. Mocenigo's insistence on defining the situation in such terms was mostly because, on the eve of war, he was more concerned with immediate needs than future supplies. Nonetheless, he did not even consider the new growth worthy of mention during his appearance before the Senate.

In retrospect, the question that arises from Mocenigo's report is not why the mainland forests were in such terrible condition in 1704. Rather, one might ask why Mocenigo could not see that in many respects the

Venetian forest patrimony was in good health. Certainly it was not due to lack of information. He had personally inspected most of the mainland forests that supplied the Arsenal with material for naval construction and the city with firewood. Moreover, in the early eighteenth century, Venice boasted the oldest and most sophisticated forestry bureaucracy in Europe. Although northern European foresters, especially in German-speaking lands, would soon claim to possess the greatest and most comprehensive knowledge of forestry in the Western world, in 1704 Venetian forest managers could still confidently assert their singular expertise in this important field of bureaucratic knowledge. Forests in Venetian territory were overseen by a set of institutions whose sole purpose was to collect, analyze, and act upon information about the timber resources available to the Republic. Indeed, Leonardo Mocenigo had conducted his inspection partially under the aegis of those very institutions. Yet despite the fact that Mocenigo was well acquainted with the workings of Venice's forestry regime, he returned from his inspection convinced that Venetian institutions had failed, and that the Republic faced an immediate and almost irremediable problem with deforestation.

The situation, as I have already indicated, was far more complex than Mocenigo's report might suggest. In the centuries before Mocenigo departed on his inspection tour, the forests of northeastern Italy, which were almost entirely under the control of Venice, had already been intensively, extensively, and repeatedly exploited by commercial interests, local communities, private landowners, ecclesiastical and secular institutions, as well as the agents of the Venetian Republic. Beginning in the early fifteenth century, the Venetians had begun to develop a coherent set of ideas about local practices of forest exploitation and a set of policies to govern them that would largely determine the condition and composition of the region's forests in the coming centuries. By 1704 the effects of nearly 300 years of direct Venetian interference were clearly visible in the landscape. But as Mocenigo's report illustrates, the results of Venetian efforts to regulate regional patterns of forest exploitation were not always exactly what the policies' architects might have hoped for. The gap between results and expectations lead to periodic efforts to reform the system through new laws governing mainland forest exploitation practices. Mocenigo's report represents one such instance, and it did, in fact, lead to an attempt to reform existing laws. Thus Venetian policies constantly sought to respond to perceived changes in the regional environment, resulting in still further changes to the forest cover, in an ongoing dialectic between politics and environment in which Venice played the leading role between 1350 and the fall of the Republic in 1797.

The panic expressed by Mocenigo and other members of Venice's ruling class was in part the product of looking at the constantly changing forest landscape as if it were static. The limits of Mocenigo's understanding of the temporary nature of the crisis led him and many other Venetians to overstate the scarcity of timber on the mainland. Such overstatements have drawn many historians of Venice into the erroneous belief that the Republic faced a permanent timber crisis, when in reality the problems were both more complex and more fleeting. To gain a better perspective on the forest landscape under the control of the Republic, then, historians must look beyond a report written in 1704, or any other year for that matter, to the long-term trends in forest exploitation that produced the forests seen by Mocenigo. In other words, scholars need to pay close attention to the ongoing interaction between Venetian knowledge concerning forests, the policies produced by that knowledge, local practices of forest exploitation throughout the northeast, and the regional environment itself to gain a fuller understanding of why mainland forests looked the way they did when Mocenigo inspected them in 1704—to say nothing of evaluating what prospects may have existed for solving the problems he identified.

During the three centuries leading up to Mocenigo's inspection, European demand for timber, fuelwood, and other forest resources was higher than it had ever been before. The list of commodities that Europeans routinely extracted from their forests is too long to elaborate here, but the preindustrial era was very much the age of wood. In most of Europe, it provided the building blocks for every town and city, fueled nearly every industry, and heated nearly every home. The forest also yielded fruit, game, summer pasture, winter fodder, and green fertilizer (or mulch) for agriculture. Even if the forest was not always at the center of people's thoughts, it was at the center of their existence.

Timber was especially crucial for Venice. Its centrality to Venetian life and prosperity was almost universally apparent to Renaissance observers. Venetian chroniclers of the period made a point of remarking on particularly conspicuous instances of timber consumption, precisely because they understood how difficult it was to secure, extract, and mobilize forest resources. In a famous example, one of the Venetian witnesses to the Ottoman capture of Negroponte in 1470 described the Turkish fleet of some 300 ships that presented itself at the entrance to the harbor as "a forest on the sea: when described incredible, but when seen stupefying."[1] For a Venetian reader, the image of a forest on the sea functioned simultaneously as a metaphor for the impressive size of the enemy fleet and as a literal account of the astonishing volume of timber required to build it. The turn of phrase could easily apply to Venice itself: a Republic built on forests, a forest on the sea. The city stands on a foundation of millions of wooden piles brought in from the mainland. Larch, alder, and oak beams compose the structural core of Venice's famous palaces and churches. The thousands of boats that supplied all the basic services to the city—including food and fresh water from the mainland—and the tens of thousands of mooring pylons to which the boats were tied were likewise manufactured from material that originated in mainland forests. As one of the largest centers of manufacturing in the preindustrial world, Venice was also one of Europe's largest commercial consumers of wood-based fuel. The city's 150,000 inhabitants relied exclusively on firewood to supply the thermal energy needed for survival—cooking as well as domestic heating in the bitter cold of the Venetian winter. The Republic also built and maintained extensive breakwaters on the littoral islands to fend off winter storm surges and regulate seasonal flooding, an effort that required ever-increasing numbers of oak piles each year. Finally, Venice continued to operate one of the largest merchant and military fleets in the Mediterranean, a fleet built almost entirely at public expense from timber harvested in public reserves on the mainland.

Two additional factors must be kept in mind in order to place Venetian demand for timber in proper perspective. First, unlike other European naval powers of the eighteenth century, Venice possessed a fixed resource base. The Dutch, English, French, and even the Spanish all had access to extensive foreign supplies of naval-grade timber—whether through the Baltic trade or from overseas colonies. Venice did not enjoy access to either. Venice's lack of colonial timber sources emphasizes that while scholars have traditionally referred to the Republic's maritime possessions as an empire, Venice's limited imperial reach paled in comparison to those of its Atlantic rivals. The Venetians acquired nearly all of their fuel and timber from their Italian territories. More importantly, they did so within the context of a shared set of legal and political traditions and with the active cooperation of the residents of their subject towns and villages. Venice's relationship with the *terraferma* may escape easy definition, but it was emphatically not that of an imperial metropole to its colonial possessions. Second, Venetian demand for timber resources was not static. If the limits to urban growth imposed by the lagoon environment kept the city's population from expanding, then industrial growth, changes in naval technology, and the worsening effects of seasonal flooding in the lagoon ensured that Venetian timber consumption continued to increase, reaching its peak in the first half of the eighteenth century—long after most scholars suppose that the Republic ran out of usable timber resources.

Given the long-term trajectory of Venetian demand for timber and the lack of opportunity to expand the resource base, it should come as no surprise that the forests in the region controlled by the Republic had been dramatically altered when Leonardo Mocenigo departed on his inspection tour. What is perhaps surprising is that any forests of significant size still stood in Venetian territory. In some areas of the Venetian *terraferma*, only a few small patches of community forest remained by the late seventeenth century. The Venetians, however, had not sat idly by while forests were cleared. Between 1350—when the first piece of legislation related to timber consumption was passed—and the fall of the Republic in 1797, Venice went from an isolated city completely dependent on foreign suppliers for timber and firewood to a regional state with a sophisticated system of administrative controls aimed at preserving forests. As accelerating agricultural and industrial growth, as well as increasing state consumption, put pressure on the region's forests, the Venetian government attempted to expand its control over the environment to preserve dwindling forest resources and prioritize their use. The result was that despite ever-increasing pressure to harvest, many large forest preserves, some of which still stand today, survived under state protection.

Taking into account the unprecedented demands placed on the forests and forest resources under the control of the Republic of Venice, a strong case can be made that Mocenigo asked the wrong question as he formulated his report. Instead of inquiring why there were so few forests left, he might just as easily have asked why there were so many. What Mocenigo does not seem to have considered is that the Venetian Republic had done far more than any other European state to implement a program of forest conservation, and it thereby managed to preserve what, by eighteenth-century standards, amounted to an impressive public forest patrimony—especially considering the small size of the Republic's territorial state. There was, in fact, no obvious ecological calamity occurring or about to occur, even though the conditions for such an event were clearly present. By all rights the Venetians should have been facing a grave timber shortage—accompanied by widespread land degradation, sheet erosion, and alluvial sedimentation—yet they were not.

How is it that the Republic of Venice managed, for the most part, to avoid a major timber crisis? This is a problem worth thinking about, and it is the central question this volume attempts to answer. *A Forest on the Sea* explores the Republic's forestry regime from two main perspectives. First, it examines the problem of forest conservation from the standpoint of the state. Venice had to overcome a vast array of practical, legal, and institutional challenges in order to exert direct control over the most important forest resources in its territories. The book analyzes these challenges and deciphers the administrative logic that informed Venetian efforts to monitor and manage local practices of forest exploitation in order to understand the presuppositions about the relationship between human action and the natural world that underpinned those efforts. Second, it investigates the problem of forest management from the point of view of a growing cadre of bureaucratic experts possessing special knowledge about forests in general as well as about specific forest landscapes. In an attempt to track the most important and the most vulnerable timber resources, the Venetians developed a fully articulated bureaucracy dedicated exclusively to forests. *A Forest on the Sea* uncovers Venetian assumptions regarding what constituted reliable expertise about the natural world, and it inquires into the empirically-based technologies of knowledge production used by this new forest bureaucracy to construct meaningful narratives about environmental changes in the most important forest landscapes. Venetian forestry officials employed two basic technologies for monitoring changes in mainland forests: quantitative surveys and mapping techniques. The book examines the way in which the Venetians wielded these two technologies in order to uncover how they understood the operations of the natural world. Ultimately, this volume argues that Venice's forest bureaucracy developed a unique view of the relationship between humans and the natural world that stressed the preservation of nature, as opposed to the more familiar philosophy of profit-driven improvement that characterized northern European attitudes towards nature in the seventeenth and eighteenth centuries. This uniquely Venetian attitude, which I call "managerial organicism," offers an important corrective to standard accounts of changing European attitudes towards the natural world during this period—especially Carolyn Merchant's seminal work, *The Death of Nature*—nearly all of which argue that European efforts to manage nature were universally a product of some combination of Baconian mechanism and colonial encounters with new and unfamiliar landscapes.[2]

States, Economies, and Nature

Venice was not the only European state to register alarm at the prospect of shortages in timber and timber products. From the English royal forest ordinances of the thirteenth century to Colbert's famous forest reforms of the seventeenth, the history of medieval and early modern Europe is replete with examples of rulers expressing concern over the condition of forests in their domains. Yet Venice remains the most remarkable instance because, prior to the late seventeenth century, Venice was the only European state to implement a large-scale forest conservation regime backed by a professional bureaucracy devoted entirely to its enforcement. The Venetian case merits our full attention for this alone. That the Venetian system was in many respects a success makes it all the more worthy of study.

Environmental historians have long been interested in landscape as an index of social, political, and economic transformation. This topic has attracted significant scholarly attention, from the early works of Alfred Crosby, William Cronon, and Carolyn Merchant to more recent works by Richard Grove, Warren Dean, Robert Marks, Brett Walker, John Richards, and Paul Warde. The relationship between the emergence of market economies backed by strong centralized states and global environmental change is now widely recognized as one of the most distinctive and important developments of the seventeenth and eighteenth centuries.[3] From Brazil's Atlantic forest to southern China's river valleys, from New England's farms to Russia's steppe frontier, early modern communities everywhere were irrevocably altering the landscape in the service of growing core populations and emerging commodity markets. This was especially true in sparsely populated frontier regions—what Jason Moore has called the "commodity frontier"—where settlers and merchants alike could extract apparently underexploited resources for the use and benefit of a growing economy of consumption centered on Eurasian metropoles.[4]

In spite of the existence of a broad consensus regarding the historical importance of changes to the global environment in the sixteenth through eighteenth centuries, environmental historians often disagree on their origins and larger significance. Many scholars have situated their narratives in the context of European expansion to other parts of the globe. The idea that a new European rational-scientific view of the natural world coupled with emergent capitalism drove alterations to the environment on a global scale during these centuries has long constituted a basic assumption for historians such as Merchant, Crosby, and Cronon.[5] As Robert Marks has pointed out, while the work of these scholars was often intended to critique celebratory accounts of the rise of the West, they nonetheless take it for granted that the engine of historical and, in this case, environmental transformation had its origins in European power and European culture.[6] The environments and peoples that Europeans encountered as they expanded into other regions of the globe, so the story goes, had to either bend to the imperatives of European markets and European views of nature or perish. Such accounts make tidy and satisfying narratives, but they also assume that there was a monolithic European view of the relationship between humans and the natural world that led inexorably down a single path to the unfettered exploitation of nature. Here the Venetian story is especially instructive, because it reveals that European culture, whatever one takes such a phrase to mean, could lead down multiple paths.

In Venice, as elsewhere, an expanding state and a new economy were transforming the regional environment. Yet Venice stands out from the rest of Europe because of the way that the Republic chose to approach the period's challenges. With limited opportunities to expand into the nearby Balkan frontier and no alternate sources of energy or building material, Venice charted a course that diverged significantly from those being pursued by many other European states in the early modern era. As demographic and economic pressures increased, the Republic opted for a strategy of conservation rather than one based on securing and exploiting foreign sources of timber. While the rest of Europe sought critical resources, including timber, in ever-more-distant locales, the Venetians concentrated on making the most of what was close at hand. This fact alone ought to single out the Venetian case for attention, because it demonstrates that there was no normative European response to the challenges posed by resource scarcity in the sixteenth and seventeenth centuries. By examining the history of Venetian forest management, it becomes possible to see that there is nothing inherent in European scientific or economic culture during this period that dictated the kinds of destructive exploitation of natural resources that occurred in other parts of the continent and globe. Such developments were contingent on a host of local political, social, and environmental conditions; they were not the necessary and inevitable result of a monolithic worldview based on the new philosophy of the seventeenth century.

Carolyn Merchant calls the form of forest exploitation that emerged in England and other northern European states in the late seventeenth century "a new managerial approach to nature" that "represented an accommodation of the old organic philosophy to the new mechanism."[7] While Merchant is undoubtedly correct in noting that European states adopted increasingly manipulative approaches to the natural world, the history of the Venetian forestry regime casts doubt on the universality of her explanation for two reasons. Despite the fact that when it came to questions of resource conservation, the Venetians rejected most of the fundamental assumptions about nature that underpinned the new mechanism, the Republic's forestry regime remained every bit as managerial as those found in England, France, or Prussia. Indeed, the Republic had already developed a highly regulatory approach to the forests of the *terraferma* by the 1560s, long before the triumph of the new philosophy or Baconian mechanism. Consequently, no link exists between Baconian mechanism and the Venetian version of managerial forestry. In addition, far from rejecting the traditional organic view of the natural world in favor of a managerial approach, the Venetians remained committed to an organic understanding of the world well into the eighteenth century—a view that emerges quite clearly in the writings of the Republic's forest bureaucrats. Thus Venice's forestry regime was not an example of what Merchant calls "the sell-out of organicism."[8] Rather, it represented the persistence of traditional organicism in a managerial context. The peculiar form of managerial organicism that emerged out of Venetian efforts to survive as a small republic in a world that was increasingly dominated by large national monarchies with access to the Atlantic trade and its vast commodity frontier was clearly a product of the Republic's particular geographical and political circumstances. But in this context Venetian exceptionalism serves to emphasize the contingency of northern Europe's mechanistic turn in the seventeenth and eighteenth centuries. The Venetian view of nature was the product of an insular society, deeply conscious of its limitations and of the fragility of its natural resources. But Venetians also believed that solutions to its most pressing environmental problems could be found through state-directed efforts at environmental conservation, informed by a set of republican institutions that sought to preserve nature rather than improve it.

While the Venetian case stands out in the European context, it is not unique in the broader history of forest management. A remarkable analog to the Venetian forestry regime during this period was developing on the other side of Eurasia, in Tokugawa Japan. The Tokugawa forestry regime is better known and understood than Venice's, thanks in large measure to the pioneering work of Conrad Totman. In *The Green Archipelago*, one of the classic works of forest history, Totman traces the emergence of institutions and practices of forest conservation in early modern Japan.[9] The parallels with Venice are striking. The resource base available to the Japanese was largely static, while demand for a variety of timber products—including construction material, green fertilizer, and fuelwood—was on the rise due to an expanding economy backed by an increasingly centralized political authority. Like the Venetians, the Japanese responded by implementing a variety of conservation measures aimed at preserving and renewing timber resources. The Tokugawa forestry regime attempted to curb consumption by restricting access to timber resources, as well as to promote forest renewal through new management techniques, including selective thinning and commercial replanting of prized species. While there are differences between the two forestry regimes—the Venetians were better cartographers, while the

Japanese were far more successful at reforestation, for instance—the similarities far outweigh them.

The remarkable parallels between Renaissance Venice and Tokugawa Japan reinforce an argument that Asian historians such as Robert Marks have been making for some time: that most, if not all, claims to European exceptionalism are a result of a lack of perspective on the part of historians of the West. Environmental historians of Asia have been particularly successful at demonstrating how patterns of environmental transformation and exploitation that historians have long associated with European expansion were, in fact, emerging in Asia well before the putative rise of the West.[10] So despite the fact that this book focuses on a relatively small region of Europe, the story it tells is one, I believe, that has global resonance.

Such apparently disparate states as Renaissance Venice and Tokugawa Japan, responding in such similar ways to a common set of environmental constraints, suggests that environmental historians need to pay more attention to structural factors when constructing their narratives. It also implies that environmental history offers a particularly promising avenue through which to pursue world history, because environmental historians can effectively situate local and regional studies in a comparative global context. To make such comparisons possible, however, historians must undertake their regional and local studies with an eye towards similar developments elsewhere on the planet, something that can only happen if we consent to read outside of the traditional geographic limits of our fields. These comparisons also assume that the cases being studied, such as Tokugawa Japan and Renaissance Venice, are equally well understood.

If the Tokugawa example is well known, the history of Venetian forest management remains relatively obscure. There are several reasons why historians have ignored the Venetian forestry regime for so long. The most obvious is that for practically all of the last century, Venetian history has too often been taken to mean the history of the city. Only in the last two decades have scholars systematically begun to investigate the relationship between Venice and its subject territories, both on the peninsula and in the Mediterranean.[11] The proliferation of studies of the Venetian *terraferma* and *stato da mar* clearly constitutes a much-needed development in Venetian historiography. Nevertheless, most of these studies have tended to focus on a single city or, in the case of the *stato da mar*, a single island. Historians of Venice have yet to tackle the problem of the Venetian mainland state as a whole. Consequently, a subject like the Venetian forestry regime, which perforce requires a broader regional perspective, still lies outside the frame of reference employed by most *Venezianisti*.[12] I argue, however, that the role the mainland territories played in securing the material underpinnings of Venetian life was at least as important as the political institutions, culture, and maritime trade that constitute the traditional concerns of Venetian studies. Any account of Venetian history that does not, in some way, acknowledge this basic fact only tells part of the story.

The lack of attention paid to Venice as a regional state has contributed to the marginalization of the Venetian Republic in the wider literature on early modern state development by making it easy for scholars to dismiss it as a historical anachronism. Indeed, by the eighteenth century, Venice was something of a curiosity by European standards: a small, independent republic in a political landscape dominated by much larger national monarchies. Moreover, it does not seem to have possessed many of the institutional markers that scholars have identified as distinctive in larger northern European states. In short, Venice does not fit into many traditional narratives of European political development.

Venetian exceptionalism has conditioned the way historians think about the Republic and its relatively small territorial state. Because it does not conform to the northern nation-state model, Venice is seen as a failure in the realm of state development. This presumes that there was ultimately a single organizational path to political modernity—whether or not one assumes that political modernity is a desirable outcome.[13] To maintain this position, scholars must argue that smaller states, such as Venice, that do not conform to the northern European model can be explained away as anomalous survivors of a bygone era. Variance from the nation-state model explains failure in the scramble for political and military supremacy in seventeenth- and eighteenth-century Europe.

This emphasis on difference elides the important ways in which a small state like Venice was similar to a large national monarchy like France. The attempt to organize the administration and distribution of natural resources such as timber is one important similarity between all human societies, regardless of size or institutional organization. If anything, the need to create a workable system for the exploitation of timber was far more pressing in Venice, with its small, isolated state, than it was for northern European states, nearly all of which enjoyed access to foreign sources of timber or, in the case of Britain, alternate sources of fuel such as peat and coal. It is not surprising, then, that an organized institutional response to timber and fuelwood shortages emerged in Venice well before similar developments in northern Europe. Moreover, the Venetian response to the administrative challenge of forest management was at least as effective as the later responses of larger European states—at least if the measure of effectiveness is the preservation and reproduction of critical forest resources. The Venetian approach to forest management bears scrutiny, therefore, not only for the perspective it offers on global environmental history, but also as the basis for a meaningful understanding of the premodern European state that escapes the Weberian trap of the nation-state model in favor of a model based on a comparison of the processes by which different states sought to solve common problems.

Chronology

The chronological sweep of this book is necessarily vast. This is unabashedly a work of *longue durée* history, and it is, therefore, inevitable that many readers will be unhappy with the lack of detail on certain points. Perhaps a far more expansive version of this book could satisfy all readers by explaining at greater length all the local variations and exceptions to the procedures and policies described herein, but only at the cost of a coherent narrative and accessibility. I would only point out that if one looks at the book in terms of the maturation of the durmast oak the Venetians needed to build their ships and breakwaters, the bulk of it covers a mere five or six generations. Moreover, because the focus here is on the lives of institutions and the ideas that they produced, only a broad focus will do.

I should also explain the major events that frame much of what follows. These will be familiar to Venetianists, but may require some explication for others. Before 1400, Venice had direct control of virtually no mainland territory. Venice's political and economic ambitions focused almost exclusively on the sea. Between the Fourth Crusade in 1204 and the end of the War of Chioggia in 1380, Venice was principally concerned with achieving a dominant trading position in the eastern Mediterranean. To this end, the Venetians fought a series of wars against the Genoese, culminating with the *Serenissima*'s victory at Chioggia. This victory emphasized Venice's control of the seas, but it also exposed its vulnerability on the mainland. The Genoese, aided by their Paduan allies, had successfully cut the Venetians off from the mainland for nearly two years. The lagoon prevented Venice's enemies from entering the city, but it also helped the besieging forces isolate the city and its inhabitants from the mainland. The Venetian victory came just in time to stave off defeat.

More than anything else, it was the experience of near defeat in the War of Chioggia that drove the Venetians to expand onto the mainland. While the Venetians remained cautious at first, by 1404 they had committed to the conquest of a mainland state. In 1424 the boundaries of their mainland state were largely established. The Venetians had carved out a territory stretching from Bergamo in the west to the Friuli and parts of the Istrian peninsula in the east.

Despite this mainland conquest, the Venetians remained fully committed to the sea. The fifteenth century was a golden age for Venetian trade. The Italian states had apparently achieved political and military stability following the Peace of Lodi in 1454; the Levant was also relatively stable under the Ottomans and the Mamluks; the Ottomans had not yet become a naval power capable of disrupting Venetian trade; the Portuguese had yet to round the Cape of Good Hope; and the Habsburg and Valois had not yet begun to use Italy as a battleground.

The conditions underpinning economic and political stability disappeared in rapid succession at the end of the fifteenth century. In 1494 Charles VIII of France descended into Italy, forever disrupting the balance of power between the Italian states. In 1498 the Portuguese discovered the Cape route, marking the beginning of the end of the Venetian stranglehold on the Eastern luxury trade. In 1499 the Ottomans handed the Venetians their first major naval defeat in two centuries at the battle of Zonchio. Then, in 1509 at Cambrai in France, the Pope brought all the major European powers except England into an alliance against Venice. The French returned to Italy and routed the Venetians at the battle of Agnadello, temporarily driving them back to the shores of the lagoon. But unlike the situation 1494, this time the French did not leave, and Italy became Europe's battlefield for the next fifty years.

In spite of the continued presence of French and Habsburg troops on the peninsula, the Venetians recouped their mainland state relatively quickly. By 1517 they had recovered nearly all that they had lost in 1509. Moreover, the Venetian Republic was the only Italian state to retain its political and military independence in the face of French and Spanish power. Political survival, however, could not hide the devastating effects of Agnadello. Venetian pride and confidence were shattered. In little more than twenty years, Venice fell from the ranks of the great European powers to second-class status. In 1494 Venice had been the dominant naval and commercial power in the Mediterranean and an important regional force in continental politics. By 1517 it had lost both distinctions.

The events of these two decades open up the third phase of Venetian history. The loss of economic preeminence in the Mediterranean and Europe, along with a new feeling of military and political vulnerability on the mainland, drove the Venetians to refashion their state. Political and fiscal control of their mainland territory, which had only been loosely exercised in the fifteenth century, became a dominant consideration in Venetian politics during the sixteenth century. In addition, the decline of the Mediterranean carrying trade drove many Venetians to invest in manufacturing and mainland property at unprecedented levels. Thus in the sixteenth century Venice, for the first time, became inextricably entwined with its mainland state. This transformation was felt not only in the political and economic arenas, but in the social and cultural ones as well, as Venetian patricians began to imitate the tastes and activities of their mainland counterparts. Traditionally this period has been seen as one of decline, but more recently this characterization has been qualified. The sixteenth century is now understood to have been a period of intense political, economic, social, and cultural transformation in Venice. Moreover, the continued prosperity of the Republic and its patriciate would seem to argue against the simplistic notion that Venice had declined, at least outside of the larger realm of European politics.

The term "decline" is now normally reserved for the next phase of Venetian history, which began in the second half of the seventeenth century with the loss of Crete to the Ottomans during the War of Candia (1648–69). Crete was the Venetians' last significant eastern Mediterranean possession, and the loss of prestige that accompanied its capitulation to the sultan's forces far outweighed its by-then minor economic and military importance. In the fifteenth century, Crete had been essential to Venetian ambitions in the East because it furnished a safe harbor where the great galleys with their immense crews could take on supplies and refit. By the seventeenth century, the Venetians had largely made the transition to square-rigged merchantmen, whose greater autonomy made the Cretan harbors superfluous. More important than the loss of Crete was the seventeenth-century economic depression that afflicted the entire Mediterranean region. The depression hit Venice's sizeable manufacturing sector particularly hard and thereby significantly reduced the Republic's tax base, which relied heavily on imposts on manufactured goods and trade.

Despite the loss of political and economic power, the Venetians struggled to preserve and consolidate what remained of their maritime possessions. They fought two more major wars against the Ottoman Empire, commonly referred to in Venice as the two wars of Morea (1684–99 and 1704–18). The wars resulted in a temporary expansion of Venetian territories in western Greece and the Peloponnese and the permanent acquisition of parts of inland Dalmatia. The cost of these adventures, however, was enormous. To meet the mounting expenses associated with a constant state of war, the Venetians were forced to sell off significant tracts of public land. Consequently, they loosened their grip on the mainland state, reversing, to some degree, the administrative reforms that had followed in the wake of the Cambrai crisis.

The economic news was not all bad. In the wake of Venetian naval victories in the two wars of Morea, maritime commerce regained some of its previous luster. The Venetian carrying trade experienced a resurgence that lasted until the 1750s. It was in these years that the city on the lagoon also became a serious tourist attraction. If Venice had become definitively second class, it was comfortably so after 1718.

The eighteenth century is one of the least understood periods in Venetian history. Aside from the opera, Goldoni's theatrical productions, and a few remarkable characters such as Casanova and Vivaldi, the Venetian *settecento* has not attracted the attention of Anglophone scholars. This is somewhat understandable, as Venice was no longer a great political or economic power, but it has led to the unfortunate notion that the Republic became politically static and reactionary, even as it entered a period of great cultural production. On the contrary, the eighteenth century was a time of both political and intellectual vitality for Venice. A new class of serious-minded bourgeois intellectuals emerged on the mainland, and by the middle third of the century they began to replace the traditional bureaucracy of the Renaissance Republic. Trained in law as well as new scientific disciplines, they imposed Enlightenment ideals of good and efficient government on the aging state through a series of bold administrative reforms. Naturally, the stage for Venetian reform was small in comparison to the global arena in which the great European powers operated, but the ideas and ambitions were similar.

Fueled by the enthusiasm of their new bourgeois administrators, the Venetians turned with renewed vigor to the governance of their mainland territories. Among other pressing issues, Venetian legislators became extremely interested in increasing the productivity of agriculture. Regional agricultural academies helped introduce new commercial crops such as rice and maize—"traditional" staples of the regional diet—and new farming techniques, with the result that Venice became a net food exporter for the first time in its history. While Venice itself declined as a manufacturing center, the Venetians successfully refashioned the agrarian sector of the mainland economy over the course of the eighteenth century. The Venetians also remained active in the Mediterranean carrying trade, even though the relative importance of that trade was no longer what it had been before the rise of the Atlantic powers.

It was against this backdrop of long-term political, economic, and intellectual transformation that the Venetian forestry regime developed. Beginning in 1350, with a single law governing the market for oak timber, progressing at first with small steps but then with ever-increasing sophistication, and ending in 1792 with a major reform of the regional administration of timber resources, the Venetians built an unprecedented system for monitoring, managing, conserving, and exploiting timber resources. *A Forest on the Sea* is the story of that enterprise.

CHAPTER ONE

Forest Exploitation before the Venetian Conquest

> Because, as everybody knows, oak is of the first
> importance to our Republic.

O N 7 SEPTEMBER 1381, the terms of the Peace of Turin were read aloud in the Piazza San Marco. The Republic had just survived its fourth and final war against Genoa, a grueling affair that stretched Venice to its very limits. The Venetians weathered a complete blockade of the lagoon by the combined forces of the Genoese fleet and the armies of the Dukes of Padua and Austria and the King of Hungary. The Republic's hard-fought victory established it as the dominant naval and commercial power in the eastern Mediterranean. Despite the many hardships of the war, Venice remained one of the wealthiest states in the Mediterranean and, with a population approaching 150,000, it was also one of the five largest cities in Europe. As the chronicler Daniele di Chinazzo put it, "as soon as the peace was published, wealthy cargoes began to arrive in Venice from all over, just as it was before the war."[1] Yet Chinazzo's optimism masked a worrisome reality. To secure the peace, Venice had ceded its only mainland Italian possession, Treviso, to the Duke of Austria and agreed to annual payments to the King of Hungary in exchange for staple rights in the northern Adriatic. Venice was also forced to acknowledge Hungarian sovereignty over the eastern shore of the Adriatic. To make matters worse, the Duke of Austria sold Treviso to the Carrara Dukes of Padua, who had been allies of the Genoese during the war. The acquisition gave the Carrara the power to cut off the lagoon from the mainland at any time, a perilous proposition for the Venetians, who could not survive long without access to the region's many agricultural products and natural resources, especially timber and other forest products.

Venice's situation in 1381 illuminates the contradictory status of the Republic as a Mediterranean power at the close of the fourteenth century. On the one hand, the Venetians were unmatched as a naval power: masters of the Levantine trade, and capable of sending trading fleets as far as London, Bruges, and Antwerp. On the other hand, the *Serenissima's* primacy on the seas and the very existence of the city itself depended on a wide variety of mainland resources, almost none of which the Venetians actually controlled. And of all the resources that could come only from the mainland, wood was perhaps the most important. Without timber to build its fleet, the commercial and naval power of the Republic would be in jeopardy. Without combustible material to fuel its several growing industries, the Venetian economy would grind to a halt. And without wooden foundation piles, the striking built environment of Venice would, quite literally, sink back into the muck of the surrounding lagoon. Venice, the great maritime republic, could not survive without constant and reliable access to mainland forests.

In the fifteenth century, Venice attempted to resolve its dependence on mainland products by conquering most of the Italian northeast, carving out a territory that stretched from Bergamo in the west all the way to the river Isonzo in the east (see map on p. xii). Together with Venetian Istria, the mainland possessions, or *terraferma*, eventually yielded nearly all of the vital resources necessary for the Republic's survival, despite Venetian fears that those resources were always on the verge of running out. Long before this conquest, however, the Venetians had already become inextricably bound to the mainland through their efforts to acquire forest resources such as construction timber, shipbuilding materials, charcoal, and firewood. The emergence of a major market for forest commodities meant that the Venetians were deeply involved with mainland forests long before many Venetian patricians had given much thought to one of the most important sources of the Republic's power and prosperity. Indeed, the majority of Venetian aristocrats rarely traveled on the mainland, and many had probably never laid eyes on a large forest of any description.

Despite the relative ignorance of most Venetian legislators concerning the sources of the forest products on which their very survival depended, the Venetian Republic had developed a complex relationship to mainland forests by the thirteenth century at the latest. As the largest regional consumer of high-quality timber, firewood, and charcoal, Venice profoundly transformed the patterns of forest exploitation that contributed to shaping mainland landscapes. Moreover, because the Venetians employed such a broad range of forest products, Venetian merchants came into contact with a wide variety of mainland institutions and groups. These ranged from small village councils to large, well-endowed convents; from feudatories with extensive rural holdings to local investors who produced charcoal and other forest products for sale in local markets. These individuals, groups, and institutions were the gatekeepers of the forest resources the Venetians so desperately needed. Some local actors were merely interested in the profits that could be derived from leasing the forests under their control and were happy to allow anyone to harvest in their woods. For example, in 1495 the bishop of the town of Belluno sued the Republic over the extraction of large quantities of beech from Episcopal lands, not because he wished to preserve the resources, but because he was unhappy with a recent reduction in the tariffs that the See was accustomed to collecting on the timber traffic along the Piave River.[2] Others wished to preserve local forest resources for their own use and viewed outsiders with skepticism. In one early sixteenth-century instance, several villages sued the Republic to prevent the alienation of public forestland (a case that will be dealt with in detail in chapter 3).[3] Such examples highlight the fact that although the Venetians were the dominant economic power in the region, they were nonetheless beholden to a multiplicity of local interests with the power to both aid and thwart Venetian efforts to secure critical forest resources— especially in the centuries before the conquest of the *terraferma*.

The woodland environments in which Venetian merchants and local users operated also varied in important ways, from heavily exploited deciduous stands scattered throughout the coastal plain to huge, contiguous coniferous forests in the sparsely populated, high mountain plateaus. The unusual variety of tree species and environments in the northeast meant that the *Serenissima* could count on the region to supply everything from tall firs for mast timbers to oak for the hulls of its ships, and from beech for galley oars to alder and larch for building foundations. At the same time, this regional variety also made Venetian efforts to secure forest resources far more complicated than they would have been in a more homogenous landscape. Each of the region's forest environments presented unique challenges to anyone seeking to exploit them, including different growth rates, stand densities, species distributions, and ease of access to navigable waterways. The varied combinations of mainland ecological, social, political, and economic structures generated distinctive local ecologies of forest exploitation, which largely determined not only the types of forest resources available to the Venetians, but the quantity, price, and even the intervals at which they could gain access to those resources. A clear understanding of the diverse local conditions the Venetians encountered in their difficult pursuit of fuel, timber, and other woodland resources makes it possible to grasp the root causes of the recurring supply crises that the *Serenissima* experienced, beginning in the fourteenth century and lasting until the fall of the Republic in 1797. While scholars have investigated isolated forest resources —such as charcoal, firewood, and Arsenal timber—there is no comprehensive account of the timber economy of the northern Adriatic. A careful analysis of the regional interaction of the geography, economy, and ecology of timber resources can substantially alter our understanding of the Venetian Republic's efforts to control the mainland. It will also challenge many common assumptions about European ideas of nature during this period.

The earliest interactions between the Venetians and the many local ecologies of forest exploitation on the mainland forever altered Venetian ideas about trees, forests, and forest products. The Venetians tended to interpret temporary shortages arising from local problems on the mainland as a symptom of a permanent condition of scarcity. Indeed, the most important legacy of the period was the perception that mainland timber was in perpetually short supply—a perception that was only enhanced by many senators' propensity to employ overwrought rhetorical devices in their assessments of the situation. Describing problems in the timber supply in terms such as "famine" and "catastrophic lack" probably served to sway votes in the Senate chamber, but it also contributed to an overwhelming sense that temporary shortages were about to become permanent. The fear of constant, irremediable scarcity lay at the heart of the Renaissance forestry regime that the Venetians created in the sixteenth and seventeenth centuries, but that fear had its origins in the crises of the fourteenth century. Venetian concerns about scarcity also led to the emergence of a well-defined hierarchy of species and end uses that Venetian legislators frequently employed as a lens through which to evaluate potential forestry legislation until well into the eighteenth century. It is crucial, therefore, to appreciate how the complex relationship between Venetian demand for timber and the multiple local ecologies of forest exploitation shaped the region's forests in the two centuries preceding the Venetian conquest of the mainland. The need to understand these local ecologies drove the Venetians to create the world's first comprehensive forest bureaucracy, complete with dedicated forestry experts and a set of survey and mapping technologies designed to track critical forest resources at the level of the individual tree.

This chapter examines the development of Venetian demand for forest resources prior to the fifteenth century. Through a detailed analysis of the complex interplay between local practices of forest exploitation and Venetian efforts to secure critical supplies of timber and fuel, the chapter demonstrates that fourteenth-century shortages were not, as the Venetians believed, the result of disappearing forests. Instead, timber and firewood shortages depended on a complicated set of interlocking variables, including local demographic patterns, property distribution, geography, weather, and forest composition. The chapter also illustrates how choices made by Venetian merchants and local actors not only altered the region's forest ecologies in significant ways, but also set the stage for the development of the Renaissance forestry regime by framing the terms under which political debates over forests would take place in the future. Subsequent chapters will demonstrate that the sixteenth- and seventeenth-century forestry bureaucracy was driven, in many ways, by fourteenth-century perceptions of timber scarcity.

It is also worth pointing out that the Venetians' mistaken conviction that mainland forests were disappearing has powerfully influenced the historiography of the Republic. Scholars, following the lead of Frederic Lane, have tended to accept at face value Venetian declarations concerning the scarcity of oak, beech, and fir—especially those found in the records of the Venetian Senate.[4] Such an uncritical analysis of what was, after all, political rhetoric is somewhat understandable, as it appears to confirm long-standing assumptions about the trajectory of European deforestation in the Middle Ages and Renaissance. The medieval agricultural revolution, which introduced the three-field system to much of Europe, undoubtedly led to a significant expansion of arable land at the expense of forests throughout the continent, although the extent and nature of that deforestation has become a subject of scholarly debate in the last decade.[5] Yet Venice's reputation as the locus of major deforestation remains intact. In his magisterial work, *Deforesting the Earth*, Michael Williams claims that "the Venetian Republic may have held 'the gorgeous east in fee,' but part of the price of that domination was the stripping of the forests from the mountains around the rim of the Adriatic."[6] Likewise, Lane asserts that "as the forests which had once surrounded the lagoons . . . were cleared away, shipwrights followed them back to the foothills of the Alps."[7] Such accounts fuel the common stereotype that the Venetians clear-cut their way through the mainland and down the Dalmatian coast to sustain their naval supremacy. This chapter demonstrates why the scale and reach of the medieval Venetian timber economy was insufficient to cause that kind of destruction. The rest of the book advances the claim that by the time the Venetians had become capable of consuming all the available timber in their territories, they had also created an elaborate system of legal, bureaucratic, and technological safeguards aimed at preventing just such a catastrophe.

Three dimensions of the problem of evaluating the effects of Venetian timber and firewood consumption should be kept in mind at this stage. First, no hard data exist on medieval deforestation in northeastern Italy, so any categorical statements should be viewed with skepticism. Second, the first year for which real data are available is 1569—when a large team of forestry experts under the leadership of the patrician Nicolò Surian completed the first comprehensive survey of oak forests in Venetian territory. These data show that regional forests contained more than enough oak to meet Venetian demand, in spite of the fact that consumption was far higher in 1569 than it was in 1400 and would continue to grow steadily in the seventeenth and early eighteenth centuries. Third, Venetian declarations concerning timber scarcity were the product of a combination of real ignorance concerning the mainland landscape and conscious political calculation. In the sixteenth and seventeenth centuries, the assumption of a supply crisis helped justify aggressive legislation aimed at removing forests from local control and placing them under the supervision of the Republic's institutions. None of this is to say that deforestation did not occur prior to the sixteenth century. One could even argue that the demographic crises of the fourteenth century allowed the region's forest cover to bounce back from a long period of contraction. This view has merit, but the abject failure of sixteenth- and seventeenth-century attempts at reforestation show that it is dangerous to assume there was a major expansion of forest cover in the second half of the fourteenth century. Chapter 2 discusses the most compelling evidence for the kind of localized deforestation claimed by Lane, but with no way of knowing exactly how much forest cover was lost during the Middle Ages, the data contained in the later cadastral surveys suggest that it is simply inaccurate to present Venice as a paradigmatic example of late medieval deforestation. The thirteenth- and fourteenth-century evidence of wide-spread clear-cutting is far from conclusive, consisting as it does of a small handful of shrill declarations by senators who mostly lacked any first-hand knowledge of mainland forest landscapes. Moreover, a careful analysis of the regional forest economy demonstrates that it would be rash to assume that anything resembling a major wave of deforestation occurred in northeastern Italy prior to 1400.

Venetian Demand for Forest Products

Significant Venetian demand for many forest products began to develop in the twelfth century, when the city rose to prominence as a commercial entrepôt. The emergence of Venice as one of the major Mediterranean ports created two different sources of demand for high-quality timber, especially the durmast oak that grew throughout the region. The construction and expansion of the city itself relied on regular and predictable access to large numbers of whole oak trunks for structural piles. Further-more, Venice's involvement in the Eastern carrying trade drove the creation of a large shipbuilding industry in the lagoon, one which consumed vast quantities of oak, beech, fir, larch, and elm timber. In addition to construction material, Venice also required increasing volumes of fuel of all descriptions. As the city's population steadily grew during the High Middle Ages, the demand for firewood intensified in a corresponding fashion. Likewise, the Venetians actively sought to expand manufacturing in the city, which increased demand for high-quality charcoal to generate the necessary thermal energy for industrial processes. Venice's famous glass industry was one of the major consumers of wood-based fuel, but the city also became a major center of silk cloth production—

which required significant amounts of thermal energy for the dyeing process—not to mention various metallurgical industries and, of course, the shipbuilding industry, which needed heat for caulking, forging, casting, and more.[8] Thus virtually every sector of the Venetian economy—from shipping to manufacturing—depended on a ready supply of imported timber and wood-based fuel.

Between 1100 and 1300, as the wealth of Venice increased, the urban core of what would become the Renaissance city took shape. What had originally been a collection of small islands scattered around the area that is now Rialto was slowly built up and expanded through landfill.[9] To resolve the problem of ground subsidence, both on the original islands and the new landfill, the Venetians drove wooden piles, called *tolpi*, into the ground to establish a stable foundation upon which to build. Oak and larch were the preferred species for piles because their dense grain was highly resistant to worms and rot—a key consideration, since once the *tolpi* were driven into the ground and built over, they could not be replaced. If the piles gave way, they brought down whatever structure stood on top of them, so durability was paramount. Large buildings such as churches and patrician palaces required prodigious numbers of piles to create adequate load-bearing foundations. It is no exaggeration to say that tens of millions of tree trunks lie hidden beneath Venice's Renaissance *palazzi*. And every one of those trees was harvested in a forest somewhere on the mainland.[10] Although the trees that supplied the piles were cut down over several centuries, the total amount of timber consumed represented a significant drain on regional forest resources.

Before the fifteenth century the Venetians possessed no forests of their own, relying entirely on foreign sources to supply them with the material needed to build their city. Venice enjoyed proximity to several rivers capable of moving timber across significant distances. Theoretically, this network of rivers—which included the Adige, Brenta, Piave, Sile, Livenza, Tagliamento, and Isonzo—gave Venetian merchants access to timber resources across a vast area stretching from the Duchy of Tyrol in the west to the Friuli in the east. But in reality, not all rivers were equal in terms of the availability of forests and forest resources, and the majority of the forest products consumed in Venice came from the Piave, Livenza, and Tagliamento rivers. This uneven geography of extraction was due to the fact that the Adige and Brenta passed through the northern reaches of the Po plain, an area that had largely been deforested in antiquity. Consequently, even though both the Adige and Brenta were major commercial arteries, they were limited in terms of the types and quantities of wood they could yield. On the Adige, the timber trade centered exclusively on the upper reaches of the river in the Tyrol. This region supplied conifers such as fir and larch, but no oak or other hardwoods.[11] Likewise, the Brenta River brought some softwoods down from the mountains above Bassano, but with the exception of the large oak forest near Padua known as the Carpeneda and a handful of stands near Vicenza, this area did not supply the Venetians with any important hardwood species.[12] In the east, the Isonzo, Tagliamento, and Livenza offered oak and beech from the coastal plain and hilly interior, but their sources were either too low or their flow too weak to supply any fir or larch from the high mountains.

The Piave was the only river in the northeast capable of supplying a complete range of forest resources, including *tolpi*, fuel, mast timbers, and other ship-grade material. From its source deep in the Alps, and all along its 220-kilometer course until its mouth in the northern lagoon, the Piave passed through a series of well-forested areas. The upper reaches of the river were connected through tributaries to a series of high alpine valleys containing extensive fir and larch forests. The middle section of the river, running past the prealpine town of Belluno, offered access to massive beech forests. Finally, in the coastal plain the lower course of the river passed near a series of significant mixed deciduous forests containing substantial quantities of valuable oak. It was to the Piave that the Venetians turned time and again to supply themselves with critical timber resources as well as fuel in the form of both firewood and charcoal. From a very early date the Piave region assumed a key role in Venetian attempts to acquire forest resources as the merchants who supplied the city with building material moved up the river in search of timber.

As Venice took shape as a major commercial center, the city developed an insatiable need for several other forest products beyond the lumber used for *tolpi*. By the thirteenth century Venice was one of the five largest cities in Europe, and its inhabitants consumed correspondingly voluminous quantities of fuel for cooking and, in the damp cold of the Venetian winter, heating. Since Venice lacked forests from which to draw crucial fuel, every bundle of firewood consumed in Venice had to be imported from the mainland. The constant need for domestic fuel was one of the most pressing issues facing the commune and its leaders. Like many Italian towns and cities, Venice established a community firewood reserve, housed in warehouses at San Biasio and near the Arsenal. The reserves fulfilled two main purposes. They helped the poor get through the winter months, when fuel prices were at their highest, and they provided for the needs of public institutions such as the mint and the Arsenal. By the sixteenth century the firewood warehouses also supplied annual allotments for religious institutions that could not afford to meet their own needs. In a city whose population fluctuated between 120,000 and 150,000, the decision to supply domestic fuel not only to the poor but to convents and monasteries represented a major commitment of public resources. To meet that commitment, the Republic's leaders sought to deploy every source of combustible material they could by recycling any and all cast-off wood as fuel. In a striking example of reuse, the Arsenal routinely broke up the hulls of decommissioned ships into small pieces for distribution to the city's poorest residents and to deserving convents.[13]

In addition to firewood for domestic use, Venice required increasing amounts of thermal energy for the city's growing manufacturing sector. The expansion of industries such as silk and glassmaking consumed large quantities of both low-grade firewood and high-grade charcoal. As with construction timber, Venetian merchants fanned out across the mainland in search of firewood. Significant supplies of fuel were widely available throughout the region east of the Brenta River. Forests as close as the area around Mestre and as far as the Tagliamento River in the Friuli were capable of providing low-grade fuel. In years when the price of firewood was high, the Venetians even crossed the Adriatic to Istria to acquire firewood. Charcoal, on the other hand, came from a far more restricted area. Charcoal suitable for industrial applications such as glassmaking and iron smelting had to come from high-quality hardwoods such as oak or beech, because low-quality charcoal from other species would not produce the predictable temperatures necessary for delicate manufacturing processes. The production of good charcoal also required significant technical expertise.[14] In addition, charcoal was fragile and did not always hold up to long-distance transportation. As a consequence, the charcoal sold in Venice tended to come from lower and middle sections of the Piave River, where good oak and beech forests yielded the crucial raw material for high-grade charcoal and local merchants possessed the skill needed to turn out a good product. For these reasons, long before the Venetians conquered the surrounding areas of the mainland, the market for piles, firewood, and charcoal had already bound the region together.

But it was the demand for high-quality timber by Venice's shipbuilding industry that generated the most powerful impetus for establishing a managed system for the procurement of forest resources. Shipbuilding involved everything from firewood and charcoal to high-quality oak, beech, and fir; it forced the Venetians to confront the full spectrum of challenges involved in acquiring forest resources. In the late thirteenth and early fourteenth century, Venice expanded and centralized the production of large commercial and military vessels in the Arsenal, Europe's largest industrial complex at the time.[15] Two key developments in maritime commerce propelled the expansion of the Arsenal. The first was the invention of a new type of ship—the great galley—that combined elements of the traditional longship, or light galley, powered by large banks of oars, and the medieval round ships, powered by sail.[16] With hulls made entirely of durmast oak—traditional galleys had used fir—these ships were more durable but also more expensive than earlier vessels.[17] The second development was the organization of Venetian trade into state-controlled convoys making annual voyages on the best routes, using a combination of great galleys for cargo space and light galleys for protection from corsairs and enemy fleets. The shift towards larger ships offered an important incentive for the organization of publicly financed convoys. The great galleys required far more timber to manufacture and maintain than either light galleys or round ships, making it difficult for even the wealthiest individuals to bear the costs associated with them. The new maritime system called for some form of collective financing and the Venetians opted for a public solution: the state built the galleys and organized them into annual convoys. The Republic recouped its costs by leasing the cargo rights in publicly held auctions open to all citizens. The Arsenal did not completely supplant private shipyards, which continued to produce round ships and the occasional light galley for individual shipowners. Nevertheless, the Arsenal dwarfed even the largest private yards. In the centuries prior to the naval reforms of the 1740s, the total output of the public shipyard exceeded that of all the private yards combined. On the one hand, state control of naval production placed the Republic in a position to dictate the price of shipbuilding materials brought to market in Venice, as well as to make critical decisions about the size and composition of the fleet. On the other hand, the Arsenal placed a significant strain on public resources, especially in times of war, when the state was forced to bear the burden of producing new warships with little assistance from private interests.

The assumption of public responsibility for the production and maintenance of what was by thirteenth-century standards a large fleet constituted a particularly Venetian response to the need for larger, more seaworthy vessels for trade and warfare. Other maritime powers—most notably the Venetians' principal Italian rivals, the Genoese—continued the traditional practice of relying on wealthy merchants to build their own ships in private yards and then leasing them in times of emergency. The Venetians drew a significant advantage from public ownership of the galleys, especially in wartime, when a convoy could be instantly transformed into a war fleet at no additional cost beyond lost shipping revenues. The Venetians believed that the public production of the fleet demonstrated their collective spirit, a critical component of the famous "myth of Venice."[18] Many scholars support this view, concurring that while the myth was a self-conscious creation of Venice's ruling class, it nevertheless reflected the fact that Venice did not suffer from the factionalism and civil discord that plagued other Italian cities throughout the Renaissance. Élisabeth Crouzet-Pavan even goes so far as to suggest that Venice's unique and demanding lagoon environment forced its patriciate to cooperate out of pure necessity.[19] While such an argument risks slipping into environmental determinism, it is undeniable that geography played a crucial role in the Venetian decision to build fleets at public expense. In the Genoese case, the persistence of private production was in some measure due to the difficulties involved in massing the necessary material for naval construction in one place. Venice not only drew timber down several rivers directly into the lagoon and the Arsenal, it also enjoyed access to every species of wood needed for galley construction. The choice to finance the fleet publicly was not inevitable, but the geography of the northeast made it possible. By contrast, the Genoese had to bring timber from several relatively small forests that were spread out along hundreds of kilometers of coastline and contained none of the astounding variety of species of the northeastern forests that supplied the Venetians.[20] As a result, the private yards in which the Genoese built their ships were dispersed along the Ligurian coast and not concentrated in the city itself. Thus for the Venetians, the rivers, plains, and mountains of the northeast became the very foundation of their commercial and naval power.

The decision to make the manufacture and maintenance of a significant portion of the fleet a public concern forced the Venetian state to assume responsibility for what would very quickly become the single largest manufacturing concern in Europe. Paramount among the new administrative tasks facing the Republic was the acquisition of all the primary materials for naval construction. In theory this task presented relatively few problems, at least as far as timber was concerned. The four principal species employed in naval construction—oak, beech, fir, and larch—were widely available along the rivers east of the Brenta. The Piave generated ample stocks of all four of these species, with additional oak and beech coming from the Livenza and Tagliamento Rivers. The Isonzo could provide beech, and Istria contained significant quantities of oak, elm, chestnut, and firewood—although higher transportation costs meant that these were generally seen as secondary options. Nonetheless, events such as the Chioggia crisis taught the Venetians that access to the region's bountiful forests could not be taken for granted. Indeed, by the middle of the fourteenth century it became evident to many that in the absence of mainland possessions, Venice needed to take a greater interest in the flow of timber into the city.

Despite the apparent wealth of forest resources on the mainland, efforts to assure the timely arrival of critical timber and fuel into the Arsenal were hampered by the state's relative ignorance concerning the location, distribution, and condition of forest resources on the mainland. With the exception of merchants who were involved in the forest-products trade, few in Venice had a precise conception of where critical forest resources came from or how they arrived in the city. This imperfect knowledge meant that legislators were not always in a position to make informed judgments about how best to secure those resources. The lack of concrete and reliable information was exacerbated by realities on the ground. The forests of the northeast were not evenly distributed throughout the region, which made it difficult for even experienced merchants to distinguish between a local shortage and more widespread problems with the supply. To further complicate matters, local practices of forest exploitation were not uniform, which meant that in superficially similar environments human actions were helping to produce forests that contained trees of very different types, age distributions, and sizes. These three factors hampered the understanding of Venetian legislators, who lacked the necessary information about local conditions on the mainland to make sound judgments about the root causes of the occasional timber shortages that plagued their city. The limited perspective of most patricians led them to the reasonable yet erroneous conclusion that if timber and fuel were not making their way to the lagoon, reserves must have been dwindling at the source. Even after the Venetians took direct control of many large mainland forests, legislators never completely abandoned the idea that supply problems were invariably a symptom of disappearing woodlands. Although this view of forests in jeopardy continued to play an important role in Venetian policies well into the eighteenth century, the emergence of a cadre of bureaucratic forestry experts in the middle of the sixteenth century provided an increasingly powerful counterweight to legislators' fears of scarcity. Chapters 4 and 5 will assess the Venetian timber bureaucracy in greater detail, including the empirical technologies of knowledge production its members used to develop a nuanced view of the local conditions that produced timber and firewood shortages. Such detailed knowledge of the specific details of forests, ranging from the number and size of trees in a stand to their distribution and overall quality, would have been unimaginable to their medieval predecessors.

Regional Forest Ecologies and the Venetian Timber Supply

Venetian demand for forest resources of all descriptions continued to rise throughout the Middle Ages, and the city's merchants struggled to meet the increased demand. As Venetian agents travelled throughout the northeast in search of timber for construction and shipbuilding, in addition to firewood and charcoal for domestic and industrial use, they encountered a complex and ever-changing set of forest landscapes.

These local forest ecologies—the product of interactions between specific human practices and the non-human environment—determined the kinds of forest resources that Venetians could obtain in a given area, the price they paid for them, the quantities that were available to outsiders in a given season, and the level of exploitation that specific forests could sustain.

Four main variables—two geographic and two social—shaped the composition of local forests throughout the mainland and thereby affected the Venetians' ability to secure forest resources. The first and most obvious geographical factor was the species distribution in a particular area. The Venetians sought to acquire very specific types of timber. Consequently, if an area contained no oak, beech, larch, or fir, it remained relatively unaffected by Venetian demand—even if heavily forested. Second, the proximity to transportation routes was a key consideration. A fantastically endowed forest was useless unless the timber could be transported to a navigable river and thence to Venice at a reasonable cost. For instance, according to the 1569 survey of the Friuli, a medium-sized forest belonging to the Count of Spilimbergo in the vicinity of the village of Barbagian contained 2,451 good oak poles. But with the nearest river sixteen miles away, the stand was adjudged useless as a source of Arsenal oak.[21] Therefore, rivers with a strong year-round flow, such as the Piave and Livenza, presented major advantages over rivers with a fluctuating seasonal flow, such as the Tagliamento. Likewise, because the Piave and Livenza rivers emptied into the northern Adriatic very close to the Venetian lagoon, timber rafts floated down these two rivers moved easily and directly into the city. By contrast, timber floated down the Tagliamento and Isonzo rivers in the Friuli, or the Quieto River in Istria, had to be towed by galleys—either loaded in barges or towed as strings of rafts—across the northern Adriatic. Not only did this entail significantly higher transportation costs for fuel and timber from these regions, it meant that the shipments were vulnerable to a variety of mishaps—ranging from bad weather to piracy—that did not threaten supplies brought down the Piave and Livenza rivers.

Beyond these geographical variables, social and political factors also played an important role in determining the types of forests that Venetian merchants encountered as they travelled on the mainland. Local population densities heavily affected the availability of wood. Harvesting timber and fuel was a labor-intensive process, and merchants relied almost exclusively on the local peasantry for the human capital necessary to extract resources from the forest. Therefore, in less-populated areas—such as the Cadore and the Istrian peninsula—it was often difficult to marshal a sufficient number of workers to harvest the quantities of timber sought by the Venetians. But in areas with high population densities—such as the lower Piave region near Venice—Venetians confronted a different set of problems. Competition from local residents who also needed forest resources drove up prices, and village authorities in densely populated parts of the mainland often sought to limit access by outsiders in order to guarantee local supplies. Patterns of land tenure, which varied significantly throughout the northeast, also had important consequences for local woodlands. In many areas of the mainland, forests on community property tended to be better managed and contained better-quality timber than those standing on private property or on land belonging to institutions such as convents and hospitals. But communal ownership also placed more restrictions on the actions of Venetian merchants, which meant higher operating costs. These factors often left Venetian merchants choosing between cheaper, more permissive leases in impoverished private forests and more restrictive leases in better-preserved common lands.

While local conditions varied considerably, the geographical distribution of species in the northeast followed certain general patterns. The region's forests stood in four distinct topographical bands. In the coastal plain to the north and east of Venice, mixed deciduous stands of oak, elm, alder, and ash tended to dominate. In the hills along the Livenza and Tagliamento rivers, chestnut and beech appeared alongside the other deciduous species. At around 350 meters in elevation, mixed deciduous forests gave way to extensive beech stands and mixed coniferous forests of fir, larch, and pine. In the high alpine valleys that lay at elevations above 800 meters, enormous larch and fir forests dominated, especially along the southern slopes of the mountains. In Istria, mixed deciduous forests of oak, elm, and chestnut were prevalent, particularly in the steep valleys of the interior.

The distribution of critical timber species in the region had important consequences for Venice. First, although oak was the most valuable type of wood for the Venetians, it was also available across a relatively wide area in comparison to other species. When the Venetians sought oak timber and fuel, they searched for it first in the nearby plains before resorting to supplies in the hills of the Friuli or, as a last resort, in the interior valleys of the Istrian peninsula. The broad area covered by oak forests also meant that forests that had been intensively harvested could be allowed to recover as merchants moved on to other areas. In later centuries the wide range occupied by oak allowed the Venetians to preserve much of the total forested area by shifting harvests from region to region. Supplies of beech were abundant but, unlike oak, they were distributed across a fairly narrow geographical range. The limited extent of beech forests rendered the supply of this important species much more vulnerable to natural disasters, social upheaval, and deforestation. The most plentiful and cheapest beech forests stood in valleys and plateaus near the middle Piave and upper Livenza rivers. Together, these two transportation corridors accounted for nearly all the beech brought to Venice throughout the Renaissance. Finally, meaningful quantities of conifers such as larch and fir were limited to the high mountains of the Cadore in the upper reaches of the Piave River, and any disruption of the Piave trade threatened to cut the Venetians off completely from their supply of these key species.

The Venetians could gain access to the main timber-producing areas of the northeast and Istria by means of five significant transportation routes: the Piave, Livenza, Tagliamento, Isonzo and Quieto rivers. The Livenza—a lowland river whose source lies a mere fifty meters above sea level—only passed through the first two bands of mixed deciduous forest. Nonetheless, its numerous tributaries ensured a consistent volume of water in the riverbed, making it a reliable route in the sixteenth and seventeenth centuries for hardwoods such as oak and beech. Its value as a transportation corridor for forest products was enhanced by the fact that its mouth lay only forty kilometers from Venice, near the town of Caorle, making it possible to move large timber rafts into the lagoon without resorting to expensive barges and galleys.

The Tagliamento, which flowed through the eastern reaches of the *terraferma*, originates in the nearby Carnic Alps at an elevation of about 1,200 meters, but only the lower part of the river was useful for transportation. The volume of water in the Tagliamento also fluctuated dramatically throughout the year and was only occasionally sufficient to carry timber rafts downstream. Moreover, its outlet lay a considerable distance from Venice, which meant that once timber rafts reached the Adriatic they had to be strung together and towed by galleys to the city. The Isonzo flows from a source in the Julian Alps at about 1,100 meters in elevation. Its source lies just on the Italian side of the Danube watershed and near the alpine passes leading to the river Sava and the Hungarian plain, all of which made the Isonzo important for trade. Like the Livenza, it is a large river, with a consistent flow, but its mouth is even farther from Venice than the Tagliamento's. In addition, only the last section of its course ever transited through Venetian territory, further reducing the river's value as a source of timber and other forest products. Lastly, in Istria the Quieto River allowed access to the heavily forested valleys at the center of the peninsula. The most important of these valleys was the Montona, which boasted one of the largest oak forests in the northern Adriatic. But the Quieto was a narrow, shallow river with an irregular flow that presented enormous challenges for floating whole trunks far enough downstream to be loaded into barges and towed to Venice. In combination with the distance, these difficult conditions made Istria the most expensive option available to the Venetians.

Given the constraints of the other rivers, from an early date the Piave emerged as the most important transportation corridor for timber and wood fuel bound for Venice. The Piave represented an ideal source of forest products, due to its particular geography. The river passed through all four bands of forest growth, which made it the only route capable of transporting every useful species of tree and wood product found on the mainland. Prior to the fifteenth century, when the Venetians relocated its mouth several kilometers to the north, the Piave emptied directly into the lagoon, further simplifying the process of moving large, heavily laden timber rafts into the Arsenal. Even after the shift, the raftsmen, or *zattieri*, who brought timber rafts down the river only made a brief transit outside the lagoon.[22] In addition, the upper reaches of the river were connected to a series of high alpine valleys that lead to the Brenner Pass. The Piave offered a sustained flow throughout the year, making it navigable in almost all conditions. It provided ample water for extensive irrigation networks as well as hundreds of mills to process the region's grain production. The river brought timber, charcoal, and iron from the mountains to market in Venice, it sustained agriculture and industry, and it offered an important connection to northern European trade routes. It also made the towns in the plains to the north of Venice quite prosperous. The Venetians were keenly aware of their economic reliance on the Piave corridor, which was one reason why their first attempt to exercise sway over the surrounding mainland was the 1339 purchase of the city of Treviso, which controlled a significant stretch of the lower Piave.

The prosperity of the lower Piave region supported a relatively large population. The area bounded by the Brenta to the west and the Livenza to the east was the most densely populated timber-producing area on the mainland. In addition to Treviso, which had around 10,000 inhabitants, the region contained a number of flourishing smaller towns—including Asolo, Feltre, and Mestre—which were centers of both manufacturing and agriculture. Still, the bulk of the population lived in villages, where agriculture was the most important local activity. Despite the large number of inhabitants, the region still contained several large deciduous forests in the fourteenth century. The Montello forest, which occupied a hilly stretch of land on the west bank of the river and covered an area of approximately ninety-five square kilometers, contained huge quantities of oak timber. The area surrounding the town of Asolo also featured significant oak forests. Farther east, along the upper reaches of the Livenza River, there were more deciduous forests that held impressive quantities of oak, and the prealpine hills to the north and west of the town of Conegliano were host to several large beech forests.

Because the Piave and Livenza rivers were important transportation corridors as well as home to a large human population, the area's forests were subject to a number of competing pressures. Local residents consumed large quantities of firewood for domestic and industrial use, charcoal for industry, and green fertilizer for agriculture. Communities both large and small throughout the region also required major quantities of timber to build and maintain the complex network of irrigation channels that drew from the Sile, Piave, Livenza, and scores of smaller tributaries to feed their fields and mills. With so much local competition, Venetian merchants sometimes found it difficult to gain access to sufficient quantities of timber and fuel to satisfy Venice's growing needs, even though the region contained several vast oak forests and a plentiful supply of labor.

Patterns of land tenure exacerbated the challenges posed by local competition for the region's forest resources. Unlike other parts of the northeast, the Piave and Livenza watershed contained almost no feudal demesne. Community property and private lands dominated the territory, although the amount of land under the control of lay and ecclesiastical institutions would increase steadily throughout the Renaissance. In addition, most of the region's legal codes gave local communities significant control over their commons, making it difficult for even local elites to usurp access rights to common land.[23] And because the largest and best-endowed forests were almost all on community property, Venetian merchants had to negotiate for access with scores of community officials who had a vested interest in preserving the region's forest resources for the benefit of their fellow villagers and other local users. As a consequence, the Venetians were not always able to purchase oak along the Piave and Livenza rivers, forcing them to look to other parts of the mainland and Istria to satisfy their ever-increasing hunger for timber.

East of the Livenza River, population densities fell significantly. The towns of the Friuli were smaller and far less prosperous than those to the west of the river. The region's hilly terrain and rocky soil could not support agriculture or industry on the same scale as the lower Piave region.[24] The lack of year-round flow in the Tagliamento and its tributaries also limited the carrying capacity of the land, because there was little water to sustain agriculture or to power mills. The combination of a smaller agricultural footprint and lower population density had allowed a good deal of deciduous forest—primarily oak, elm, and chestnut—to survive throughout the region. The relatively small pool of available labor and difficult transportation conditions hindered access to many of these forests, but as a general rule timber was more plentiful and less carefully husbanded than in the west.

Much of the woodland in the Friuli stood on feudal demesne, and the aristocrats who held the rights of usufruct to those lands were far more liberal about leasing them to outsiders than the small communities of the Piave. Aristocratic claims were aided by the fact that the legal framework of property ownership was very weak in the Friuli—especially when compared to the lower Piave. Disputed claims of ownership, which were quite common in the Friuli, often allowed merchants to secure favorable leases on forests.[25] The towns and villages of the Friuli were also less protective of their commons than their counterparts west of the Livenza. With a smaller population and none of the complex infrastructure of canals to support, Friulian communities relied heavily on the income that could be derived from leasing their commons to outsiders. Venetian merchants found a receptive audience for their overtures in the Friuli, and the relative abundance of forest resources there made up, to some degree, for the higher costs and inconveniences of using the Tagliamento as a transportation route. The firewood trade in particular thrived in the Friuli, because it was less vulnerable to higher transportation costs than the traffic in timber. Firewood bundles could be loaded onto small boats that made regular trips to Venice, whereas merchants specializing in timber had to organize galleys and barges—with their large and expensive crews—to ferry their bulkier merchandise across the Adriatic.

Farther east, on the Istrian peninsula, the Venetians encountered still more difficult conditions. Istria was even less densely populated than the Friuli, and beginning in the fourteenth century it experienced a demographic decline that would last until the late seventeenth century.[26] The small itinerant population made it difficult to organize work crews to harvest forest products, and, as outsiders, the Venetians lacked the power to coerce the local peasantry into compliance. As a contested frontier region, Istria also did not possess an institutional or legal system capable of consistently managing land use or property rights.[27] The lack of juridical mechanisms for legitimating usufruct and property rights discouraged Venetian merchants from investing in the Istrian timber trade. Losing the lease on a forest at the whim of a local lord was a constant risk, as was the danger posed by Austrian forays across an increasingly militarized frontier. There was also the matter of a scarcity of good river routes. The Quieto River provided the best access to the natural wealth of the Istrian interior, but it was a shallow river with an unreliable flow. The tributaries that fed the main river were weak and often subject to blockage by sediment, making it impossible to lash harvested timber into large rafts.[28] On the rivers of northeastern Italy such rafts conveyed firewood, charcoal, and other commodities downstream —a practical impossibility in Istria. Instead, the Venetians had to gather all the loose logs at a collection point near the town of Pinguente and load them into barges to be towed across the Adriatic to Venice. The combination of these barriers meant that while hardwood timber—especially oak, but also elm and beech—was plentiful on the Istrian peninsula, it was also often more expensive than wood from the timber-producing areas of the Italian mainland. Only Istrian firewood, which could be shipped at a lower cost in smaller craft, was consistently competitive with *terraferma* supplies.

In spite of the risks involved, the Venetians still sought to exploit Istria's dense oak and elm forests. And although Venetian merchants tended to be unwilling to invest in such a risky environment, there was no shortage of local proxies ready to do business with representatives of the Venetian government. Reliance on local agents was intended to minimize the risks that made Venetian merchants wary of sinking capital into Istrian forests. Local proxies had the necessary connections to marshal labor for the harvest, and they were presumably less vulnerable to the unilateral revocation of leases by local lords. Moreover, they did not face the mistrust and outright hostility that was often directed at Venetian merchants. At the same time, reliance on local factors entailed a different set of risks. Corruption and timber theft were the most common charges leveled at Istrian proxies. But while many were doubtless guilty of abusing their position for personal gain, the Venetians found it very difficult to establish effective legal or contractual deterrents against such behavior. Istrian agents held a virtual monopoly—especially in the firewood trade—and the Venetians were forced to accept the loss of a certain percentage of the harvest as the cost of accessing Istrian hardwoods.

Beech was the only deciduous species in relatively short supply in the lower Piave and in Friuli and Istria. Fortunately for the Venetians, it was available in great quantities in the middle reaches of the Piave River, in the area surrounding the town of Belluno. In the prealpine valleys and plateaus of the middle Piave, the oak and elm that dominated forests at lower elevations gave way to large stands of beech timber, with some conifers, such as larch, mixed in. Like the Friuli, the region around Belluno was more sparsely populated than the neighboring lower Piave area. Belluno was the only urban center of any size, and the scattered mountain hamlets of the region supported only small populations and controlled relatively small areas of common land. Most of the land was either feudal demesne held by the Bellunese aristocracy or ecclesiastical property controlled by the local bishop, but because the region was not capable of supporting much agriculture, a significant proportion of that land was unprofitable. The local economy relied instead on a variety of extractive activities, including timber production and charcoal manufacture. Mining was also an important source of income for the Bellunese. Some of this production was needed to support Belluno's metallurgical industries, but considerable quantities of timber, charcoal, and raw ore were exported along the Piave River corridor.

The Bellunese timber industry was already well developed by the early fourteenth century. Despite the difficult terrain and small population, the middle Piave benefited from a fortunate geographical situation for forest exploitation. The river's many tributaries connected the main course of the Piave with the valleys and plateaus that held large beech forests, which meant that a considerable area could be put into production. The flow in these tributaries was reliable enough to float large numbers of logs down to the main river, making it possible to harvest larger poles. Sawmills were constructed on many of the fastest-moving streams to process cut timber into board lengths.[29] At collection points near Belluno, raftsmen bound whole poles into rafts, loaded them with milled lumber, bundles of firewood, and charcoal, and then set off downstream to the wealthier towns of the lower Piave and Venice.[30] Tariffs on the raft traffic helped sustain both the commune and the episcopal diocese of Belluno.[31]

The active trade in forest products meant that the middle Piave represented one of the most appealing sources of timber and fuel for the Venetians—even if the area's beech charcoal was not quite as good as the oak charcoal produced in the lower Piave. The many timber merchants based in Belluno were eager to sell their products downstream, and reasonable tariffs on river traffic encouraged the export of the region's natural resources. The main barrier to access was the small rural population. The scarcity of labor limited both the total yield of the annual harvest and the volume of secondary products (such as charcoal) that could be produced following the harvest. The population—like that of all mountainous areas of Europe—was extremely vulnerable to famine and disease. Consequently, the region's fuel and timber production fluctuated significantly from year to year, especially during periods of acute crisis, such as in the second half of the fourteenth century.

If the area under Belluno's control helped satisfy Venice's need for hardwoods, Venetian merchants still had to face the challenge of acquiring sufficient quantities of critical softwood species such as fir and larch—which yielded masts and *tolpi*, respectively. The middle Piave generated limited quantities of larch when harvests occurred in mixed stands, but not nearly enough to satisfy the building trades in Venice. As for the large, straight-grained fir used to make masts, the Venetians needed to look to still more distant sources. The Tyrol trade was capable of supplying some fir, but the mainstay of critical mast timbers was the Cadore region north of Venice. Huge fir and larch forests grew in the high mountain valleys of this region, especially along the southern slopes. Tributaries connected several of the high alpine valleys of the Cadore to the upper reaches of the Piave. During the spring melt, these tributaries carried large fir poles down to the main alpine confluence of the Piave near the strategic town of Pieve di Cadore, where they could be bound together and sent downriver to Belluno. The tiny human population in the Cadore was concentrated in a handful of small mountain villages, such as Auronzo, Dobbiacco, and Pieve. Regional agrarian production was marginal and insufficient to support even the modest requirements of the local populace.[32] Timber was one of the few products—along with silver and lead—capable of sustaining the local economy.[33] Like the Bellunese, then, the Cadorini became willing exporters of their forest wealth.

Most of the forests in the Cadore stood on community lands rather than feudal demesne. However, since the local population relied so heavily on timber exports for its survival, community leaders placed few restrictions on access by outsiders. Merchants could secure leases on forestland with relative ease. Nonetheless, there were still significant barriers to overcome for anyone seeking to access the region's wealth of fir and larch. The fragility of the area's population alone turned regular, large-scale timber harvesting into an uncertain enterprise. The labor pool was so small that even a minor demographic shock was enough to hinder the harvest, sometimes for several years. The local environment also posed challenges to anyone seeking to profit from the extraction of high-quality timber resources. For all of the region's immense wealth of forests, the alpine tributaries down which large fir logs had to travel to reach the Piave only held sufficient water for a very brief period—sometimes as little as two or three weeks—in the early spring. Work crews were under immense pressure to have the harvest ready to float in advance of the spring runoff in the mountains. A delay of even a few days in marshaling labor could spell the difference between a successful harvest and no yield at all if felled trees had to be abandoned on the ground to rot. So despite the eagerness of the Cadorini to lease their forests, alpine timber remained a risky investment for Venetian merchants.

Taken as a whole, the forests of the lower Piave, Friuli, Istria, middle Piave, and Cadore provided an unusually rich source of critical timber and fuel supplies. The hardwood forests of the three lowland regions offered a wealth of oak and other important hardwood species. The two higher regions made up for the lack of beech at lower elevations and also offered plentiful supplies of fir and larch, the two most critical softwood species. Each of the five regions featured a distinctive forest ecology and presented a different set of challenges to anyone hoping to exploit local forests. In the lower Piave the oak forests were large, labor was plentiful, and transportation corridors were inexpensive and efficient. The majority of good forests in this territory stood on community land. Merchants seeking access to those forests had to contend with a property regime and legal tradition that favored local users over outsiders. Timber was abundant but not always easy or cheap to purchase. In the Friuli, feudal demesne and institutional property dominated. Local demand was low, so landowners and communities were happy to lease forestland to Venetian merchants. Yet a lack of labor and relatively poor transportation routes made it both expensive and challenging for Venetian buyers to move large quantities of timber across the region. But firewood, which was easier to transport, remained widely available in the Friuli. In Istria, deciduous forests were plentiful but the small population and poorly defined system of property rights kept all but the most daring Venetian investors out of the peninsula. Local proxies stepped in to fill the void, but rampant corruption, theft, and endemic problems with the Quieto River made Istrian timber relatively costly—although the peninsula's fuel prices remained competitive. In the middle Piave, expansive beech forests stood on a combination of community property, feudal demesne, and church lands. The region served as a major center of timber production and relied heavily on income generated by forest exploitation. Local merchants dominated the trade in forest commodities, including charcoal, but demographic fluctuations had a significant effect on timber harvests, and regional yields could vary considerably from year to year.

Finally, in the Cadore region, extensive fir and larch forests stood on large tracts of community property. Tiny and poor, mountain hamlets leased these forests freely. But the narrow window for harvesting, combined with an unreliable labor pool, created a situation in which annual yields could fall to nothing in response to even minor food shortages or other forms of social distress.

In theory, the combined yield of these five timber-producing areas should have been sufficient to provide the raw material required to meet both local and Venetian needs for construction timber and fuel—even taking into account the fact that demand increased steadily on all fronts until the economic slowdown of the early fourteenth century. Yet in practice, geographic and social barriers often drove local prices for timber and fuel to levels that merchants were unwilling to meet, leading to periodic shortages in Venice. The Republic's leaders were in no position to address the problem of recurring shortages, because they lacked a clear understanding of the root causes. Their ignorance of mainland landscapes and environments—especially in remote areas such as the Cadore—was astonishing, and it was only made worse by the fact that they had no way of gathering reliable information about the real condition of *terraferma* forests except through second- and third-hand reports. The complexity of the problem also hampered Venetian legislators' attempts to grasp the issues. With so many merchants facing such diverse challenges in their efforts to secure fuel and timber, it was nearly impossible for senators to draw solid conclusions about the causes of periodic shortages. The only thing they could determine with any certainty was that timber and firewood appeared more difficult to locate and more expensive to purchase than at any other time in the Republic's history. As a result, the assumption that the supply was failing at the source took hold in the chambers of the Ducal Palace.

Local Practices of Forest Exploitation and Venetian Shortages

In addition to the specific forest ecologies of the five timber-producing regions of the northeast and Istria, a number of more widespread conditions and practices affected the availability of timber and fuel in Venice. Regardless of location, the timber harvest was a delicate mechanism, easily disrupted. The arrival of forest commodities in Venice was the consequence of a complex series of events. Several factors affected not only the yield of a given harvest, but how much of it eventually made its way to Venice. These included the weather, problems with the labor supply, local competition for forest resources, and local practices of forest exploitation.

Throughout the mainland and Istria, forest exploitation followed a common seasonal pattern. Lumbering and large-scale firewood harvesting could only occur in the late summer and midwinter months, when peasants were not busy with the agricultural tasks that constituted their main occupation. Cutting timber and firewood on behalf of the Venetians represented a lower priority for peasants than the spring planting or fall reaping that followed close on the heels of the two timber-harvesting periods. If the task of getting large poles down to local rivers and streams for transport was unfinished at a time when the fields needed tending, peasants would simply walk away from their work in the forest, leaving valuable timber stacked by the side of roads and rivers, where it became vulnerable to theft and exposed to the weather. The later archival sources are replete with reports of abandoned timber rotting in forests and embarcaderos.[34] The willingness to abandon timber also arose from the fact that, prior to the sixteenth century, in most places the work was unremunerated. Work gangs were organized under the auspices of *angarie*, a type of corvée that communities—and later the Venetian state—demanded from the peasantry as a tax.[35] Communities owed a certain number of workers, based on the number of residents in their jurisdictions. In the case of the firewood harvest, every household received a share of the harvest as partial compensation for the labor. In later centuries the Venetian forest bureaucracy began to pay the workers a piece rate for harvesting certain types of wood—especially Arsenal timber. But prior to the Venetian conquest, most of the labor was performed gratis. Of course, once sufficient fuel and timber had been gathered to meet the needs of the village, there was little incentive—except perhaps fear of punishment—for peasants to continue working, which further contributed to the problem of abandoned timber.

The weather also affected how much time the peasants had to complete the harvest. During winter harvests, work had to begin in February, in order to take advantage of the higher water levels in local streams and rivers generated by the seasonal runoff that usually began in March. In late summer, the aim was to have the timber ready to float at the end of September, when autumn rains usually raised water levels throughout the northeast. The larger the trees being harvested, the more critical it became to fell and to move them down to riverbank embarcaderos in time to take advantage of higher volumes in local streams and rivers. Moreover, the greater the distance that large poles had to travel from forest to riverbank, the greater the importance of beginning the harvest in a timely manner—which is why forests more than two or three miles from a river were useless as sources of high-quality timber. Low precipitation levels in a given year—to say nothing of extended periods of drought—reduced the available time for floating large logs, often to the point where it became almost impossible to deliver the harvest to the river on time. For these reasons, the shortcomings of *angaria* labor, combined with the difficulties of coordinating the arrival of timber with the moment of maximum affluence in local waterways, created a situation in which even the smallest misstep had the power to disrupt the timber harvest. And even tiny disruptions had painful consequences for the Venetians, as local residents were always sure to look to their own needs before sending timber or fuel downstream.

The delicate timing of the harvest and the vicissitudes of the *angarie* were not the only factors affecting the availability of timber and fuel in Venice. Local market conditions did much to determine regional supplies. The summer and winter harvests involved more than just getting large poles down to the embarcaderos; they also created the raw material for lime, charcoal, and other processed forest commodities (such as green fertilizer) that were produced in the weeks and months following the harvest. Because the finished products were easier to transport than the raw material—be it large pieces of wood for charcoal or leafy material for fertilizer—such commodities were invariably produced in the immediate vicinity of the forests where the material had been collected. The time it took to create the finished product meant that by the time it was ready for market the timber rafts that carried merchandise downstream had already departed. And unless the area of production was located in the coastal plain where small boats regularly moved bulk cargo around, merchants were left with the choice of making an immediate profit by selling their wares locally or waiting several months until the next harvest season in the hopes of getting a better price from Venetian buyers. The lag time created disincentives to sell charcoal and other finished commodities outside of the area of production, which could then lead to significant shortages in Venice that had nothing to do with the availability of oak and beech timber—the two most common species used to make charcoal.

Local consumption also had discernable effects on the Venetians' ability to secure vital forest resources. A significant portion of the yield of any harvest went to satisfy local demand for domestic firewood, industrial charcoal, and construction timber destined for buildings and critical infrastructure such as bridges, mills, and irrigation canals. The more densely populated an area, the more local requirements affected how much material would be left over for Venetian merchants to buy. But even in a less-populated region such as the middle Piave, local consumption could affect Venetian supplies. For example, according to Andrea Pasqualigo—the Venetian *podestà* of Belluno—the town's metallurgical industries consumed upwards of 104,000 baskets—approximately 7,500 cubic meters—of charcoal a year in 1575.[36] He also estimated that the average charcoal furnace turned out around 360 baskets—approximately 26 cubic meters—which meant that Belluno alone consumed around 289 furnaces' worth of charcoal per year. Since the total production of charcoal in the region varied significantly—depending on factors such as the availability of labor, weather, and the number of merchants investing in charcoal production—in a bad year local industries could consume all of the local supplies, leaving nothing for Venetian merchants to purchase. Likewise, the hundreds of irrigation canals—whose walls were shored up by massive numbers of wooden piles—and bridges in the lower Piave consumed a significant share of the region's annual harvest of construction timber.

Local needs also altered practices of forest exploitation in ways that affected the supply of forest resources in Venice. Mainland residents often prized different kinds of wood than the Venetians, and sought to shape their local forests—especially community forests—accordingly. The most significant example of this phenomenon was the firewood harvest. For most *terraferma* communities—regardless of size—domestic fuel was perhaps the single most important forest commodity. Delays in the maintenance of bridges and irrigation networks were tolerable.

Shortages of industrial fuel affected the profits of merchants and artisans. But a lack of domestic fuel, especially in winter, meant potential death for many, not to mention the risk of severe peasant unrest that could jeopardize the social order. It is no coincidence that access to firewood was always among the first demands made in peasant revolts throughout the medieval and early modern periods, and village authorities were right to fear the possibility of violence. To forestall such threats to civic order, communities throughout the mainland distributed a fixed share of the firewood harvest to all local households and maintained additional stockpiles that could be distributed to the needy in the event of a bad winter.

Because of the critical importance of firewood, local officials generally preferred to rely on community forests rather than private suppliers to keep the common reserves fully stocked. On the one hand, this meant that community leaders—especially in densely populated areas—tended to remain attentive to the protection of community stands, which in turn helped preserve regional forest cover. On the other hand, the importance that local authorities placed on firewood meant that these stands were managed in ways that increased yields of fuel while reducing yields of the large poles coveted by the Venetians for construction and shipbuilding. The most common strategy to increase firewood yields in deciduous forests was to coppice—cutting trees low to the ground and allowing many shoots to grow out of the stump. Heavy coppicing generated reliable yields of the small and medium-sized branches needed to make bundles of firewood and produce charcoal, but it discouraged the growth of the large, straight-grained trees needed for naval construction and the building trades. Depending on the size of the community forest, the terrain remaining for intact trunks could be quite small, which usually meant that only the biggest community forests were capable of producing a surplus of large poles for export to Venice.

Coppicing was not the only strategy available to villages seeking to ensure that their community forests remained capable of providing the necessities of life to local residents. Another common approach was to employ a system of rotational harvesting in community stands. Throughout the mainland, villages and towns divided their forests into sections called *prese*. Each *presa*, or coupe, would be used for a season, and then allowed to rest while each subsequent coupe was harvested in turn. Depending on the size of the forest and local norms there could be as few as six and as many as fifteen coupes in a given stand. The rotation of coupes, at least in theory, prevented the overexploitation of any single section of the forest while preserving the total area.

Not all villages were equally successful at preserving their community forests. Commons were subject to a variety of conflicting pressures from both within and without the community. During periods of crisis, leasing commons to merchants—or in drastic cases selling off community forests to private parties—served to mitigate fiscal shortfalls for many villages and towns. Traditional practices also put pressure on community forests. During the summer, for example, villages often allowed livestock to enter community forests to take shelter from the heat and to permit the open pasture to recover from heavy grazing. This practice conflicted with the desire to preserve the forest, because domesticated animals had the unfortunate habit of eating seedlings and damaging saplings, thereby threatening the integrity of the forest. Attempts to limit the damage through imposing head limits and restricting the period that stock could spend in the woods only worked as long as local officials made the effort to enforce such regulations. But corruption was common, and village leaders often turned a blind eye to abuses.[37] Likewise, there was little to prevent individuals from entering the forest outside of the official harvesting periods to collect fuel or timber for personal use. The cumulative effect of such abuses could sometimes be devastating for community lands, especially in the Friuli where herds tended to be larger. But as a general rule, local communities managed to preserve substantial areas of forestland in the centuries leading up to the Venetian conquest.

Because community forests were so often closed to outside interests, Venetian merchants preferred to avoid commons in their efforts to secure forest resources. Private property owners, feudatories, and institutions were usually eager to lease unprofitable forestland to outsiders. Leases typically lasted a decade and, better still—at least from the Venetian perspective—rarely required the leaseholder to respect harvest limits or the sequential exploitation of coupes. Indeed, for some landowners, leasing a forest to a merchant was sometimes simply a cost-effective way to clear-cut, with the ultimate goal of converting it to arable land. Consequently, as Venetian demand increased throughout the twelfth and thirteenth centuries, so, too, did the rate of deforestation on privately held lands. In some parts of the mainland the result was an emerging imbalance in the distribution of forests—with an increasing proportion of the best forests on community land and a decreasing proportion on private land.[38] Chapter 4 details how one of the tangible achievements of the Venetian forestry regime was to reverse this trend by forcing at least some private and institutional landlords to employ the same conservation measures as local communities.

Nevertheless, it is important not to exaggerate the degree to which unscrupulous individuals destroyed private and institutional forests. Venetian merchants found that the limitations imposed by labor and the seasonal nature of the work still applied on lands they leased that otherwise had no harvesting restrictions of any kind. Workers remained in short supply—especially during the fourteenth century—and more often than not, merchants relied on their landlords to provide them with *angaria* labor for the harvest. Even in those cases where they paid workers a wage, merchants were no more successful than community authorities at preventing peasants from abandoning the timber harvest in favor of work in the fields. In addition, the timeframe for the harvest remained just as tight. If the timber did not make it to the river in time, merchants were no better positioned than anyone else to move it downstream. So despite the fact that the terms of private and institutional leases tended to be quite liberal, problems with the labor supply and the timing of the harvest limited the extent of the resultant deforestation.

During the various economic and demographic crises of the fourteenth century, what had been occasional shortages of timber and fuel in Venice became increasingly frequent. The supply shortages were particularly acute during outbreaks of the plague, because the ability to organize and deploy labor on a very tight schedule constituted one of the main factors that made the difference between surplus and shortage in Venice. As successive waves of plague devastated Italy after 1348, the Venetians faced not only a frightening demographic crisis but serious shortages of timber and fuel as well. Indeed, it is not surprising that the first efforts to find a legislative solution to timber shortages occurred in 1350, when the Great Council passed a measure regulating the sale of oak in Venice.[39] The law gave the Arsenal right of first refusal on any naval-grade oak sold in the city. Venetian legislators believed that restricting the market for high-quality oak would guarantee that the Arsenal, at least, would remain supplied, even if private yards might suffer. And the Great Council did not stop there. Soon beech joined oak as a regulated species. In 1372 the Great Council established a fine of nine *grossi* per lost or broken oar, to be collected from the captains of every returning galley.[40] Again, legislators believed that they could help the Arsenal avoid a timber shortage, this time by attempting to limit wasteful use of critical resources. The conviction that problems with the timber supply could be addressed through restrictions on the sale and use of oak and beech was based, in part, on the flawed conception that supply problems were the consequence of a lack of adequate supplies in mainland forests. Yet as I have already shown, timber and fuel shortages were largely tied to a combination of mainland labor shortages, the harvesting cycle, local practices such as coppicing, and the various regional barriers that Venetian merchants faced in their efforts to secure forest resources. That the Venetians feared sources of timber and fuel were disappearing was understandable, but the fact that none of these other factors—especially the shortage of labor—were considered worthy of mention by legislators illustrates the degree to which they were misunderstanding the problem.

Restricting the market on Arsenal-grade oak and beech, while based on faulty premises, was not necessarily a damaging decision. Unfortunately for the Venetians, the perception that supplies on the mainland were dwindling led legislators to take a far more problematic step than simply assessing fines on lost oars. Legislators feared that if the price of oak rose too high, the Arsenal would no longer be able to afford to manufacture ships, placing the cornerstone of the Republic's prosperity in jeopardy. Along with market restrictions, the Great Council decided to impose price ceilings on oak—and eventually on beech and firewood too. The intent of the price ceilings was to prevent merchants from taking what the Republic's leaders saw as unfair advantage of the shortages. Later, when the Senate extended the ceilings to the firewood trade, the fear was that predatory pricing would literally leave Venice's poor out in the cold. But in both cases the laws had the effect of exacerbating shortages. Capping the price simply discouraged merchants from seeking timber and fuel in any but the most easily accessible forests. Suddenly the high transportation costs associated with Istrian timber became an insurmountable obstacle to its purchase. Likewise, price ceilings all but prevented merchants from seeking timber in areas such as the Friuli, where labor was scarce and therefore expensive. Not only did this limit the total amount of timber that the Venetians could purchase, but it also led to the depletion and outright destruction of some of the most easily accessible stands along the Piave and Sile rivers. For these reasons the Venetian response to shortages—the price ceilings—made the effects of the fourteenth-century crises on the timber supply even worse than they otherwise would have been. The Arsenal and the city continued to experience shortages, and as for the end-user legislation, the captains of the great galleys restricted themselves to the absolute minimum number of oars, preferring to rely on the wind rather than risk the fines.[41]

The Venetian reaction to cyclical shortages in the timber supply was understandable, in spite of its obvious flaws. The Venetians were responding to what they thought were dwindling supplies of oak and beech timber throughout the *terraferma*. The inability of the Senate and the Great Council to control local practices of forest exploitation or the effects of the weather, combined with their misperception of the causes of recurrent shortages, led them to what they considered to be their only alternative, controlling consumption. Market controls, coupled with rules dictating the use of the finished product, had little in common with the programs Venetian legislators developed in the following centuries that were aimed at the regulation and conservation of timber resources, but the legal precedents they set would remain important for the future. The lesson that the Venetians drew from fourteenth-century supply crises was that the available supply of oak and beech timber was finite and perpetually in jeopardy. This assumption would lead them, in the following century, to adopt a strategy aimed at drastically limiting access to forests when they were finally able to begin controlling timber at the source. While such a strategy would be successful in terms of preserving the total forested area on the mainland, in many places it would also hamper the growth of important species such as oak and beech, a contradiction that chapter 5 examines in greater detail.

Perceived Shortages and the Emergence of the Market Hierarchy

It is not enough to say that Venetian legislators believed that the timber supply was finite, or even that it was an important resource, without stopping to define the terms that major Venetian magistracies used to understand that resource. After all, timber was a material with hundreds of potential applications. In the fourteenth century, however, the Venetian government was largely unconcerned with most other applications for timber outside of shipbuilding, because of the importance of maritime commerce and the fact that Arsenal timber appeared to be the most difficult material to procure. By the early fifteenth century, firewood and construction material for urban growth and infrastructure would also appear on the legislative horizon, but in the minds of most fourteenth-century legislators, timber simply meant ships.

Three tree species used in naval construction—oak, beech, and fir—have already been mentioned, but shipyards also required considerable quantities of larch, elm, and walnut. Oak was used for the hull, main bulkheads, structural ribs, and knees, as well as the keel of galleys and round ships. The galley oars were made of beech, the masts of fir, the deck and minor bulkheads of larch, the spars of elm, and the rudder of walnut. The Arsenal could not build a ship without adequate supplies of all of these species, but oak and beech represented a special concern, because together they comprised most of the timber consumed in naval construction. Durmast oak accounted for over three-quarters of the timber in a Venetian ship. A great galley required at least 200 mature oak poles twenty-four feet or more in length and between four and six feet in circumference to produce the over 800 separate planks and fittings that made up the hull.[42] As for beech, a light galley carried at least 120 oars, and a great galley employed up to 180 oars at a time. An unusually large and perfectly structured beech tree yielded, at best, six large oars of the type used in the galleys. Of course, such trees were rare, and a single galley required at least 50 mature beech poles for its initial store of oars. Regular refits consumed many more. By contrast, a single ship required only three or four high-quality fir poles for its masts, and perhaps five lesser-quality poles for planking. A dozen good larch poles furnished the decking, and the same number of walnut and elm poles yielded the raw material for the rigging and rudders of several ships.

Not only was oak the most important species used in naval construction, it was also the most complicated to prepare. Before oak could be sawed into planking for the hull, it required seasoning. Green timber was not reliably watertight, and ships made of poorly-seasoned timber frequently experienced catastrophic hull failures.[43] The Venetians seasoned oak in the Arsenal by weighing down bundles of logs and sinking them to the bottom of bays set aside for that purpose. After allowing the logs to sit underwater for anywhere from six to eighteen months, workers recovered the poles and skilled sawyers cut them into the planking that made up the hull of a new ship. Supplying the Arsenal with oak was not merely a question of harvesting poles and floating them downstream; it also required a significant amount of advance planning. More importantly, a substantial stockpile of seasoned oak needed to be on hand in the event that a large number of vessels had to be commissioned at once—as occurred, for example, during the War of Chioggia. The fact that the yield of mainland harvests fluctuated so much from year to year made it almost impossible for the Arsenal managers to plan ahead, a problem that grew far worse during the uncertain years following 1348.

In short, there were six species of trees, two of which were constantly in short supply, and a single important end user: the Arsenal. These were the terms in which Venetian legislators understood timber in the fifty years leading up to the Republic's mainland expansion. This schema offers one of the keys to understanding many subsequent developments in Venetian forestry policies. The notion that Arsenal-grade oak and beech were especially difficult to find became a basic, unquestionable fear for most Venetian legislators. The scarcity of oak and beech recurs as a constant refrain in the language employed by the various Venetian councils. In the preambles to legislation it was never merely want of timber, but rather it was a literal famine—*carestia*—that was said to afflict the state and its shipbuilding center. Typical language included such phrases as "knowing that the famine of timber threatens our liberty"; "recognizing the importance and necessity of timber for the Arsenal and the well being of our republic"; "because, as everyone knows, oak is of the first importance for our republic"; and, "the Arsenal, as everyone knows, is of singular importance to our liberty." Language explicitly linking forest resources with the survival of Venice and its republican liberty continued to dominate discussions of timber until the fall of the Republic, even in times when the yield of mainland harvests was more than adequate to meet overall demand. Such expressions became increasingly common in sixteenth-century legislation, when legislators began to employ this vocabulary of scarcity to a whole slate of important commodities such as saltpeter, hemp, and iron. In the fourteenth century, however, that vocabulary was reserved for a select few critical resources: wheat, salt, and Arsenal timber.[44]

The vocabulary of scarcity reveals a crucial aspect of the Venetians' understanding of the supply problems that the Arsenal began to experience in the fourteenth century. The market and end-use legislation was aimed at restoring the supply of essential species, either by reserving what was available on the market or preserving the equipment that was manufactured using a particular species of wood. By assigning oak and beech a privileged position in the market, the Venetians assigned them a privileged position in political debates as well. In later centuries, what should have been debates about problems with the supply of timber and fuel in general were consistently transformed into debates about oak and beech. Timber was routinely referred to as oak, as if this were the only species of tree growing in the mixed deciduous forests of the coastal plain. And in the minds of most Venetian legislators, it may as well have been.

The privileged political position of oak established a hierarchy of market priorities. Controlling the timber trade meant controlling the oak trade first and the beech trade second. Venetian legislators' focus on two species to the exclusion of others had a lasting effect on local patterns of forest exploitation and renewal throughout the mainland, following the early fifteenth-century Venetian conquest. Price ceilings actively discouraged timber merchants and local communities from expanding their harvests into new stands—especially those that stood in more difficult terrain. As a result, merchants slowed the rate at which they harvested oak and beech on the mainland, which had the paradoxical effect of preserving oak forests at the very moment that the Venetians were afflicted with a severe timber shortage and would have done anything to secure new supplies. This paradox helps illustrate the most important shortcoming of the hierarchy of markets: it offered a distorted lens through which to view the region's forest cover. In the mind's eye of most Venetian legislators, the market hierarchy created an imaginary mainland ecology in which even-aged, single-species climax stands stood under the constant threat of extinction at the hands of unscrupulous people. The physical landscape of the region did not, unfortunately, contain forests of this sort. It had never contained them. Therefore, the political values that the Venetians had assigned to oak and beech did not reflect the environmental context within which those two species were being exploited and reproduced.

In the fourteenth century, the distorted vision produced by the market hierarchy was exacerbated by the utter lack of concrete and reliable information about the nature and extent of mainland forest resources. Better information might have provided legislators with a more nuanced understanding of the supply problems. Because the Venetians controlled little or no mainland territory, they were forced to rely on second- and third-hand reports for their decisions. Very few senators, Collegio members, and other decision-makers had any idea what the mainland environment looked like or what kinds of local conditions and practices created timber shortages in Venice. Nonetheless, the politically determined market hierarchy had lasting consequences for the future of the forestry regime. When translated into forest-use legislation, the market hierarchy would only acknowledge a handful of uses among hundreds. By continuing to privilege the Arsenal, the hierarchical scheme prevented Venetian legislators from seeing the larger environmental context of forest exploitation in the *terraferma* and Istria, even as a new class of Venetian officials ventured onto the mainland in search of the sources of critical forest resources. It is to this search, and the new knowledge about forests that it produced, that the next chapter will now turn.

CHAPTER TWO

The Venetian Discovery of Mainland Forests

And their actions did more harm than good.

IN 1441 THE VENETIAN PATRICIANS Marco Cornaro, Francesco Garzoni, and Orio Pasqualigo set out from the city to inspect the condition of mainland forests along the Sile, Piave, and Tagliamento rivers. For centuries this region had served as a reliable source of firewood for Venice. But in the wake of a series of severe fuel shortages in the city, the Venetian Senate had become increasingly anxious about the availability of combustible material. In an effort to alleviate the growing crisis, the Senate commissioned the elected heads of the three Venetian magistracies whose areas of responsibility had a bearing on the firewood trade to inspect mainland forests and identify possible new sources of fuel.[1] Cornaro and his companions spent two months touring the mainland in the hopes of finding a solution to the dearth of fuel in Venice. While the inspection was a collective affair, only Cornaro felt compelled to write extensively about what he had seen. The resulting document was both a work of remarkable technical sophistication and a surprisingly flawed view of several important forest landscapes.[2] On the one hand, Cornaro's treatise represented an extraordinary development, because in it he offered the first coherent analysis of ongoing firewood shortages that did not identify the impoverishment of mainland forests as a primary cause. The work was also noteworthy for its powerfully reasoned account of the complex relationship between the mainland environment and the lagoon—specifically his treatment of the linkages between deforestation, erosion, and sedimentary accumulation. On the other hand, despite the fact that Cornaro made sweeping claims about the availability of good firewood throughout the lower Piave region, he included virtually no useful information about the actual state of the forests in his work. In large part this was because, as a Venetian, he viewed water as the most important component of the landscape and forests as a secondary feature. His emphasis on water also reflected his possession of an elaborate technical understanding of the ways in which water and land interacted, but he lacked a corresponding grasp of the complicated relationship between forests and the surrounding environment. The shortcomings of Cornaro's understanding of forests ultimately limited his ability to imagine possible solutions to the problem of cyclical fuel shortages.

Cornaro's treatise offers a valuable window into the ways in which Venetian legislators interpreted the information about mainland forests that began to flow into the Ducal Palace in the wake of the conquest of the *terraferma*. The treatise clearly demonstrates that after nearly four decades of mainland rule, the Venetians still knew relatively little about the sources of the city's timber and fuel. It also highlights the limits of the Republic's power to control, preserve, or otherwise alter mainland forests. By all accounts the Republic's leaders should already have been familiar with the nearby mainland by the time they dispatched Cornaro, Garzoni, and Pasqualigo on their mission. Venice had first taken possession of the area around Mestre a century earlier in 1339, lost it at the Peace of Turin in 1381, and then reconquered it in 1404. By 1441 Venetian rule over significant sections of the lower Piave region was anything but a novelty. Yet Cornaro's treatise reveals a striking lack of familiarity with many features of these critical landscapes. Moreover, the fuel shortages that prompted the inspection illustrate the degree to which the conquest of the *terraferma* had failed to address any of the endemic problems with the supply of forest commodities that had plagued the Venetians in the fourteenth century.

Through a careful analysis of three crucial problems enumerated in Cornaro's writings, this chapter explains why the Venetians continued to struggle to secure forest resources after the conquest of the mainland; how those struggles drove them to seek possible new sources of firewood; and how ongoing problems with the timber and firewood supply drove them to take tentative first steps towards the creation of a comprehensive program of forest management. Cornaro's treatise demonstrates the ways in which Venice's peculiar geography powerfully influenced the way that residents of the lagoon viewed mainland landscapes. The chapter will also analyze how Venetian ideas of geographic space affected the efforts of officials such as Cornaro to interpret what they saw when they looked at forests, sometimes leading them to faulty conclusions about the integrity of those forests. In addition, Cornaro's writings reveal how the Venetians gradually developed a regional perspective on environmental change that helped them understand the connections among diverse mainland landscapes in the coming centuries. By linking firewood shortages to a more familiar set of problems having to do with alluvial sediment, Cornaro offered a persuasive argument that the flow of forest resources into Venice could only be understood as a small piece of a much larger and more complicated economic and environmental puzzle. This chapter shows that the Venetians began to translate their extensive experience with water management into a new set of ideas about the maintenance of mainland forests.

Finally, the official response to Cornaro's arguments underscores the reasons why the conquest failed to ensure the flow of critical forest resources into Venice. Cornaro proposed a number of quite sensible solutions to what he saw as the root causes of ongoing fuel shortages. These suggestions included conducting dredging operations in inland waterways, reforesting the region's riverbanks, and reforming the system of market controls that the Great Council had established during the crises of the fourteenth century. This chapter demonstrates that the persistence of local privileges and property rights on the mainland prevented the Senate from acting on most of Cornaro's suggestions in any meaningful way—even though action probably would have helped guarantee the arrival of forest commodities in the lagoon. Powerless to impose new regulations governing land use, legislators ignored Cornaro's call for forced reforestation. Likewise, instead of reforming or eliminating the market regulations, the Senate attempted to strengthen them. This approach proved no more effective than it had been in the previous century, but its continuing failure was instrumental in finally forcing the Republic's leadership to accept the necessity of a new approach to the problem of forests—one that entailed interfering with the property rights of the mainland residents who controlled the resources that the Venetians so badly needed.

Water Management and Venetian Interpretations of Mainland Landscapes

In 1441, when the Senate selected him to inspect nearby sources of firewood, Marco Cornaro held the office of *provveditore alla giustizia vecchia*. As a relatively young officeholder at age 29, his election to the position represented an important first step along the standard *cursus honorum* followed by countless ambitious Venetian patricians at the outset of their political careers.[3] Competent service in the office would prove to senior members of the government that a young man such as Cornaro was worthy of nomination to more important positions within Venice's republican system.[4] As a *provveditore alla giustizia vecchia*, Cornaro's most important responsibility was to oversee the maintenance and well-being of the lagoon—including the city's famous canal network.[5] Judging by his later writings, it is safe to conclude that Cornaro took these responsibilities very seriously indeed. His 1442 treatise, "On Forests," displays an intimate knowledge of the complex geography and hydrology of the waters surrounding Venice. Nor did the treatise mark the end of Cornaro's involvement in the administration of water. He later served for multiple terms as *savio alle acque*, and in 1457 he proposed the relocation of the mouth of the Brenta River—a project that would not be completed until the following century.[6] In 1460 he also penned the treatise "On the Lagoon," which included a lengthy natural history of the northern Adriatic coastline.[7] He died of the plague in 1465. As this brief biographical sketch indicates, Marco Cornaro made pondering the lagoon and the surrounding watershed his life's work.

Massive reclamation projects such as the Dutch polders may enjoy pride of place in historical narratives about European efforts to reshape the environment, but in the fifteenth century Venice's lagoon was among the most painstakingly managed environments in the world.[8] The lagoon had been the site of an ongoing struggle against alluvial sediment for almost as long as humans had lived there. In antiquity the Venetian lagoon was the largest single element in an extensive system of wetlands stretching along the Adriatic coast from Ravenna to Aquilea. By the time the Venetians expanded onto the mainland in the early fifteenth century, their lagoon was the only contiguous body of water remaining along that stretch of the northern Adriatic. The rest of what Pliny the Elder famously referred to as "the seven seas" had long since been reduced to marshland or entirely swallowed up by the mainland.

The survival of the Venetian lagoon was almost entirely due to constant and tireless efforts on the part of the humans living there. The landfill that had allowed the Venetians to expand the urban core of the city in the preceding three centuries was created from alluvial sediment laboriously dredged up from the lagoon floor. Urban expansion, however, did not consume enough sediment to offset the progressive terrestrialization of the lagoon. Despite ongoing dredging efforts, the Venetians recognized that the lagoon and the port remained under constant threat from effluvium. Eventually, the rate of sedimentary accumulation prompted the Venetians to consider major alterations to the lagoon environment aimed at eliminating—or at least minimizing—the problem.

Beginning in the late thirteenth century, the Venetians undertook a series of reclamation projects in the lagoon that dwarfed all previous interventions. Instead of removing accumulated silt as they had done in the past, the Venetians aimed at eliminating the main sources of sediment by transforming the lagoon from a brackish delta marsh into a saltwater tidal body.[9] To accomplish their goal the Venetians had to divert the two river systems that fed into their lagoon—the Brenta to the south and the Piave-Sile system to the north—so that they discharged their silt-laden water directly into the Adriatic.[10] The Republic did not complete this immense undertaking until the mid-seventeenth century, but by the early fifteenth century several important diversions had already been finished and the rate of siltation in the lagoon visibly reduced. Even so, the Venetians remained vigilant, as the many irrigation canals and smaller streams that fed off the Piave and Sile still dumped silt-laden fresh water into the upper lagoon, and part of the Brenta's flow still entered the lower lagoon.

The river diversions set an important legal precedent for Venetian interference on the mainland that the Republic would later exploit to justify confiscating large areas of forestland for public use. To build the new channels along the lagoon littoral, the Republic had forcibly seized and destroyed significant tracts of agricultural land belonging to Paduan subjects. Initially the Senate limited its trampling of local property rights to areas directly affecting the lagoon. But those actions served as a model for the extension of state sovereignty over forests in the late fifteenth century.

The river diversions also affected mainland forest cover in more tangible ways. The levees and embankments that protected the new riverbeds consumed mammoth quantities of timber in the form of *tolpi*, almost all of which came from the lower Piave region. And the demand for *tolpi* did not abate with the completion of the diversions. The fourteenth- and fifteenth-century alterations to the watershed introduced major tidal fluctuations into the lagoon. To counter the pernicious effects of the tides—which bore heavy silt loads, especially during the autumn high-water season—the Venetians constructed a new system of earth and timber breakwaters along the lagoon's littoral islands. Unlike the inland system of embankments, which was fairly stable, the breakwaters annually suffered extensive damage from winter storm surges. Each spring and summer the Venetians labored to replace thousands of *tolpi* that had been washed out to sea during the most recent season. The need to rebuild the breakwaters created a sustained demand for construction timber that lasted until permanent stone structures were finally built in the middle of the eighteenth century.

The long struggle to shape and maintain the lagoon had a powerful influence on how Venetians viewed the natural world. Most importantly, it created a familiar lens that Venetian officials such as Cornaro could employ to interpret any change in the mainland environment that had a discernable effect on the waters surrounding the city. Indeed, Cornaro and others had observed a notable increase in the volume of sediment accumulating in the lagoon after 1424—the year that the conquest of the *terraferma* was complete. To the Venetians, the increase in alluvial sediment presented a clear symptom of dangerous changes underway in the mainland environment. And while there was not yet any clear connection between the sediment and the problems with the firewood supply, the Senate considered it best to proceed with caution and include a representative of the *provveditori alla giustizia vecchia* among the officials dispatched on the 1441 inspection tour. The Senate also selected one of the heads from the *provveditori al commune* and another from the *ufficiali alle rason vecchie*, Garzoni and Pasqualigo. The first magistracy was in charge of customs revenues on all traffic entering the lagoon, including timber and fuel. The second was responsible for auditing government expenditures, including bulk purchases of firewood and timber.

The Senate's original commission to the three young patricians called on them to inspect the forests along the Sile, Piave, and Livenza rivers, with the aim of identifying possible new sources of fuel for the city. The winter of 1441 had been an especially trying one for the city's firewood warehouses. As Cornaro recalled in a 1442 letter, "there was, at that time, a very great famine of firewood in the city, such that firewood . . . could not be had."[11] During the two months that he and his two companions spent looking at mainland forests, Cornaro painstakingly recorded what he saw. He also reflected on the possible connections between the increasing rates of siltation that his office had been witnessing in the lagoon and the forests he was inspecting on the mainland. The result of these ruminations was a lengthy treatise on the relationship between the watershed and the firewood supply. The Senate would hardly have been interested in a lengthy technical report of the sort Cornaro was intent on preparing. As a rule, senators preferred that reports be brief and formal. The most senior officials might have license to address the body at length. But the three younger patricians were expected to offer a quick summary of their activities, preferably one that confirmed what the Senate already believed—that mainland forests were running out of firewood at an alarming rate. The trio's job was simply to locate new sources of combustible material, not to discourse at length on what most legislators perceived as the well-known causes of the crisis.

As Cornaro pondered what he was seeing on the mainland, he gradually came to the conclusion that cyclical fuel shortages were not the product of dwindling supplies in the woods. Rather, Cornaro reasoned that the shortages had two main causes. In the opening of his treatise he blamed the fourteenth-century system of market controls, arguing that price ceilings combined with the overzealous and at times corrupt application of customs duties and transportation tariffs had made the trade so unprofitable that few merchants were willing to risk investing in it any longer. Referring to the officials who—supposedly following the explicit instructions of their superiors in Venice—had "enforced the tariffs without exception," he said that "their actions did more harm than good."[12] Cornaro then proceeded to argue that while some deforestation had indeed occurred on the mainland, it was only indirectly to blame for the collapse of the firewood trade. Specifically, his treatise contended that extensive riverbank deforestation throughout the lower Piave region had led to erosion, which in turn had raised the amount of silt suspended in local waterways to dangerous levels. The increased volume of sediment was, he posited, the cause of the alarming rise in the rate of siltation in the lagoon observed by the *provveditori alla giustizia vecchia* in recent years. For Cornaro, higher sediment loads were the other principal cause of the firewood shortages. The silt, he said, had almost entirely blocked many of the smaller streams and canals used by the boatmen who transported firewood to Venice, effectively crippling the trade. Without these small waterways the boats could not reach the embarcaderos or move firewood collected in area forests on to Venice. In other words, in Cornaro's estimation there was no fuel shortage, just a poorly conceived set of market controls and a large number of badly managed inland waterways that together prevented firewood from reaching the lagoon.

Cornaro's analysis was remarkably lucid. He attributed the treatise's scope and clarity to his personal experiences, noting that "it had pleased God that I should have been *giustiziere vecchio* the previous year, such that I was then able to address my spirit to this problem, take note of the source of corruption, and make provisions in the hope that such a great inconvenience might not repeat itself."[13] Cornaro proceeded to emphasize the importance of his tour of the nearby watershed in the formulation of his ideas, claiming that his ability to comprehend the causes of firewood shortages was "also because I possessed a good and worthy experience of the countryside of the Trevigiano, Cenedese, and even the Friuli."[14] Despite grounding his claim to authority in an important series of personal experiences, the treatise placed him in an extremely awkward position with regard to his superiors in the Senate. After all, he had been charged with locating new sources of fuel, not with reevaluating a set of policies that dated back nearly a century to the 1350 law restricting the market on oak. As an ambitious young patrician Cornaro had every incentive to keep his theories to himself and simply move on to his next assignment. But Cornaro felt strongly enough about his ideas that he was willing to risk voicing them in public, even if he was not foolhardy enough to present them to the entire Senate. With over 200 members— many of them his rivals for political advancement—it would have been far too difficult to convince a majority of senators that the traditional understanding of timber and fuel shortages was misguided. Instead, Cornaro decided to approach the smaller Collegio, an executive body made up almost entirely of the most senior members of the government. The Collegio might ultimately reject his suggestions, but the more restricted and secretive venue would insulate him against some of the political risk involved in openly criticizing long-standing policies. With that in mind, he convinced his friend Hieronimo Molin—one of the three heads of the Forty—to secure him an audience before the assembled Collegio to present his findings.[15]

The product of both serious rumination and political machination, Cornaro's treatise was a carefully calibrated piece of rhetoric. He spent relatively little time on his critique of the market controls and tariffs. While his argument was both reasonable and accurate, it would not do for a young patrician to be seen undermining a set of policies that enjoyed a broad consensus among the Republic's leadership. Indeed, he devoted most of the very brief section on the firewood market to attacking the tax farmers and minor officials who collected money from the boatmen and merchants. Criticizing corrupt officials was always a safe approach in a republican system that was fairly obsessed with guarding itself against the undisciplined passions and interests of its citizens.[16] He left it to his audience to draw the obvious conclusion that the actions of subordinate officials reflected larger flaws in the policies governing the firewood trade and were not merely the result of individual malfeasance.

Having protected himself against the most politically dangerous objections to his argument, Cornaro then proceeded to undertake a lengthy and exhaustive analysis of silt blockages in the dense network of inland waterways between Treviso and the lagoon. Here he found himself on safer ground. By couching his theory in terms of threats to the watershed, Cornaro firmly situated his argument within the well-respected tradition of Venetian water management. Whether or not his audience accepted his assertion that siltation was one of the main causes of firewood shortages, the idea that it posed a threat to the lagoon—and therefore to the Republic—was guaranteed to be uncontroversial. At worst, the Collegio would reject his proposals while praising him for his zealous concern for the integrity of the lagoon and the city.

The bulk of Cornaro's treatise consisted of an exhaustive account of siltation. As in his earlier letters, he stressed his personal, first-hand knowledge of every stream and canal. His description of the network of inland waterways was so comprehensive that it would have been possible to retrace his itinerary step by step with nothing more than a copy of his treatise in hand. By cataloging the extent to which alluvial sediment had obstructed inland waterways, Cornaro clearly hoped to make his case more persuasive. Yet in spite of its almost excruciating detail, his analysis also served to expose its almost complete lack of any meaningful information about the forests he had been sent to examine. If his description of the stream and canal network was precise enough to act as a map, his description of the forests did not even furnish the most elementary information about their size, density, or composition. At several junctures he expressed "pleasure at having seen so many places so full of wood," but he did not consider it important to specify either what kind of wood or how much wood existed in those places.[17] He simply assumed that the forests he was seeing were suitable sources of firewood. And while he may have been correct in that assumption, he supplied no useful information to support it. The Senate had sent him to look at the forests of the lower Piave, but Cornaro had seen the region's waterways instead.

As a Venetian who had lived most of his life in the lagoon and had served as a *provveditore alla giustizia vecchia*, looking at water must have seemed like a logical and natural way to analyze the mainland landscape. After all, to a resident of the lagoon, water was the most important feature of any landscape. At the same time, this perspective was fatally flawed as a basis for surveying forest resources, because it failed to take into account any of the crucial factors that determined the yield of a given forest. Not every species of wood was suitable for use as firewood, so even if a place was indeed "so full of wood," it might be full of the wrong kind of wood and therefore unsuitable for exploitation. In addition, for a forest to generate reliable yields of fuel, it needed to be heavily coppiced. Large hardwood poles, while potentially useful for any number of purposes—including shipbuilding material, construction timber, and piles—were all but useless as fuel because of the labor required to reduce them to an appropriate size. The total size and stand density of a given forest also influenced the kinds and sizes of trees that would grow there. If the forest was too small, it might not tolerate heavy exploitation because it could not be divided into a sufficient number of coupes. If a less-valuable species such as elm dominated in the stand, then it would never become a reliable source of oak or beech. In addition, the flooding that inevitably results from the type of siltation that Cornaro described is lethal to the most valuable hardwood species—such as oak, which needs dry, well-drained soil to thrive. Finally, Cornaro made no mention of what kind of property the forests stood on. Were they community forests reserved for local needs, or were they privately or institutionally owned stands that firewood merchants might lease? He did not say and the Collegio did not ask. At a minimum, a survey of forest resources had to take these five factors into account if it was going to provide even a rough idea of how much firewood a forest might yield. But Cornaro, like most Venetians, lacked even the most basic understanding of what he was looking at when he stood before a wooded area.

Knowing that in 1441 even an extremely thoughtful and sophisticated Venetian observer such as Cornaro could not see beyond the superficial aspects of mainland forests highlights the fact that the Republic's leaders then were no better informed about the sources of timber and fuel than their fourteenth-century predecessors. If after two months of inspecting forests Cornaro still knew so little about them, how could a senator in the Ducal Palace be expected to possess any kind of meaningful knowledge? The treatise also shows that gathering useful information about the *terraferma* forests was not simply a matter of sending officials out to have a look and waiting for them to report back. To produce effective catalogs of forest resources, Venetian officials needed to abandon an existing set of assumptions about the landscape rooted in centuries of living in the difficult lagoon environment and extracting a living from the sea. They needed to stop seeing water and start seeing trees.

In spite of the limited perspective that Cornaro brought with him on his tour of mainland forests, his treatise still reflected an impressive conceptual breakthrough. Not only had he produced one of the first truly comprehensive analyses of a complex watershed, but he also drew some extremely sophisticated conclusions from what he had seen. For even if he could not say with certainty that any of the forests he had surveyed contained useful material for firewood or were available to lease, he was nonetheless correct to argue that because so many streams and canals were obstructed by sediment, it meant that those forests could not be exploited on behalf of the Republic. Nor did he end his analysis there. Cornaro proceeded to make a startling set of assertions about the causes of the worrisome increase in siltation. For while Cornaro implicitly dismissed the traditional view that deforestation was the source of timber and fuel shortages, he assigned a prominent place to clear-cutting in his account of what had been occurring in the watershed.

Cornaro argued for a two-pronged solution to the problem of siltation. The first part involved extensive dredging operations to liberate the obstructed waterways and once again make the region's forests accessible to boat traffic. Here Cornaro was still hewing closely to a traditional set of concerns and solutions—the Venetians had been dredging in and around the lagoon for centuries. It was with his second prescription that Cornaro pointed to radically new possibilities. Cornaro asserted that while he saw no reason to think that widespread deforestation had affected the firewood supply, he had witnessed substantial evidence that localized deforestation of riverbanks had led to significant erosion. This erosion, Cornaro argued, was the source of the sediment that was blocking inland waterways and threatening the well-being of the lagoon. In light of these facts he concluded that only a long-term strategy that combined dredging with reforestation of the riverbanks would effectively reduce the amount of sediment suspended in local rivers and streams. Cornaro also hoped that such a strategy would resolve Venice's problem with cyclical fuel shortages by reopening the region to boat traffic.

The most striking feature of Cornaro's argument is the way he situated the question of the firewood supply within a broader environmental context by correlating the problems of water and forest management and exposing the connections that bound them into a single regional ecology. From his perspective, the lagoon, the rivers, and the forests were merely three faces of a single problem—a problem requiring an integrated response on the part of the Republic. Although he did not understand the effects of species distribution, local practices of exploitation, and property rights on forest yields, he nonetheless developed a complex view of the interconnections between the region's waterways, agrarian landscapes, and forests. He also clearly understood that alterations to one part of the environment—in this case forests—could precipitate significant changes in the others. In this regard, Cornaro saw much more than either his colleagues in the Ducal Palace or his fourteenth-century predecessors. His landscape was still dominated by water, but he understood that water as part of a larger regional system.

While Cornaro's treatment of the lagoon as the nexus of a regional ecosystem that included the mainland was clearly a product of Venetian concerns, it was also related to a broader set of ideas about the relationship between human action and the natural world. Indeed, his writings echo the concerns of an earlier anonymous writer who penned a brief three-folio tract on the lagoon in 1413.[18] Originally attributed to Cornaro, the pamphlet echoes many of the same themes that appear in the 1442 treatise, even if it lacks the later work's technical detail and sophistication.[19] Like Cornaro, the 1413 anonymous was interested in the origins of sedimentary deposits in the lagoon. And, again like Cornaro, this earlier writer argued that intensified riverfront agriculture led to increasing silt loads in the region's rivers and irrigation networks. While the 1413 author was not interested in firewood, he did argue that silt blockages threatened to halt riverine transport throughout the region, which would, in turn, limit local access to regional markets. He concluded that if left unchecked, the disruption of transportation networks by siltation would eventually begin to affect even Venice's economy.

Despite the brevity of his tract, the anonymous author did not limit himself to describing the immediate and future problems created by recent agrarian activity in the *terraferma*. He also made specific recommendations for alleviating them. Like Cornaro, his most radical proposal involved forced reforestation along riverbanks and irrigation canals. Tree-lined rivers and canals, he argued, would help retain the soil, even in the face of intensified plowing and planting. Furthermore, the public benefits of his plan were, he claimed, obvious. Venice would be safeguarding the city and its economy, not to mention avoiding the significant public expenditure that would otherwise be required to dredge the lagoon and the inland waterways. To delay would be folly, he admonished, for the problem was getting worse by the day and repairs would soon be beyond the fiscal and physical capabilities of the Republic. The increase in sedimentary deposits, he concluded, represented a potential crisis with profound consequences for the Republic.

The similarities between the 1413 tract and Cornaro's treatise are remarkable. In some ways, the earlier writing reveals even more about the ways in which fifteenth-century Venetians perceived and understood the challenges of environmental change. The author's analysis of the threats posed by alluvial sediment was rooted in two important assumptions about the character and source of the problem. First, he contended that the impending crisis was caused by humans who had altered the environment in ways that violated the internal logic of nature's workings. He was particularly concerned that riverfront deforestation represented an untenable deviation from nature's norms, and severe land degradation was the inevitable result of such deliberately unnatural activity. Second, he claimed that the ill-considered deforestation and intensive plowing that was upsetting the region's balance was relatively recent and thus potentially reversible. Based on both assumptions, he concluded that the best possible solution was to "imitate nature" by restoring the region's forests and watercourses to their ideal condition.[20]

The call to imitate nature is not remarkable in and of itself. The idea that nature constitutes an appropriate and orderly model for human activity has its origins among the Socratic philosophers of antiquity. In the mid-thirteenth century, Saint Thomas Aquinas adapted this idea from Aristotle to argue that the order of nature reflected the divine plan. By the fifteenth century, humanist scholars throughout Italy had begun to advance the claim that nature was the best model for architecture and urban planning. In 1416, interest in this notion led to the publication of an emended edition of the works of the second-century Roman author Vitruvius, who had employed a similar line of reasoning in his architectural writings. The publication of Vitruvius inspired new architectural treatises by Leon Battista Alberti and Antonio Averlino (known as Filarete) among others. These Renaissance authors made the case for a new architecture based in large part on the imitation of nature.[21] Thus when the 1413 anonymous penned his brief treatise, the concept of *imitatio naturae* was already circulating widely among literate circles in Italian cities. The related notion that the proper application of human ingenuity could build upon and improve nature, however, remained unexpressed both in the treatise and in virtually all subsequent Venetian writings on the topic. Even though one might argue that the Venetian lagoon management schemes of the past century had, in some sense, attempted to improve nature to better serve human ends, the 1413 author and his contemporaries tended to think of such projects as imitating—not altering—nature. This view continued to dominate Venetian conceptions of nature until the fall of the Republic. Chapter 6 will address the development of a uniquely Venetian understanding of the relationship between human action and nature at length. For now, suffice it to say that the anonymous tract was typical not only of early fifteenth-century Italian thought in general, but of Venetian thought in particular.

If the writer was not convinced that humans could improve on nature, he clearly feared that they could destroy it by acting without proper reflection. This belief formed the core of his second claim: that the degradation caused by human activity in the region was relatively recent. Nevertheless, in keeping with his optimistic belief that the damage was still reversible, he advised his readers to develop new solutions to the challenges of lagoon management. Cornaro's 1442 treatise demonstrates that the 1413 anonymous was correct to claim that significant ecological changes—including limited deforestation and increased erosion—had occurred in conjunction with the Venetian conquest. Whether or not he was right to believe that those changes might yet be reversed is a far more debatable proposition. Certainly Cornaro's observations suggest that not much had been done in the intervening twenty-nine years to arrest inland siltation, which had only grown worse. The most interesting feature of the 1413 anonymous' claim, however, is the notion that human activity in the region had suddenly become unnatural. Unfortunately, he furnished no motive for the sudden shift in the form of human exploitation of the environment, nor did he accuse anyone or anything for the supposed change. This omission was surely not due to a shortage of potential scapegoats. He might have blamed the conquest, the greed of landowners intent on short-term profits, or a general moral decline among the Venetian ruling class—all of which were commonly expressed concerns in fifteenth-century Venice. Moreover, the author seems to have purposefully overlooked the possibility that the Venetians' deliberate alterations to so many nearby waterways might have contributed to the current crisis. Indeed, it is striking that the author ignored the obvious contradictions in his appeal to restore the region to its "natural" state. The very conditions he wished to restore had been created through unprecedented human intervention in the landscape. The author's perception of what was natural was a product of the Republic's political and economic concerns. By invoking nature, he did not intend to suggest nostalgia for what a modern writer would call a wilderness uncontaminated by human influence. Rather, he was promoting the restoration of an ecological situation—now jeopardized by human negligence—that had been deliberately created to favor a particular set of Venetian commercial and civic interests.

The 1413 anonymous and Marco Cornaro stand out as early examples of a growing interest among the Venetian patriciate in the condition of the regional environment. As concerns over environmental change mounted, the Senate commissioned numerous surveys of mainland property and resources, and scores of officials participated in the process by which the Venetians discovered essential aspects of their new territories. Cornaro was the only patrician to produce a lengthy and elaborate technical treatise in this early period, but he was joined by a growing body of officials who sought to acquire and transmit new knowledge about the workings of the mainland landscape. In the years following Cornaro's report, Venetians travelled throughout the mainland at the behest of the Senate and the Collegio. One of the main purposes of such tours was to locate sources of critical supplies of timber and fuel. As each successive group of surveyors moved farther inland, they learned to ask new questions and draw fresh conclusions about the landscapes that confronted them. For example, a 1456 survey of rural property near Aquilea named the species of trees found in some of the surveyed forests and even attempted to describe the composition of individual stands by identifying the dominant species within them.[22] The inspectors still did not consider it important to record the type of terrain on which each forest stood, nor did they include any remarks concerning the total area covered by the forests, the sizes of trees, the soil composition, or the distance from the forests to the nearest navigable river. In other words, the information gathered remained fairly rudimentary, but it represented a major improvement over Cornaro's vague allusions to "places full of wood." In the scant fourteen years that had passed since Cornaro had put pen to paper, a select group of Venetian patricians had already learned to ask more precise questions about mainland landscapes.

The knowledge acquired by fifteenth-century patricians in government service was neither systematic nor programmatic. It still resided primarily with individuals rather than in the institutions they served and, therefore, varied significantly. Nevertheless, the differences between Cornaro's 1442 treatise and the 1456 survey of woods near Aquilea show how individual patricians had begun to develop increasingly specific and localized knowledge about particular forest landscapes in the decades following the conquest of the *terraferma*. The two reports also underscore the emergence of a regional perspective on environmental change that eventually formed the basis of Venetian attempts to regulate forests. Cornaro grounded his treatise in an important set of concerns about the relationship between human action and the natural world that were quite specific to Venice and its peculiar geographic setting. Yet this very local knowledge allowed him to assemble a sophisticated argument that made explicit and specific linkages between human practices far upstream and important changes in the delicate environment of the lagoon. He was able to describe the connection between particular agrarian practices, forests, erosion, and the accumulation of alluvial sediment in considerable detail. As a Venetian, his focus remained firmly on water. But his analysis of many of the connections between waterways and the lands that surrounded them was quite sophisticated, even if his understanding of forests left a good deal to be desired. Men such as Cornaro gradually transformed their sophisticated local knowledge of water into a larger set of ideas about the interconnectedness of the regional environment. Indeed, by 1456 many officials scrutinized the landscape with new eyes. The members of the *rason vecchie* who traveled to Aquilea that year pointed out many features of the forest landscape—species and stand composition—that Cornaro never noticed. Just as Cornaro recognized that Venice's liquid landscape was part of a complex and far-flung hydrological system, a select group of officials was beginning to recognize that mainland forests were part of an equally vast and complicated set of connected landscapes that were continually being reshaped by both human action and the behavior of the forests themselves. This growing realization lay at the heart of the forest management regime that the Republic would attempt to impose on its mainland subjects starting in the second half of the fifteenth century.

Local Property Rights and the Limits of Venetian Power to Preserve Forests

Reaction to Cornaro's appearances before the Collegio was mixed. Cornaro later recalled with pride that the Doge himself had "asked me who I was . . . called me by name and touched my hand while saying to me: 'Marco, my son, you have touched on the very heart of this matter.'"[23]

Real action, however, was not forthcoming. As expected, his proposal to reform the market controls was not politically viable. If the members of the Collegio had any thoughts on the matter, they did not express them for the record. Likewise, Cornaro's suggestion that the Republic undertake forced reforestation of riverbanks and canal embankments did not elicit a single official comment. The reasons for the Collegio's silence seem clear. Even if the political will had existed to pursue such a strategy, no legal mechanisms existed for the Senate or the Collegio to force mainland property owners to undertake such a difficult project. Like Cornaro's intimations about the failures of the market controls, his reforestation plan was simply outside the realm of political possibility. On the question of dredging, however, the Republic's leaders proved quite receptive. Again, this was to be expected. Dredging represented a traditional response to a very well-understood set of problems. Unfortunately, it was one thing for the Collegio to agree that dredging was necessary, but quite another for it to take the necessary steps to see it through. Dredging in canals and tributaries had to be done in the dry. Workers dammed up either end of a portion of a watercourse, drained the section, removed the soil, destroyed the dams, and then repeated the process in the next section of the stream. As a consequence, dredging was so costly that the Venetians could only attempt it in a limited number of carefully chosen cases. Dredging on the scale suggested by Cornaro would have been so expensive—not to mention labor intensive—as to be beyond even the considerable means of the Republic. The Collegio instructed the Senate to approve a far more modest program and to place Cornaro in charge of it.[24]

The fact that reforestation constituted an outlandish idea in fifteenth-century Venice was not simply due to the legislators' limited understanding of mainland landscapes. To facilitate the conquest and absorption of a large number of previously independent cities and towns—each boasting its own particular legal traditions and social practices—the Venetians opted to not create a uniform legal or administrative system. The decision was largely a function of the fact that the Venetians were half-hearted conquerors. James Grubb has argued convincingly that "only with reluctance did Venetian councilors abandon a long-standing policy that emphasized diplomacy over conquest and preferred client *signori* to direct rule."[25] Whatever their reservations, by the late fourteenth century most Venetian patricians had reconciled themselves to the inevitability of some level of political and military entanglement with the mainland. The aftermath of the War of Chioggia had made the need for action apparent to all but the most conservative patricians. Faced with a rapidly changing and increasingly dangerous political and military situation, the Republic's leaders felt they had no choice but to protect their interests by stabilizing as much of the northeast as they could. Beginning in 1404, with the acquisition of Vicenza, the Republic slowly expanded its control of the nearby mainland. In 1405 the Venetians conquered Padua, in the process exterminating the Carrara dynasty.[26] From 1410 until 1424, they fought a series of minor wars with the Holy Roman Emperor, eventually extending their northern and eastern frontiers to include much of the Istrian peninsula, the Friuli, and the entire Piave basin as far north as Cadore in the Alps. Finally, they fought a short war against Milan, adding Brescia and Bergamo to their dominion.

The extent and rapidity of the Venetian annexation of the mainland may appear stunning, but they owed much of their success to a series of external factors. The emperor was unable to fully commit himself to defending the Friuli and Istria because the continent-wide crisis caused by the Great Schism was reaching its climax at the Council of Constance. The Milanese, for their part, had to protect their southern flank against the Florentines and, therefore, could not meet the Venetians at full strength. The Venetians also enjoyed strong support from the local nobility and urban commercial oligarchies almost everywhere they went. The nobles were dissatisfied because they had lost many privileges under German and Milanese rule, while the oligarchs' business interests had been hurt by an imperial boycott of Venetian goods.

Despite the apparent success of this mainland expansion, there were also very real problems that were not immediately apparent in 1425. To secure the support of mainland elites in their struggles against the Carrara, Milan, and the Empire, the Venetians had been forced to concede considerable local autonomy. In the long run, such local compromises undermined the Republic's ability to exercise central power and authority in the *terraferma*. For historians the question has been to what degree the Venetians ever intended to become involved in direct rule on the mainland. In the words of Grubb, "from the beginning . . . the Venetian state was marked by limited central ambitions. Certainly expansion was not intended to absorb mainland cities into a greater union."[27] John Law has also observed that "doubts and opposition followed the growing military, fiscal and political burdens that attended the Republic's increasing involvement on the *terraferma*."[28] For Grubb, Law, and others, the political and legal strategies that the Venetians followed and the political compromises they sought reveal ambivalence towards, if not outright distaste for, direct rule. Gaetano Cozzi counters that the Venetians were openly preparing themselves for permanent mainland expansion as early as 1403.[29] Cozzi contends that what appears to be a haphazard approach to mainland rule was actually a way for the Venetians to bridge the cultural gap that divided them from their subject territories and deploy a juridical and administrative web across the new mainland state.[30] However, even if one accepts Cozzi's assertion that the Venetians followed a deliberate and thoughtful strategy of conquest, the undeniable fact remains that the legal framework that emerged in the wake of expansion was intrinsically weak. It created frequent local resentments and protected local privileges without significantly enhancing central authority.

The inherent structural instability of the *stato di terraferma* carried implications that went well beyond the Venetians' ability to retain political and military control over their new territories. The loose character of mainland rule also presented major problems for the Republic's efforts to control critical resources—especially timber and fuel—at the point of production. With the exception of Padua, where all traces of the former Carrara rulers were removed from the city, the Venetians tried to leave local institutions and customs in their new dominion intact. It was this decision to favor local privileges over central prerogatives that prevented the Republic's leaders from pursuing Cornaro's ambitious program of reforestation. Nothing in the local statutes of the recently conquered territories justified forcing landowners to manage their forests in unaccustomed ways. And having promised to respect local privileges, the Senate balked at imposing new rules governing land use in community forests. Venetian officials might collect taxes—a traditional privilege accorded to central authorities—and use the resulting revenues to perform maintenance on a recognized public resource such as a bridge or an irrigation canal. But they had no power to force landowners to plant particular crops, preserve woodlands, or replant trees in areas where local residents had cleared forest cover. This weakness of central authority constituted one of the major differences between the dredging program proposed by Cornaro and his reforestation scheme. In most *terraferma* jurisdictions, water was an acknowledged public resource, subject to the control of political authorities, while forests—with the sole exception of community forests—were still seen as a private resource.

Even if they had been interested in reshaping the laws that governed property rights and land use, the Venetians were ill equipped to understand the issues involved. They had no legal tradition of their own for the regulation of usufruct rights and other technical aspects of land use because they had never held enough agrarian land to make it a pressing issue.[31] And while certain medieval interpretations of Roman law incorporated plants and animals into the political community—making it possible to legislate particular forms of land use—Venetian common law had no mechanisms for doing so.[32] To further complicate matters, the mutual unintelligibility of Venetian common-law and mainland Roman-law traditions was not the only challenge that the Republic's officials faced. Each commune followed its own particular customs, traditions, and legal definitions of property. The laws governing land use varied enormously, even between neighboring jurisdictions. Uniformity, therefore, represented an elusive and potentially explosive goal for the Venetians to pursue. To standardize land tenure and usufruct systems throughout the emerging Venetian territorial state would have created far more problems than it ever would have solved. The Venetians had also promised their new subjects considerable local political autonomy, making any attempt to impose sweeping reforms of property rights risky. The Venetians could hardly afford to alienate the residents of their recently acquired territories and undermine their still-tenuous hold on the *terraferma*. Moreover, even if the Venetians had been willing to take that risk, they lacked the resources to enforce new laws. In other words, the prospects of forcing local residents to respect unfamiliar conventions appeared dim at best. From the Venetian perspective the best policy, at least at first, appeared to be supporting the status quo.

Even forcing local residents to maintain a public resource such as a waterway proved devilishly difficult. When Cornaro returned to the mainland to oversee dredging operations in some of the streams and canals he had inspected the previous year, he found himself facing recalcitrant locals, unhappy with being forced to perform service on behalf of their new rulers in Venice. As with so many public projects, canal and river maintenance relied on *angaria* labor. But drawing on the local peasantry to work on a dredging project meant taking them away from work they would have been doing on behalf of their communities or their landlords. Cornaro and his masters in Venice might have felt a strong sense of urgency about clearing up some of the streams and canals in the area south of Treviso, but few local residents shared their enthusiasm.

Cornaro's experience of local resistance to Venetian mandates was entirely consistent with that of other officials sent out onto the mainland to monitor the watershed. From the very outset of the conquest, the Venetians had been eager to enforce local statutes concerning the maintenance of canals and associated infrastructure. In 1410, for example, the Venetian *podestà* at Legnago on the Adige River was ordered to collect an extraordinary tax on local landowners to finance the repair of levees and boat landings, many of which were reported to be in terrible condition. Local *statuti*—or legal codes—already called for the tax in times of need, but it had rarely been imposed in the past. When local landholders refused to comply, the Senate tried to levy punitive fines without success. In the face of fierce resistance, the Venetians persisted in their attempts to collect the tax and repair the damaged levees. In 1412, after a barrage of local appeals had been exhausted in Venetian courts, the Senate was finally able to compel the local landowners to comply with the original order. Sporadic efforts to overturn the tax continued until at least the end of the sixteenth century, but on the issue of water management the Venetian courts proved steadfast.[33]

Disputes over the Republic's power to enforce local statutes governing water use constituted an important exception to the Venetian policy of limited interference in the *terraferma*. Venetian concerns over the lagoon, combined with a preexisting body of law on the mainland at least allowed the Republic to attempt imposing its will on reluctant landowners and communities. Forests were another matter entirely. With no local legal traditions offering useful precedents for central control over forest use—again with the exception of community forests—the Venetians soon confronted a considerable challenge when it came to subjecting new territories to the Republic's rules while at the same time addressing Venice's pressing need for timber and fuel. The Senate's reluctance to interfere with local privileges or alter existing property rights severely restricted the options available to Venetian officials eager to ease the flow of forest resources downstream to the lagoon. The lack of legal mechanisms to enforce new forestry regulations is one reason why Cornaro's treatise focused primarily on dredging. Reforestation was simply not an option. Bound by the terms of their agreements with subject cities from tampering with land use patterns, the Venetians had created a major obstacle to their own efforts to secure reliable access to crucial supplies of timber and fuel.

The conflict between the desire to preserve local autonomy and the need to supply the Arsenal with timber and the city with fuel continued to inform Venetian attitudes towards issues of forest exploitation for the rest of the fifteenth century. The rights of private and institutional landowners remained largely off-limits until the sixteenth century. However, during the second half of the fifteenth century the Venetians began interfering forcefully in the management of community forests. Like waterways, community forests constituted a public resource, which created the political and legal opening the Republic needed to justify infringing on local practices of forest exploitation.

The Failure of Market Regulations

Before the Venetians decided to regulate community forests in the same fashion as they regulated waterways, they turned once again to the system of market regulations. Since the various market restrictions imposed in the second half of the fourteenth century had consistently failed to resolve timber and firewood shortages, Venetian legislators first attempted to shore up those regulations through renewed enforcement efforts and increasingly elaborate regulatory strategies. Imposing constraints on the market for forest commodities remained a viable option, because the existing structure of price ceilings and tariffs did not impinge on local rights. Instead, market controls fell under the rubric of tax policy, the one area where the Republic's leaders had had no compunction about asserting central authority from the very outset of the conquest.[34] The Senate believed that the most obvious solution was to extend the fourteenth-century laws governing the sale and consumption of timber products from the city into the *terraferma*. The Venetians moved aggressively to regulate local markets for timber and firewood and establish annual quotas for delivery to the lagoon.[35] The Senate first imposed such regulations on the cities and towns of the lower and middle Piave regions, before ultimately extending them to other parts of the mainland. For example, the establishment of a central timber market in Belluno was among the first official acts following the conquest of that district in 1404, so that all available Arsenal-grade timber there—principally beech in this case—could be earmarked for direct transport to Venice.[36]

The Venetians quickly recognized the problems inherent in extending market controls onto the peninsula. Legislating the routing of timber and fuel to Venice did not ensure their appearance in the lagoon, especially in light of the Venetian habit of imposing price ceilings along with market quotas. The Senate responded to shortfalls by attempting to ascertain the extent and availability of forest resources throughout the mainland. In addition, officials in timber-producing regions also sought to gauge the local capacity to produce finished products such as charcoal and milled lumber. In 1408, for example, the *provveditori al commune*—one of several magistracies that regulated commerce in Venice—commissioned an inventory of all sawmills and other buildings pertaining to the timber trade in the *contado*—or rural hinterland—of Belluno.[37] Officials intended such inventories to furnish a more accurate idea of how much timber they might expect to acquire for the city's needs. But since local yields fluctuated so much from year to year in response to weather and to demographic and social factors, simply counting sawmills constituted an extremely inaccurate predictor of future production. In addition, forcing local merchants to obey market mandates issued in Venice proved far more difficult than anyone in the Ducal Palace had imagined. In 1410—as hostilities with the Empire began anew—a stern letter from the Doge reminded the local Venetian governor at Belluno of his responsibility to ensure shipment of all timber earmarked for Venice. Apparently local residents had been diverting the timber to black markets, where it presumably fetched higher prices than it would have in the heavily regulated Venetian market.[38] The price ceilings created black markets even in Venice. In 1411, for example, the Senate established severe fines for merchants in the city who used the ongoing shortages as an excuse for ignoring the price ceilings on firewood.[39] As they settled into their new role as rulers of a mainland state, the Republic's leaders soon discovered that possessing the *terraferma* did not make market controls any more effective. Resistance to the regulations on the part of merchants and local residents, as well as the structural factors that governed local and regional yields, dulled an already blunt instrument to the point of uselessness.

Beyond the resistance of mainland residents and the peculiarities of local forest ecologies, the Venetians confronted additional obstacles as they sought to extend existing market regulations into their new dominions. Institutions and officials accustomed to operating within the close confines of the city had trouble coping with the scope and geographical reach of the timber and firewood trades. For example, the responsibilities of the office of the *ufficiali alle rason vecchie* not only encompassed price monitoring, but also included auditing the expenses of every Venetian official—including ambassadors and governors. With the proliferation of mainland governorships that were created in the wake of the conquest, the *rason vecchie's* responsibilities swiftly outstripped the magistracy's surveillance capabilities. Similarly, the *rason vecchie* simply lacked the manpower to monitor the dozens of firewood markets throughout the *terraferma*, to enforce market regulations, to prevent merchants from violating price ceilings, and to clamp down on corrupt tax farmers and other minor officials. Overburdened and overwhelmed officials and institutions could not keep pace with their increasing responsibilities, much less impose order on unruly markets.

In such a chaotic, complex, and ever-changing marketplace, abuses were rampant and perverse incentives abounded. Tax collectors, local customs inspectors, and other individuals responsible for collecting tariffs and duties found firewood to be a lucrative bailiwick, rife with opportunities for illicit gain. Because fuel was a basic necessity, mainland residents and Venetians alike found it impossible to refuse extortionate demands on the part of merchants and tax collectors. Likewise, even well-intentioned officials could not keep up with developments in the mainland's hundreds of local firewood markets, especially when supplies remained tight and demand high. For its part, the *ufficiali alle rason vecchie* found itself subject to a number of conflicting pressures. The magistracy auctioned off the rights to collect certain taxes and other duties and relied on the proceeds for a substantial part of its budget. The incentive to maximize the income generated from these auctions led the *ufficiali alle rason vecchie* to turn a blind eye to some of the more egregious behavior on the part of those who had purchased a tax. Only when the courts intervened would the *ufficiali alle rason vecchie* act to curb profiteering by tax farmers and local officials. But prosecuting a few individuals did little to stem more widespread and systemic abuses. This kind of petty corruption served to squeeze firewood merchants even harder by cutting into their already meager profit margins. The laments of local authorities and firewood merchants eventually became loud enough to draw the attention of the Senate, the courts of the Forty, and even the Council of Ten. The most common complaint accused tax collectors of excessive zeal. Many petitioners claimed that tax farmers and local officials had suddenly revived duties and exactions that had fallen into disuse for centuries. The residents of Venice also felt the effects of profiteering, and had it not been for the Senate's price controls, the cost of a bundle of firewood would have reached historic highs. As profit margins fell perilously low, merchants abandoned traditional areas of firewood harvesting. Finally, as the area of production contracted, painful shortages became the norm in the city.

By 1437 the situation had become critical. After a winter of extreme firewood shortages had emptied Venice's public warehouses, the Senate took direct action. It began by renewing and strengthening some of the existing market controls.[40] In March of 1438 the Senate lowered the price ceiling on the firewood market within the city, in an attempt to keep fuel affordable. The Senate also responded to some of the merchants' complaints by temporarily lifting some of the more onerous tariffs on inland traffic. Never intended as a permanent measure, it was the expressed intention of legislators to restore the taxes once the crisis had passed. The Senate also tried to relieve some of the administrative burden on the *provveditori alle rason vecchie* in order to promote more effective oversight of the firewood trade. Two months after altering the market regulations, it created the *provveditori sopra il fatto delle legne*, or firewood managers. The sole responsibility of this brand-new magistracy was the requisition of combustible fuel.[41] The Senate elected three patricians—Francesco Garzoni, Orio Pasqualigo, and Andrea Gritti—to serve eighteen-month terms. The *ufficiali alle rason vecchie* were still responsible for auditing the trade and overseeing firewood markets—both on the mainland and in Venice—but they were no longer in charge of deciding how much fuel the city needed each year. The new firewood managers assumed responsibility for monitoring the stocks of firewood in the public warehouses, issuing licenses to draw wood from the warehouses, and informing the *ufficiali alle rason vecchie* when supplies were falling short of projections. Monitoring the firewood warehouses was a major undertaking, so the Senate's decision did in fact take pressure off of the already overburdened *rason vecchie*. In other respects, however, splitting control of the firewood trade between two separate bureaucracies created unnecessary confusion. For example, the Senate ordered the firewood managers to tour the mainland and scout out fresh sources of firewood at the outset of their term of office, even though the *rason vecchie* remained responsible for monitoring the flow of firewood through mainland markets.[42] In practical terms, the new officials took charge of fuel at the source and at the point of consumption, while the existing officials supervised everything that happened in between. The Senate, meanwhile, made no provisions for the two magistracies to share information or otherwise cooperate in their efforts to regulate the firewood trade. The results were predictably chaotic.

Dividing responsibilities between different magistracies constituted a typical early fifteenth-century Venetian response to the challenges of mainland rule. The decades following the conquest brought the creation of several new offices as the Senate attempted to lighten the administrative burden borne by patrician officeholders and their citizen assistants. The decision to divide the responsibility for fuel and for Arsenal timber strongly influenced the Venetian forestry regime's management of woodlands. Overlapping jurisdictions also led to bureaucratic competition as the elected heads of institutions sought to gain control of the tariff revenue generated by mainland markets. In the case of the new firewood managers and the established *ufficiali alle rason vecchie*, supervising the market for fuel brought with it control over lucrative tax concessions, transportation tariffs, and the power to collect fines from sellers and boatmen. A clever patrician officeholder could exploit any or all of these revenue streams for personal gain. As a result, the *ufficiali alle rason vecchie* had no incentive—with the dubious exception of an altruistic spirit of public service—to cooperate or share information about the fuel trade with the firewood managers. The *provveditori sopra il fatto delle legne* and the *ufficiali alle rason vecchie* were rivals vying for control of tax income and institutional power, not two halves of a coherent institution sharing a common goal of administering firewood resources for public benefit.

Following the creation of the new firewood managers, the Senate continued to make incremental adjustments to market controls and tinker with the division of bureaucratic responsibilities. At the end of July 1438 the Senate lowered the price ceiling on firewood even further, citing "the great disorders that arise from the high cost of firewood, especially for the poor of our city."[43] At the same time, the Senate also expressed concern over market conditions on the mainland, and ordered one of the *ufficiali alle rason vecchie* to conduct an inspection tour to observe tax collectors and other local officials first hand. The Senate was concerned that such officials were not respecting the March measure temporarily lifting many intermediate tariffs. All of these instructions were in keeping with the division of responsibilities that the Senate had drawn when it created the *provveditori sopra il fatto delle legne*. However, the Senate also instructed the leader of the inspection party to keep an eye out for possible new sources of firewood in mainland forests—a task that should have fallen to the firewood managers. The Senate's action bolstered the *ufficiali alle rason vecchie*'s authority at the expense of the *provveditori sopra il fatto delle legne*. The exclusion of firewood managers from the inspection tour also made it possible for the *rason vecchie* to take sole credit for any subsequent improvements in Venetian fuel markets.

At first the *ufficiali alle rason vecchie*'s inspection tour appeared to produce incredible results. Firewood once again to flowed into Venice's dangerously depleted warehouses. Undoubtedly the sudden presence of a Venetian patrician and his entourage at mainland embarcaderos and marketplaces had done much to hasten the movement of firewood down the region's rivers. Tax farmers and other local actors who might otherwise have violated the temporary suspension of inland tariffs would certainly have respected the new rules in the presence of a representative of the *Serenissima*. Merchants would also have taken advantage of the opportunity to move cargo safely to the lagoon in the hopes of making a profit before conditions changed once again. The positive effects of the inspection inspired the Senate to revisit its recent decision to expand the administrative apparatus dedicated to the firewood supply. In the wake of the *rason vecchie*'s apparent success, many senators decided that the firewood managers were simply superfluous. The *ufficiali alle rason vecchie* supported this position. In their report on the inspection they recommended that the *provveditori sopra il fatto delle legne* be disbanded and that full control of the firewood trade be restored to their own office.[44] In 1441—on the eve of Marco Cornaro's tour of the mainland forests—the Senate acted, disbanding the *provveditori sopra il fatto delle legne* after a mere three years of existence. Clearly the effects of the inspection tour had given the Republic's leaders hope that the city's cyclical fuel shortages could be solved through a more judicious application of market regulations, combined with periodic inspections of mainland markets. To that end, the Senate instructed the *rason vecchie* to send a representative to inspect points of sale and embarcaderos every four months.

The *ufficiali alle rason vecchie's* victory over its bureaucratic rivals was painfully short-lived. Within a few months of the Senate's disbanding the *provveditori sopra il fatto delle legne*, the Venetians once again found themselves in the grip of a serious fuel shortage. Many senators had clearly mistaken a set of temporary effects associated with the 1439 inspections for a permanent solution to cyclical firewood shortages. By 1441, the window of opportunity that the inspection had opened for merchants to move their wood to Venice had closed, and the market for firewood collapsed again. The *ufficiali alle rason vecchie* had not even had the opportunity to implement the newly mandated inspection regime before the trade came to a virtual halt. Still, it was difficult to shake the Senate's faith in market regulations. With no other legal mechanisms at its disposal, Venice's main legislative body tried to duplicate the success of the 1439 inspections through a second major inspection effort, the 1441 survey in which Marco Cornaro participated.

It was against the backdrop of this institutional rivalry that Cornaro wrote his treatise. The infighting between the firewood managers and the *ufficiali alle rason vecchie* had led to the disbanding of one magistracy and the discrediting of the other. Nevertheless, the Senate remained fully committed to shoring up market controls, even if it meant sending a continuous stream of officials onto the mainland to force local compliance with central mandates. Cornaro had to choose his words carefully to avoid incurring the legislators' wrath. He began by addressing the continuing problems plaguing Venetian officials in their attempts to police an unruly trade beset by corruption and profiteering. Cornaro divided the blame for the ongoing crisis between local actors, such as tax collectors and village authorities, and the *ufficiali alle rason vecchie*. In so doing Cornaro hewed closely to an officially accepted version of the ineffectiveness of market regulations, stressing lack of enforcement rather than flaws in the underlying regulatory structure. Yet while he acknowledged that the failure of the *rason vecchie* to follow up on the successes of the 1439 survey with additional spot checks certainly contributed to the renewal of fuel shortages, he also intimated that the market regulations themselves might be partially to blame. He observed that "the Senate's provisions were such that [in the years since 1438] officials had imposed fines and fees totaling more than 11,000 Venetian Lire and collected around 2,000 Ducats. And their actions did more harm than good, for the poor people dared not move firewood for fear of such fines, with great damage to [Venice]."[45] He followed this brief but scathing observation by launching directly into his elaborate analysis of siltation. In essence he was arguing that if the Republic would only invest in infrastructure rather than in attempts to enforce flawed regulations, the market controls could be scaled back and drastic measures such as price ceilings could be reserved for the occasional emergency. Increased supply would ensure that the price of fuel remained affordable. This is not to suggest that Cornaro was a free-market booster *avant la lettre*. Certainly he supported the idea that in the face of shortages the Republic's leaders were right to cap prices to maintain civic order. Rather, his argument against market regulations closely mirrors his arguments in the rest of the treatise. By stressing the harmful effects of excessive fines, Cornaro was simply claiming that the power of the purse alone could not resolve the problem of fuel shortages. Without an active effort on the part of the Republic's institutions to address access problems at the source, there could be no long-term solution to the problem of cyclical crises. Market regulations by themselves were insufficient to resolve one of the city's most pressing problems.

Cornaro's carefully worded critique of the fourteenth-century system of market controls met with mixed reactions. While not a single member of the Collegio supported the idea of scaling back market regulations, the argument that effective enforcement of the rules was beyond the power of the *ufficiali alle rason vecchie* proved convincing. The willingness of the Republic's leaders to believe that the *rason vecchie* were to blame was not simply due to Cornaro's rhetorical brilliance. The Collegio had heard a stream of similar laments from merchants and boatmen in the firewood trade. Ultimately, the combination of Cornaro's arguments and local complaints convinced the Collegio to take action. In June of 1443 the Senate—at the behest of the Collegio—revoked the *ufficiali alle rason vecchie*'s right to inspect mainland forests and restricted its authority over the firewood trade to tariffs and duties collected at the entrances to the lagoon.[46] Of course, this action did little to resolve the causes of the supply crisis, and soon the stock of firewood in the city's warehouses dropped so low that the legislators feared the possibility of riots if a solution was not found quickly.

Meanwhile, the boatmen who plied the region's waterways with their cargoes of firewood and charcoal petitioned a variety of Venetian courts with increasing fervor in search of redress for the abuses they had endured from profiteering tax collectors. Like Cornaro, the boatmen argued that the proliferation of duties and tariffs threatened to make their participation in the firewood trade untenable. Many of the plaintiffs also objected to the price ceilings, complaining that the continual application of price controls made it impossible for any of the active participants in the trade to survive. Some even accused the *ufficiali alle rason vecchie* of conspiring with tax collectors to increase the amount collected in tolls—and presumably to then split the profits. The success of the 1439 inspections suggests that such accusations were probably ill-founded, but the underlying argument—that tolls and tax levies were choking the trade—caught the attention of the Republic's leaders. Still the Senate delayed, unwilling to give up its one sure point of leverage over the fuel supply. Finally, it could no longer avoid the reality of the situation. In December of 1450 the Senate permanently annulled all intermediate duties on the transportation of firewood along inland waterways. In their place it established a single tariff—to be collected by the *rason vecchie*—on fuel brought into the lagoon.[47] Eight years after Cornaro presented his treatise before the Collegio, the Senate at last did away with some of the market restrictions in an effort to encourage the flow of firewood into the city.

Although the Senate eventually acted to limit the market-control system that had developed since the middle of the fourteenth century, tax collectors still managed to find ways to extort the highest possible fees from the boatmen. Under the new system, boatmen carrying fuel reported to the *pallade*—customs houses placed at the inland entrances to the lagoon. Here an inspector examined the cargo manifest—known as a *bollo*—and collected a tariff based on the value of the firewood in the hold of the boat. The officials manning the *pallade* were not salaried employees of the *ufficiali alle rason vecchie*. Rather, they worked for a share of all collected monies. During this period, Italian states frequently employed such men in the hopes that giving them a stake in the rigorous application of customs duties would guard against corruption. Unfortunately for the boatmen, experienced tax officials knew precisely how to compute the volume of a cargo so as to maximize their own take of the proceeds. A clever inspector on the *pallada* could apply any or all of several variables to his calculation, such as comparing the amount of firewood on the manifest with his own estimate based on the length or beam of the boat, the depth of the hold, or even how much water the boat happened to be drawing when it arrived at the inspection station. Depending on which variables the official decided to count—not to mention the weight he assigned to them—he could adjust the final figure to his own benefit. Understandably, the boatmen claimed that such practices constituted a form of extortion, no different than if the inspector had offered to take a bribe in exchange for overlooking the tariffs.[48] In the sixteenth century, the Collegio and Senate moved to refine the collection of taxes at the *pallade* by forcing each boatman to carry logbooks that included an official measure of the cargo capacity of his vessel.[49] The logs and the ratings became a source of contention and were the subject of a number of court cases beginning in 1532, some of which dragged on until the fall of the Republic.[50]

The Senate's inability to restrict the market-distorting actions of the customs officials and other representatives of the *ufficiali alle rason vecchie* highlights the limits of the Republic's coercive power in the fifteenth century. Just as Marco Cornaro's lack of specific knowledge concerning forest landscapes prevented him from providing a meaningful account of the condition of the woodlands he encountered on his tour, the *ufficiali alle rason vecchie*'s lack of knowledge concerning the activities of local tax collectors kept that institution from forming a coherent picture of why the firewood market was faltering. And without the ability to gather such information in a systematic fashion, the *uffi-*

ciali alle rason vecchie remained perpetually beholden to the whims and private interests of innumerable local actors. In other words, the Republic's lack of surveillance power helped to prolong the ongoing cycle of firewood shortages. And as the firewood trade continued to suffer, so too did the stocks in the Venetian warehouses. Eventually, following four more years of frustrating shortages, the Senate decided to try a different approach. The legislators still preferred to intervene in the market, rather than at the level of local land use, to try to increase fuel supplies. Nevertheless, rather than attempting yet another adjustment of the tariffs and price controls, the Republic's leaders decided to turn to someone from outside the government to resolve the problem.

In 1454 the Senate commissioned a timber merchant by the name of Pietro Valier to seek out and purchase firewood on behalf of the state.[51] The Senate awarded Valier a two-year term of office, a stipend of 1,000 ducats, and its official protection. In return, the legislators required Valier to use every means at his disposal to ensure that the city's warehouses remained fully stocked. Valier's commission included a strongly worded warning to the *ufficiali alle rason vecchie* not to interfere with his activities—unless specifically ordered to do so by the Senate or requested to do so by Valier—or pay a 100-ducat penalty. The decision to hand over responsibility for the fuel supply to a firewood merchant emerged as the Senate's last remaining option for using market levers to ensure that the warehouses remained stocked. Rather than creating new market regulations, Venetian legislators turned to Valier, an individual with extensive experience in the offending market for combustible material. If none of the many inspectors who had been dispatched from Venice had been able to locate new sources of fuel, then the assignment of the task to an individual with a professional stake in the firewood supply was a logical decision. The risk of corruption was very real—it is difficult to imagine that Valier failed to use his position to make a handsome personal profit—but a sufficient number of senators saw that risk as worth the potential reward of resolving the problem of firewood crises once and for all. The measure passed handily and the Senate's faith in Valier was rewarded. He proved successful enough that at the conclusion of his two-year term, the Senate selected another timber merchant named Giorgio Venier to take his place and accorded him the same responsibilities and privileges.

Despite the undeniable success of the merchant managers, the Senate remained deeply concerned about corruption and abuse of office. Rotating the commission among several firewood merchants offered a short-term solution by preventing the creation of a private monopoly at public expense. But the Senate recognized that it would soon run out of suitable candidates for such a crucial position. The public warehouses were far too important to leave in private hands indefinitely. Nonetheless, the fact that Valier and Venier had apparently managed to resolve the fuel crisis forced the Republic's leaders to ponder the possibility that a merchant from outside the governing elite could better facilitate the flow of firewood into the lagoon than a large and powerful magistracy such as the *ufficiali alle rason vecchie*. So it was that at the conclusion of his term in 1458, the Senate asked Giorgio Venier to accept the conversion of his extraordinary commission into an officially recognized office with a title, salary, and support staff of citizen secretaries.[52] Venier accepted and received an annual salary of 250 ducats, a 350-ducat supplement to cover personal expenses, and a two-year term of office with the title of *provveditore alle legne*. By establishing a new institutional home for Venier and his fellow firewood merchants, the Senate sought to take advantage of their personal knowledge of the fuel trade while subjecting their activities on behalf of the state to the same scrutiny as other public officials.

The second incarnation of the *provveditori sopra il fatto delle legne* bore little resemblance to the magistracy created in 1438. Not only had the number of elected officials been reduced from three to one, but the Senate made every effort to select men for the position who had specific knowledge of the firewood trade. For several election cycles after the Senate had transformed the office from an ad hoc commission to a regular magistracy, only individuals with particular knowledge of the trade held the office. The Senate reelected Venier in 1460 and 1462 before choosing another firewood merchant named Jacopo Coppo to succeed him in 1464.[53] However, the Senate recognized that it could not go on relying on such dealers forever. The risk of corruption was too great, and the supply of eligible merchants was ultimately limited. The Republic's leaders understood well that they needed to find a way to institutionalize the private knowledge possessed by merchant managers such as Valier, Venier, and Coppo. In 1468 the senators sought to resolve this problem through the addition of a second patrician officeholder to help bear the growing burdens of the office. The legislators staggered the two *provveditori*'s terms of office so that "the new officeholder might acquire the appropriate knowledge and information from the old."[54] Although the office continued to be the nearly exclusive province of timber merchants for at least the next two decades, by the time the office became more venial, the Senate had firmly established a system that would allow patrician officeholders to acquire the necessary knowledge about the firewood trade, in the event that they were sufficiently motivated to do so.

One other factor should be kept in mind when considering the accomplishments of the merchant managers and their successors in the new office of *provveditori alle legne*. Not only did Valier bring significant personal knowledge and experience to bear on the problem of recurring fuel shortages, he also significantly expanded the reach of Venetian firewood markets. Prior to the 1460s much of the firewood consumed in Venice had come from forests that stood in the region bounded by the Brenta River to the west and the Livenza River to the east. Cornaro and his companions had covered this very area during their 1441 inspection tour—as had all the other early mainland surveys. Because this region boasted a relatively high population density, along with a well-developed agrarian regime supported by a dense and complex network of irrigation canals, it was unlikely that any group of inspectors would discover untapped sources of firewood there. Certainly the fact that this region formed the nexus of the watershed that fed into the Venetian lagoon—as well as the complexity of its irrigation network—allowed Cornaro to see the connections between mainland agriculture, riverbank deforestation, and sedimentary accumulation. But despite his optimistic assertion that the region abounded with "places so full of wood," the truth was that his twin prescriptions of dredging and of lifting some of the market regulations ultimately could not provide more than a short-term solution to the dearth of combustible material in Venetian warehouses. The only real solution to cyclical shortages was to seek new sources in more distant forests.

By the end of the fifteenth century Venetian merchants and the new firewood managers routinely traveled into the eastern reaches of the Friuli and across the Adriatic to the Istrian peninsula to secure the firewood that the city so desperately needed. By contrast, in 1442 Cornaro and his fellow inspectors had "decided not to cross the Tagliamento to see the many streams and ditches full of wood there, due to the bad roads and so as not to spend Holy Week away from home."[55] This shift would have important long-term consequences for the Republic's system of forest management. In the centuries to come—particularly in the seventeenth century—the Venetians developed a highly segmented approach to the acquisition and management of crucial forest resources. Beginning in the last quarter of the fifteenth century, the center of the firewood trade shifted definitively to the east. Because moving bundles of firewood cost far less than moving timber, the Republic's leaders reasoned that it would be better to purchase firewood in the eastern Friuli and in Istria and to reserve the forests of the lower Piave for shipbuilding material and construction timber. Additionally, by the 1460s Venetian inspectors had learned enough about the mainland forests that no one in the Ducal Palace could cling to the illusion that heretofore unknown sources of fuel were waiting to be discovered in the region west of the Livenza River.

The creation of the new *provveditori alle legne* and the elimination of most of the inland tariffs largely resolved the problem of cyclical firewood shortages in Venice. Nevertheless, the specter of running out of fuel—especially high-quality fuel for manufacturing applications—continued to haunt the Republic's leaders. With the growth of industries such as silk, metallurgy, and glassmaking throughout the lagoon, the city's basic fuel requirements continued to grow well into the eighteenth century. The streamlining of market regulations and the establishment of a bureaucracy whose sole responsibility was monitoring the fuel supply represented significant steps towards ensuring consistent supplies for the foreseeable future. Yet the limits of Venetian political power on the mainland continued to hamper the new firewood managers' efforts to regulate local practices of forest exploitation. The *provveditori alle legne* continued to operate exclusively through the marketplace. So, beginning in the 1470s, the Venetians turned their attention to the problem of local practices affecting the availability of firewood and Arsenal timber.

CHAPTER THREE

Venetian Forestry Laws and the Creation
of Public Forest Reserves

> Let it be determined that nobody shall cut or
> have cut timber of any sort in that forest for any
> reason except the needs of our Arsenal.

O N 27 DECEMBER 1471 THE Venetian Senate overwhelmingly voted
to ban a large complex of community forests known as the Bosco
del Montello that stood on hilly ground in the northern part of the
territory of Treviso.[1] The measure, which passed with 140 votes in favor
and only eight in opposition, stripped the local villages of the power to
regulate the thirteen contiguous community stands that made up the
forest, assigning it instead to the *provveditori all'arsenale*—the Arsenal
managers. The Montello ban represented a dramatic break with past
regulations and signaled the beginning of a new era of forestry legislation. By confiscating common lands, the Senate forever abandoned the
policy of minimal interference in the realm of property rights. By limiting access to what had previously been a locally controlled resource,
Venetian legislators announced their intention to begin directly regulating access rights to certain mainland forests. No longer would the Venetian authorities remain content merely to interfere in the market in their
attempts to ensure critical timber and fuel supplies. Increasingly, they
aggressively reserved the best oak, beech, and fir forests for the Arsenal,
creating a network of state forest reserves intended to secure supplies of
necessary shipbuilding material in perpetuity. To safeguard the fuel supply, the Senate and the Council of Ten eventually opted to set aside many
smaller forests for the use of the firewood managers. Viewed in this
context, the 1471 Montello ban provided the opening wedge for an am-

bitious and intrusive legislative program that had as its ultimate aim direct state control of key forest resources.

Additional legislation followed close on the heels of the Montello ban. In 1476, the Senate passed six laws governing the exploitation of community forests throughout the *terraferma*. Eventually, Venice's leaders extended these same rules to oak forests on private property, feudal demesne, and even ecclesiastical lands. By the middle of the sixteenth century the Venetians had created a complex set of forestry laws governing every aspect of oak and beech exploitation on the mainland. The forestry laws not only limited access to the new network of Arsenal and firewood reserves, they also dictated with considerable precision what communities, individuals, and institutions could do with even the smallest forest, copse, or windbreak containing oak or beech. Remarkably, the Council of Ten even attempted to force landowners to replant oak forests on land that had previously been cleared for use as pasture and for growing crops.

This chapter examines the emergence and development of Venetian forestry legislation in the late fifteenth and sixteenth centuries. A careful analysis of the Republic's legislative program reveals a gradual shift away from indirect attempts to control resources via the marketplace towards an aggressive program of direct administration of specific mainland forests. Initially, the Republic's leaders saw the regulation of forestry practices as an extension of their previous attempts to control the markets for timber and firewood. The result was a set of land-use laws modeled on the previously established market hierarchy that favored oak and beech over other species that were bought and sold on the mainland. Beginning in 1476, Venetian forestry legislation similarly privileged oak and beech forests over all others. This paradigm shaped the earliest forestry policies and exerted a powerful influence on the extent and composition of mainland forests in the three centuries that followed. In accordance with the laws, Venetian officials limited their enforcement efforts to forests containing oak and beech while allowing communities and private landowners to exploit other forests in any way they wished—including clearcutting them to make way for new arable land. The pattern of selective clearing that resulted contributed to the creation of a patchwork landscape of small forests belonging to local residents and institutions interspersed amongst large state and community forests under the protection and control of the Venetian forest bureaucracy. These large tracts of common land assumed the ever-increasing burden of satisfying Venetian demand for critical forest commodities. And it was primarily in these lands that legislators sought to extend the state's sovereignty. In this fashion, the Republic's laws helped shape virtually every forest landscape in the northeast, even those that did not contain the species of timber coveted by the Venetians.

The forestry laws also posed enormous practical problems for the Republic's institutions and the officials who staffed them. The combination of strongly guarded local privileges and a lack of any effective enforcement mechanisms undermined the new legislation from the outset. Mainland residents of all social and economic classes actively tried to circumvent and undermine Venetian laws, and without reliable local allies, forestry officials were hard pressed to impose the will of the Senate and the Council of Ten. The fact that *terraferma* communities were so often successful at hampering the enforcement of the new forest regulations illustrates how officials still largely lacked the coercive power to impose the Republic's will on mainland landscapes. The perpetual struggle to enforce new rules powerfully conditioned the perceptions of legislators in the Ducal Palace. Beginning with the very first market controls in the mid-fourteenth century, the Venetians had feared that the timber supply would one day run out. By the turn of the sixteenth century that anxiety had come to be closely identified with mainland communities and landowners. Many Venetian patricians became increasingly convinced that local residents exploited their forests in an unrestrained and short-sighted fashion and that left to their own devices they would soon consume all the available timber in the *terraferma*. Consequently, forestry legislation began to focus on the regulation of specific activities that the Venetians viewed as threatening the timber supply. In addition to routine firewood harvesting, these other actions included pasturing livestock; producing lime, charcoal, and tannin; and manufacturing barrels and other products. For local residents these activities represented traditional and reliable modes of forest exploitation, and the Republic's efforts to limit their long-standing practices of forest use only bred resentment against Venetian rule. In this regard, the new laws illuminate an increasing divergence between the political and economic values that the Venetians assigned to mainland forests and the corresponding values embodied by the traditional practices of the Republic's mainland subjects. As the Venetian conception of what constituted appropriate practices of forest exploitation came into increasing conflict with traditional modes of forest subsistence on the mainland, the Republic's leaders responded by redoubling their efforts to curtail what they saw as the wasteful habits of their subjects. By the middle of the sixteenth century, the Council of Ten had expanded a legal structure originally intended to apply to a single large forest—the Montello—to include any forest containing oak, regardless of ownership or location. These laws would form the foundation of the forest management system that the Venetians continued to develop over the course of the sixteenth century, as the Republic sought to reshape the mainland landscape to serve Venetian needs.

The Creation of the *Boschi Pubblici*

When the Senate gathered in December of 1471 to consider a ban on the Montello forest, many Venetian patricians were deeply concerned about the Arsenal's timber supply. Although legislators had focused most of their energy on securing adequate supplies of firewood in the immediate wake of the mainland conquest, by midcentury they began to express anxiety over the supply of ship-quality timber for the Arsenal as well. The Republic had been the dominant naval power in the eastern Mediterranean ever since the victory at Chioggia nearly a century earlier, but that dominance was under increasing threat from a new power in the region, the Ottoman Empire. The preamble to the Montello ban captures the uneasy mood in the Ducal Palace perfectly: "Our Arsenal is currently in the greatest need of timber. In fact it has never had such great necessity as at the present time due to current events."[2] With the size and war-readiness of the fleet suddenly becoming a major concern for the first time since the 1380s, the Senate expressed a renewed and keen interest in the supply of naval-grade timber.

In the middle of the fifteenth century the Venetians still relied almost exclusively on market regulations to ensure that the Arsenal remained fully stocked with critical timber resources. If prior to the 1470s legislators had not expressed the same level of concern about Arsenal stores as they had about the firewood warehouses, it was not because market regulations were any more effective in the domain of shipbuilding material. Instead, the apparent lack of concern was due to the fact that the Arsenal faced relatively little competition for high-quality oak and beech timber, making it easier to secure—at least initially—than fuel. Great quantities of beech remained accessible in the middle Piave region, allaying any fears that the shipyard might run out of oars. In addition, oak remained relatively plentiful throughout the region east of the Brenta, and if need be the Arsenal could always look to Istrian sources to make up for any shortfalls in the supply. The main difficulty that the Arsenal managers faced was maintaining adequate stockpiles of oak in useable condition.

Oak timbers had to be seasoned underwater for about eighteen months after their arrival in the Arsenal, so it was essential to maintain a regular and predictable flow of material into the yard, even in years when shipbuilding activity slowed or stopped altogether. A serious shortfall in seasoned oak could literally shut down the yard for months at a time while craftsmen waited for green timber to harden sufficiently to be sawed into board lengths. If such a crisis were to occur in wartime, the consequences could be devastating. To avoid jeopardizing future production, officials had to exercise a good deal of foresight. The need to acquire oak timbers well in advance of when they would actually be employed in naval construction became a major headache for the Arsenal managers in later years. In the fifteenth century, however, the *provveditori all'arsenale* succeeded in maintaining adequate stocks of fully seasoned timber in the yard. While the Arsenal managers occasionally expressed concern about future supplies, they did not once complain that they had been forced to build ships with green timber—a problem that would come to the fore 250 years later during the second war of Morea.[3]

Fir for mast timbers, rather than oak for hulls, presented the main challenge for the *provveditori all'arsenale* at midcentury. The fir supply appeared more vulnerable because the Venetians could only purchase mast-quality fir from suppliers in the Cadore region near the headwaters of the Piave River. Control of the Cadore had been a major objective of the mainland conquest, and the Venetians finally absorbed the area into their mainland dominion in 1420, when the governing council—the *consiglio generale*—of the town of Pieve di Cadore voted to accept the Republic as the sovereign authority throughout its territory. Possession of the Cadore promised to open up access to the large fir and larch forests that grew along the slopes of the high alpine valleys whose tributaries flowed into the Piave River. Venetian merchants had long operated in the area precisely because of the presence of those forests. Indeed, when Pieve's elite recognized that they would have to choose between rule by Venice and rule by the Holy Roman Empire, the geographic and economic links to the lagoon made the Republic the obvious choice. When the council announced its decision to the crowd gathered outside the municipal palace, the mob is reported to have shouted its approval saying, in part, "Such has long been our will. Does not our river run to and emerge in the Venetian lagoons? Are not our main and principal interests with the Venetians? Are not the Venetians the buyers of our timber?"[4] While the story is almost certainly apocryphal, its circulation makes it clear both why the Cadorini chose Venice and why the Venetians desired the Cadore.

The Venetians offered generous terms to the citizens of Pieve di Cadore and their subject villages in the outlying valleys—terms that were formalized in a *capitulum* issued in 1424.[5] The Senate commuted all sentences that were pending in Venetian courts against citizens of Cadore and Venetian exiles resident in the territory. It also exempted goods originating in the Cadore from many taxes and most commercial tariffs. Finally, the Venetians allowed Pieve's *consiglio generale* to retain the right of nomination to the vicariate and even permitted it to elect a local citizen as the territory's *capitano*. Although the Cadorini had enjoyed the prerogative of electing the *capitano* in the past—when they had been subjects of the patriarch of Aquilea—it was not a foregone conclusion that the Venetians would allow the practice to continue. The Venetian Senate traditionally elected a patrician to an eighteen-month term as *podestà*, or governor, in the larger mainland towns. Typically the *podestà* was responsible for collecting taxes in the town and its territory and acted as a court of appeal for local disputes. However, the town council retained most of its previous administrative and legislative functions. In smaller frontier towns, the Venetians often sent a patrician to act as a *capitano* instead. The *capitano* was mainly responsible for the fortifications, militias, and other military preparations in his territory. The most important mainland cities, such as Padua, often boasted both a *podestà* and a *capitano*. That the Senate entrusted the military security of the Cadore to a local resident was fairly unusual and even risky. After all, while the economic and geographic ties that bound Pieve to Venice were strong, the loyalty of the Cadorini could not be taken for granted—especially with the presence of powerful imperial lords in nearby valleys.

In return for the Senate's many concessions, the *consiglio generale* awarded Venetian merchants exclusive rights to purchase the district's most important commodity, timber. In essence, the Republic's leaders chose to grant the area an unusually large measure of political independence in return for a monopoly on fir and larch trees harvested in the valleys ruled by Pieve. On the surface, such an agreement might appear odd. After all, regardless of the Cadorini's political loyalties, the region's timber could only travel down the Piave River to Venice, no matter who sat in the *palazzo comunale* in Pieve. However, by assigning a monopoly on the trade to Venetian merchants and making shipments bound for Venice tax exempt, the Senate hoped that the Arsenal would receive all the fir and larch it needed. Of course, the Senate's optimism was based on the somewhat naive presumption that Venetian merchants would be honest brokers and not divert tax-exempt timber to unauthorized mainland buyers during the long journey down the river. The Cadore monopoly was a distant cousin to the controls for the firewood market. In both cases—firewood and fir—the Senate remained unwilling to interfere in either local property rights or usufruct rights in community forests. This reluctance made it nearly impossible for the Venetians to influence local patterns of forest exploitation. Instead, the Venetians hoped that market regulations alone would guarantee the city's supply of a crucial forest resource. And in the case of fir, as in the case of firewood, the Republic's leaders would be sorely disappointed.

The shortcomings of the Cadore monopoly were not as apparent as the problems with the firewood trade. Whatever fir was lost to the black market, it was not enough for the Arsenal managers to raise an alarm in the Senate. The stocks of mast timbers in the Republic's shipyard remained adequate to meet the routine requirements of the fleet. Unfortunately, conditions changed quite suddenly and dramatically in 1453. With the fall of Constantinople to the armies of Mehmed the Conqueror, the Venetians decided that they needed to prepare to face the possibility of an Ottoman challenge to their dominance in the eastern Mediterranean. In the case of the Arsenal, preparedness entailed stockpiling sufficient timber to build a large military fleet on short notice in the event of war with the Porte. The Republic's leaders apparently did not feel comfortable entrusting the task of providing such an extensive number of spare mast timbers to the merchants who held the Cadore monopoly. Instead, the Senate turned directly to Pieve's *consiglio generale*—asking it to donate the needed material as a gesture of thanks for the Republic's protection. The fact that the Cadorini delivered the requested timbers only served to emphasize both the strength of the ties that bound them to Venice and the region's importance to the Arsenal's supply system.

The Republic's leaders were clearly intrigued by the possibility that the Arsenal could receive mast timbers from the Cadore without the costs and risks of relying on merchants. In 1463, the Senate again turned to Pieve's *consiglio generale* for help. This time, though, the Venetians went a step further. Claiming *diritto di riserva*—the traditional right of the *res publica* to seize all unclaimed resources in its territory—the Senate asked the Cadorini to designate a large fir forest near the villages of Auronzo and Dobiacco as a mast reserve.[6] The forest was known as the Bosco della Vizza, a legal term describing a piece of community property that could be leased for periods of up to twenty years. Eventually it became known simply as the Vizza di Cadore.[7] The Venetians chose the forest because it contained an unusually large number of high-quality fir poles that met the Arsenal's stringent requirements. It also happened to stand near one of the largest tributaries of the Piave, which meant that even in years with below-average precipitation, crews would be able to move at least some timber down to the main course of the river.

The legal claim of *diritto di riserva* was somewhat tenuous. While most mainland communities in the northeast had traditionally exercised the *diritto di riserva* within their own jurisdictions, it was far from clear that the Republic was entitled to those same rights by virtue of its regional dominion. Moreover, under normal conditions the *diritto di riserva* only applied to unclaimed or spontaneously growing resources. Certainly in the case of the Vizza di Cadore—which was a community forest jointly controlled by Auronzo and Dobiacco—defining the timber it contained as unclaimed stretched the term to the limits of credibility. The Venetians might have tried to make a case based on the theory that the fir trees in the forest were spontaneously growing and therefore subject to the *diritto di riserva*. But such legal sophistry relied on all concerned ignoring the fact that trees were not defined that way in any other community forests. Both the Senate and the *consiglio generale* seem to have recognized the somewhat questionable nature of the claim, since neither body placed any restrictions on the traditional usufruct rights enjoyed by the residents of Auronzo and Dobiacco. In essence, the Venetians did not claim sovereignty over the entire forest. Nor did they claim ownership of all the mast-quality timber within the forest. In sharp contrast to later practices, the best fir trees were neither marked nor cataloged in any fashion. Rather, the Senate used the *diritto di riserva* to assert the Republic's right to exploit the forest as the Arsenal's needs dictated and without seeking the permission of either Pieve's *consiglio generale* or the village leaders in Auronzo or Dobiacco. In other words, Venice, Auronzo, and Dobiacco enjoyed equivalent rights in the Vizza di Cadore—including the right to appropriate labor for timber harvests in the form of *angarie*. The act of designating the Vizza di Cadore as a timber reserve served to formalize the arrangement that the Senate had struck with the *consiglio generale* a decade earlier. The Venetians and the Cadorini had simply agreed that in the future the Arsenal could requisition mast timbers from this specific forest at will and without consultation.

The new arrangement presented several advantages. It gave the Republic some assurance that in the event of a war with the Ottomans, the fleet would not find itself short of masts. Moreover, the agreement offered such assurance without requiring the Arsenal managers to become involved in directly supervising the harvest or making any of the critical decisions about when to harvest and which trees to take. The Cadorini remained responsible for organizing the *angarie*, harvesting the timber, getting it into the river, and moving it to the collection point at Perarolo, near Pieve di Cadore, where raftsmen lashed the poles together and prepared them for the journey downstream to Venice. There were also a few sawmills at Perarolo that, during periods of high water, were capable of processing some of the timber into board lengths for the construction trade. The raftsmen stacked the milled lumber on the assembled rafts and delivered it to markets downriver.[8] The only phase of the harvest for which the Venetians remained directly responsible was contracting with the raftsmen who would move the timber from Perarolo to the lagoon. The Vizza possessed many of the advantages of a dedicated reserve with almost none of the organizational problems. Such an arrangement could work in the Cadore because the combination of low population density and large forests meant that it was plausible for the Arsenal to claim privileged access to large fir poles without abrogating local rights. In the more densely populated areas of the middle and lower Piave, the Venetians remained reluctant to share forests in quite the same way, because they feared that the woods held insufficient stocks of timber to support multiple uses.

The arrangement that the Venetians struck with the Cadorini for access to the Bosco della Vizza established the important legal precedent that in times of public emergency the Republic could apply the *diritto di riserva* to mainland forest resources. It placed the Venetian courts in a position to back even more aggressive claims in the future. So it was that a mere eight years after the designation of the Vizza di Cadore as a mast reserve, the Senate decided to establish a similar reserve for oak timber along the lower course of the Piave River. Just as they had in the case of the Vizza di Cadore, the Venetian legislators invoked the Ottoman threat and the need to ensure the readiness of the fleet. By framing the legal question in terms of naval security, the senators were able to exploit the Cadore precedent to the Republic's advantage and claim the right to establish a new reserve. Even so, creating an oak reserve presented a far more complex set of challenges than the fairly straightforward process that had led to the establishment of the Vizza di Cadore. As a rule, the territories where the best oak grew were more densely populated than the Cadore, and local elites were far less likely than the Cadorini to agree that the Venetians had the uncontested right to claim the *diritto di riserva*. In addition, these local residents used their forests far more intensively than the Cadorini.

The Senate must have known that sharing access with local villages was going to be a much greater challenge than had been the case in the high mountain valleys of the upper Piave region. The Venetians could certainly have avoided some of these problems by choosing to establish their first oak reserve in the eastern Friuli or Istria, where demographic conditions were similar to those in the Cadore. Yet in spite of the potential difficulties, the lower Piave region presented too many important advantages for the Senate to ignore them and look elsewhere. The Piave was the only river that offered both a reliable year-round flow and access to a number of large community forests containing oak. Furthermore, its proximity to Venice made the region more secure than the

Friuli and Istria and far more appealing from the point of view of transportation costs.

All that remained was to identify the best forest in which to assert the Republic's claims to the *diritto di riserva*. The Arsenal managers sent a master carpenter named Domenico Lion to inspect community forests along the Piave and recommend the one with the best oak for conversion into an Arsenal reserve. Lion's report does not survive, but in the legislation banning the Montello he is quoted as saying that the forest contained "timber for more than 100 excellent galleys of great quality."[9] This statement reveals that in the second half of the fifteenth century the Venetians still possessed a limited understanding of mainland forests and their role in supplying the Arsenal with timber. Lion had just inspected what would become the single most important source of shipgrade oak for the next 350 years, yet he assessed its potential solely in terms of how many galleys the shipyard could build with the timber that stood in the forest at that moment. Neither he nor his superiors in Venice saw this most important of all oak forests as a sustainable source of timber. They still thought about woodlands in fairly crude terms. In particular, the fact that they assessed the forest in terms of the number of oak it contained, rather than in terms of its overall size, soil quality, or species distribution, illustrates how they continued to think of timber as a resource that was rapidly disappearing from mainland landscapes, and not as a potentially renewable feature of those landscapes. Of course in 1471, amidst the fear of an impending Ottoman attack, the idea that a forest could provide the material for over 100 ships must have been so comforting to all concerned that no one thought to broach the question of future yields.

Having identified the forest it wished to designate as a reserve, the Senate then faced the problem of how to apply the Cadore precedent to the Trevigiano. In other words, the Republic's leaders had to decide whether to claim the same rights to harvest oak in the Montello as those enjoyed by local communities, or to claim the *diritto di riserva* over the entire forest and administer it entirely from Venice. If they opted for the latter arrangement, the state would be faced with the problems of organizing the annual oak harvest and managing the forest—including determining such minutia as how much firewood each village could harvest and in which coupe, as well as how much winter fodder and green fertilizer the villagers could remove from the wood. Such concerns were hardly trivial, since whatever fears the Senate may have harbored about the fragility of the resource, it could hardly strip thirteen villages of all of their traditional usufruct rights and then also expect them to labor happily on behalf of the Arsenal in the bargain. Asserting the *diritto di riserva* over a forest the size of the Montello was a momentous decision that would place the burden of administering a vast and complicated forest landscape squarely on the shoulders of the Arsenal managers. And in 1471 there was no reason to assume that they were equipped to accept that burden. Perhaps there were a few timber merchants in Venice who knew how to organize a large harvest, but none were likely to be elected *provveditore all'arsenale*—an office that usually went to senior members of the Senate. And there were certainly no Venetian patricians possessing any experience with the challenges of managing a large forest, especially the contentious issue of allocating and distributing common resources among local residents. Nevertheless, the Senate opted to turn the Montello over to the Arsenal and charge the shipyard's managers with the task of regulating access to the forest through a system of licenses. The Senate made its reasons clear in the legislation by again referring to Lion's report and stating that

> the forest has been reduced to a poor and terrible condition due to the
> fact that many local residents disobediently—and in the hopes of
> profit—cut and tear out a great quantity of the best timber to make
> barrels and charcoal that could be purchased elsewhere. This practice
> does the greatest harm to the forest, especially considering how useful
> and fruitful it could be for our Arsenal.[10]

This passage justifies the Senate's unprecedented decision to apply the *diritto di riserva* so as to limit severely the access rights of the thirteen villages surrounding the Montello. The villages would still be allowed to petition the Arsenal for licenses to collect firewood and green fertilizer, but they could no longer pasture animals or take other kinds of wood out of their own commons. In essence the Senate claimed that because local residents had proven themselves to be poor stewards of a forest that had the potential to supply the Arsenal with critical material, the Republic was within its rights to confiscate the resource and manage it on behalf of itself and the villagers both.

By banning access to the Montello, the Senate sought to establish the precedent that failure to manage a forest properly was the legal equivalent of allowing livestock to escape from a pasture and wander unclaimed across the countryside—in both cases the resource was untended and therefore subject to the application of the *diritto di riserva*. This argument bears a strong resemblance to some of the assertions regarding water made by Marco Cornaro in 1442 and the earlier anonymous scribe of 1413. Just as both authors defined proper water management on the mainland in terms of a specific set of Venetian interests in the lagoon, so too did the Senate in 1471 define proper forest management exclusively in terms of the Arsenal's needs. By this rationale, any practice that impeded the growth of the large, straight, even-grained oak poles needed for shipbuilding constituted a failure to manage forest resources correctly. Of course, the Republic's view of failure was often at odds with local ideas and practices. For example, pollarding, which was a perfectly reasonable practice when seen from the perspective of local demand for firewood and the raw material for charcoal production, suddenly appeared to constitute a profligate use of a scarce resource when viewed through the eyes of Venetian officials. Likewise, running livestock in the forest during the summer might have helped villages manage their open pasture better, but to the Venetians the practice clearly threatened oak seedlings and consequently had to be banned completely. Furthermore, because legislators had already established that timber constituted one of the cornerstones of the Republic's liberty, the Montello ban opened up the possibility of linking a specific form of forest management —one that promoted the growth of Arsenal-grade timber—to traditional Venetian definitions of the public good. Conversely, the ban also paved the way for defining many local practices as antithetical to the interests of the *res publica*. As the Venetians became more familiar with local practices of forest exploitation, they began to draw explicit connections between specific forms of forest management and a republican conception of the public good.

Where the Montello ban differed from Cornaro's ideas concerning water management was in the depth and breadth of the knowledge underpinning the arguments. While Cornaro possessed significant experience in the arena of lagoon management, nobody in the Ducal Palace had much in the way of practical knowledge that could be translated into a set of specific policies governing a complex forest landscape such as the Montello. The decision to ban was instead a product of longstanding Venetian fears that oak and other critical resources were disappearing and the correlated belief that the only way to preserve such resources was to prevent competing users from enjoying unfettered access to them. In this sense, the Montello ban resembled fourteenth-century market controls more than it did Marco Cornaro's sophisticated prescriptions for managing mainland waterscapes. Nevertheless, the ban furnished the Republic's leaders with a powerful instrument to use when protecting the interests of the Arsenal. By creating a broad definition of mismanagement, the Senate not only shifted the blame for timber shortages from its own market policies to the misdeeds of mainland residents, it also established a future legal pretext for unilaterally imposing the *diritto di riserva* over other forests.

Altering local practices in such a drastic fashion presented Venetian authorities with a number of serious challenges. Local residents were unlikely simply to surrender many of their traditional usufruct rights, nor were they going to accept easily the idea that long-established practices of forest management suddenly represented poor stewardship. Anticipating a good deal of local resistance, the Senate established what it considered stiff penalties for individuals who failed to comply with the Montello ban. Violators incurred a fine of 25 *lire di piccoli* for each "piece of wood they might cut" as well as two months in prison for each violation of the ban. Informants split the proceeds of the fine with the Venetian authorities—in this case either the *podestà* of Treviso or the Arsenal managers. Since a piece of wood was not clearly defined in the measure, there was ample room for the Arsenal or the *podestà* to impose extortionate fines. But what made the penalties truly draconian was the fact that individuals convicted under the statute could not, under any circumstance, appeal the resulting fines to another court. All sentences stood in perpetuity. The Senate was well aware that Venetian citizens and mainland subjects alike were extremely adept at using the Republic's labyrinthine court system to delay unfavorable judgements, sometimes for decades. Historians such as James Grubb and Edward Muir have demonstrated how the system of seemingly infinite appeals greased the machinery of state by creating a relatively safe space for mainland subjects to push back against abuses perpetrated by their Venetian rulers.[11]

But in the case of the oak timber in the Montello, the Senate was unwilling to risk the possibility that local residents might destroy precious oak and then take refuge in the courts. Consequently, the only way to make the penalties truly intimidating was to prevent violators of the Montello ban from pursuing an endless series of appeals. And even that provision ultimately proved to be an insufficient deterrent. Indeed, throughout the sixteenth and seventeenth centuries the Senate and the Council of Ten found themselves regularly ratcheting up the penalties until it finally became a capital crime for unlicensed individuals to enter the Montello with cutting tools in hand.[12] Such an extreme punishment reflected both the Venetians' real sense that the ban had failed to alter the villagers' destructive habits and the locals' continuing belief that they should enjoy traditional rights of usufruct in the Montello in spite of the Republic's claims to exclusive sovereignty over the wood.

The problem was not limited to the Montello. Throughout the seventeenth and eighteenth centuries, small communities in areas that boasted large and abundant state forests expressed considerable displeasure at being denied access rights to resources that sometimes went unexploited for years at a time. For example, in 1734 the patrician Bertuccio Dolfin inspected a number of smaller state reserves along the Piave River, some of which had been ignored by Venetian officials for over a century. Unsurprisingly, Dolfin discovered that many of those forests had been long since been pressed into service by local villagers, none of whom were old enough to remember that the woods in question were Arsenal reserves. Worse still, at least nineteen forests had "vanished from all memory, leaving not a vestige of their former selves."[13] Dolfin expressed dismay at the loss of so much timber but admitted that "the usurpers and abusers are protected by about a century and a half of official neglect ... and may live unpunished."[14] Equally unsurprisingly, the villagers were none too happy to discover that what they had always presumed to be a community resource was actually under the direct control of the Venetian Arsenal, and Dolfin was forced to admit that "it will be most difficult, perhaps impossible, to fully restore these forests to the public patrimony."[15] Dolfin's reports highlight the degree to which exercising sovereignty depended on the consistent presence of Venetian officials, and how easily the state could lose its hard-won authority in the face of local resistance.

The Vizza di Cadore and the Bosco del Montello were the first of the large state-owned forests—called *boschi pubblici* or *boschi di San Marco* —that would become the mainstay of the Arsenal's timber supply by the middle of the sixteenth century. The establishment of state reserves represented a sea change in the relationship between the Republic and its mainland subjects. The power to apply the *diritto di riserva* in a unilateral fashion irrevocably altered the way in which Venice's leaders thought about the problem of accessing forest resources. Suddenly it was not merely possible for officials to interfere in local practices of forest exploitation, but it had become an obligation to step in to save vital resources from profligate local users. For the Arsenal managers the change was even more dramatic. The directors of the Republic's shipyard went from acting as privileged timber consumers whose market position was guaranteed by the fourteenth-century regulatory regime to being responsible for the administration of a large and growing collection of mainland forests—including everything from ensuring the integrity of those forests to deciding what share of the forest resources should go to local communities, and to marshalling and supervising the workers who performed the annual harvests. These new administrative responsibilities placed a considerable financial burden on the Arsenal, which now bore all of the costs of the harvest as well as the expense of employing forest guardians and other local officials. The Senate never completely abandoned market regulations, but the focus of its legislative efforts increasingly shifted towards a policy of direct state control over the management of timber resources. Initially Venetian interventions focused exclusively on state forests, but community forests fell under state scrutiny in 1476, and by the middle of the sixteenth century the Senate and the Council of Ten had begun attempting to impose stricter regulations on private and ecclesiastical landowners whose properties included oak forests.

After 1471 the Council of Ten—the smallest and most powerful committee in the Venetian Republic—took an increasing interest in Arsenal reserves. The Council was in charge of state security, and its members increasingly viewed keeping the Arsenal supplied with timber as a vital part of that brief. The Ten worked steadily to expand the Republic's forest patrimony. By the end of the fifteenth century the Council had added two more large oak forests to the Arsenal's growing mainland possessions. In a series of rulings enacted in 1488, the Council of Ten claimed *diritto di riserva* over a forest near Padua called the Carpeneda.[16] Soon thereafter the Council also declared the Montona—a large wood near the geographical center of the Istrian peninsula—an Arsenal reserve. In both cases the Montello ban served as the template for imposing direct control over public resources. As with the Montello, the Carpeneda ban allowed the surrounding communities that traditionally controlled the forest to collect firewood with the permission of the Arsenal managers.

The terms of the Montona ban were not as clear. One side of the forest ran along the imperial frontier, and local residents often had ties to communities on both sides of the poorly defined border. In the unlikely event that they were caught stealing from the reserve, lawbreakers could reasonably expect to escape prosecution by taking shelter outside of Venetian territory. Entire villages occasionally threatened to pick up and move if it meant receiving better treatment from an imperial lord or Ottoman sanjak.[17] Keeping tabs on activity in the reserve was also extremely difficult, as the nearest Venetian official—the *capitano* at Raspo —had to travel for two days over difficult and dangerous terrain just to lay eyes on the forest. Consequently, the Council of Ten could not and did not expect the Arsenal to exert the same degree of control over the Montona as it did over the Carpeneda and Montello reserves. If anything, the Montona was a more lawless version of the Vizza di Cadore—a large commons where the Venetians uneasily shared privileges with unruly villagers.

The emerging involvement of the Council of Ten had a dramatic effect on the development of the state forest reserves. Because the Council's main constitutional role in Venice's republican system was to oversee matters that affected the security of the state, its growing interest in forests and forestry legislation made clear that the *diritto di riserva*—as it applied to Arsenal timber—was a matter of signal importance.[18] Moreover, because the Ten also functioned as the Republic's highest court of appeal, its involvement guaranteed that the Republic's right to seize poorly managed community forests could withstand most legal challenges mounted by local communities. The Council's small size, great prestige, and immense institutional power also placed it in a far better position to make quick decisions concerning forest exploitation than the larger and more divided Senate. By the end of the fifteenth century the Council of Ten had assumed the task of proposing and ratifying new forestry laws. The Council also established itself as an overseer with respect to the Arsenal managers' administration of the new public forests. The Ten demanded that the Arsenal submit all requisitions from the state reserves to it for approval. Beginning in the middle of the sixteenth century, the Ten also took control of the process of issuing licenses to harvest firewood and timber in the reserves. The daily records of the Council during this period provide a precise chronicle of formal requests for permission to harvest oak timber. The surviving petitions cover a wide range of projects, from the seemingly trivial (four oak trees of inferior quality to repair a mill) to large institutional projects (500 oak poles to build the foundation for a new church bell tower) to major public works on the mainland (600 oak poles to repair river embankments) to the maintenance of the lagoon infrastructure (10,000 oak poles to rebuild damaged breakwaters on the barrier islands of Lido and Pellestrina).[19] The volume of requests was enormous. In a typical year the Council might receive as many as 400 requests to cut oak—and the Ten heard, debated, and voted on each individual case. Lastly, the Council's power allowed it to aggressively employ the *diritto di riserva* to expand the size of the Arsenal's oak patrimony. Thanks to the Council of Ten, by the middle of the sixteenth century the Republic had seized control of over forty separate forest reserves in the northeast and in Istria. But the *diritto di riserva* was only one aspect of an emerging set of legal precedents that Venetian legislators established in the second half of the fifteenth century, precedents that formed the basis for the Venetian forestry regime of the sixteenth and seventeenth centuries. In fact, even as the Council of Ten concerned itself with expanding the Arsenal reserves, the previous problems with the firewood supply increased the Senate's interest in the management of the community forests that still constituted the main source of fuel for the residents of the lagoon.

The 1476 Forestry Laws and the Hierarchy of Forest Utilization

In January of 1476 the Senate passed six provisions governing the use of community forests in the *terraferma*. The new laws addressed both the collective and individual exploitation of community woodlands.[20] The statutes, which are summarized below, covered a wide variety of forest uses and became the single most commonly cited precedent in Venetian forestry legislation well into the eighteenth century. Each of the new laws established the right of the *res publica* to regulate a specific set of practices in community forests throughout the mainland. Moreover, the statutes placed the Republic in the role of guardian of community forest resources with a pressing interest in preserving both the total area covered by the woods and the specific forest resources that the Venetians most needed for the city and the Arsenal.

1. Mandatory coupes: The Senate mandated the division of all mainland community forests into ten coupes for rotational harvesting. All communities would have to harvest a coupe for one year and then allow it to rest for nine.

2. Restrictions on the sale of common land: The Senate established that community forests could not be alienated or sold under any conditions, but leases were still allowed under carefully controlled conditions. Communities caught breaking the law would have to pay a fine of 100 ducats for each violation. The Senate also offered amnesty to all those who had illegally purchased a community forest, provided that the offenders returned the land to the commons within a month of the publication of the laws.

3. Bans on pastoralism and swidden: This measure outlawed both traditional swidden agriculture in the commons and the use of community stands as summer pasture. The Senate established a fine of 100 ducats and six months in the galleys for anyone who used fire to deliberately destroy community forests. It established a further penalty of 40 *soldi* per animal for those caught pasturing in the forests. In addition, the Senate authorized Venetian officials to place a moratorium of up to five years on harvesting in forests that had been heavily damaged by fire or pasturing.

4. Restrictions on the sale of wood from the Montello: Boatmen transporting firewood harvested in the Montello on behalf of the Republic had to bring it directly to Venice and could not sell it anywhere en route. The Senate established a 100 *lire* base fine and 40 *lire* per *passo* of black-market wood from the Montello, along with the confiscation of the cart or boat transporting the bundles.

5. Expansion of the public warehouses: Because of past problems with the supply of firewood, including the delay of shipments due to inclement weather, the Senate ordered the expansion of the firewood warehouse at San Biagio and near the Arsenal.

6. Primacy of the Arsenal: The Senate also dictated that the Arsenal's needs for oak and other wood should always take precedence in any disputes over the application of the new laws.

The following day the Senate passed an additional measure requiring a two-thirds majority in the Great Council to overturn or suspend any of the six provisions.

The 1476 legislation addressed a number of key issues concerning the exploitation of mainland forests. It also initiated a significant shift in Venetian policy. Neither the Senate nor the Council of Ten had ever laid down any guidelines for how the two original Arsenal reserves—the Montello and the Vizza di Cadore—should be managed. Beyond mandating that the Arsenal managers issue licenses to cut timber and firewood in the Montello, the Republic's leaders had not established any specific practices for the new reserves. Moreover, the licensing requirement only applied to Montello oak. The Senate had never intended either reserve to serve as a model for the management of community forests—or any other mainland forests for that matter. Even though the 1471 Montello ban criticized mainland residents for their mismanagement of precious resources, legislators had nevertheless allowed them to continue to employ traditional modes of exploitation outside of the confines of the oak reserve. In this respect, the 1476 laws reflect a major change in Venetian attitudes towards forest use. For the first time, the Republic's lawmakers had attempted to create a universal system of local-access rights in community forests rather than acting to reserve specific trees in a limited number of specially designated stands.

Despite the Senate's use of strong language and apparently harsh penalties in the new legislation, it still failed to address several significant issues. None of the rules laid out in the measures applied to private or ecclesiastical property, thereby limiting the power of the laws to preserve forest cover. Nor did the laws provide for any systematic controls to ensure their enforcement beyond the occasional inspection tour by a representative of the *provveditori alle legne* or the Arsenal. And without any means of tracking changes at the local level, inspectors could do relatively little to correct violations of the new rules. Lastly, the laws did not offer any positive measures to encourage reforestation—only negative proscriptions against specific uses and activities. In this last sense, the 1476 laws bore an important resemblance to the Montello ban five years earlier, which proscribed common local practices such as using the woods for summer pasture, but did not establish any positive measures designed to encourage renewal of the crucial oak resources that had inspired the ban in the first place.

Without any real mechanisms for enforcing the new rules, the relatively modest negative proscriptions contained in the 1476 legislation expressed more of a hope than an actual plan for preserving community forests. The first law, mandating the maintenance of ten coupes in all community forests, stands out as the only positive prescriptive measure among the six statutes. Yet the Senate hoped the rule would preserve the total forested area rather than intending it to promote the regeneration of important species, meaning that the Venetians still held relatively limited prescriptive ambitions. It should also be noted that this law did not represent an innovation. It merely formalized what was already a nearly universal practice in community forests throughout the region.[21] In this regard, the Senate did not impose a new mode of forest exploitation on ignorant villagers. Rather, the measure emerged from the recognition that whatever the needs of the Arsenal, local residents retained the right to extract fuel and a limited number of other necessities from community forests. The Republic's leaders simply demanded that mainland communities respect and follow their own traditional practices when doing so. Nevertheless, that legislators were even aware of the possibility of using the coupe system does indicate that Venetian officials had learned something about local practices of forest exploitation in the half century since the conquest.

Whatever its shortcomings, the new legislation constituted the first systematic attempt to regulate local practices of forest exploitation and was therefore unlike any of the stopgap measures and market controls that the Venetians had imposed in the past. More importantly, the 1476 laws became the template upon which the Council of Ten and the Senate based almost all forestry legislation until the middle of the seventeenth century. And even in a later era, when legislators possessed a more sophisticated understanding of forests, the 1476 laws remained one of the state's more important legal precedents until the fall of the Republic. In this regard, the 1476 laws were the most significant piece of forestry legislation ever passed by the Senate. These six simple rules for managing community forests framed almost all future debates concerning the regulation of local practices of forest exploitation, and established the legal foundation of the forestry regime in the sixteenth and seventeenth centuries.

In the 1476 laws, the Senate clearly identified what it believed to be the two primary causes of deforestation in community forests: running livestock and using fire to clear the forest. In keeping with the idea that these practices constituted particularly egregious forms of mismanagement, the Republic's leaders established that the aim of all forestry legislation should be to curb these two abuses as much as possible. The Senate reserved the heaviest fines for those who burned forestland in order to expand pasture or cropland. The legislators established only slightly less punitive penalties for anyone caught pasturing animals in the forest—at 40 *soldi* per head, even a small herd of ten or fifteen animals could lead to prohibitive fines. The structure of the pecuniary penalties reveals that Venetians drew distinctions among various local practices based on how destructive they believed the actions to be. If they saw employing coupes as a beneficial practice that ought to be encouraged, they saw pasturing and the use of fire as grave threats that needed to be stamped out at any cost to preserve vulnerable resources. The emphasis placed on livestock and deliberate forest clearance highlights how the Republic's leaders had begun to form a coherent image of the profligate mainland resident whose actions threatened the *res publica*. The selfish peasant appropriated or destroyed common resources for personal gain, while the civic-minded peasant utilized the forest in cooperation with his fellow villagers and always with an eye towards its preservation for future applications. And peasants were not the only targets of the 1476 laws. The Senate clearly and deliberately aimed the laws at those members of the landowning classes whose property bordered on community forests. The Venetians recognized that individuals and institutions alike had a vested interest in clearing forests to expand their own holdings, so they attempted to situate such practices within a moral economy of nature that placed a higher value on forestland than the agrarian economy could. In nearly every respect, the 1476 laws articulated the idea that local practices of forest exploitation had meaningful consequences for Venice.

The 1476 laws also set up an important and enduring opposition between pastoralism and the kinds of forests the Venetians hoped to see preserved. The Venetians uncritically viewed all pastoralism as threatening mainland oak reserves—especially the delicate seedlings that represented future galleys and round ships. The senators' fears were not entirely unfounded. A sizeable flock of sheep was capable of consuming almost all the low-lying vegetation in a small forest if the animals were allowed to roam free. Nevertheless, not all livestock threatened oak seedlings, and pasturing some animals in the forest could have beneficial effects. For example, allowing pigs to consume the acorns and pass the seeds through their digestive tracts promoted the renewal of oak trees. For precisely this reason, local authorities in many parts of northern Europe often allowed peasants and villages to release their pigs into the forest during the fall.[22] But the Senate drew no distinctions between the behavior of different domesticated species, since concerns over the destructive potential of livestock overrode any arguments in favor of pastoralism—even when such arguments originated in Venice. For instance, in 1775 the chair of physics at the University of Padua, Simone Stratico, wrote a short treatise comparing the shipbuilding theories and techniques he had observed during an extended stay in England with the methods employed in the Venetian Arsenal. In a section devoted to forest management, Stratico took the time "to consider the question of *stortami* which are so important in the construction of ships, and which are generally in short supply in the Arsenal."[23] *Stortami*—literally crooked timbers—were the rarest and most important of all Arsenal-grade oak. The Republic's shipwrights used *stortami* to fabricate the structural knees and ribs that braced the hull. In an attempt to convince the Senate to reconsider the blanket policy forbidding local residents from pasturing animals in oak forests, Stratico observed "that in uncultivated areas and other fields accessible to animals, the oak trees grow in an irregular and crooked manner due to the wounds they receive from the animals and from the force of the wind."[24] In other words, Stratico argued that the natural behavior of the cattle as they scratched themselves against trees encouraged the growth of *stortami*. Consequently, he believed that the Republic ought to encourage peasants to pasture livestock in oak forests by lifting the long-outdated proscriptions contained in the 1476 legislation. The Senate declined to consider his proposal.

The Senate viewed farmers with a similarly jaundiced eye. The third 1476 law did not distinguish between clearing forest for pasture and clearing it for arable land, and farmers were subject to the same sanctions as shepherds. The Venetians also directed the second measure—which prohibited the alienation of common lands containing forest—against individuals and institutions who owned agricultural land. The Venetian conquest had unleashed a significant redistribution of rural property in the northeast, and a new class of urban-based landowners was eager to extract profit from agriculture. Most leased their new properties and allowed the tenants to make critical decisions regarding what to plant and how to manage the land.[25] An increasing number, however, were becoming interested in directly managing their rural holdings. Many of the new owners saw an opportunity to increase their agrarian investments by purchasing marginal lands from poor villages and then improving them through either reclamation or forest clearance.[26] Like pastoralism, the Venetians saw this type of land investment as being inimical to their goal of preserving valuable forest resources. Consequently, the Republic's leaders sought to stop the alienation of common lands in timber-producing regions. In fact, the Venetians had already attempted to limit the power of villages and towns to sell and lease their commons prior to 1476. In 1463 the Senate enacted a law calling for a thirty-year banishment for anyone caught usurping community property with the intention of purchasing, selling, leasing, or otherwise profiting from its alienation. But there were two main distinctions between the earlier law and the 1476 statute. The 1463 legislation penalized the buyer, while the new rules punished the local political authorities who had presumably allowed the usurpation. The new law also drew an explicit connection between the sale of common lands and deforestation by creating additional prohibitions that only pertained to woodlands. The 1476 laws thus framed the relationship between agriculture and forestry as an antagonistic one—a view that dominated the writings of sixteenth- and seventeenth-century forestry officials.

Unfortunately, the sheer scale of the problem of surreptitious privatization of common lands meant that no law, however strongly worded, could prevent the sales from continuing. In the second half of the fifteenth century it was up to local councils in cooperation with resident Venetian officials—either the *podestà* or the *capitano*—to ensure that the commons remained under the control of the community to which they belonged. Of course, local councils were almost always composed of the very same wealthy merchants who wanted to profit from the purchase and conversion of common lands, so the Senate could expect no help from that corner. To make matters worse, most of the best forestland stood in minor jurisdictions—such as Feltre, Belluno, Conegliano, and Raspo—which the Senate generally used as proving grounds for young patricians who had never held an elected office before.[27] Such men were inexperienced and lacked the personal authority to force powerful local elites to comply with central edicts. It was simply foolhardy for the Senate to imagine that "the wealthiest and most important local families took much notice of a Venetian youth who had just arrived in town."[28] So unless a more senior and powerful official representing the Arsenal or the Council of Ten passed through on an inspection tour, youthful *podestà* lacked the authority to enforce the laws, which meant that community forests remained vulnerable to privatization well into the sixteenth century.

Venetian legislators also lacked the necessary understanding of mainland property rights to enable them to craft legislation capable of effectively protecting community forests. The Senate based both the 1463 and 1476 laws governing common lands on the assumption that mainland towns and villages possessed a single type of commons that could be subjected to a uniform set of rules. In reality, community property took at least two distinct forms in the legal traditions of most northern Italian towns—the local council could lease or sell one type but not the other. In theory, such arrangements protected the villagers' basic interests in the commons while allowing local authorities to use parts of the community's patrimony to raise needed revenue. The new Venetian regulations severely curtailed the traditional rights of local communities to use a portion of their commons for the fiscal well-being of the village or town. Town councils and wealthy landowners throughout the *terraferma*—all of whom shared the desire to protect and maintain traditional rights in the face of Venetian aggression—moved quickly to challenge the new laws. By bringing the issues into the courts, mainland residents forced

Venetian tribunals and *podestà* to rule repeatedly on whether or not the new rules applied to specific pieces of land. Such proceedings threatened to spiral out of control, clogging dockets and involving the Republic in contentious disputes with local elites and village councils alike. In 1488 the Council of Ten finally conceded that the 1476 legislation did not apply to all community lands. By using the court system, mainland residents of all classes successfully argued that the traditional rights of communities to alienate a portion of their common lands protected those lands from both the 1463 and 1476 legislation. The Ten ultimately acknowledged the existence of two forms of community property, each subject to its own rules. *Beni comuni* became the legal term used to refer to those common lands that could be alienated by local governments and were not subject to Venetian regulations. A second category, known as *beni comunali*, could not be disposed of by local councils and remained subject to the Venetian ban on leases and sales. Identifying and regulating these lands presented Venetian officials with so many problems that in 1574 the Senate created an entire bureaucracy devoted solely to cataloging and preserving community property—the *provveditori sopra beni comunali*.[29]

Despite the apparent success of their efforts to limit the scope of the 1476 laws, challenging the new legislation proved to be a double-edged sword for many mainland elites who chose to wield it. The Council of Ten and other Venetian courts and administrative bodies took advantage of their new understanding of the distinctions between different forms of community property to bolster central control over oak forests that stood on community lands. Relying on the 1476 statute, Venetian officials aggressively pursued individuals who had taken advantage of Venetian rule to usurp community forests by arguing that any wooded area containing oak fell, by definition, under the rubric of *beni comunali*. In a 1495 ruling, the Council of Ten established that all *beni comunali* should remain perpetually "to the common benefit and usufruct of the communities in which they are located."[30] The Ten also established stiffer penalties for those individuals convicted of illegally alienating *beni comunali* and encouraged local authorities to appoint guardians to protect community forests from future abuses.

Like the laws banning livestock from community forests, the conflicts over control of common lands reflect the differences between the ways

that the Venetians and their mainland subjects understood forest resources. Local residents of all social classes did not view the clearing and
conversion of a limited amount of common forestland to arable land or
pasture with the same concern as their Venetian rulers. If the forest was
marginal to begin with, then no harm could come to the community by
allowing leaseholders to clear it. In fact, open land—whether pasture or
cropland—generated far higher rates of return than woodlands when
leased or sold, creating a powerful incentive for poor villages and towns
to permit such clearing. If the cleared forest had previously been a regular source of firewood or fodder, this usually meant that local authorities
simply planned to press a previously marginal section of the forest into
service as a source of woodland staples. In either case, the community
realized profits without much risk of local shortages of fuel and other
crucial forest resources. To the Venetians such practices looked quite
different. In the 1471 legislation banning the Montello, the Senate had
justified confiscating the forest by arguing that local communities had
been badly mismanaging their most valuable timber resources.[31] For the
Republic's leaders, any local benefits that might be derived from leasing
or clearing community forests were outweighed by the possibility that
those forests might no longer yield reliable surpluses of fuel and timber
for Venetian consumption. By the end of the fifteenth century the Venetians were increasingly willing to intervene aggressively to protect those
surpluses.

The Venetian position was not without merit. Allowing leaseholders to
clear common forests was wasteful because even modest clearing could
make a dramatic difference in terms of the total area covered by the
community's stands. And while a properly managed smaller stand might
still meet local needs in most years, it could never supply the Venetians
with the resources they required. Even if local officials made a good-faith
effort to preserve the large, straight-grained poles used by the Arsenal, a
small stand might no longer contain sufficient numbers to justify the
expense of mobilizing labor for a harvest. Widely scattered poles, however tall and straight, were all but useless because of the higher costs
associated with their removal. Likewise, a smaller community stand divided into relatively tiny coupes could still supply fuel for a village, but the
Venetians wanted such forests to generate a healthy surplus for export to

the lagoon. Little wonder then that the Venetians became so intent on limiting the alienation of community forests.

Still, the Venetians bore some responsibility for the situation. Widespread clearing in community forests in the fifteenth century was both cause and effect of the endemic fuel shortages in the city on the lagoon. Venetian tariffs and price ceilings discouraged merchants from harvesting in less-accessible areas, which only served to place an unbearable demand on the most easily reachable sources of firewood. In many ways Cornaro had framed his 1442 treatise around the relationship between market controls and forest depletion. He argued that there was plenty of potentially useful firewood that simply was not being exploited effectively, due to elevated transportation costs caused by obstructed inland canals and the imposition of excessive fines and tariffs by Venetian officials. In the same way that the Senate had repeatedly attempted to force locals to clear sedimentary deposits in inland canals to improve access to underexploited stands, the 1476 laws attempted to force mainland subjects to harvest firewood in underutilized sections of the forest so that they might produce an adequate surplus to satisfy the growing needs of the metropole.

What the Senate failed to include in the measure was any aid to the affected communities. Legislators made no attempt to ease the transportation costs borne by the merchants, much less to compensate the peasants who furnished the labor for the extra time and effort involved in exploiting a broader area of forestland. In 1476 the Venetians remained either unaware or unconcerned that the new laws might place an untenable burden on mainland residents. In fact, the 1476 laws only paid attention to local conditions and practices in cases where a clear connection existed between the perceived effects of a traditional practice such as the coupe system and the Republic's need for a particular set of forest commodities. By the middle of the sixteenth century the Republic's leaders would begin to take better account of local conditions. For example, in 1530 the Council of Ten ordered the destruction of a public mill that blocked a navigable stream and repairs to several roads because "the present shortage of firewood in our city is not due to a lack of abundance in the local forests, but on account of transportation difficulties and the condition of the roads leading to them."[32] Unfortunately, in 1476 the occupants of the Ducal Palace did not enjoy access to the type of detailed information about the *terraferma* that could lead them to take such an action.

Because the 1476 laws attempted to regulate forest use, they held long-term implications for the future of Venetian forestry legislation and practice. With this legislation, the Venetians formally established the terms under which they would begin interfering with local rights and customs in order to secure critical forest resources. In essence, the Senate articulated what had always been implicit in the market controls from an earlier period. The 1350 law regulating the sale of oak on the open market, for example, had created a purchasing hierarchy for high-grade timber that favored the Arsenal over all competing buyers. Likewise, legislators had designed price-fixing, tariffs, and point-of-sale regulations to give the state warehouse a competitive advantage and guarantee regular supplies. With the 1476 laws, the Senate created an analogous hierarchy for forest use. As the Venetians sought to impose a uniform set of forest exploitation practices on their mainland subjects, this hierarchy of uses influenced the framing of almost every new piece of forestry legislation. Until the middle of the seventeenth century, laws governing forest exploitation rarely innovated or deviated from the template established by the 1476 laws. Subsequent laws tended to reinforce or raise the penalties for violators, further clarify the rules governing use, or extend the regulations to different types of property. By the end of the sixteenth century, the Senate subjected private and ecclesiastical woods to the same regulations as community lands. In short, the 1476 laws established the model of forest use that the Venetians eventually expected landowners to follow everywhere in the Republic's domains.

The Arsenal remained rigorously atop the Senate's list of priorities, even though the firewood supply had been one of the driving forces behind most previous efforts to locate and control forest resources. The final provision, the shortest and simplest of the six that comprised the new legislation, clearly stated the shipyard's importance: the Arsenal's needs took absolute priority over any other consideration. Nonetheless, firewood retained some of its previous importance. By stressing the necessity of the coupe system, legislators recognized that providing firewood for Venetian consumption remained a key issue. The Senate and the Council of Ten had created a bureaucracy (the *provveditori alle legne*), mandated the expansion of the firewood warehouses at San Biasio, and attempted to force mainland residents to take steps to guarantee at least a small surplus for the Venetian market. Major problems remained, including market controls that created disincentives for local residents to produce a surplus, but the 1476 laws still represent a significant step in the development of Venetian forestry policies.

It is not difficult to understand why firewood never displaced Arsenal-grade timber as a concern for Venetian legislators. Despite the complications that arose as firewood officials journeyed to ever-more-distant locations in their search for fuel, the issues involved remained relatively simple compared to those encountered when bringing Arsenal timber to market in Venice. Workers could break up firewood in the forest and pack the bundles out of even the most difficult terrain on the backs of animals or humans. But crews could only fell and successfully extract Arsenal timber from forests that stood close enough to waterways of sufficient size, depth, and flow to float entire logs. These waterways, in turn, had to lead to larger rivers that could carry the logs, lashed together into large rafts, downstream to the Adriatic, where they could then be ferried to Venice.[33] Finally, the water necessary to carry the timber rafts was usually available only in two seasons—during the spring snowmelt and again during the September rains. Thus the window of opportunity for the acquisition of naval stores was relatively narrow, making a more programmatic approach imperative. Whatever logistical difficulties pertained to the firewood supply, they paled in comparison to the complications involved in harvesting, processing, and transporting Arsenal-grade timber. Consequently, to prevent the most accessible stands from degrading to the point where they could no longer produce high-quality wood, the Venetians attempted to broaden the area under exploitation. Forcing local residents and leaseholders in community forests to pack firewood out of the deep woods was one way the Senate imagined it could ensure the integrity of more accessible stands.

If the Arsenal and the firewood warehouses stood atop the new hierarchy of uses, nearly all local applications lay near the bottom. The two local uses that suffered the most in the 1476 legislation were pasturing and agriculture. The Venetian Senate believed both practices were fundamentally incompatible with the two main goals of the new laws—limiting local activity in community stands and preserving the total wooded area. Venetian legislators might have been largely ignorant of the complexities of local patterns of forest exploitation, but they felt that they understood the threat that agriculture and pastoralism posed to forests. The Republic's leaders thought they could curb the mainland tendency to clear forests and create new pasture or arable land by outlawing the use of fire and regulating practices they believed led to overharvesting. The same held true, from the perspective of the senators, for the common habit of pasturing animals within the confines of the woods during the hot summer months—even if the actual effects of that custom were actually ambiguous. However important these activities may have been to local economies, they had to give way to the needs of the metropolitan economy. The hierarchy of forest exploitation created by the 1476 laws was one that favored the economic interests of Venice over those of mainland villages. Moreover, the Venetian interests in question were inextricably linked to the preservation of a specific ecological order in community forests—an order in which there was no room for livestock or fire.

While the 1476 legislation and the creation of state forest reserves placed severe new burdens on mainland residents, it would be a mistake to assume that the Republic and its institutions remained unaffected. Because the new hierarchy of uses privileged the Arsenal above the firewood warehouses, the new laws also forced the state to alter many of its own traditional modes of acquiring forest resources. When the Senate and the Council of Ten acted to expand the Arsenal's forest patrimony in the last quarter of the fifteenth century, they were also inadvertently limiting the scope of the firewood managers' operations. And as the Council of Ten placed more and more tracts of oak forest off limits— especially in the area bounded by the Piave and Livenza rivers—it forced the *provveditori alle legne* to range much farther afield in their efforts to locate and secure reliable sources of fuel to meet growing demand in Venice. By the early sixteenth century, the new forestry laws and the hierarchy of uses had produced a dramatic change in Venetian efforts to obtain forest resources. The firewood managers looked increasingly to the Friuli, the Istrian peninsula, and parts of the Dalmatian coast as the primary sources of firewood, while the Arsenal managers concentrated their efforts to secure shipbuilding material on the forests of the Piave and Livenza watersheds. Nonetheless, some overlap remained. The Montona reserve in Istria provided an important source of Arsenal timber well into the eighteenth century, and firewood merchants in Piave towns such as Feltre sold large quantities of combustible material to the residents of the lagoon. But for the most part, by the end of the sixteenth century the Venetians sought Arsenal timber in the west and fuel in the east. In the meantime, the precedents that the Republic had established with the aggressive application of the *diritto di riserva* and the 1476 measures created a legal framework for the extension of state sovereignty over ever-increasing areas of forestland in the following centuries.

The Cambrai Crisis, Fiscal Reform, and the Expansion of the State Reserves

The precedents that the Senate set with the 1471 Montello ban and 1476 laws governing the exploitation of community forests paid handsome dividends for the Republic in the sixteenth century. The Council of Ten in particular invoked fifteenth-century precedents to increase significantly both the size of Venice's forest patrimony and the power of its institutions to regulate local practices of forest exploitation. Much of this expansion of the state reserves occurred in the years following the invasion of the *terraferma* by the forces of the League of Cambrai. Between May of 1509—when French forces routed the Venetian army near Agnadello on the Adda River—and 1524—when the Venetians finally recaptured virtually all of their lost territories—the Republic faced its most serious political and military crisis to date. By the time the Venetians had reorganized their army and pushed the French and Habsburg forces out of the *terraferma*, the Republic had suffered a terrible fiscal and political blow. Most modern historians agree that Agnadello and its aftermath marked a watershed moment in Venetian history, even if they might differ as to the reasons.[34] Certainly the leaders of the Republic recognized that they had fallen from the ranks of the leading Christian powers in the aftermath of the war. The lengthy struggle to reclaim the mainland also placed a heavy financial and social strain on the Venetian patriciate. Without the *terraferma* to draw on for money and material support, the state had forced Venetian patricians to finance the Republic's costly military effort through multiple rounds of forced loans. Several banks failed under the pressure of repeated runs. The war also cut into maritime trade, as the public galleys often failed to sail during the war years.[35] Other consequences were more positive for the Republic. The defeat allowed the Venetians to chart a new institutional and political course in their newly reconquered territories. The *stato di terraferma* that emerged from this process was quite different from the one the Republic had ruled in the fifteenth century. In spite of the diminishment of their ambitions on the European stage, the Venetians took advantage of their second conquest of the northeast to establish a degree of central control that would have been unimaginable to their predecessors.

The Republic's leaders faced several pressing problems as they attempted to reestablish their political power in the *terraferma*. The war had exposed hidden resentments against Venice, especially among mainland aristocrats who felt they had lost many of their traditional freedoms and privileges under republican rule. The strain on Venice's coffers had also brought to light the fact that the Republic's uncertain finances were badly in need of reform if it was going to face up to the new challenges of the sixteenth century—especially the need to maintain a strong standing army to counter ongoing Habsburg and Valois military activity on the Italian peninsula.[36] The Republic's decision to address these two problems had significant consequences for the Arsenal's forest reserves. Fiscal reform finally made it possible to finance the administration of the Arsenal reserves effectively, especially the costs associated with organizing and conducting large oak and beech harvests. Moreover, the confiscation of land belonging to individuals and families who had been disloyal to the Republic during the war allowed the Council of Ten to raise badly needed capital and add vast and potentially valuable acreage to the Arsenal's forest patrimony through the exercise of the *diritto di riserva*.

Among the most urgent issues facing the Senate at the conclusion of the war was the massive public debt that it had accumulated in the defense of the Republic. Property belonging to mainland elites who had openly welcomed the invaders created a convenient source of revenue for the cash-starved state. The Council of Ten, under the pretext of restoring security to the *terraferma*, confiscated significant tracts of land and then auctioned them off to raise badly needed capital.[37] Occasionally the Ten distributed the land to subjects who had remained loyal during the war but who could not afford to participate in the auctions.[38] In the case of property that included forests, the Council often took advantage of the situation to add to the Arsenal's reserves through the application of the *diritto di riserva*. In addition, Venetian patricians exploited the chaotic situation in the *terraferma* to invest heavily in land—something they had been reluctant to do in the past. Certainly a few Venetians had purchased mainland property during the fifteenth century, especially in the areas around Padua and Treviso where pre-existing patterns of land owner-ship had been altered by the conquest, but it remains difficult to gauge the actual rate of Venetian investment during the first century of main-land rule with any precision.[39] What is certain is that both the scale and scope of sixteenth-century purchases of mainland property were unprecedented.

The redistribution of property on such a massive scale forced the Venetians to contemplate reforming fiscal systems throughout the main-land. Most local governments maintained tax rolls called *estimi*, which they used to calculate routine annual assessments as well as extraordi-nary taxes and forced loans. From the perspective of the forests, the most important tax was the *carratada*, which was used to finance the *angarie* for timber and firewood harvesting in community forests and for other public projects. The *estimi* were based on the total value of land in the district, and each village was responsible for a fixed contribution when-ever the Venetians called for an assessment. It was up to local authorities to collect the tax from whomever they could. Given the fragmentary nature of property in the *terraferma*—as well as the fact that so much land was owned by distant urban residents—village authorities con-fronted numerous difficulties as they sought to identify debtors and force them to pay their fair share of the tax. The lack of accurate property registers shifted much of the tax burden onto the poorest mainland residents, a problem that had become increasingly acute in the latter half of the fifteenth century when urban residents from the larger mainland towns had begun investing heavily in rural property. Indeed, by the turn of the sixteenth century the imbalance between urban and rural tax obligations had become untenable, and the massive shift in ownership that occurred as a result of the war dealt the final blow to an already fragile tax system.

The Venetian Senate recognized the need to reform the Republic's rev-enue system, especially if it wished to improve its ability to rule and de-fend the Republic's territory. Consequently, the Senate made the *estimi* one of its first orders of business, even before the reconquest had been completed. In the fifteenth century, local civic councils had established the *estimi* independently of Venice, and the process had often been vitiated by local elites eager to protect their investments. In the post-Cambrai era, the Senate sought to reform both the manner in which the *estimo* data were collected and the process of translating those data into useful tax rolls. To accomplish these goals, the Venetians had to navigate carefully between alienating local urban elites, addressing the fiscal crisis, rewarding those members of the old aristocracy who had not betrayed them, and meeting the increasingly urgent demands of smaller communities for tax relief. These communities—along with the remnants of the landed aristocracy—were especially eager to help the Venetians reform a tax system that penalized rural residents. In many areas of the mainland, rural residents formed organizations—known as *corpi territoriali*—to promote fiscal reforms that benefited smaller-scale rural landholders and villages that were subject to the larger towns.[40] Together, the Venetians and the *corpi territoriali* managed to revise the *estimi* in ways that reflected the increasing shift towards urban ownership of rural property.[41] The net effect of these reforms was to make it far easier for local authorities to collect the *carratada* and other taxes that supported the timber and firewood harvests. The funds collected by local authorities constituted the lifeblood of Venice's system of forest management, for without the money to pay for the harvesting and transportation of forest resources, the Arsenal could not build ships and the city's firewood warehouses would soon have been empty.

Tax reform was not the only avenue the Venetian government explored in its attempts to raise new revenue. Many leading Venetian patricians saw mainland community property as a potential source of funds for the Republic's coffers. But before community lands could be sold, they had to be identified, cataloged, and restored to the communities that had once controlled them. This process represented one of the most difficult and most important challenges facing Venetian authorities in the aftermath of the Cambrai crisis. Community property had suffered heavily during the war, and the chaos of wartime had provided an opportunity for many abuses and usurpations. Invading armies had foraged for fuel and timber in community forests without regard for such niceties as which coupe was due for harvesting that season. Urban residents also attempted to take advantage of the confusion and destruction of local records to claim common lands as private property. Restoring the status quo ante presented Venetian officials with a daunting challenge, but one far too critical to ignore. Prior to the war, community forests had formed the backbone of Venice's firewood supply. These forests had also been at the heart of many of the disputes that arose between Venice and its subject territories in the latter decades of the fifteenth century, especially once the Council of Ten had begun to apply the *diritto di riserva* widely. Therefore, gaining control of community forests and coming to some sort of acceptable compromise over the rights and privileges enjoyed by local residents and the Venetian Republic was a crucial step in the process of reestablishing the system of timber and firewood supply.

The fifteenth-century disputes over the status of community lands that led to the 1463, 1476, and 1495 laws governing the alienation of community property—as well as the division of community property into the two categories of *beni comuni* and *comunali*—provided Venetian officials with a legal framework for dealing with lands where ownership had been usurped in recent decades and during the war. As disputes over the alienation of community property—especially forests—appeared on the dockets of Venetian courts in the years following the War of Cambrai, the Council of Ten often stepped in to ensure the return of forests to the affected communities. Immediately after the reconquest of the district of Belluno in 1514, for example, an appeal of a local judgment made its way to Venice, where it was heard by the *Avogaria di Comune*, the main court of first appeal in most civil cases.[42] An association of small rural communities brought the case against the local Venetian authorities in Belluno who, the plaintiffs claimed, stood idly by as prominent members of Belluno's urban aristocracy alienated community property at will.[43] Not surprisingly, the local *podestà* had rejected the case. Not only had the plaintiffs implicated him in the wrongdoing, but he was probably hesitant to challenge publicly the most powerful local families so soon after the reconquest. Faced with prevarication from the local seat of government, the plaintiffs appealed the decision directly to Venice. In response to their complaint, the Council of Ten issued a *ducale*—a type of ducal decree—warning landowners in the Belluno and Seravalle area to cease making illegal claims on community property or face immediate prosecution by the Ten.

The Belluno case illustrates how younger resident Venetian officials remained reluctant to intervene too forcefully in local disputes, especially if their actions might anger members of powerful elites in their territories. However, the case also reveals how the complaints of the Republic's least powerful subjects often offered higher Venetian authorities an opportunity and a justification to stop the most obvious abuses. The Council of Ten did not intervene every time it heard that a peasant's rights had been abrogated, but it was not afraid to castigate local elites when it served the interests of the Republic. Throughout the sixteenth century, the Council of Ten exploited the complaints of the least important mainland residents to exert greater control over the powerful, and one of the issues that frequently established common ground between humble rural residents and the members of the Council was the erosion of community property.[44] For peasants, the dissipation of the commons threatened their ability to heat their homes, feed their livestock, and supplement their own meager diets—especially in years when the countryside experienced shortfalls in grain production. For the Council of Ten, the loss of common lands meant the loss of forestland, which in turn threatened the Republic's ability to acquire the resources it relied upon to preserve its liberty.

Although general agreement existed in the Ducal Palace that establishing central control over the commons was a necessary enterprise, no consensus existed on what to do with the lands once they had been successfully recovered. Some senators favored auctioning off *beni comunali* to help reduce the public debt—arguing that the fifteenth-century laws dividing community property between state and local jurisdictions gave them the authority to sell such lands in the same way that local communities could sell their *beni comuni*. However, the legislators who favored such policies faced serious obstacles in their attempts to implement them. Even assuming the Senate could persuade local communities that it had the unilateral authority to sell local common lands at auction, distinguishing between *beni comuni* and *comunali* with any precision was difficult at best. No maps or land surveys existed to establish the exact boundaries between state and local demesnes within the commons. Many villages took advantage of the ambiguity to thwart Venetian plans by using the courts to contest the Republic's claims to particular parcels of land.[45] And although Venetian officials believed many such claims were spurious, litigation took years and the Republic's financial need was immediate. Local residents correctly calculated that even a short delay could effectively block a sale forever by forcing the Venetians to turn their attention elsewhere in search of easier sources of revenue.

The land sales also met with considerable criticism within the walls of the Ducal Palace. Many senators opposed any attempt to sell commons, making it difficult to marshal the necessary votes to authorize an auction. Opponents of the sales pointed out that confiscating and selling community property could only lead to more resentment against Venetian rule—especially given that the Venetians had used the plight of mainland towns and villages to justify the confiscations in the first place. Putting the recovered lands on the auction block and potentially selling them back to the individuals or institutions that initially usurped them promised to accomplish little in ensuring the future loyalty of Venice's mainland subjects. The most powerful argument against the sales, however, was that they threatened the Republic's supply of critical forest resources. That argument carried weight because it framed the problem as a conflict between the demands of the short-term fiscal crisis and the well-established idea that forest resources on the mainland were disappearing. Alternate sources of revenue could be found, but forest resources were ultimately finite. This position generated considerable support within the chambers of the Ten. Because the Council had taken the lead in the fifteenth-century efforts to control and regulate community forests, its members were predisposed to accept the idea that a clear link existed between preserving community forests and preserving Venetian liberty. In this sense, the Council understood the laments of local communities to be symptoms of a wider set of problems affecting both the stability of the *terraferma* and the availability of forest resources. The danger was that selling reclaimed lands at auction would undermine the confidence of mainland residents in Venetian rule at a very delicate moment, as well as increase the risk to the Republic if the timber supply were to fail, and these proved to be the deciding factors in the debate.

The Ten's concerns forced the Senate to explore alternatives to unilateral auctions of common lands. For example, in 1517 several local communities in the territories of Brescia and Verona petitioned Venetian authorities for help in recovering community lands from usurpers. The Senate agreed to help prosecute the offenders, but in the same breath it decreed that the communities would have to repurchase the lands at a rate to be determined by a Venetian court.[46] The strategy was clearly designed to satisfy all parties. The mainland elites—and any Venetian patricians who might have bought the lands illegally—were offered some measure of compensation for the lost property. At the same time, the financial burden was shifted to the communities that had filed the claim, which was more than a simple convenience. In the face of such a severe fiscal crisis, the Senate could hardly afford to take on the additional burden of repurchasing usurped commons. But by attempting to satisfy everyone, the Venetians ended up angering all parties involved. Venice was not the only city facing revenue shortfalls. Most *terraferma* towns, especially the smaller communities that had lost significant portions of their commons in the war, were practically bankrupt. Indeed, many town councils may have hoped to sell the lands to raise money in much the same way as the Venetian Senate contemplated doing. Consequently, Venetian attempts to avoid financing the recovery of usurped lands failed in the face of the local communities' inability to commit even modest sums of money to the effort. Furthermore, the 1517 decree made no mention of how, without the active help of the central authority, small local towns were meant to disentangle the usurped lands from the complex web of powerful local interests. The Senate provided legal and moral support for local efforts to regain lost lands, but it committed no Venetian resources to the task. Ultimately, the measure proved divisive. Venetian magistracies were inundated with requests for clarification from all parties involved in disputes—the local elites and the communal authorities—none of whom were satisfied with the Senate's position on the matter. Finally, in 1530 the Collegio ruled once and for all that the intent of the law had been to allow towns and villages to recover their lost lands, thus placing the state irrevocably on the side of the communities.[47]

Another important moment in the debate over the fate of the commons occurred in December of 1527. In response to the ongoing fiscal crisis, Leonardo Emo, the *provveditore sopra i denari*, proposed the sale of up to half of all community lands in the district of Treviso to reduce the public debt.[48] According to the diarist Marino Sanuto, the Senate did not get to vote on the measure because the Council of Ten claimed jurisdiction. Four days later, when the measure was introduced in the Ten, it passed by a margin of 14 votes in favor, 10 opposed, and 3 abstentions—a narrow margin in a body where near unanimity was the norm.[49] In early 1528 the Senate sent the patrician Antonio Giustinian to the Trevigiano and Friuli to survey all the woods and fields that had been state demesne and to recover usurped community property.[50] As his first reports trickled in, the Senate made plans to sell the confiscated lands at auction. The first proposal to reach the Senate floor called for the sale of 1,000 *campi* —about 380 hectares—of forest near the town of Motta on the Livenza River. The Senate planned to reap at least 10,000 ducats from the auction. The Council of Ten initially intervened to block the measure on the grounds that the forests in question contained Arsenal oak and therefore could not be sold.[51] The measure was introduced a second time the following morning, and the three heads of the Ten again moved to block it, but its supporters mustered enough votes to carry the day.[52] Undaunted, the Ten persisted in its efforts to stop the auction from moving forward. The following week the Council had one of the Arsenal managers speak out against the sale on the Senate floor, reiterating the claim that the alienation of these specific forests would destroy precious Arsenal supplies. The plan's architect, Leonardo Emo, responded that "we have 17,000 troops to pay and no way to raise the money. And besides, the timber in those forests is not for the Arsenal."[53] In the end, the opposition had the last word. Only 150 of the 1,000 *campi* were put on the block, as the Arsenal managers working in concert with the Council of Ten successfully halted further sales.[54]

The Council of Ten ultimately imposed a compromise solution that addressed local concerns about the erosion of common lands while expanding the Republic's control over community forests containing oak and firewood. The Ten allowed towns to reduce a portion of their community forests—usually around a third of the total area—to pasture or arable land, which they could then lease, sell, or keep as commons at their discretion. Another third had to be left as forest in perpetuity, where it would continue to serve local needs as well as generate firewood for Venice. While these forests remained as local demesne, the Ten placed the firewood managers in a supervisory role by granting them the authority to both vet the terms of any leases and collect a share of the proceeds. The final third of these forests devolved to the Republic as state demesne. The Council of Ten sold some of this land to bridge the ongoing shortfalls in state revenue. However, any forests that contained oak were set aside as *boschi pubblici* and subjected to similar rules as the Montello and other Arsenal reserves—although some were designated as firewood reserves and placed under the control of the *provveditori alle legne*. In this way the Council extended central control over community forests and significantly expanded the forested area under the direct control of the Arsenal and the firewood managers. Initially, the Council of Ten attempted to apply the measure only in the area between the Piave and Livenza rivers—the traditional mainstay of the Arsenal's oak supply. The Ten dispatched Antonio Giustinian to survey community lands along this corridor and subsequently sold a small portion the Republic's third of the land on the basis of his survey. The Council then converted the remaining forests into public Arsenal and firewood reserves.[55] After this trial run proved successful, the Ten extended the rule to other parts of the *terraferma* until it became the standard template for Venetian management of community forests.[56] The process also set a crucial legal precedent for the expansion of the state forest system throughout Venice's mainland territories. Most of the new state forests created through this mechanism lay between the Piave and Tagliamento rivers—an area destined to play a crucial role in Venice's forestry system over the next two centuries.

The new measure differed drastically from past proposals because it addressed both the Republic's and the local communities' fiscal crises. Small communities received two important benefits from the new regulations. First, they were allowed to alienate some proportion of their property to raise revenue for their own needs. Second, they were assured that the Republic's most powerful institutions would help local authorities protect the remaining community forests from local elites eager to get their hands on them. From the Council of Ten's perspective, the measure softened the effects of the immediate revenue shortfalls while expanding the Republic's legal authority over critical forest resources. The Ten saw the imposition of stricter central control as necessary because, in keeping with the framework of the fifteenth-century laws, it viewed mainland residents as poor stewards of their own forests. From the perspective of the Council, the state was the only entity with an interest in forest resources that possessed both the power to preserve them at the local level and the desire to do so. By the first third of the sixteenth century, the Venetian leadership had come to believe that a concerted effort on the part of the Republic to preserve forestland furnished the sole means of guaranteeing that the Arsenal's reserves and the city's firewood supply would not be consumed by profligate mainland residents of all social classes. Only the state and its institutions could protect and balance the interests of all parties with a claim on scarce forest resources—local residents, property owners, Venetian investors, and the state itself. Following the post-Cambrai recovery of the mainland, the era of limited interference by the Republic was effectively over.

The Expansion of Forestry Legislation and Its Consequences

By 1530 the Council of Ten had firmly established a legal basis for regulating access to community forests. Although the state's power to enforce effectively its own legislation remained extremely limited and varied significantly from place to place, the important precedents that the Council set in the aftermath of the Cambrai crisis remained vital to Venetian ambitions in mainland forests until the fall of the Republic in 1797. Nevertheless, while the Ten aggressively asserted the power of the state to alter local practices of forest exploitation in unprecedented ways, it remained faithful to the spirit—and most of the assumptions—of the fifteenth-century laws. The Republic's leaders still presumed that critical forest resources were disappearing at an alarming rate; they still saw the greed and profligacy of mainland residents as the main causes of the disappearance of those resources; and they continued to rely on the six 1476 laws governing the practices of forest exploitation in community stands as the principal template for subsequent efforts to regulate local patterns of forest use.

Still, significant lacunae remained in terms of the scope and reach of the forestry laws. The most important shortcoming of the legislation was that it only applied to community forests and Arsenal reserves, leaving private and institutional landowners free to dispose of their forests in whatever manner they pleased. In many ways this situation was the logical consequence of the strategy that the Senate and the Council of Ten had pursued in establishing state control of large tracts of community land. Legislators built the edifice of existing forestry laws in part on the presumption that the Republic had the right to regulate access to the most important common resources, such as water and forests. The Montello ban and the 1476 laws may have been unprecedented in terms of their intrusiveness, but the Venetians had acted within a legal tradition that recognized the right of the *res publica* to regulate common lands. Private property and lands belonging to institutions such as the church or lay confraternities lay beyond the reach of that body of legal precedent. In other words, the Venetians had legislated themselves into a corner when it came to regulating forest exploitation practices outside of common lands. Indeed, aside from confiscating the property of rebels in the wake of the Cambrai crisis, the Council of Ten did little to extend the state's authority over privately owned forests and nothing at all with respect to institutionally owned woods. To some degree the Council of Ten must have seen little reason to move in the direction of regulating the exploitation of forests on private property. The system of Arsenal reserves appeared to be working as intended. In 1527 the Arsenal managers even boasted of a surplus of larch and fir timber in the shipyard, prompting the Council of Ten to suspend all supply contracts for those two species until further notice.[57] The deliberations over the disposition of community lands also drew the Ten's attention away from private and institutional property in the 1520s. By 1528, however, most of the debates surrounding community forests had been settled, and the Council began to concentrate on the significant changes that had been taking place in private and institutional forests since the turn of the sixteenth century.

While the Arsenal managers enjoyed the fruits of the new reserves, the firewood managers once again experienced substantial difficulties in their efforts to secure fuel from mainland forests. The early sixteenth century witnessed a dramatic expansion of manufacturing industries, both in Venice and on the mainland.[58] Many industrial processes required thermal energy that could only be generated by firewood or charcoal. Thus, despite the absence of real population growth in the region, demand for fuel had increased steadily since the late fifteenth century. And with the attention of the Council of Ten riveted firmly on the region's community forests, merchants shifted their focus to private and institutional forests in their efforts to secure fuel supplies. As the thermal energy demands of industries such as cloth dyeing, metallurgy, tanning, glass manufacturing, and paper, lime, soap, and gunpowder production increased, the price of fuel throughout Venice's territories soared. In January of 1531, the Council of Ten reported that the price of a *passo* of firewood on the mainland had more than doubled in the past year—from 6 *lire* to well over 14 in some areas.[59] The Council laid the blame at the doorstep of private landowners who had—the Ten argued—allowed merchants to clear-cut their forests for industrial fuel and then converted them to cropland. Representatives of the Council reported that fuel "cannot be found due to the fact that many *campi* have been deforested and converted to arable, despite the fact that everyone is aware that our laws forbid deforestation."[60] Earlier reports—including a 1514 survey conducted by one of the Arsenal managers, Giacomo Querini—corroborate the Ten's account. Querini told the Senate that although he had found the Arsenal reserves in good condition, private parties had clearly taken advantage of the chaos of wartime to clear-cut large tracts of forestland along the Piave and Livenza rivers in an effort to expand their arable landholdings.[61] The surge in forest clearance made itself felt through an increasingly tight market for fuel both in Venice and throughout the *terraferma*.

In Venice the situation threatened to spiral out of control. Successive winters of severe firewood shortages left the public warehouses empty and the city's manufacturing industries in danger of closing. In 1530, the Council of Ten stripped the firewood managers of their authority to open the warehouses to the city's poor, handing the keys to their own chamberlain instead.[62] In January of 1531, the Council observed that the dearth of fuel had reached the point where "our mint cannot function, nor can many artisans such as glassmakers, dyers, and metalworkers. And unless opportune and proper provisions are made, no one can doubt but that there will no longer be a shortage, but an absolute lack of fuel in our city."[63] The prospect of running out of fuel was terrifying to the Republic's leaders, and they were determined to resolve the fuel crisis at any cost.

The Ten took several steps to address what it perceived to be the principal causes of the crisis. First, it attempted to crack down on black-market sales of firewood and charcoal by establishing severe penalties—including loss of office and banishment—for Venetian officials who overlooked illegal exchanges at mainland embarcaderos.[64] In areas of firewood production along the Livenza River, the Council also allocated a percentage of the income derived from the firewood managers' leases to the improvement of public roads.[65] The Ten expected these measures to lower the price of fuel by improving access to abundant sources of firewood and preventing corruption at the point of sale. At the same time, the Council recognized that if it really wished to restore the price of fuel to previous levels, it needed to take steps to regulate forest exploitation practices on private and institutional property, not just in community forests.

As the situation in Venice worsened, the Council of Ten decided to confront the problem of clear-cutting in private forests head on. To do so, the Ten needed to establish firmly that the forest exploitation practices the Venetians deemed wasteful also represented a threat to the Republic's security. In this way the Council could create a legal justification for an unprecedented abrogation of the rights of private and institutional landowners. In the fifteenth century Venetian legislators had supported the establishment of Arsenal reserves on the grounds that the destruction of key species used in shipbuilding—oak, beech, and fir—threatened the fleet and, therefore, state security. However, with the Arsenal enjoying unprecedented surpluses, the Council could no longer resort to this line of argument. Instead, it proffered a different set of claims that dated back to fifteenth-century treatises by such authors as Marco Cornaro and his anonymous 1413 predecessor. The Ten posited that clear-cutting on private and institutional lands threatened the Republic's security in three ways. By contributing to fuel shortages and price spikes, deforestation threatened "the health of the inhabitants of Venice," who would no longer be able to heat their homes and "purify the air of malignant winter vapors."[66] Moreover, shortages of industrial fuel threatened several key industries that underpinned the city's economy. Finally, the Ten argued that "the aforementioned deforestation is a most manifest cause of siltation in our lagoons, because those forests no longer provide any obstacle or restraint against the rains and other inundations."[67] In the Council's estimation, the gravity of these three threats justified state intervention to preserve forests not only on common lands, but on private and institutional property as well. In the decree that followed, the Ten extended all existing laws governing forest exploitation to every forest "whether ecclesiastical or under any other title one can name . . . in the Friuli, as in Trevigiano, Mestrino, Padovano, Colognese, Polesine, Rovigo and throughout the Dogado."[68]

The Council of Ten's new position represented the culmination of over half a century of legal precedent. Ever since the Montello ban in 1471, the Republic's leaders had used the language of state security to justify regulating local practices of forest exploitation in the commons. More recently, the Council had used the argument to spare community forests from the auction block in the aftermath of Cambrai. With this new measure, the Ten expanded the connection between forest conservation and state security to the point where the Republic could intervene to protect virtually any forest in the *terraferma*, regardless of whether it contained critical species or not. Because deforestation damaged public health, the economy, and the lagoon, no forest was exempt from regulation. In practice, of course, the Venetians primarily concerned themselves with preserving hardwood forests capable of providing fuel for local and regional consumption and stands containing Arsenal-grade oak. Conifer stands, which were fairly common in parts of the coastal plain, remained outside the field of vision of Venetian legislators and inspectors.

The Council of Ten did set one important new precedent in 1531. Previous laws, including the 1476 legislation, had sought to impose uniform practices of forest exploitation aimed at preserving the existing area covered by forests containing oak and other hardwood species. With the new measures, the Council also attempted to reverse recent deforestation and restore mainland forests to what it trusted was the status quo ante. The 1531 legislation proceeded to mandate that "all those who, in the last forty years, have clear cut forests of whatever sort . . . are obligated to restore to forest eight *campi* for every 100 cleared."[69] Furthermore, the Ten instructed that "the fields that will be restored to forest should be the ones closest to rivers and the salt water for the benefit of our lagoon."[70] The Council also decreed that landowners plant trees in two percent of the areas that had not previously been forests. With the inclusion of both reforestation and afforestation requirements in the 1531 decree, the Council of Ten inaugurated a policy forcing mainland residents to adopt positive practices aimed at increasing the total area covered by forests. Previous laws, dating back to the 1471 Montello ban, had largely consisted of negative proscriptions against customs and behaviors that the Venetians saw as detrimental to their own economic, military, and ecological interests. Strikingly, the 1531 measure allowed landowners to replant any species they chose, so long as they restored eight percent of the cleared area. While the Council offered no explanation for its lenience, the Arsenal's timber surplus probably contributed to the loose character of the requirement. Future restatements of the eight percent rule would require landowners to replant oak.[71] Regardless, the 1531 law represented a major turning point in Venetian forestry legislation, precisely because it turned away from exclusively negative measures towards positive practices designed to create a forest landscape consonant with Venetian political and economic priorities.

The move towards positive measures did not entail the abandonment of negative proscriptions, however. On the contrary, the Council of Ten's decision to extend the reach of the 1476 laws to private and ecclesiastical property coincided with the creation of even more specific proscriptions against local activities the Venetians viewed as detrimental to the Republic's interests in forest resources. In 1524, for example, the Ten extended the 1476 prohibition against using fire to clear forest to include all open land within a one-mile radius of any Arsenal reserve.[72] In this instance the Council was responding to reports that shepherds deliberately allowed the burns they employed to promote the renewal of their pastures to spread into reserved woods so as to expand the available grazing area. The measure effectively used the Republic's right to regulate activities in the Arsenal reserves to create a buffer zone in which traditional land-management practices that conflicted with Venetian interests were outlawed, even if those practices were central to sustaining local pastoral economies. Subsequent legislation built on the 1524 precedent and expanded the list of forbidden activities, as well as the area of control. In 1540 the Council of Ten forbade the use of fire in all marshlands that bordered on commons, because landowners often conducted such burns to prepare areas for reclamation.[73] The Venetians had a long-standing interest in preserving the marshland surrounding the lagoon because it created the crucial backwater necessary to flush the lagoon of waste with each tidal cycle.[74] Now the Republic's leaders linked concerns over preserving marshland with concerns over the integrity of mainland forests—just as they had linked deforestation to siltation in the 1531 legislation. Then in 1557 the Council outlawed charcoal and lime production within the same one-mile radius of *boschi pubblici* as the 1524 edict, citing the fire hazard created by the burning chambers used to produce both commodities.[75] In all three instances, the Ten sought to alter traditional practices in order to preserve an economic and ecological order that supported Venetian interests. The Ten based this series of laws on the assumption that the actions of profligate and irresponsible mainland residents were to blame if the region's forest landscapes remained under threat of disappearing.

By the middle of the sixteenth century, the Venetians had used the 1476 precedents to extend the Republic's power to dictate not only local practices of forest exploitation in all mainland forests, but also many land management techniques in agricultural land, pastures, and swamps that bordered on forests. They had also created a set of laws that drew clear connections between deforestation and environmental changes in the lagoon—exactly as Marco Cornaro had recommended in 1442. Increasing awareness of the links between forests and the rest of the mainland environment is evident in the 1548 law banning the enormous beech forest nestled in a high plateau above Belluno, known as the Bosco del Cansiglio or Bosco del Alpago. The Cansiglio was the last major Arsenal reserve the Council of Ten would establish, and the terms of its creation represent the culmination of nearly a century of forestry legislation.

In June of 1548 the Council of Ten dispatched two of the Arsenal managers—Bernardino Vettori and Francesco Duodo—along with Alessio di Mathio, Luca di Nicolò, and Marco di Zuane—three of the shipyard's master oarmakers—to inspect beech forests in the *terraferma* and in Istria, with an eye towards establishing a beech reserve modeled on the Montello. In the words of Duodo and Vettori, "because of the difficulty there has been for the last few years in supplying the Arsenal with beech, it became necessary to acquire timber from foreign sources and especially from the jurisdiction of the King of the Romans."[76] Duodo and Vettori began in Istria before proceeding to the middle Piave region because, "having listened to those possessing knowledge, we had heard that there was a large and beautiful forest in that region. We also knew from the *proto* and other oar makers that the oars made from timber originating in that forest were of most perfect strength."[77] What they saw astonished the entire party. "To tell the truth we can affirm to your excellencies that we found a thing greater and better than we could have ever imagined."[78] They proceeded to describe in some detail the forest's sixteen-mile perimeter and abundant growth. Most of all, they argued, the wood afforded far better access to transportation—in this case the

Piave River—than comparable forests they had seen in Istria, where they did "not know how it would be possible to move whole trunks."[79]

In a separate report, the three *proti* seconded the judgment of their superiors. They also revealed that they had seen even more of the forest than the two patricians, pointing out they had visited "places where their magnificences did not accompany us."[80] They asserted that in their estimation the forest contained "beech timber of great size and excellent for making oars," and claimed the forest "is of such size . . . that we believe we can promise your excellencies that it will provide oars for your needs for many tens, no hundreds of years at a rate we would conservatively put at between six and ten thousand oars a year."[81] They also stated that the Cansiglio timber was of far higher quality than similar timber they had tested in Istria. The *proti* concluded with an appeal to the Council of Ten, stating that "we know that it will be a great expense, but we hope that out of reverence for God your excellencies, through your prudence and generosity, will provide that such a beautiful jewel will not be ruined."[82] After receiving both reports, the Council of Ten voted that "the aforementioned forest of Alpago be placed under the protection of this council with all the provisions and conditions that apply to the Montello, Carpeneda, and Montona reserves."[83]

The Cansiglio ban highlights many of the key aspects of the legal apparatus governing the practices of forest exploitation developed by the Venetians since the establishment of the Vizza di Cadore in 1463. Compared to the 1471 Montello ban, which entered into considerable detail concerning the rights of the Republic to place restrictions on local access, not to mention the specific practices that were no longer permitted, the Cansiglio ban appears terse and perfunctory. The measure's single sentence offers no justification for the Council of Ten's decision to ban the forest, for the simple reason that by 1548 none was needed. The decree merely cites the earlier bans on large Arsenal reserves, which had long since established the necessary legal precedents for such a seizure. Nor did the members of the Ten feel the need to elaborate on the specific management measures to be imposed on the forest—they simply took them for granted. By 1548, general agreement existed in the Ducal Palace as to the need for forest reserves, as well as to the steps that should be taken to safeguard them. The Arsenal managers divided the Cansiglio into sixteen coupes, and the Council forbade the standard list of destructive practices within one mile of the forest. Both Duodo and Vettori's report and the report filed by the three *proti* argued that local residents would destroy the forest before long if the Council did not intervene. The belief that the Republic was the appropriate guardian of valuable public resources was no longer a matter for debate. The idea that the most desirable landscapes were those managed to meet Venetian needs first and foremost required no elaboration. As the master oarmakers put it, the Ten had an obligation to act "lest the forest be dissipated and ruined as is already occurring on a daily basis by the production of charcoal and the extraction of firewood."[84] Only the Republic could save the "jewel" that was the Cansiglio from the depredations of mainland residents. By 1548, the Venetians had successfully created an elaborate set of legal precedents that firmly established the Republic's right to regulate and even outlaw traditional practices of forest exploitation on any type of property anywhere on the mainland and in Istria. The Venetians had become—in theory at least—the masters of all forests in their domain. However, enforcing the new laws presented the *Serenissima's* institutions with an immense challenge, a problem the next chapter will explore.

CHAPTER FOUR

The Venetian Forest Bureaucracy

I believe that it is disgraceful and unjust to
condemn a poor peasant who out of desperation
to keep his children warm and fed has stolen oak,
while at the same time absolving people in
authority who have eradicated entire forests.

IN A LETTER TO THE Council of Ten dated 4 November 1602, the *provveditore sopra boschi* Giovanni Garzoni gave a progress report on his
continuing efforts to survey and catalog oak resources in the lower Piave
and Friuli regions. Garzoni had spent the previous six months supervising a large team of Arsenal craftsmen, land surveyors, and stone cutters
as they engaged in the onerous undertaking of counting, measuring, and
marking every single oak tree in the lower Piave region. The task was so
involved that nearly two more years would pass before Garzoni saw the
shores of the lagoon again. To add to an already difficult survey mission,
Garzoni was also responsible for locating areas where significant illegal
clearance had taken place since the previous comprehensive cadastral
survey in 1586. In addition, he was charged with identifying the per-
petrators and convening special courts to prosecute them.[1] Lastly, the
Council of Ten expected Garzoni to make substantive recommendations
for improving the administration of what had become, by the turn of the
seventeenth century, an immense forest patrimony covering a wide area
of the northeast and Istria. Created in the mid-sixteenth century, the
office of the *provveditore sopra boschi* was primarily responsible for con-
fronting the increasingly complex problem of monitoring Venice's ever-
expanding system of state forests—a challenge that had proven beyond
the capacities of both the *provveditori alle legne* and the *provveditori
all'arsenale*. The *provveditore sopra boschi*, then, embodied both the

power of the state to regulate local practices of forest exploitation and the collective knowledge of Venice's increasingly complex forest bureaucracy. In his interactions with mainland residents the *provveditore sopra boschi* presented the most important public face of the Republic's forestry laws, and he assumed the duty of enforcing those laws, through violence if necessary. In his interactions with the Senate and the Council of Ten, he served as the official spokesman for the institutions charged with ensuring the flow of critical forest resources into the lagoon, and his task was to keep the Republic's leaders apprised of the exact condition of the public forests as well as to offer advice for improving their management. In other words, the *provveditore sopra boschi*—and by extension the entire Venetian forestry bureaucracy—performed a double act of interpretation. For mainland residents he interpreted the intent and scope of the Venetian forestry laws, and for the Republic's leaders he interpreted the extent and composition of the forest landscapes of the *terraferma*.

Garzoni's term as *provveditore sopra boschi* offers an excellent vista on the most pressing problems facing the Republic's forest bureaucracy, both on the mainland and in the Ducal Palace. The immense extent and reach of Garzoni's survey reveals how complex the task of managing the state forests had become since the fifteenth-century Montello ban. As the previous chapter demonstrated, the size and geographical scope of the new Arsenal reserves, combined with the need to enforce the more intrusive forestry legislation that accompanied the establishment of those reserves, presented the Republic's institutions with an immense administrative challenge. This chapter will examine how this challenge drove the Venetians to develop a highly sophisticated and articulated bureaucracy for managing forest resources, culminating in the creation of the office of *provveditore sopra boschi*. It will also illustrate how the structure of the Venetian bureaucracy reflected both the long-standing legislative emphasis on Arsenal timber and the specific challenges awaiting Venetian officials in mainland forests. But traditional Venetian ideas about timber influenced more than just the Republic's bureaucratic organization. As Garzoni's many letters make clear, the belief that Arsenal-grade timber would eventually run out powerfully informed the Venetian approach to managing the new reserves. For example, by the turn of the seventeenth century, an accumulation of evidence pointed towards the wisdom of allowing multiple users to gain access to state forests. Nevertheless, the Republic's leaders continued to insist that *boschi pubblici* should be preserved for the exclusive benefit of the shipyard, primarily because of the persistent fear that oak might disappear entirely. Complete exclusivity remained an illusion, of course. In most cases the Venetians had no choice but to allow local residents to extract the bare necessities of life—limited quantities of firewood, green fertilizer, fruit, and game—from nearby public forests. Yet they drew the line at sharing the Arsenal's bounty with the firewood managers, as well as with mainland elites and institutions. Thus the specific mode of forest exploitation favored in the Ducal Palace forced one arm of the forest bureaucracy—the *provveditori alle legne*—to shift its center of operations to less secure frontier regions in Friuli and Istria to make way for the further expansion of the Arsenal's reserves. Finally, Garzoni's contentious correspondence with the Council of Ten underscores the perpetual tension between the inevitably schematic and abstract understanding of forests in the Ducal Palace and the increasingly nuanced view of officials on the ground. This information gap caused many *provveditori sopra boschi* like Garzoni no end of frustration, as legislators repeatedly rejected their carefully considered plans for reforming the state forests in favor of more simplistic schemes that consistently failed to account for the importance of local social and ecological factors.

This chapter analyzes the four crucial problems raised by Garzoni's reports to the Ten. It explores the ways in which the expansion of state reserves and the imposition of laws restricting local practices of forest exploitation quickly overwhelmed the fifteenth-century institutions charged with managing the flow of timber and fuel into the lagoon. It proceeds to explain why the Venetians chose to meet these new challenges by reducing the role of the firewood managers, reinforcing the primacy of the Arsenal in the formulation of forestry policies, and creating a new institution—the *provveditori sopra boschi*—devoted entirely to surveying forests and using criminal prosecutions to enforce the laws governing forest exploitation. Then it investigates the reasoning behind the Venetians' dogged pursuit of a forest management strategy based on the creation of exclusive Arsenal reserves designed to bar most users— including the *provveditori alle legne*—from sharing access, even to trees that had not been earmarked for the shipyards. Finally, it illustrates the ways in which the emerging expertise of the *provveditori sopra boschi* was increasingly at odds with the fairly simplistic ideas about timber and forests circulating in the Ducal Palace. The chapter advances two related arguments. First, that the Venetian forestry bureaucracy represented the logical outgrowth of traditional Venetian ideas and concerns about the fragility of forest resources. And second, that its policies were peculiarly republican, both in terms of the way in which those policies defined the common good, and in terms of whom the forest bureaucrats chose to exclude from the state forests.

A Divided Bureaucracy

In 1471—when the Senate created the Montello reserve and assigned its administration to the Arsenal managers—the Republic's leaders made the momentous decision to exclude the firewood managers from participation in the management and exploitation of the new state forest. Given the controversy swirling around the ban's unprecedented abrogation of local privilege, the question of which Venetian magistracy would superintend the reserve may have seemed relatively inconsequential to most senators. Yet the decision profoundly and permanently shaped the development of the Venetian forestry regime in the sixteenth and seventeenth centuries. Prior to the establishment of the first real Arsenal reserve, the responsibility for the acquisition of forest resources fell to a combination of magistracies. These institutions included the *provveditori e patroni all'arsenale*, the *provveditori alle legne*, and—for a time —the *provveditori alla giustizia vecchia* and the *ufficiali alle rason vecchie*. The fragmented nature of Venetian administrative efforts had contributed to the fuel crises of the mid-fifteenth century by making it especially difficult for legislators to form a coherent picture of a complex problem that included such factors as river siltation, tariffs, and species distribution in the forests of the lower Piave region. But a growing number of forest surveys such as Marco Cornaro's 1442 inspection helped legislators develop a more coherent picture of the multiple linkages between siltation, deforestation, market distortions, and the firewood supply. The legislators' growing awareness of the complexity of the problem of securing sufficient quantities of fuel eventually led them to the decision to reestablish the *provveditori alle legne* in 1458, under the direction of the firewood merchant Giorgio Venier.[2] In so doing the Senate attempted to simplify the difficulties of regulating markets by dividing responsibility for the timber and fuel supplies between two magistracies —the *arsenale* and the *legne*, respectively—rather than leaving them in the hands of several different offices.

The Arsenal and firewood managers held separate but parallel jurisdictions over the sale of a specific set of forest commodities, both in Venice and on the mainland. On the surface, they appeared to be coequal partners in the Republic's newly streamlined efforts to ensure the flow of critical resources into the lagoon and the city. Yet there were significant differences between the two offices that had important consequences for the development of the forest management bureaucracy. The Arsenal was one of Venice's most important institutions, and the Senate tended to nominate relatively senior members of the Republic's elite as candidates for the office of *provveditori e patroni all'arsenale*.[3] The merchants elected to the post of *provveditore alle legne* in the first decades of its existence came from outside the corridors of power in the Ducal Palace. Whatever importance the firewood warehouses may have held, the *provveditori alle legne* could not hope to match the *provveditori all'arsenale* in terms of prestige or political influence. Indeed, the *provveditori alle legne* did not even enter the Senate ex officio until 1487, while both the *provveditori* and the *patroni all'arsenale* had long held that right as well as a voice in Collegio meetings.[4] In addition, the priority accorded to Arsenal timber in the market hierarchy—and later in the hierarchy of uses—meant that fuel could never match timber in either political or economic importance. Thus from the outset, the firewood managers found themselves in a subordinate position with respect to the Arsenal managers.

In spite of their somewhat lower political status, the *provveditori alle legne* shouldered a significantly higher administrative burden in the early years of Venetian interference in mainland forests. The *provveditore alle legne* was not only responsible for monitoring the market for firewood, but also for locating and inspecting new sources of fuel and timber on the mainland. Only ten years after the establishment of the office, its duties had become so onerous that the Senate opted to add a second patrician *provveditore* to ease the burden.[5] And for many years following this 1468 addition, the two *provveditori alle legne* probably possessed more extensive personal experience with mainland forests than almost any other patrician holding elected office. Indeed, the Senate deliberately staggered the terms of office of the two *provveditori* so that "the one might acquire the appropriate knowledge and information from the other."[6] In other words, the measure expanding the size of the office both recognized the value of the firewood managers' direct experience with mainland forests and sought to capture and preserve that knowledge in some way so as to assist future officeholders in the effective discharge of their duties. By contrast, the Arsenal managers' many duties in the shipyard did not always allow them to participate in the forest surveys that in many cases constituted the only source of concrete information about forests available to legislators in the Ducal Palace.[7] Many of the *provveditori* and the *patroni all'arsenale* were well versed in specific aspects of naval construction, to be sure, but it was the *provveditori alle legne* who regularly travelled to see the actual sources of timber and fuel first-hand. The combination of their experience in the trade and their active participation in survey expeditions made the firewood managers the most knowledgeable patricians in the fledgling timber bureaucracy. Certainly they knew more about the mechanics of harvesting and moving large quantities of timber than anyone else within Venice's republican apparatus. Moreover, the personal nature of the *provveditori alle legne's* knowledge of forests also worked in their favor, because the Venetians prized empirical knowledge above all.

In theory, at least, their substantial empirical knowledge should have been sufficient to give the *provveditori alle legne* at least a voice in the management of the Montello reserve, yet it was not. Instead, the Senate chose to assign full responsibility for overseeing the exploitation of the new state forest to the *provveditori all'arsenale*. Handing the oversight of the public forests to the Arsenal managers need not have meant excluding the firewood managers. However, the Montello ban specified that the Arsenal alone would enjoy unfettered access to the new reserve because "it is in the greatest need of timber."[8] The Senate made minor concessions to the needs of the thirteen villages surrounding the reserve, but it did not allow the *provveditori alle legne* any share of the Montello's yield. From the very outset, then, Venice's leaders established that as each new reserve was added to the reserve system, it would be open to a limited number of uses. The Senate and the Council of Ten resolved to protect only the most essential local usufruct rights and the Arsenal's privileges, and nothing else. They deliberately excluded both mainland elites and other state consumers, such as the firewood managers. In the middle of the sixteenth century, the Council of Ten began to requisition oak piles for the maintenance of the complex flood-control system in the lagoon as part of the regular Arsenal harvests, but it made no further exceptions until the eighteenth century. Exclusivity became the watchword for the management of the state forests. Just as the firewood and the Arsenal managers divided the task of regulating the markets for fuel and timber, respectively, after 1471 they divided their control over exploitation practices in mainland forests. By excluding the *provveditori alle legne* from the Montello, the Senate ensured that in the future the best oak, beech, and fir forests became the exclusive province of the Arsenal. The firewood managers and mainland elites were forced to settle for access to what remained, which increasingly meant undesirable scrub and heavily coppiced community stands.

This division mirrored the ideas about mainland forests that held sway in the Ducal Palace in the winter of 1471, especially the unshakeable assumption that crucial forest resources were in constant peril. Market distortions, in combination with the Venetians' overall lack of familiarity with mainland landscapes, reinforced legislator's fears that high-quality timber was disappearing at a rapid rate. Neither the Arsenal representatives sent to survey the Montello nor the senators who voted on the measure banning the woods appear to have had any concept of forest renewal or of the factors that might speed the process by which harvested oak could be replaced by new growth. Therefore the decision to exclude all but the most essential local uses and users meshed perfectly with the long-standing Venetian perception of scarcity in mainland forests.

The decision to bar most users from the state forests also fit well with traditional Venetian ideas about what constituted the public good. Dating back to the earliest fourteenth-century market controls, Venetian legislation consistently and explicitly drew a rhetorical connection between the Arsenal's need for timber and Venice's survival as a free republic. The Republic's leaders frequently invoked such phrases as "knowing that the famine of timber threatens our liberty," and "because, as everyone knows, oak is of the first importance for our republic." In other words, Arsenal oak was more than just an important resource for Venetians; it was the physical embodiment of republican liberty. As important as fuel was to the survival of Venice as a city and as an industrial center, the Republic's leaders never uttered the words firewood and liberty in the same breath. By contrast, the traditional political and ideological connections between protecting the lagoon and safeguarding the Republic informed the Council of Ten's decision to merge the Arsenal harvest with the harvesting of oak piles for the lagoon's infrastructure.[9] The lagoon and oak timber both possessed an almost mystical quality in Venetian legislative rhetoric. And while it would be fair to point out that fifteenth- and sixteenth-century Italians wasted no opportunity to discourse at length about republican liberty, it is also apparent that in the case of Venetian forestry policy there was a clear and unambiguous connection between the political rhetoric concerning the Arsenal and the lagoon and the actual management practices the Venetians pursued in the *boschi pubblici*. Likewise, the decision to protect the rights of local communities while excluding powerful individuals and institutions fits perfectly into traditional Venetian ideas about the relationship between the state and its mainland subjects, which tended to regard *terraferma* elites with suspicion.[10] In this sense, defining the common good in terms of local access served Venetian ambitions very well, because it allowed the Council of Ten to employ the state forests as a bludgeon against powerful mainland interests by excluding them from access to important resources in their own territories.

If the Arsenal managers could congratulate themselves on their acquisition of such an outstanding resource, the firewood managers had serious grounds to lament the specifics of the new ban. For centuries the Montello had been a valuable source of firewood and finished charcoal for Venice. Now the *provveditori alle legne* faced the formidable task of having to locate new sources to make up for the loss of such an important production site. Furthermore, because the Montello ban set the key precedent for all future applications of the Republic's *diritto di riserva* over critical forest resources, every expansion of the Arsenal's reserves came at the mounting expense of the firewood managers' ability to obtain high-quality fuel. Even though the *provveditori alle legne* and their subordinates remained at the forefront of efforts to locate new sources of timber and fuel into the first decade of the sixteenth century, their exertions often benefited the Arsenal rather than the firewood warehouses. Ultimately, the exclusion of the firewood managers from access to the ever-growing system of Arsenal reserves served to undermine further the authority of that magistracy, with the result that the opinions and desires of the Arsenal managers began to drive the conduct of surveys and other forest inspections. By 1569, when the Republic undertook the first of several full-scale cadastral surveys of mainland oak trees, it was a former *provveditore all'arsenale* who supervised the survey and zealously guarded the Arsenal's interests. Through their close connection to the Council of Ten, the Arsenal managers also successfully maintained the upper hand over the firewood managers in debates over which local practices of forest exploitation to regulate. Again, these developments echoed preexisting ideas about how to regulate the flow of forest commodities into the lagoon. Thus, just as the regulatory hierarchy of species discussed in chapter 2 favored the Arsenal over the firewood warehouses, the division of institutional responsibilities that emerged from the 1471 Montello ban gave the shipyard's managers—in cooperation with the Council of Ten—a privileged position in determining future forestry policies.

The exclusion of the *provveditori alle legne* from policy debates and management decisions came at a hidden cost. By dividing the fledgling forest bureaucracy along traditional lines, the Venetians missed a crucial opportunity for bureaucratic cooperation. A system in which high-grade timber would go to the shipyard while the scraps and lower-quality poles would get divided between local communities and Venice's firewood warehouses had the potential to benefit all parties. However, by forcing the *provveditori alle legne* to venture ever-farther afield to find fuel, the very policies intended to alleviate what the Senate referred to as Venice's "famine for timber" instead reinforced the perception of severe scarcity in mainland forests by making fuel harder to obtain. By the time the patricians in the forest bureaucracy changed their minds about the policy of exclusion, during the late sixteenth century, it was too late to sway the Council of Ten. For the Republic's leaders, the notion of maintaining exclusive Arsenal reserves had become an unquestionable cornerstone of forestry policy, and no amount of protesting on the part of the forest bureaucracy could alter their opinion. The pernicious effects of the policy of exclusion became one of the most important sources of friction between the forest bureaucracy and the Council of Ten in the seventeenth century. It was not until the eighteenth century that it became standard practice to use thinning operations in Arsenal reserves to extract firewood for local residents and the Republic's warehouses alike.

A New Role for the *Provveditori alle Legne*

The process by which the Arsenal managers took the lead in virtually every aspect of forestry policy took several decades to unfold. In the meantime, the *provveditori alle legne* continued to make contributions to the search for still-untapped (by Venice) forest resources. As the Arsenal expanded its grip on the best forests in the lower Piave region, the firewood managers were forced to venture to the outermost edges of Venetian territory in their quest for fuel to stock the warehouses. By the beginning of the sixteenth century, most of Venice's firewood came from the Friuli and Istria. The state's lengthening reach in the firewood market led to a corresponding increase in the scope and importance of forest surveys. In September of 1507, for example, the Council of Ten dispatched one of the secretaries of the *provveditori alle legne*—a *cittadino* named Ludovico Bon—to the Friuli to conduct a comprehensive survey of the community forests there.[11] The following year the Ten extended Bon's commission to include Istrian forests as well.[12] Bon's wide-ranging tour of community forests opens a window not only onto the expanding territorial reach of Venice's forest bureaucracy, but also onto the escalating complexity of the tasks it faced. Earlier firewood surveys, such as Marco Cornaro's 1442 inspection, rarely strayed far from the territories bounded by the Piave and Livenza rivers, because this area was largely capable of satisfying the Republic's hunger for combustible material. However, with the expansion of the Arsenal's exclusive forest holdings in that very region, the firewood managers found themselves forced to range ever more eastward in search of new sources of precious fuel. Bon's two-year tour of the eastern reaches of the Republic's northern Adriatic possessions underscores just how prominent the Friulian and Istrian forests had become in the nearly four decades since the Montello ban. By the turn of the sixteenth century these forests constituted the very mainstay of the city's fuel supply.

Bon's mission also highlights the degree to which the 1476 legislation had placed a major administrative burden on the firewood bureaucracy.

Like earlier fifteenth-century surveys—including Cornaro's—Bon's principal task was to ascertain the quantity and quality of firewood sources in a specific region. In comparison to his predecessors, however, Bon operated across a far greater area—Cornaro had only surveyed a relatively small region of the lower Piave and Livenza watersheds. Moreover, it is worth noting that Bon's assigned territory included some of the Republic's most unruly possessions, places where the authority of Venetian officials was only grudgingly accepted.[13] As if this were not enough, the Council of Ten also expected Bon to ascertain whether local officials and residents were complying with the practices laid out in the 1476 legislation governing the exploitation of community forests. Not only was he obliged to ensure that community forests had been divided into the canonical ten coupes, he also had to assume responsibility for the restoration of any recently usurped community forests and initiate legal action against the offenders—provided they could be identified. Bon went armed with a Ducal letter issued by the Ten instructing all local officials —including the various Venetian *capitani* and *podestà*—to give him their full cooperation in these important matters.[14] But whatever weight a *ducale* from the Council of Ten may have carried with the residents of Venice's imperial frontier, Bon lacked any of the personal authority a patrician *provveditore* could have brought to bear in touchy situations. With his power thus limited, Bon clearly faced a Sisyphean task. Conducting an effective survey across such a wide area represented a serious challenge for a lone official, regardless of rank or social status. Weighed down by onerous survey duties, Bon also had to shoulder a difficult and delicate set of judicial responsibilities. None of his reports survive, but it is safe to assume that his efforts at imposing Venetian ideas of proper forest management met with limited success in the hardscrabble mountains and valleys of Istria.

Bon's commissions offered a brief but significant view of the increasing administrative burdens the 1476 laws placed on firewood managers, but they are not the only available evidence. Indeed, the first serious indication of the mounting pressures faced by the firewood managers came nearly two decades earlier and much closer to home. On 11 February 1488, in the midst of a heated debate over allegations of widespread fraud in the city's firewood markets, the Collegio suggested that henceforth the firewood managers should no longer be drawn from the ranks of veteran firewood merchants, but rather "from expert judges and auditors so that they may better hear and adjudicate court cases."[15] At issue in the Collegio's discussion was the recent rash of cases in which the boatmen who hawked firewood at Rialto and other points in the city had been discovered selling undersized bundles to the public. Each bundle, or *passo*, had to meet minimum length and circumference standards, and every boatman was supposed to carry a measuring chain so customers could verify that the *passi* they were purchasing met these norms. Unannounced inspections by representatives of the *giustizia vecchia* revealed that many boatmen had tampered with their chains so as to defraud their customers. The proper length of a *passo* had long been a matter of considerable dispute in the trade. In the halcyon days of the fourteenth century, when firewood was widely available, a bundle four-and-a-half-feet long was considered a *passo*.[16] By 1488 the Republic's officials demanded that the bundle be no less than three feet in length—reflecting the fact that high-quality firewood was becoming harder to acquire. The offending boatmen stood accused of passing off bundles as short as two-and-a-half-feet long as a standard *passo*. The Collegio did not take the matter lightly. It imposed a heavy fine on dishonest sellers, with the further threat of exclusion from the trade for repeat offenders.[17] Moreover, the Collegio ordered that a permanent measuring line be carved onto the doorposts of the *provveditori alle legne's* offices near the Piazzetta, so concerned buyers could subject suspect chains to immediate inspection. Later on, a similar measuring line was placed on the doorpost of the offices of the *collegio alle acque* near Rialto, where it is still visible today.[18]

The drive to create a set of universally recognized standards for a *passo* of firewood can be understood as part of a larger process by which the Republic strove to impose commonly recognized measurements on a wide variety of trades.[19] Such efforts met with only partial success, to which the survival of a bewildering number of local weights and measures throughout Venetian territories attests.[20] However, the fact that the Collegio also advised changing the criteria for electing the *provveditori alle legne* shows more was at stake than attempting to rein in a few crooked boatmen. In essence, the Republic's leaders were arguing that if endemic shortages of firewood in 1458 had dictated that the firewood managers possess specific knowledge of where and how to acquire fuel, the increasing problems with market justice demanded different types of experience and knowledge. Chapter 5 will take up the problem of bureaucratic expertise as it affected forest management in a more systematic way, but for the time being, it is important to note that the Collegio's collective judgment in this matter represents a crucial transitional moment in the development of the *provveditori alle legne*. The merchant managers had secured sufficient supplies of fuel for the city, so the specter of shortages no longer loomed quite so large in the minds of the senior leadership in the Ducal Palace. Now the court dockets—which were rapidly filling with complaints over fraud in the firewood trade— posed a more immediate concern for the Republic's ruling elite, leading them to consider the possibility of substituting experienced jurists for knowledgeable merchants in the office of *provveditori alle legne*.

As the identity of the patricians who held the office of firewood manager changed, so too did the issues on which the bureaucracy focused its energies. Gradually the firewood managers ceased to participate in expeditions to locate and survey mainland and Istrian forests, concentrating instead on enforcing market regulations, punishing illegal activity in the firewood trade, and overseeing the auctions that assigned contracts to harvest firewood in those common forests—the *beni comunali*—over which the Republic could exert direct control. Even these scaled-down responsibilities proved sufficiently onerous that in 1533 the Senate opted to add two more elected patrician officials, the *sopraprovveditori alle legne*, to the bureaucracy in a new effort to relieve the burden on the existing *provveditori*.[21] The Senate then mandated that the two newcomers divide the responsibilities of the office with the original officials. The new *sopraprovveditori* assumed control of the judicial affairs of the office, while the two *provveditori* remained responsible for the collection of fines, the assignment of supply contracts, and all the other longstanding oversight functions of the office. To discourage corruption and embezzlement, control of the bureaucracy's finances rotated among its four patrician members on a monthly basis. With the 1533 reform, the office of the *provveditori alle legne* definitively lost any active role in surveying and managing forests. It also lost its voice in policy debates. Thereafter, the institution's day-to-day responsibilities kept its patrician supervisors firmly in situ in Venice, where they busied themselves hearing court cases and conducting surprise inspections at the customs *pal-*

lade and the various *fondamente* where firewood was sold. This shift ultimately served to sever the *provveditori alle legne's* experiential connection to mainland forest landscapes, removing them to a metropolitan location where they could no longer participate directly in the process whereby the Republic asserted control over distant forest resources.

After 1488, the *provveditori alle legne* rarely strayed far from the lagoon. Instead they sent subordinate officials to conduct inspections in their place, in much the same way that the Arsenal managers often sent a *proto* from the shipyard rather than traveling in person to survey prospective reserves. Ludovico Bon's survey was the last and most important inspection to be conducted by one of the firewood managers' secretaries. It thus marked the end of the era of active involvement on the part of the *provveditori alle legne's* office in surveys and inspections of mainland forests. While it was not unheard of to send a secretary in place of a patrician, this usually occurred only when the secretary possessed unusual knowledge or an indispensable skill. The best-known examples of this phenomenon were the famous *dragomanni*—the Turkish speakers who conducted most of the face-to-face diplomacy between Venice and the Porte.[22] The Arsenal's reliance on master craftsmen should be understood in the same light—in the fifteenth century the Republic's leaders recognized that the *proti* were better qualified than their patrician supervisors to judge the quality of timber in mainland forests.

The Senate, however, had always dealt with firewood in a different fashion. Dating back to Marco Cornaro's 1442 inspection, it consistently entrusted firewood surveys to patricians with significant personal experience in the matter at hand—what the Senate was accustomed to refer to as *optime informati*, or best-informed men. The firewood merchants who populated the office of the *provveditore alle legne* in its early years clearly qualified as *optime informati* in the realm of forests, even if the Senate maintained lingering reservations about their potential conflicts of interest. Thus Bon's expedition constitutes concrete evidence of an important transformation in the expertise of the *provveditori alle legne*: from knowledge of forests and the firewood trade to knowledge of Venice's byzantine court system. The ultimate effect of this transition was to exclude the *provveditori alle legne* from debates over forestry policy.

The shift away from direct patrician involvement in Venetian forest inspections reveals three important dimensions of the changes that occurred in the offices of the *provveditori alle legne* after 1488. The Council of Ten's unwillingness to release one of the patrician managers from his duties to travel on what was clearly a critical mission reveals just how full the firewood managers' court docket had become by the turn of the sixteenth century. Moreover, after 1488, the gradual transition from electing merchant managers to choosing from among experienced jurists meant that the patricians who held the office of *provveditore alle legne* no longer possessed any particular knowledge of forest landscapes. The firewood managers' lack of personal familiarity with forests and with practices of forest exploitation became a liability on a long and delicate survey mission, where the ability to make critical distinctions between different landscapes remained crucial. And on a purely practical level, the firewood managers' eighteen-month term of office now represented a significant obstacle to their traditional role as supervisors of forest inspections. Ludovico Bon departed Venice for the Friuli sometime in the late summer of 1507 and did not return from Istria until nearly two years later, when the outbreak of the War of Cambrai forced him to cut short his activities on the peninsula. Under these conditions, even if a firewood manager departed on the first day of his term of office, he could not expect to complete such an ambitious survey before the expiration of his mandate. And sending a new *provveditore* out to take charge of an ongoing survey would have meant wasting valuable time getting the newcomer up to speed, thereby making the secretary the more logical choice in the minds of the Council of Ten. Simply put, the combination of new reserves, new laws, and the ever-expanding geographical scope of Venice's search for critical forest resources irrevocably altered the manner in which Venetian officials conducted forest inspections. By the turn of the sixteenth century, surveying forest resources had become an extremely complex and time-consuming enterprise, requiring increasingly specialized knowledge and the personal authority that only a senior patrician could bring to bear on recalcitrant locals and inexperienced *podestà*. Under such conditions, officials who had responsibilities in Venice and limited terms of office, such as the firewood managers—or the Arsenal managers for that matter—could no longer participate in the process of identifying and cataloging forest resources. The Venetians clearly needed a new solution to the challenges of locating and securing new sources of timber and fuel.

Sixteenth-Century Forest Surveys

After Ludovico Bon's Istrian survey was cut short by the outbreak of war in 1509, it would be five difficult years before the Council of Ten could afford to turn its attention once again to the question of evaluating the condition of mainland forests.[23] When it did, the Ten decided to try a new approach to the problem of surveying forests and ensuring that local communities and individuals obeyed the laws defining acceptable practices of forest exploitation. The Council did not turn to the overburdened firewood managers or their staff again. Nor did the Ten fall back on the other traditional approach by asking the Arsenal managers to appoint a group of reliable master craftsmen to travel onto the mainland and report back on what they had seen. Instead, the Council of Ten opted for a completely novel approach: it commissioned Giacomo Querini—one of the outgoing *provveditori all'arsenale*—to lead an inspection team onto the mainland to begin the process of restoring order to the Republic's forests.[24] Querini did not have an official title; in his correspondence he refers to himself as a *provveditore all'arsenale* even though he no longer held that office. His was an extraordinary commission that combined the power and prestige of the Arsenal with an indefinite mandate to remain in the field for as long as it took to complete his inspection. Unlike Ludovico Bon, who—even armed with a letter from the Ten—did not present an imposing figure, Querini possessed the personal authority necessary to demand the cooperation of local officials. In particular, he could happily issue orders to the younger Venetians patricians who sat in the governor's palace in minor centers such as Feltre and Conegliano, because they would not want to cross someone with the power to derail their political futures back in Venice. Querini was a forest surveyor who could also enforce the 1476 laws by sitting in uncontested judgment over local residents and Venetian officials alike. In short, he was everything his fifteenth-century counterparts were not.

Although Querini held no particular title, his commission set a crucial precedent for the future. Querini's mission marked the moment when, with rare exceptions, the Republic's leaders entrusted all future forest surveys to an outgoing *provveditore all'arsenale*, whom they invested with judicial authority as well as an open-ended mandate to spend as much time as it took to complete his inspection tour. Beginning in 1569, these surveys primarily took the form of periodic cadastral surveys of every oak tree on the mainland, but the Council of Ten and the Senate occasionally commissioned inspections of beech and fir forests as well. The patricians who led the large survey teams responsible for collecting the cadastral data were known as *provveditori sopra boschi*. Unlike the two older components of the forest bureaucracy—*legne* and *arsenale*— the *provveditori sopra boschi* did not head up a permanent magistracy. Nor did they possess any authority or responsibilities outside of their mandate to inspect specific forests and convene judicial proceedings to punish those who had committed crimes against the forest, whereas both the Arsenal and the firewood managers voted in the Senate ex officio. Instead, whenever the Senate or the Council of Ten commissioned a forest survey, it elected a *provveditore sopra boschi* from a slate of candidates who had recently served as Arsenal managers. The newly minted *provveditore sopra boschi* retained his mandate until the successful conclusion of the survey, at which time the office would cease to exist until the Republic's leaders decided that a new survey was necessary. It was common for several years to pass between the expiration of one *provveditore*'s mandate and the election of another. In the interim, the *provveditori all'arsenale* and *provveditori alle legne* continued to manage the flow of high-grade timber and fuel into the lagoon, as well as to oversee the prosecution of lawbreakers in the city and on the mainland.

At this juncture, a brief detour into the Venetian state archive is necessary. Due to a nineteenth-century cataloging error, the records and correspondence of the various *provveditori sopra boschi* are mixed in with the records of the *provveditori alle legne* in two different document series: *Amministrazione Forestale Veneta* and *Provveditori sopra Boschi*. As a consequence, previous historians have failed to distinguish between the two offices.[25] The fact that in their original incarnation the *provveditori alle legne* were called the *provveditori sopra il fatto delle legne e boschi* has only served to augment the confusion. The similarity between the two names may even be the source of the original error. As a result, scholars such as Frederic Lane and the eminent nineteenth-century forest historian Adolfo di Berenger all have labored under the mistaken assumption that the *provveditori alle legne* and *provveditori sopra boschi* were one and the same, and that the firewood managers were responsible for the mammoth cadastral surveys of oak analyzed in chapter 5.[26] In fact, the *provveditori sopra boschi* who produced the cadastral surveys were not concerned with firewood and excluded the *provveditori alle legne* from any form of participation in cataloging and quantifying mainland forests. In addition, because the officeholders were drawn from the ranks of the Arsenal managers, the *provveditori sopra boschi* consistently and vigorously promoted the interests of the shipyard at the expense of the needs of both Venice's firewood warehouses and mainland institutions. In this sense, the failure to recognize the existence of two different institutions devoted to the acquisition of forest resources has blinded scholars to the fact that the component parts of Venice's forest bureaucracy often worked at cross-purposes, thereby contributing to the perpetuation of cyclical fuel shortages in the lagoon.

Let us now return to Giacomo Querini, who was a *provveditore sopra boschi* in all but name in the summer of 1514, when the Council of Ten dispatched him onto the mainland to survey the damage that the war had wrought on Venice's forests and to initiate judicial proceedings against lawbreakers. On 1 January 1515, Querini sent a letter from Treviso to update the Council of Ten on his progress. He had examined most of the accessible forests in the lower Piave region, and while they were not in ideal condition, he confided that "it is not as I feared."[27] In Querini's judgment, the two most pressing tasks were reestablishing all the Venetian laws that pertained to forest exploitation practices and creating mechanisms for their continued enforcement. To that end, he proudly reported that he had "left instructions that the laws of 1476 be read aloud in every market in the Trevigiano once a month on the day when it is customary to announce the laws."[28] More importantly, he ordered that village leaders—usually the *degano* or *meriga*—whose common lands bordered on the reestablished Arsenal reserves "be held personally liable for all future damage inflicted on our Republic's forests."[29] Finally, he appointed local forest guardians "to protect the public patrimony."[30] In most of the northeast it was customary for villages with extensive community forests to employ a forest guardian to protect common resources from poachers and other miscreants. Querini attempted to extend this practice to those forests over which the Republic had exercised the *diritto di riserva*. The Venetians had torn the Arsenal reserves away from local communities, so Querini's notion that members of those same communities could be trusted to guard the state forests may seem disingenuous. Indeed, nearly a century later the *provveditore sopra boschi* Giovanni Garzoni still had occasion to claim that state forests went largely unguarded, suggesting the degree to which Querini was out of his depth in 1514. Nonetheless, the idea that state forests should have permanent guardians made an impression on the Council of Ten and the Collegio, with the result that by midcentury every public forest on the mainland had at least one guardian—usually called a *capitano del bosco*—appointed by the Arsenal managers. In larger forests, such as the Montello and the Cansiglio, the *capitano del bosco*—who was usually a retired Arsenal craftsman—was assisted by several armed lieutenants drawn from the local populace.

Giacomo Querini's commission, then, represented a watershed moment in the development of the bureaucratic institutions charged with governing the Republic's forest patrimony. Henceforth all forest surveys and inspections had to be conducted under the aegis of a similar extraordinary appointee. The emergence of the *provveditore sopra boschi* as an arm of the state solved many of the problems that had come to light with Ludovico Bon's inspection of the Friuli and Istria. The creation of the *provveditori sopra boschi* relieved both the *provveditori alle legne* and the *provveditori all'arsenale* of any responsibility for participating in the important task of locating and quantifying mainland forest resources—responsibilities for which, by the turn of the sixteenth century, they no longer had the time or the knowledge. The *provveditori sopra boschi* also resolved the problem of authority that had limited Bon's effectiveness, as it placed a senior member of the Republic's governing elite in a position to impose personally and directly the will of the state on forest landscapes. Finally, the *provveditori sopra boschi* solved the problem of the declining personal expertise of the *provveditori alle legne* and *provveditori all'arsenale* by becoming the repository for specialized knowledge of mainland forests. In this regard, the *provveditori sopra boschi* became a new, third pole in Venice's divided forest bureaucracy.

Yet as actors in the unfolding struggle for control of the region's forests, the *provveditori sopra boschi* remained closely aligned with the Arsenal managers, if for no other reason than they had all served as *provveditori* or *patroni all'arsenale* immediately prior to accepting their commissions as forest inspectors. The clear bias these men held in favor of the interests of the shipyard only served to further marginalize the firewood managers from important debates over forestry policy. Just as the expansion of the Arsenal reserves forced the *provveditori alle legne* out of the lower Piave to the furthest reaches of Venetian territory in their search for fuel, so too did the creation of the powerful new office of *provveditore sopra boschi* leave them waiting in the antechamber whenever the Council of Ten took up the topic of forest management. Seen in the light of later developments, Querini's appointment not only signaled the emergence of a new institution in the Republic's growing forestry regime, it also marked the end of the firewood managers' direct involvement with mainland forests.

From the second decade of the sixteenth century on, the *provveditori alle legne* acted almost exclusively through the market to secure and preserve the forests that supplied the city with its indispensable combustible material. The market levers at the *provveditori alle legne's* disposal included not only the traditional manipulation of prices and tolls, but increasingly involved complex supply contracts with local merchants in regions of firewood production such Istria and the Friuli. Nevertheless, these instruments paled in comparison to the growing forest patrimony under the direct control of the Arsenal managers and the *provveditori sopra boschi*.

Harvests, Local Resistance, and Perceptions of Scarcity

By creating the office of *provveditore sopra boschi*, the Republic's leaders addressed several pressing issues involved with surveying forests. They did nothing, however, to resolve the more practical problem of supervising the harvest of timber and firewood. Prior to the creation of the Arsenal reserves, the merchants with whom the *provveditori* and the *patroni all'arsenale* contracted assumed the responsibility of organizing and paying the labor, harvesting the timber, and moving it down to the nearest river. Once there, raftsmen, who were organized into their own corporation, lashed the poles together to make the rafts that they floated downstream to the lagoon.[31] The Arsenal managers' involvement in the process was limited to paying the merchants and the raftsmen. In a similar fashion, the *provveditori alle legne* contracted with firewood merchants, who were then responsible for leasing forests from local communities, organizing the labor, bundling the firewood into *passi*, and moving it down to the nearest riverside embarcadero. From there, boatmen collected the bundles and transported them to Venice. Farther upstream, in areas that were inaccessible to small boats, the crews would load the bundles onto the rafts of Arsenal timber bound for Venice.

Chapter 1 discussed several interrelated factors that affected the costs faced by timber merchants. These included the forests' distance from navigable rivers, seasonal variations in the water levels in those rivers, the distance between the river mouth and the lagoon, and the availability of peasant labor in the area where harvesting was to take place (which, in an era of chronic demographic instability, was difficult for merchants to predict with any accuracy). The merchants bore almost all of the risks associated with the harvest. Most Arsenal suppliers operated under a five-year contract—known as a *condotta*—that paid them a fixed annual rate for delivering a predetermined quantity of timber to the shipyard. If the contractor failed to deliver the timber on time, or if the timber did not pass an inspection by the shipyard's master craftsmen, he usually incurred punitive fines. These contracts acted as a de facto price ceiling that, when combined with the 1350 law giving the Arsenal first pick of any additional timber brought to Venice, made it difficult for merchants to recoup costs associated with a difficult harvest. Occasionally individual *condotta* holders successfully petitioned for relief, as in the case of one Bernardo Corramexin. In 1501 he managed to convince the *provveditori all'arsenale* that he needed 40 ducats (he had originally asked for 100) to make up for unspecified difficulties he had encountered in the Friuli.[32] But at the turn of the sixteenth century, the Arsenal managers and the Council of Ten rarely exhibited such largesse, with the consequence that Venetian policies actively discouraged merchants from taking any risks by harvesting in politically or topographically difficult regions. In addition, because contractors preferred to return year after year to the most easily accessible forests—especially those in the lower Piave region—they depleted those forests far more than they might otherwise have done. As Giovanni Garzoni observed early in his 1602 inspection tour, "I expected the forests along the Piave in the district of Treviso to be the most impoverished because of their proximity to our city, and so they were."[33] The relative paucity of oak in nearby forests further reinforced the perception of general scarcity that governed policy decisions in the Ducal Palace, because these were the only forests that most senators would have seen in person. Indeed, the greatest defect of the Arsenal's *condotta* system was that the *provveditori all'arsenale* were rarely in a position to influence directly decisions about where and when to harvest. Such decisions had the potential to mitigate what the Venetians understood to be the more pernicious consequences of the existing system. Regularly rotating the point of extraction could limit deforestation and preserve important timber resources, as well as limit erosion and the consequently high levels of siltation in the lagoon.

Prior to the reestablishment of the *provveditori alle legne* in the 1450s, the firewood supply system operated along similar lines. Firewood merchants signed quinquennial supply contracts that paid out at a fixed price per *passo*, and they enjoyed the freedom to decide where and when to harvest. Most merchants operated in fairly restricted areas, where they maintained long-term relationships with the communities and institutions that controlled much of the available forestland.[34] And in many cases, including that of the aforementioned Bernardo Corramexin, merchants signed simultaneous contracts with the Arsenal and the *provveditori alle legne* so that they could remove both firewood and Arsenal timber in a single harvest.[35] Consequently, Venetian demand for firewood had a disproportionate effect on forest composition in the lower Piave and other regions that boasted easily accessible woodlands. The merchant managers who oversaw the operations of the *provveditori alle legne* into the last decade of the fifteenth century were able to alter this traditional pattern of forest exploitation by expanding the roster of merchants on whom the Republic relied for combustible material. In so doing, they extended the reach of the Venetian firewood market into the easternmost corners of the *terraferma* and Istria, thereby reducing the impact of central demand on the forests of any one region. The success of this strategy is evidenced by the Collegio's willingness, in 1487, to remove the merchant managers from the office of *provveditori alle legne* and replace them with judges, once the managers appeared to have set up a system that ensured the regular arrival of firewood in the city.

The establishment of the Montello reserve in 1471 set in motion a series of changes that altered the existing system of timber and firewood acquisition. The Arsenal continued to contract with private suppliers to supplement the Montello's yield. However, as the system of *boschi pubblici* expanded inexorably up the Piave and across the coastal plain to

Istria, a growing percentage of the timber that arrived in the shipyard came from state reserves. By the middle of the sixteenth century, private suppliers no longer played as prominent a role in harvesting high-quality oak, beech, and fir timber. When the Arsenal did purchase timber from private suppliers, it was usually only to make up for occasional shortfalls in the production from the state forests. But extracting timber from reserves such as the Montello presented the Arsenal managers with a serious challenge, one for which they were ill prepared, especially given their almost total lack of experience with mainland forests. And because the Council of Ten and the Senate were intent on keeping as many other users out of the reserves as possible, the Arsenal managers could not simply subcontract the harvest to private parties. Nor could they afford to send one of their number out to supervise as many as eight simultaneous harvests. In this respect, the decision to make the Montello an exclusive reserve held yet another hidden cost for the forest bureaucracy, because it created onerous new responsibilities for which existing institutions were utterly unprepared.

In his detailed study of the *arsenalotti*, Robert Davis observes that, beginning in the sixteenth century, the shipyard's craftsmen assumed an increasingly active role in the supervision of the technical aspects of shipbuilding.[36] Davis focuses exclusively on the craftsmen's role within the Arsenal's increasingly sophisticated division of labor, but they also played a pivotal part in the management of the growing system of *boschi pubblici*. With the *provveditori all'arsenale* too busy to travel, and the *provveditori alle legne* increasingly limited to courtroom duties, the Arsenal's *proti* assumed the task of supervising the harvest of Arsenal timber in the *boschi pubblici*. And when the Council of Ten ordered the Arsenal managers to appoint *capitani*—or guardians—for the most important reserves, the *provveditori all'arsenale* chose them from among their own workers. By the sixteenth century, when the Arsenal's forest patrimony included more than forty different forests—each with its own Arsenal-appointed *capitano del bosco*—as many as eight separate groups of craftsmen would travel to various parts of the mainland to extract Arsenal timber from public reserves every February and August. Each team was usually composed of one *proto* assisted by four *sottoproti*. Thus during the harvest season there were as many as forty Arsenal *proti* and *sottoproti* directly involved in the management of mainland forests, either as guardians or as harvest managers.

In a typical harvest cycle, one group of craftsmen travelled to the Cadore to see to the mast harvest in the Bosco della Vizza, another to Belluno to supervise the beech harvest in the Cansiglio, a third to beech forests in the upper reaches of the Livenza, and the remaining men to whichever oak reserves the *provveditori all'arsenale* had decided to tap that year. Because the Arsenal *proti* were commoners who held no real power, their efforts had to be supported by the local Venetian governor—the *capitano* or *podestà*. Ordinarily the Council of Ten commanded the local authorities to organize the necessary *angaria* labor in advance of the craftsmen's arrival so that work could begin promptly. The Arsenal representatives marked individual trees for felling and then observed as local laborers harvested the designated poles and moved them to the embarcaderos. Much of the success of such a complex and time-sensitive operation depended on the power of the local *podestà*. For example, the Montello reserve fell under the jurisdiction of the *podestà* of Treviso, who was invariably an older, more experienced patrician and thus in a better position to force reluctant villagers to respond to the call to labor. By contrast, craftsmen sent to the Montona reserve in Istria relied on the young and often inexperienced *capitano* at Raspo to furnish them with willing workers. As a result, they tended to encounter far greater difficulties.

The *proti* who supervised the harvests also assumed a key role in the transmission of knowledge about mainland forests to the Arsenal and the Ducal Palace. Because the Council of Ten appointed a *provveditore sopra boschi* perhaps once a decade, the *proti* who supervised the harvests were the only Venetian representatives who routinely visited the *boschi pubblici*. Even after the 1569 inception of regular cadastral surveys, which supplied the Arsenal managers with specific quantitative data concerning oak forests throughout the mainland, the craftsmen remained the principal source of detailed descriptive accounts of the condition of mainland forests. When an Arsenal report or a Council of Ten decree opened with a typical phrase such as "it has come to our attention that in the Montello Forest the trees that are specifically reserved for our Arsenal are being seriously damaged, day and night," the source of the information was almost always an Arsenal *proto*.[37] Occasionally a local *podestà* would take an interest in the local *boschi pubblici* and include reports on their condition in his correspondence with the Senate and the Council of Ten. The most prominent example was Marc'Antonio Miani, the *podestà* of Belluno, who wrote several detailed letters in 1574 about the condition of the Cansiglio reserve. However, for most patricians serving on the mainland, forests were only one of many issues that crossed their desks. As a result, most *podestà* only paid attention to the woods under their jurisdiction when the Council of Ten told them to organize an *angaria* for a harvest.

The increasingly prominent role that Arsenal craftsmen played in collecting information about the condition of mainland forests served to reinforce traditional Venetian ideas about timber and fuel. When a harvest failed to produce the desired quantities of timber, the *proti* usually placed the blame on the misbehavior of local residents or on the lack of suitable timber in the forest to which they were assigned. Venetian *podestà* also routinely accused local residents of failing to respect their orders rather than shouldering the responsibility for failed harvests themselves. As a consequence, the Arsenal managers and their superiors in the Ducal Palace developed the idée fixe that mainland residents constantly pilfered timber from the *boschi pubblici* or engaged in other practices that gradually ate away at the public stock of timber. Even the cadastral surveys failed to dislodge this idea, largely because these surveys occurred so infrequently that any positive quantitative information they contained was drowned out by the constant cacophony of complaints originating with the *podestà* and *proti*.

The criticisms directed at local residents were not entirely without foundation. Mainland peasants were understandably unhappy about being summoned to perform *angaria* labor on behalf of the distant Venetians. And it was no challenge for villagers in timber-producing regions to sabotage the harvest if they felt they were not being treated fairly. The workers engaged in the arduous labor of harvesting large oak, beech, and fir timber on behalf of the Arsenal understood well that the timing of the harvest was critical if the felled poles were to make it to the river in time for transport to Venice. Thus the most common form of peasant resistance to the *angarie* was to work so slowly that by the time the poles were moved into position outside of the forest, the period of peak flow in the river would have passed, at which point the Arsenal craftsmen would be forced to abandon the poles until the next harvest cycle. As early as 1487, Istrian peasants routinely employed this tactic to force the *provveditori alle legne* and the *provveditori all'arsenale* to pay them bonuses for delivering harvested firewood and timber to the banks of the Quieto.[38] In 1530, peasants from the villages surrounding the Montona reserve used the threat of walking away from the harvest to force Venetian authorities to pay them an advance of 50 ducats for their participation in the harvest. As the chagrined *capitano* of Raspo, Nicolò Grimani, explained in a letter to the Council of Ten, "without acceptable terms, the greater part of them will desert, on account of their ability to follow the large number of *morlacchi* who have already removed themselves to the territories of the Turkish Sultan."[39] To add insult to injury, Grimani admitted that he had emptied Raspo's modest treasury and borrowed additional funds from Capo D'Istria to pay the workers, so he no longer had sufficient money to pay for his own table. The Council had no choice but to accept Grimani's decision to pay the large advance as a fait accompli and reimburse him.

In the sixteenth century the Venetians responded to peasant resistance to *angarie* by converting the *angarie* into a system of paid labor financed by a property tax called a *carratada*. *Carratada* impositions represented an increasingly common way for Venetian authorities to underwrite a variety of public projects throughout the mainland.[40] In the case of timber, once the Arsenal decided to harvest in a particular area, the Council of Ten instructed the local *podestà* to collect the tax and use the proceeds to finance the operation. Workers were paid a fixed rate per pole in exchange for their labor. But this change in policy failed to have the desired effect. Peasants continued to employ delaying tactics to force the local *podestà* to ask Venice for additional funds.[41] So successful were these tactics that the Senate and the Council of Ten ceased to debate the issue and simply began disbursing the monies as a matter of course. The *provveditori all'arsenale* became so liberal in this regard that it caused problems for the *provveditori alle legne*, whose reliance on local merchants working under fairly rigid *condotta* contracts limited their fiscal flexibility. For example, in 1591 the *capitano* at Raspo reported that the villagers in the area surrounding the Montona reserve refused to labor on behalf of the local firewood contractor "because they claim the recent famine forces them to spend more time on preparing to sow."[42] Yet when

"Paolo Sprazza, the *proto* sent from the Arsenal, arrived, the workers readily presented themselves for that harvest, for it is a far more profitable activity."[43] This incident offers a vivid example of how the Republic's divided forest bureaucracy could often work at cross-purposes. In this case, the Council of Ten's efforts to address peasant grievances over the Arsenal harvest actually hampered the operations of the firewood merchants who labored on behalf of the firewood managers.

The shift to a system of direct remuneration for local peasant labor also created unanticipated problems for many local *podestà* assigned to a timber-producing area. The new system did little to heal the resentment many peasants felt over being forced to labor on behalf of the Republic. In addition, property-owning elites on the mainland and in Venice saw the new tax as an unjust imposition and sought to undermine the system's finances at every opportunity. If they thought they could get away with it, landowners attempted to avoid paying the *carratada* for timber harvests. Not only did they consider Arsenal harvests to be a Venetian expense brought on by Venetian policies, but they also objected to paying for a forestry regime that explicitly excluded them from sharing in the bounty of the *boschi pubblici*. By refusing to pay—or simply delaying long enough—landowners could effectively cut off the funding for the harvest. For mainland elites, sabotaging Arsenal harvests potentially fulfilled at least two aims. In the short term, it could reinforce their superior social and political status vis-à-vis a young and ambitious Venetian *podestà* by forcing him to humiliate himself before the Council of Ten, admitting that he had been unable to collect the tax on time. In the long term, if a group of landowners managed to avoid the tax every time the Arsenal sought to harvest timber in their district, they might eventually convince the *provveditori all'arsenale* that there was little point in returning. In this way, they could regain some of their lost privileges in local forests.

For their part, the Arsenal managers railed against the delays brought on by the combination of tax evaders and peasant resistance, but their exhortations rarely achieved tangible results. The Arsenal records do not allow for a precise accounting of deliveries, but the available data suggest that by the seventeenth century it took at least two harvest cycles—or about ten months—and often longer for felled timber to make its way from the point of extraction to the shipyard. Eventually, such delays in

TABLE 4.1   Oak poles delivered to the Arsenal during the War of Candia (1645–68)

Source	Quantity	Percentage
Montello	1,200	4
Montona	196	1
Other lower Piave reserves	2,500	8
Friuli reserves	11,400	37
Private suppliers	15,200	50
Total	30,496	100

SOURCES: I compiled these data by combing through the *Filze* of the *Senato Mar* and *Senato Terra* series, the *Filze* of the *Consiglio dei Dieci, Parti Comuni,* and the records in the *Provveditori e Patroni all'Arsenale,* recording every mention of a delivery of Arsenal oak to the shipyard. The data are almost certainly incomplete, but they still provide a rough idea of the provenance of oak during the war.

the delivery of critical material simply became an accepted part of the process of timber acquisition. This constituted a tolerable state of affairs in peacetime. However, in wartime the delays potentially threatened the Republic's ability to maintain the fleet and thus caused considerable alarm in the Ducal Palace. For example, in February 1667, near the end of the War of Candia, the *provveditori all'arsenale* sent an urgent report to the Senate in which they warned that persistent problems with the harvest threatened the shipyard's stock of seasoned oak timber. The *provveditori* lamented that "not a single oak tree from the last two Montello harvests has arrived in the yard. We have done all that we could with letters and threats, but now we see these delays every year even in formerly reliable areas such as Motta Trevigiana, Uderzo, and Porto Buffolè."[44] The available data substantiate the *provveditori*'s complaints. Fully half of the oak that entered the Arsenal during the war (1645–68) came from privately owned forests, as repeated failures of the public harvests forced the Republic to purchase oak from private parties instead of taking advantage of its own abundant reserves (see table 4.1). As an interesting aside, the Arsenal managers took the time to note that "the *Luogotenente* of Friuli is to be praised for his timely deliveries of desperately needed oak."[45] Again, the available delivery data substantiate this anecdotal claim. *Boschi pubblici* in the Friuli accounted for 37 percent of the total oak delivered to the shipyard during the war—as compared to only 1 percent originating from the Montona reserve in Istria and 4 percent from the Montello. While the *provveditori all'arsenale* provided no explanation for this exception, the fact that cooperative feudal lords in the Friuli could compel their peasants to perform the labor without constantly being forced to renegotiate the terms of service must have constituted an important factor in the success of the Friulian harvests during the War of Candia.

The power of mainland residents to manipulate the public *condotta* system to their advantage reinforced the Venetians' belief in the scarcity of high-grade timber. Once again the available data on deliveries of Arsenal oak and beech confirm that this idea was not totally devoid of merit. Between delays in the public *condotta*, timber left to rot by the side of the road or in the forest, and simple theft, only seven out of every ten oak poles harvested in Arsenal reserves ever made it to Venice. Therefore, the *provveditori all'arsenale* had to requisition roughly 50 percent more oak timber than they actually needed to maintain adequate stockpiles of seasoned material in the shipyard. Regardless of whether or not oak forests really were disappearing, the sheer volume of wood that went missing en route from the reserves to the lagoon represented a legitimate source of concern for the Republic's leaders. Still, their reaction revealed that they continued to view the problem in proscriptive terms. Rather than attempting to create new incentives for local residents to participate responsibly in the Arsenal harvest—such as sharing some of the yield with the workers—the Senate and the Council of Ten opted instead to increase their efforts at enforcement. In a 1667 letter to the *capitano* of Raspo, the Senate pointed to the "serious damage done by private individuals who cut and removed the very oak that the Arsenal needed most from the harvest" and ordered him to "republish the usual proclamations and prohibitions . . . and rectify the aforementioned disorders as quickly as possible."[46] There can be no doubt that crafty peasants knew how to turn their time in the service of the Arsenal to their advantage. Timber that did not make it to the river quickly enough to be bound into rafts represented a huge temptation for the sticky-fingered or, for that matter, workers who felt ill used or underpaid. As the *provveditore sopra boschi* Giacomo Giustinian reported in 1585, after having confronted a group of peasants near Asolo they responded that "when the *Podestarie* and Towns failed to pay the poor carters for their loads, they converted the timber for their own use, and now they say that next year there will be no one willing to load oak timber in the whole district of Treviso."[47] Another common ruse involved "topping" the ends of the logs before delivering them to the embarcaderos and keeping the cut ends for personal use.[48] Workers also routinely took home the scraps and stripped branches left over from the harvest, a practice that the *proti* appear to have tolerated, even if it met with disapproval in the halls of the Ducal Palace. The Council of Ten responded by calling for surprise inspections of woodpiles and ordering the Arsenal *proti* to mark both ends of every felled pole so that inspectors could verify their integrity at every stage of their journey to the Arsenal.[49]

The Senate and the Council of Ten hoped that by encouraging local authorities and the Arsenal's emissaries to crack down on the most common abuses, they would help safeguard the resources of the *boschi pubblici*. However, most officials charged with enforcing the forestry laws—especially the *provveditori sopra boschi*—tended to adopt a more tolerant stance with respect to the actions of mainland peasants. As the *provveditore sopra boschi* Giovanni Garzoni pointed out to the Council of Ten in 1602, the kinds of petty theft committed by the poor in no way endangered the integrity of the Arsenal reserves. Furthermore, Garzoni argued, the Council needed to recognize that "it is disgraceful and unjust to condemn a poor peasant who out of desperation to keep his children warm and fed has stolen oak."[50] More worrisome for Garzoni were the actions of mainland elites who, he argued, "have eradicated entire forests to satisfy their greed."[51] In other words, the poor stole a few trees that the Republic could afford to lose, while the wealthy stole forests that it could not do without.

It is telling that while the Council of Ten passed laws calling for such harsh punishments as three jerks of the rope, two years in the galleys, and up to five years of banishment for a variety of offenses against the *boschi pubblici*, the *provveditori all'arsenale*, *provveditori sopra boschi*, and *provveditori alle legne* issued almost no judgments against individual mainland peasants in the sixteenth and seventeenth centuries. And when other officials—such as local *podestà*—attempted to penalize peasants for stealing small quantities of timber, the forest bureaucracy often refused to enforce the sentences. The Arsenal managers and *provveditori sopra boschi* were even willing to stand up to the Council of Ten on occasion. For example, in 1565 the *provveditori all'arsenale* refused to send one Bartolomeo Manzini to the galleys, in deference to his poverty and age. In 1568 they again refused to enforce fines for illegal possession of oak against "the poor men and villages of Tessera" in the territory of Mestre.[52] Thus, when it came to crimes committed by the poor, the *provveditori sopra boschi* and other forestry officials sent a clear message to mainland communities that the forest bureaucracy was willing to forgive relatively petty infractions. At the same time, as Giovanni Garzoni's letters make clear, they also tried to convince their superiors in Venice that such crimes did not threaten the Republic's precious stores of timber.

The willingness of the Asolani to speak openly to Giacomo Giustinian about their motives for helping themselves to timber suggests that they did not fear punishment from the *provveditore sopra boschi*. This incident further suggests that the *provveditori sopra boschi* were at least partially successful in their efforts to convince villagers that they were disposed to be forgiving. Convincing legislators that not all crimes against the forest were equally despicable proved far more difficult. The Senate tried to hold the line on punishing any and all wood poachers, but by the middle of the seventeenth century their resolve began to weaken. In the 1667 letter to the *capitano* at Raspo in which the Senate instructed him to crack down on theft in the Montona reserve, the legislators included the caveat that "it should be done so as not to harm the poor."[53] Instead, the Senate instructed the *capitano* to concentrate his efforts on the "agents of the four boat builders in Piran and those in other Istrian ports," because they posed the most serious threat to the forest.[54] And in 1704, the Senate conceded the point and accepted the advice of the *inquisitore sopra boschi* Leonardo Mocenigo to create a formalized system for sharing the scraps and other leftovers of Arsenal harvests with the villages that had supplied the labor.[55] In so doing, the Senate sought to convince peasant communities that they could rely on the state to protect their share of local forest resources.

Instead of persecuting the peasantry, the Venetian forest bureaucracy focused most of its energies on prosecuting landowners, corrupt officials, and other individuals who did more than top the occasional pole earmarked for Venice. The surviving trial records in the Venetian archives deal with a wide range of crimes against the forest, from the 1656 case of Mattio Cornua, who organized a smuggling operation that cut oak timber in the Montona and sold it on the Habsburg side of the frontier; to the case of Pietro Brazza, a tariff agent who in 1585 turned a blind eye to firewood smuggling in exchange for six *lire* and a jug of wine; to the 1603 trial of ZuanBattista Fuliero, who stole large quantities of oak from the Carpeneda forest near Padua by passing himself off as an Arsenal official, complete with forged letters from the Council of Ten and a group of impostor *proti* by his side (he even forced nearby villages to provide him with *angaria* labor); to the 1627 prosecution of several members of Pieve di Cadore's *consiglio generale* who conspired to clear-cut four community stands by means of fraudulent leases backed by phony Council of Ten licenses.[56] In each of these trials, as in almost every major case that the forest bureaucracy chose to pursue, the scale of the crime was the single most important factor. Fuliero and Cornua did not pilfer a few scraps or help themselves to an abandoned log or two; they stole significant numbers of living oak poles from Arsenal reserves. Their actions represented a clear and present danger to an ecological order designed to favor crucial Venetian interests. The town councilors in Pieve used their positions to defraud peasants of their fair share of fuel and other critical forest resources, thereby placing Venice's interests in the Vizza di Cadore and other *boschi pubblici* in jeopardy. Likewise, in the case of Brazza, by accepting bribes he defrauded the Republic of a significant quantity of combustible material, not just a few bundles. Brazza merited prosecution because his actions called the credibility and efficiency of Venice's supply system into question.

A quick look at the thirty-three sentences handed down by Giovanni Garzoni between 30 September 1602 and 21 February 1603 confirms the impression that the *provveditori sopra boschi* sought to distinguish between serious crimes and petty offenses. Thirteen of the cases involved fewer than ten oak poles. In those instances, Garzoni either handed down a relatively minor fine to an individual perpetrator or a slightly larger fine to the community as a whole. In only one of the thirteen cases did an individual receive any form of physical punishment, and then only because the individual—Domenego Gatto—could not afford the modest fine (Garzoni sentenced him to a year in a "locked prison").[57] Garzoni reserved the most serious fines and punishments for individuals or institutions who took more than twenty oak trees at a time. Interestingly, the two largest fines were assessed against Venetian religious institutions. He fined the *Padri Crosechieri* of Venice 200 ducats for illegally harvesting oak in two forests they owned near the village of Dese and clearing a section of one of them to use as pasture. Garzoni also hit the convent of Sant'Andrea in Venice with a 90-ducat penalty for having "hired workers to cut down 90 oak trees, dig up their roots, and convert an area of 386 *perteghe* to arable."[58] In other words, when Garzoni complained to the Council of Ten that people "in authority" had been "eradicating entire forests," he meant it quite literally. More importantly, in both instances a powerful institution had committed a serious crime against the forest, thereby placing in jeopardy the ecological order that the forest bureaucracy struggled to preserve. And in both cases, those institutions felt the full force of the *provveditore sopra boschi*'s ire.

Giovanni Garzoni and other *provveditori sopra boschi* had several good reasons for favoring a lenient approach to petty crimes against the forest. Unless timber poachers were caught in flagrante, the *provveditori sopra boschi* faced an extraordinarily difficult task in proving that a particular individual was responsible for damage done to reserved oak. One solution was to punish the entire community, as the Council of Ten sought to do in the 1568 case cited above.[59] However, as the *provveditori all'arsenale* pointed out in their response to the Ten's decision in that case, harsh action risked alienating the very villages that furnished the labor that made an Arsenal harvest possible. And Garzoni's reluctance to impose heavy fines on small communities further illustrates the degree to which the forest bureaucracy wanted to protect peasants from the harsh punishments called for in most Venetian laws. In large measure, this was due to the fact that the *provveditori sopra boschi* understood that by sparing peasants the full force of the law, they stood a better chance of catching and punishing major offenders. Venetian authorities relied almost exclusively on local informants, to whom they promised anonymity and a share of any fines collected in the event of a successful prosecution.[60] By overlooking petty infractions, forestry officials encouraged peasants to cooperate in the pursuit of more serious criminals. And by forgiving lesser crimes committed "out of desperation," as Garzoni put it, the *provveditori sopra boschi* reinforced the Republic's image as the protector of "poor peasants" against abuse by the wealthy and the powerful. This image was particularly important in the case of crimes against the forest, because the lawbreakers were usually among the most powerful people in the local community, and they were willing to use force to keep their operations secret. As a consequence, if Venetian officials wanted to enforce the laws, they needed to show that they could guarantee their witnesses protection from those who were stealing Arsenal oak. In this sense, the Venetian forestry regime constituted both an imposition and an aid to mainland villages' efforts to protect their commons.

The Council of Ten's aggressive use of the *diritto di riserva* placed clear limits on communities' traditional rights of usufruct. At the same time, however, the presence of Arsenal oak in local forests supplied peasants and village leaders with a powerful lever they could use against local elites who tried to expropriate common resources for private gain. The Republic's desire to preserve timber and fuel could be harnessed by local peasants, who had their own reasons for wanting to see forests protected. And, for its part, the forest bureaucracy incorporated the villages' needs into its ideas concerning the relationship between forests and the public good, even in the face of resistance from the Ducal Palace. By linking the Republic's interests to those of village communities, the *provveditori sopra boschi* and other concerned Venetian officials partially averted the so-called tragedy of the commons that engulfed so many rural communities in other parts of Europe in the early modern period.[61]

The case of the Istrian smuggler Mattio Cornua merits additional consideration, because it highlights the critical role played by local peasants in the enforcement of the Republic's forestry legislation. The entire case hinged on information given by anonymous informants, who tipped off the *capitano* at Raspo, Antonio Barbarigo. Barbarigo "judged that it would be best to proceed in secrecy and to offer immunity, in the event that one or more of the witnesses turns out to be among the conspirators."[62] Three local men—Steffano Schulaz, Mattio Visentin, and Giacomo Grestiach—had obtained a license to remove stunted growth from a section of the Montona reserve, but instead took healthy oak trees. They then sold the trees on the Austrian side of the frontier. Because there were no witnesses willing to corroborate the story in an open hearing, Barbarigo proceeded to question the three men privately. When they refused to answer the *capitano's* questions, he "interrogated them individually and under the threat of torture, so that they might confess the truth; for without the threat of torment they only swear falsehoods out of fear of retribution and loyalty to their friends."[63] Barbarigo's tactics worked. All three confessed to working for Cornua, a local boss, who had bankrolled the operation and "kept the villagers quiet through acts of violence and threats of more."[64] Based on this information, Barbarigo decided to search Cornua's home in the town of Sovignano. Climbing into the rafters, he discovered ninety-seven beams of solid oak and elm, all bearing the Arsenal's mark. Examining the rest of the home, Barbarigo and the master carpenter who accompanied him concluded that there were an additional 265 pieces of reserved oak and elm in the walls and ceilings. Cornua had "built his house out of Arsenal timber," including, it turned out, his dining-room table.[65] The successful apprehension and prosecution of Cornua depended on the local peasants' belief that the Republic would come to their aid by protecting their anonymity and removing their tormentor. The case also shows that the *provveditori sopra boschi* were correct to draw a distinction between minor infractions and real crimes against the ecological order. Finally, it illustrates how a small village was able to exploit the Republic's concern about Arsenal oak to undermine the authority of a powerful local boss, thereby protecting the integrity of the commons.

The 1627 trial of the corrupt councilors in Pieve di Cadore further reinforces the degree to which the Republic's efforts to enforce its forestry laws depended heavily on the cooperation of the peasantry. The *capitano* of Cadore, Giovanni Battista Briani, related how "the poor of this territory have been deprived of their sustenance, through which they support their children and maintain their homes."[66] Anonymous informants had tipped him off that members of Cadore's governing council, the *consiglio generale*, had hired thugs from outside the local community to act as their proxies in leasing and stripping community forests of all useful timber. And like the Istrian peasants who successfully petitioned the *capitano* at Raspo for a pay raise, the villagers promised "to abandon their burdens and remove themselves to the adjoining Archducal territories" if Briani did not halt this abuse of power.[67] In addition to acting as titular leaseholders, the outsiders also used force to keep the villagers out of the woods while they "removed everything of use and value from the territory."[68] In his report, Briani described the interlopers as "rapacious wolves who fear neither God nor the laws . . . deprive the poor of their rights . . . destroy everything they rent . . . and then retire to the local inn, where they devour everything in sight."[69] Briani again referred to them as voracious in a passage in which he described how the corrupt councilors had tried to avoid prosecution by "sending two or three of these 'devourers' to Udine to give false testimony before the *Luogotenente*."[70] Briani effectively employed the image of the *magnadore* (or "devourer") to draw attention to the fact that the thugs—and the officials who employed them—were like locusts, destroying local forests and leaving nothing in their wake. In Briani's estimation, the corrupt councilors were guilty of serious crimes against "the public good" that "excluded the poor from the benefits of the commons."[71] Thus the *capitano* cast himself—and by extension Venice—as the protector of the peasantry's rights to the commons. In protecting those rights, the Republic also defended its own interests in the valuable resources that the community forests produced (provided the forests remained standing). Of course, if the Council of Ten could have arranged it so that no local residents enjoyed any access rights to forest resources, it would gladly have done so. However, an alliance of convenience with angry villagers offered an excellent excuse to police unruly elites who were, in the Venetian's view, the most dangerous enemies of the public good and the most irresponsible destroyers of public resources.

The Cadore prosecution also reveals a great deal about how local peasants viewed access rights to the commons, especially forests. The trial lasted for five days in September. Over that period, Briani called nineteen different witnesses to testify against the councilors. The witnesses were all peasants from local villages; some held positions of authority within their respective communities, but several were undistinguished individuals. What emerges from the testimony of these witnesses is that even in a relatively remote and extremely poor region such as the Cadore, peasants possessed a sophisticated understanding of the boundaries that defined their commons, the laws that governed their use, and even the identities of the individuals who leased them. In his interrogation of the witnesses, Briani skillfully used their intimate knowledge of the region's community forests to identify the forests where outsiders had suddenly come into possession, thus exposing the councilors' crimes. Briani's exchange with his first witness, a local wine-carrier named Giovanni de Mario, provides an excellent example of just how much local peasants understood about the common forests of the region:

BRIANI: How many common forests belong to your village?

GIOVANNI: We have four common forests.

BRIANI: Where do their borders run?

GIOVANNI: Our village possesses the four forests that stand between Campedello and Campolongo.

BRIANI: And from whom does your village receive its privileges in these four forests?

GIOVANNI: From this magnificent community of Cadore, so that we may build bridges and other things we need.

BRIANI: And to whom has your village rented these forests?

GIOVANNI: For the last 12 or 13 years we have been renting the Bosco della Digola to Signor Benetto Pellizzarolo. The Bosco de Val Maio behind Costalta we rent to Messer Zuan Battista di Mario da Campedel and his partners, that is to say Messeri Bettin de Bettin and Lorenzo de Bettin. And the other two pieces we rented to the aforementioned Messer Zuan Battista de Mario and to Messer Nicolò de Zuan Giacomo and Messer Bettin de Bettin.

BRIANI: And for how long do these leases last?

GIOVANNI: For one year at a time only.[72]

Giovanni de Mario went on to offer an explicit account of the value of the leases and explained that in the past the leaseholders had always presented harvest licenses issued by the *Luogotenente* in Udine before exercising their privileges under the terms of the lease. Several subsequent witnesses demonstrated equally specific knowledge of the common forests belonging to their villages, including highly detailed memories of who leased those woods, the precise conditions of the leases, and even how their villages had spent the profits. Not only does their testimony furnish ample evidence that peasants understood their common rights extremely well, it also shows that they kept careful track of who used the forests and for what purpose. In a world where the main actors in the local forest economy were intimately acquainted with one another, rural communities were highly attuned to violations of their rights. Moreover, this trial exposes the fact that peasants and rural communities were well aware that while they did not view forest resources in quite the same way as the Venetians, they did share with their distant masters a common hatred for the ways in which local elites exploited the forest. Local villages wanted to protect their access to critical resources, while the Venetians wished to conserve those same resources by preventing as many people as possible from utilizing them. These two different visions of forest resources found common ground in their mutual desire to prevent the destructive modes of exploitation preferred by private landowners and leaseholders eager to maximize short-term profits—or, as Briani evocatively put it, to devour all the forest's resources in a single meal. Indeed, the peasants who whispered in Briani's ear knew exactly what to tell him to get him to bring the full weight of Venetian power to bear on the foreigners, and their masters in the *palazzo comunale* in Pieve di Cadore, who had denied them their rightful share of common resources.

The *Catastico Garzoni* and the Knowledge Gap

Giovanni Garzoni's stint as *provveditore sopra boschi* brings all of the themes of this chapter into relief. His letters demonstrate just how complex the problem of managing mainland forests had become in the 141 years since the creation of the Montello reserve. The number of tasks that Garzoni juggled—combined with the sheer volume of contradictory information his survey teams, secretaries, and local administrators placed on his desk—made his duties exponentially more challenging than anything confronted by his fifteenth- and early sixteenth-century predecessors. His exchanges with the Council of Ten also point to the difficulties he dealt with as the public face of Venetian forestry laws in the *terraferma*. In his role as the official mediator between the demands emanating from the Ducal Palace and the complaints of peasants and rural communities, Garzoni also faced the formidable task of reconciling two very different views of mainland forest landscapes and ecologies. Finally, as these two understandings of the natural world increasingly diverged—especially with respect to the Venetian policy of exclusive access to the *boschi pubblici*—Garzoni and other *provveditori sopra boschi* developed new and unique knowledge concerning the best way to manage the complex forest landscapes of the *terraferma*. Over the course of the seventeenth century, the *provveditori sopra boschi* became increasingly convinced that opening up the Arsenal reserves to more intense but still carefully regulated exploitation by local communities would safeguard future supplies of oak and beech timber. By the turn of the eighteenth century, the *provveditori sopra boschi* had developed a fully articulated system of multiple-use forestry, despite continued resistance from the Ducal Palace. The development of the *provveditori sopra boschi's* expertise and their ideas about the best way to manage forest landscapes will be the focus of chapter 5. However, Garzoni's letters offer a privileged view of some of the earliest formulations of the *provveditori sopra boschi's* arguments concerning the relationship between human action and local forest ecologies.

Caught between the practical demands of administering forests and the more abstract concerns about dwindling resources emanating from the Ducal Palace, Garzoni was repeatedly forced to justify his actions (or inactions) to his superiors. Indeed, Garzoni's letters reveal just how demanding the office of *provveditore sopra boschi* had become since Querini's tour of the Friuli and Istria in 1514. Not only did the position of *provveditore* require at least a passing knowledge of timber and the timber trade, but the officeholder needed to have the personal authority both to impose the Republic's will on unruly mainland elites and prestigious religious institutions and to stand up to pressure from the powerful Council of Ten. Moreover, he had to be willing to spend upwards of two or three years in pursuing a difficult and thankless task that combined the physical hardship of personally inspecting hundreds of forests in all weather conditions with the mental and moral challenges of vicious and hard-fought legal and political battles with powerful individuals and institutions throughout the *terraferma*. At age sixty-three, Garzoni fit the profile perfectly. As a senior member of the Republic's ruling patriciate, he could demand obedience from younger Venetian *podestà* and recalcitrant local elites alike. And like almost every *provveditore sopra boschi* since the mid-sixteenth century, he had recently served as a *provveditore all'arsenale*. His service in the shipyard gave him a basic familiarity with the challenges of securing and processing the high-quality timber used in naval construction. That knowledge in turn allowed him to make sense of the quantitative and qualitative information his survey teams collected. Finally, the combination of his knowledge and social status put him in a privileged position to interpret and explain the significance of the survey data to the Council of Ten and thereby promote more effective forestry policies.

The Council of Ten's commission called for Garzoni to conduct a cadastral survey of oak in the Vicentino, Padovano, Trevigiano, and Friuli. The commission elaborated the need for such a survey, reminding the newly elected *provveditore sopra boschi* that "past experience has taught us that ordinary diligence and care is insufficient to prevent the inestimable and most serious damage that is constantly being done to oak trees."[73] In practice this meant that the Ten expected Garzoni and his survey teams to count and catalog each and every living oak tree in the northeast over eighteen inches tall, including individual trees in roadside windbreaks and village squares. In addition to counting trees, Garzoni's men used duplicate registers to record the size, location, and ownership of every forest containing oak. One master copy—containing the complete data—was stored in Venice, while individual registers containing local data were deposited in the appropriate chanceries. Garzoni and his men also had to map, survey, and mark the boundaries of every *bosco pubblico* in the *terraferma*. Garzoni then had to compare the new data assembled by his men against the information contained in the registers of the previous comprehensive cadastral survey, completed in 1586 by Giacomo Giustinian.[74] Wherever he discovered significant discrepancies in terms of the size of particular forests or their contents, the Council of Ten expected him to open an inquiry that would, if all went as planned, culminate with Garzoni sitting in judgment at a specially convened trial of the wrongdoers. Garzoni also had to personally inspect and verify every license to harvest in private, ecclesiastical, and community forests and to punish anyone caught violating the terms of their license. Lastly, the Ten ordered him to seek out all other abrogations of Venetian forestry laws and "freely slaughter any livestock illegally pasturing in restricted forests."[75]

Garzoni was, by all accounts, a dedicated public servant, yet eventually even he balked at the enormity of the task that had been assigned to him. He left Venice in the late autumn of 1601, in time to observe the harvest in the Montello and other state forests in the lower Piave region. In September of the following year he and his survey teams—he initially had four *proti* and sixteen *sottoproti* working with him—were still counting oak in the district of Treviso and observing the fall harvest cycle. The *provveditori all'arsenale* complained to the Council of Ten about the expense of keeping so many *proti* and *sottoproti* in the field for such an extended period of time.[76] The Ten responded by agreeing to allow Garzoni to skip the districts of Padua and Vicenza—districts that supplied minimal quantities of Arsenal timber in any event—and to limit his inspection to the lower Piave and Friuli regions.[77] The Ten also allowed the Arsenal managers to recall most of Garzoni's team, leaving him with only six *proti* and *sottoproti* altogether. The reduction of his staff must have severely affected the pace at which Garzoni could survey and catalog forests, yet, as he pointed out in January of 1604, "despite having only six *proti* to assist me, I have managed to accomplish in two years what Giustinian took 27 months to do with eight *proti*."[78] He also proudly confided that he saved money by declining to hire locals to survey the perimeters of individual forests, preferring instead to perform the task himself with one of his men. But even Garzoni had his limits. The following month—at the conclusion of the winter harvest cycle—he asked to be released from his office "in deference to my advanced age of 65, and because I have given such service that I have not even a spark of remorse in my mind for making this request."[79] In March of 1604 he sent an even more plaintive appeal to the Ten, asking for eight days of relief to travel to Venice to "correct a misadventure that has befallen my son Piero, who will be the ruin of me and all my posterity."[80] Shortly thereafter, the Council of Ten relented and allowed Garzoni to repatriate without fully completing his survey of Friulian forests. By that time, he and his subordinates had been in the field for two-and-a-half years; had organized over a hundred trials; had placed almost as many private forests under new bans; and had counted, marked, and cataloged nearly 750,000 individual oak trees in over 800 separate forests in the lower Piave and parts of the Friuli.

This brief overview of Garzoni's term as *provveditore sopra boschi* reinforces several of this chapter's more important points about the Venetian forestry regime at the turn of the seventeenth century. Garzoni's survey clearly reveals exactly how complex—overwhelming, even—the task of managing Venice's forest patrimony had become over the course of the previous century. Garzoni's account of his own accomplishments, self-serving though it undoubtedly was, provides an eloquent and impressive testament to the many challenges that the *provveditori sopra boschi* faced as they ventured onto the mainland. In addition, Garzoni's survey reveals precisely why the traditional forest bureaucracy could not keep up with the rapid expansion of the Republic's interest in mainland forest resources. The *provveditori* and *patroni all'arsenale* had their hands full with the daily operations of the shipyard. Likewise, the *provveditori alle legne* fully occupied themselves supervising the sale and distribution of fuel in the city, administering justice in a chaotic marketplace, and supervising the many merchants who held supply contracts with the state. At the same time, with surveys becoming increasingly complex affairs, the Republic's leaders had little choice but to create new institutional mechanisms aimed at collecting and interpreting information about mainland forests. The sheer volume of information that Garzoni and his men gathered reveals the improved skill and scope of the Venetian forest bureaucracy, which had become adept at collecting data about forests and at translating those data into useful and replicable knowledge of mainland landscapes.

Giacomo Querini's 1514 tour of the Friuli and Istria furnishes an excellent benchmark for evaluating the development of the *provveditori sopra boschi* as an institution over the course of the sixteenth century. Querini travelled extensively, saw many forests, and made a genuine effort to reinforce the Republic's power to regulate forest exploitation by appointing local guardians and mandating regular public proclamations of the laws. He also made some substantive suggestions for improving the mechanisms for regulating the exploitation of forests in Venetian territory. However, his accounts of Friulian and Istrian forests remained largely impressionistic and anecdotal, and in this sense they had more in common with fifteenth-century inspections than with the later comprehensive surveys of oak. Querini collected no quantitative data, conducted only a handful of trials, and left little in the way of useful knowledge for his successors to use as a point of comparison for their own surveys. Garzoni, by contrast, bequeathed his successors a voluminous correspondence, rich in astute observations about the social and economic dimensions of crimes against the forest, as well as a massive, specific, and presumptively precise quantitative record of the oak patrimony in the lower Piave and the Friulian side of the Livenza watershed. With surveys such as Garzoni's, the Venetian forest bureaucracy came of age.

There is no evidence that Garzoni embarked on his mission with a preconceived set of ideas about the condition of mainland forests or the root causes of the problems that plagued the Arsenal's supply system. Most likely, he joined his fellow patricians in their conviction that oak represented not only a crucial resource, but one of the cornerstones of Venice's republican liberty, or as he put it, "the principal foundation of the defense of Your Serenity's *stado da mare*."[81] He undoubtedly shared their concern that this most precious of forest resources should be protected at all costs. Beyond such commonplace ideas, however, Garzoni's letters reveal little about what he thought prior to his election as *provveditore sopra boschi*. Garzoni's cadastral survey was the third major count of oak forests undertaken by a *provveditore sopra boschi* after the *Catastico Surian* in 1569 and the *Catastico Giustinian* in 1586. But Garzoni's is the first survey for which a fairly complete record of the *provveditore's* correspondence survives, so it is the first such survey that offers real insight into how the experience of being a *provveditore sopra boschi* influenced the officeholder's ideas about the relationship between the Republic, mainland residents, and forest landscapes. A careful reading of Garzoni's letters reveals not only that he developed a sophisticated account of what was happening in the forests of the lower Piave and western Friuli, but that his account deviated in significant ways from the traditional narratives about mainland forests that dominated in the chambers of the Ducal Palace. In particular, Garzoni came to believe that peasants and peasant communities did not represent a major threat to the integrity of mainland forests, and that the Council of Ten needed to consider altering the traditional mode of managing the Arsenal reserves from a system built around exclusivity to a system of carefully monitored multiple uses. To show how such a system might work, Garzoni decided to intervene forcefully in privately owned forests, deliberately constraining the power of individual and institutional property owners to manage their woodlands.

The fundamental principles that informed Garzoni's ideas about how to reform the management of mainland forests emerged early on in his tenure as a *provveditore sopra boschi*. On 20 April 1602, a little over four months into his mission, Garzoni wrote the first of what would become a long series of letters defending the actions of peasants and other poor residents of the lower Piave. "The poor are not to blame," Garzoni wrote, "for they act out of desperation, need, and ignorance, and there is little in their actions that is not forgivable."[82] Garzoni argued that the Republic should turn its attention to the wealthy, who represented, in his estimation, "the real threat" to the integrity of the region's forests. The notion that the poor should be forgiven and the wealthy punished became one of the most consistent themes in Garzoni's exchanges with the Council of Ten. He continually expressed significant dismay at the degree to which mainland elites had brazenly violated the Venetian forestry laws without any apparent fear of punishment. He quickly set out to redress the problem, only to discover that the offending individuals and institutions were prepared to fight him every step of the way. In November, he reported that as he approached the end of his first year in the lower Piave region, he had "personally conducted a great many criminal trials. To which number I will soon add 52 more, thirteen of which will involve charges against aristocrats who are continually waging violent legal war against my person."[83]

Garzoni identified two main causes for the willingness of elites to defy the laws governing forest exploitation: the lack of any meaningful official presence in any mainland forests except the *boschi pubblici*, and a series of gaping loopholes in the system of licenses that constituted the principal mechanism for monitoring the actions of individuals and institutions in those forests. Garzoni claimed that in several instances he was the first inspector to examine many private and institutional forests since the *Catastico Giustinian* sixteen years earlier. While community and state forests benefited from the watchful eyes of guardians who were responsible for everything that happened within their bailiwick, private and institutionally owned woods containing oak had no such safeguards in place to prevent their abusive exploitation. Despite the fact that anyone wishing to harvest oak in these forests needed to first obtain a license from the *provveditori all'arsenale*, no mechanisms existed for verifying that the license holder was obeying the terms set forth in the license. The comprehensive cadastral surveys exposed violations—often long after the fact—but not the violators, since scores of licensed individuals could have stolen reserved oak in the decades between surveys. In March of 1603, Garzoni suggested that the Council of Ten "pass a new law making the owner of the property from which the oak were stolen liable for damage to his trees if he cannot offer up the individual responsible."[84] Indeed, Garzoni himself had already begun to assess liability for damages, as the hefty fines levied against the nuns of Sant'Andrea and the

Padri Crosechieri show.[85] But, Garzoni argued, such fines would only work if "the *podestà* and other local authorities personally visit the woods in question," otherwise "the informants, who cannot bear the expense and inconvenience of travel, will fail to testify and these crimes will go unpunished."[86] Against this backdrop, Garzoni moved to make local officials responsible for monitoring activity in stands containing oak during the intervals between formal visits by a representative of the forest bureaucracy. Otherwise, he contended, landowners would continue to do whatever they pleased no matter what the laws dictated.

Garzoni also argued that the lack of a consistent official presence made it easier for greedy merchants and landowners to take advantage of loopholes in the licensing system to systematically strip forests of good oak timber. Beginning with the *Catastico Surian* in 1569, the *provveditori sopra boschi*'s survey teams were supposed to stamp every oak tree more than three feet in circumference with a *bollo*—a proprietary mark or seal. Once marked, a tree became subject to the Republic's *diritto di riserva*, regardless of whether it stood on private or public property. Only harvest crews employed by the Republic could fell marked poles, unless the landowner or leaseholder could produce a license issued directly by the Council of Ten or the *provveditori all'arsenale*. Unfortunately, because the Council of Ten tended to think about forests in abstract terms, the licenses specified only the larger territorial jurisdiction where the licensee could harvest and the number of poles he could take. The Council only named the specific forest to be used when the license involved a *bosco pubblico*. Consequently, as Garzoni pointed out, license holders would take the permitted quantities from each of several forests in the same jurisdiction, "thereby fraudulently harvesting many times their allotment of oak."[87] To combat this practice, Garzoni proposed the simple solution of "naming the nearest village or, if possible, the specific forest in which the harvesting will take place on the license."[88] Garzoni also noted other shortcomings in the licensing system. For example, licensees often took advantage of vague phrasing to harvest larger and higher-quality oak than the Council of Ten gave them permission to take. This practice posed a clear threat to the "double-sealed" timber—the application of a second seal made the tree the exclusive property of the Arsenal—that constituted the mainstay of the shipyard's oak supply. Again, Garzoni argued that the licenses needed to contain more specific information to make it easier for newly empowered officials in the employ of the *podestà* to conduct surprise inspections and catch lawbreakers, as well as to "ensure that peasants who might not fully understand the law did not take the wrong trees by mistake."[89] The Council of Ten approved of Garzoni's proposals and decided to phase in his reforms of the license system. By the end of the seventeenth century, the licenses came to include all the information suggested by Garzoni and more. The improved licenses allowed the forest bureaucracy to track the progress of timber from the forest to the lagoon by recording the names of all the parties who touched the timber during its voyage downstream.

The Council of Ten's rapid acceptance of Garzoni's suggestions about licenses reflected a traditional view of the threat local users posed to mainland forests. Garzoni easily persuaded his superiors that a more intrusive system of monitoring the actions of local landowners represented a positive addition to the existing forestry regime. The Council did not, however, prove as receptive to Garzoni's subsequent ruminations on the licensing issue. In particular, Garzoni became convinced that his predecessor, Giustinian, had been overzealous in his application of the second, more restrictive *bollo*. In so doing, Garzoni argued, Giustinian had created a perverse incentive for private property owners and license holders to abuse their privileges: after the Arsenal claimed its share of oak in a district, there was none left over for local use. In April of 1603, Garzoni explained that the zealous application of the second *bollo*

> has placed all the useful trees out of reach, leaving only stunted, use-
> less trees and crooked saplings for individual use. Because these are
> useless for making bridges and mills, or even gondolas . . . when a
> *squero* or other license holder holds a license to cut six poles and he
> finds no single *bollo* trees that meet his needs because they are all too
> small, then I say that he has been forced to harvest timber with two
> *bolli* because there is nothing else for him to do. So it is necessity
> more than ill will that leads him to disdain the commandments of
> Your Serenity.[90]

To address this issue, Garzoni suggested waiting until trees reached five feet in circumference before deciding whether to apply the second *bollo*. He contended that this delay would leave a sufficient number of trees that were three or four feet in circumference available to satisfy local needs. It also allowed for a more precise assessment of the quality of the tree. According to Garzoni, it was not always possible to predict with any accuracy whether a pole with a circumference of three feet would grow into a strong, straight-grained oak suitable for naval construction or a lesser-quality pole suitable only for building mills and bridges. Waiting until the trees reached a greater size would permit the *provveditori sopra boschi* to supply a more realistic account of the Arsenal's reserves, because "a vast number of marked oak grows in your excellencies' forests, but very few will ever be good enough for the Arsenal. I am certain of this, as I am certain that I am rendering faithful service to the Republic and jealously guarding its interests by pointing it out to you."[91] So if Garzoni believed the wealthy were greedy and rapacious abusers of the precious forest landscapes of the *terraferma*, he also believed the Republic's policies made the problem worse by providing them with additional incentives to break the laws. These considerations led Garzoni to conclude that the solution lay in allowing local users freer access to intermediate-quality timber, thus placing the forest bureaucracy in a better position to preserve the highest-quality timber for the Arsenal. In other words, Garzoni proposed a limited program of multiple uses in mainland forests. Only the Arsenal would cut the highest-grade oak, while private users would take poles of intermediate quality unlikely to ever be useful for the shipyard.

Despite Garzoni's carefully crafted arguments, the Council of Ten held fast to its proscriptive approach to regulating access to oak forests. For the Republic's leaders, the idea that loosening the restrictions on oak harvesting could actually conserve Arsenal-grade timber violated the baseline assumptions about the relationship between mainland residents and dwindling resources that informed every existing law governing local practices of forest exploitation. Accordingly, the Council simply elected to ignore Garzoni's suggestions on this matter. The Ten's unwillingness to consider Garzoni's apparently radical proposition that the Republic should allow greater local access to certain types of oak provides an excellent example of the emerging divergence between the traditional Venetian understanding of forests encoded in the laws and the new knowledge being generated by the *provveditori sopra boschi* through the cadastral surveys. Garzoni clearly possessed specialized expertise concerning forests, but long-standing Venetian conceptions concerning the scarcity of critical oak and beech timber still defined the limits of policy proposals.

The Council of Ten and the Senate stood on the side of tradition and the law. For their part, the *provveditori sopra boschi* possessed an increasing store of quantitative information that gave them a privileged view of the practical effects of the law on local forest ecologies. And Garzoni did not like what he saw. He was dismayed to discover that in many instances, state forests that Giustinian had surveyed in 1586 included far fewer oak trees than they ought in 1602. For example, in early 1603 Garzoni reported that the *bosco pubblico* near Morgan "should have contained approximately 36,000 oak according to Giustinian's survey and the records of all subsequent harvests. Yet I must report that there are only 28,238 living trees, along with 1,311 dead trunks and 1,230 half-dead oak."[92] Garzoni argued that some of the apparently missing oak was only missing on paper—the product of shoddy record-keeping. In a letter written two months later, he complained, "it is with incredible disappointment that I report that . . . nowhere in the *Catastico Giustinian*, which I keep by my side at all times, is there any record of the 100,000 or more oak that have been harvested since 1586, with the exception of a single notation concerning a mere six trees."[93] But poor clerical practice only accounted for a portion of the missing oak. Using the *Catastico Giustinian* as a benchmark for his own surveys, Garzoni identified a number of privately and institutionally owned forests that had been either partially or entirely cleared; he then prosecuted the owners. For example, in December 1602 Garzoni fined a landowner named Girolamo da Poz 200 ducats and ordered him to replant the fields he had illegally created out of forestland.[94]

For the Council of Ten, such reports confirmed what it already believed, namely, that mainland communities were guilty of poaching reserved timber and wasting valuable resources. For Garzoni, however, the numbers suggested something else entirely. In the case of the state forest near Morgan, he related how,

> after investigating the causes of the great number of dead and half-dead oak, I determined that it is due to the great thickness of the forest . . . and that the best way to preserve the trees is to remove the dead and half-dead poles so that the sun, with its heat, might warm

the live oak and the ground in which they were born, without any danger that they might die. In this way, after eight or ten years they will be large enough for the important work of the Arsenal.[95]

Thus, in Garzoni's view, the *bosco pubblico* near Morgan suffered not from overuse, but rather from underuse. Once again, Garzoni attempted to convince the Council of Ten that by issuing licenses to local users to take intermediate-grade oak, mainland residents would obtain the timber they required for local projects—and therefore would be less likely to steal from the Arsenal—and the naval-grade poles in forests such as the one near Morgan would get much-needed room to grow and become useful. In other words, Garzoni believed that by opening up the forests to carefully controlled local use, the Republic would enjoy higher and more reliable yields of crucial timber resources. Once again, the Council of Ten elected to remain silent on the matter.

Because Garzoni could not persuade his superiors in Venice of the wisdom of his plan, he decided to take matters into his own hands. Over the course of 1602, Garzoni identified twenty-eight privately and institutionally owned forests in the lower Piave that had been, in his estimation, badly managed by their owners. Garzoni used his power as *provveditore sopra boschi* to ban the stands and place them under the Arsenal's control. He then used them as a proving ground for his ideas about managing oak forests. Garzoni explained that he had chosen these twenty-eight forests because they contained "50,000 oak of every size and quality" that were threatened by private interests.[96] The first step Garzoni took was to seed the stands with acorns, in the hopes of aiding their recovery from the overly aggressive exploitation they had suffered since the *Catastico Giustinian*. Garzoni then implemented a series of reforms aimed at transforming the twenty-eight stands into multiple-use forests capable of providing oak for both local and state needs. Garzoni formalized a new set of usufruct rights for the stands that allowed the owners to harvest low- and intermediate-quality oak under the supervision of an Arsenal *proto*. He also asked the Council of Ten to approve crippling penalties for "those who clear-cut and transform forest into arable, which is the most deplorable sin that can be committed in the matter of oak."[97] In an effort to persuade his superiors that he acted in good faith and not out of selfish impulses, he pointed out that he had "distributed my entire share of all fines collected to date to the poor and to pious institutions."[98] Since his share consisted of the not inconsiderable sum of 614 ducats, the gesture was meaningful. Indeed, Garzoni's accounts show that he gave almost all the money he collected to the Hospedale dei Mendicanti and Venice's magdalene house—Santa Maria delle Convertite. Even so, the Council of Ten declined to endorse Garzoni's reforms, preferring to protect the traditional approach encoded in the fifteenth- and sixteenth-century laws governing practices of forest exploitation.

The Council of Ten was not the only skeptical audience that Garzoni faced in his efforts to promote a new set of ideas about forests and forest resources. Mainland residents proved equally difficult to convince that employing a different approach to forest management could protect the resources coveted by the Venetians while at the same time providing for local needs. As Garzoni continually remarked in his letters, there was little respect for Venetian forestry laws anywhere on the *terraferma*. Nevertheless, he drew a distinction between the actions of individual and institutional landowners and those of the rural communities, claiming he "never found that villages or peasants had deforested or taken large oak at the root."[99] Like most Venetian forestry officials, Garzoni understood that subjecting peasants to harsh punishments would undermine the entire enterprise of forest management; without informants willing to cooperate with the authorities, elites were free to clear-cut forests without fear of reprisal. Thus Garzoni claimed that he always strove for leniency when passing judgment on peasants and rural communities accused of misappropriating oak.

Garzoni's leniency, however, did not stop several rural communities from appealing directly to the Council of Ten to overturn many of his verdicts. For Garzoni, the peasants' actions represented a betrayal of his trust: "Had I applied the full penalties demanded by the law, I could have destroyed these villages. I therefore believed that it would not represent an offense to Your Serenity when I gave in to compassion and applied sentences that were more pious than just."[100] Moreover, as the list of sentences he submitted to the Council demonstrated, Garzoni invariably allowed rural communities to conceal the identity of lawbreakers and instead pay a token collective fine. But rural communities remained committed to seizing every opportunity to resist what they saw as an unjust abrogation of their usufruct rights. From the perspective of mainland peasants, it mattered little whether the culprits were local elites bent on converting forest to arable land or representatives of the Republic intent on protecting Arsenal resources. If they could stop the abuse through recourse to Venetian courts, they would. And peasants were not above casting aspersions about Garzoni's good faith and loyalty to the Republic to get what they wanted. For Garzoni, this too was a personal indignity that "freezes the very blood in my veins and will, without a doubt, cause me to die of grief."[101]

Histrionics aside, throughout his tenure as *provveditore sopra boschi*, Garzoni was forced to confront the fact that he was trapped between two irreconcilable views of mainland forest landscapes. The view from Venice was of irresponsible and profligate mainland residents who should be excluded from oak forests, lest they destroy what little was left of a resource that constituted one of the cornerstones of republican liberty. The view from the villages was of an overreaching state that should limit itself to protecting the poor from predatory elites and not add to the peasants' burdens by taking away their right to extract the basic necessities of life from local forests. For his part, Garzoni failed to convince either side that the best way to protect their respective interests in critical forest resources was for everyone to cooperate in a system of carefully regulated exploitation. Nevertheless, his correspondence with the Council of Ten demonstrates that by the turn of the seventeenth century, the *provveditori sopra boschi* were well on their way to developing an integrated view of forest management that accounted for metropolitan needs and local privilege alike. The *provveditori sopra boschi* continued to struggle to overcome the traditional view of mainland forests that dominated in the Ducal Palace well into the eighteenth century. In so doing, Venice's forest bureaucracy created new forms of quantitative and cartographic knowledge about mainland forests that allowed it to make increasingly refined judgments about the condition of the most important oak and beech reserves. It is to this expert knowledge and its uses that the next chapter turns.

CHAPTER FIVE

The Preservation and Reproduction of Bureaucratic Knowledge

> At the base of hill known as San Prosdocimo
> of Treviso, in the valley of Marich, we chose a
> boulder as the third survey marker. On it we
> carved C.X.[Council of Ten]3. Turning east we
> skirted the narrow ravine that leads to the hill
> known as Forcona. After 450 *passi* we reached
> the summit of the Forcona. From there one can
> see a large swath of the Trevigiano, including the
> pastures where livestock are watered and fed.
> Outside the forest, we placed a stone marker in
> the ground and carved C.X.4 on its face.

IN APRIL 1684 THE PATRICIAN Alvise Gritti appeared before the Council of Ten to discuss his recent tenure as the *provveditore al Montello*—the patrician supervisor of the oak harvest in the Montello reserve. Gritti's report included the by-now familiar litany of complaints about the bad habits of the residents of the thirteen villages that surrounded the reserve. In Gritti's estimation, the peasants "proceed to harvest with great energy their share of the harvest, but do not work with the same diligence to mark and transport the portion destined for the Arsenal."[1] He also pointed out that villagers routinely held the harvest hostage in order to force the Arsenal to pay them a bonus for completing the work, leaving the unguarded harvest "deep in the shadows and thick of the forest" and making it easy prey for thieves.[2] According to Gritti, local forest guardians did little to stop individuals from pilfering the Arsenal harvest because the position paid too little to attract any but "the worst sort of person."[3] He concluded that the combined effect of these abuses resulted in the fact that it took two years for requisitioned timber to make its way from the Montello to the Arsenal. Judging by Gritti's complaints, little had changed in the Montello since Giovanni Garzoni's cadastral survey in 1602. Some of the details in Gritti's report differed from those contained in Garzoni's letters, but the message remained substantially the same: local residents refused to comply with Venetian dictates and the Arsenal suffered as a consequence. In many respects, Venice's forest bureaucracy had settled into a comfortable routine of blaming mainland residents for problems with the timber supply while accepting painful delays in the delivery of Arsenal material as an unavoidable fact of life.

A closer examination of Gritti's report, however, reveals that the Venetians had made significant efforts to address the problems in the reserves by altering their approach to forest management over the course of the seventeenth century. If Gritti employed the well-worn rhetoric of his fifteenth- and sixteenth-century predecessors, he also displayed much more specific knowledge about the Montello itself than any of them had, as well as a considerable command of the issues and challenges involved in managing a large oak reserve. Not even the impressively thorough Garzoni—whose 1602 letters were analyzed in the previous chapter—could match Gritti's familiarity with the Montello. Gritti had at his fingertips an exact reckoning of every oak that had been felled in the reserve over the course of the previous three years, including scrap material that the Arsenal's agents had handed over to the thirteen communes surrounding the forest. Consequently, Gritti was also able to account for every Arsenal pole that had gone missing from the most recent harvests with considerable precision. He reported that 6,701 poles had been felled, but the *capitano del bosco* had counted only 6,606 on the ground, meaning that 95 had disappeared before a single pole had been removed from the reserve. Gritti then added that 5,116 had been loaded for transport once the lesser-quality poles had been sorted out at the embarcaderos. Finally, he relayed that only 4,369 were actually delivered to the shipyard, meaning that another 747 had gone missing en route (a marginal note indicates that another 55 trickled in after Gritti's appearance, bringing the total number missing to 692).

Gritti's ability to access and present such details reveals that the cadastral surveys had finally borne fruit in the form of useful data about the location and condition of oak trees throughout the *terraferma*. But the patrician managers' new emphasis on local facts was not limited to statistics drawn from the *catastici*. Gritti took it for granted that the Montello required active care outside of the Arsenal harvests, and that the thirteen communities had a legitimate claim on the material produced by thinning operations and other routine maintenance. By contrast, in 1602 the Council of Ten had summarily rejected the notion that the Montello forest should be touched except to harvest Arsenal material, despite Garzoni's eloquent entreaties. In fact, by the end of the seventeenth century, patrician officials such as Gritti had become recognized and reliable experts on the management of the Republic's forest reserves, possessing a knowledge of mainland forests, rooted in a vast trove of empirical information, that allowed them to make critical decisions about where and when to harvest in order to maximize future yields of important species.

This chapter will examine the factors that contributed to the creation of expertise in Venice's forest bureaucracy. Venetian bureaucratic experts stood out from their counterparts elsewhere in Europe both for their strong preference for direct observational knowledge and for their firsthand experience of technical problems. My argument is that the Venetian emphasis on empirical experience influenced the way in which experts such as Gritti communicated their knowledge to their superiors in the Ducal Palace. Throughout Europe, individuals claiming expertise presented themselves as the possessors of unique knowledge. Venetian officials eschewed such claims of individual knowledge, emphasizing instead that they were the spokesmen for the collective empirical knowledge of a large number of subordinates—including citizen secretaries, Arsenal *proti*, local woodcutters, forest guardians, and other anonymous participants in the enterprise of managing the Republic's vast forest reserves. This preference for collective knowledge over individual knowledge not only reflected the Venetians' republican ideals, which emphasized collective consensus as the foundation of social and political stability, but it also underlined their unwavering belief in the superiority of concrete experience over abstract theory. The chapter then analyzes the development of a pair of related technologies aimed at producing and reproducing new knowledge about mainland forests: the cadastral surveys and the accompanying cartographic representations of *boschi pubblici*. These technologies made it possible for the forest bureaucracy to store information about mainland timber for future use and thus were crucial to the creation of new forms of bureaucratic expertise in the seventeenth and eighteenth centuries. Finally, it examines the ways in which the forest bureaucracy made use of its increasing trove of information and the conclusions about proper forest management that the *provveditori sopra boschi* and other officials drew from it. Ultimately, I will argue that while the new sources of bureaucratic knowledge gave the *provveditori sopra boschi* considerable power to shape the way that individual reserves were managed, the overall approach to forestry remained deeply conservative. Traditional fears that precious timber resources would eventually run out profoundly affected the ways in which legislators interpreted the new quantitative data produced by the cadastral surveys. In the end, the cadastral surveys generated the impetus for continued conservation rather than increased exploitation of mainland forest resources.

Venetian Bureaucratic Expertise

Chapter 2 examined the Senate's response to recurrent fuel crises, culminating in the creation of the second incarnation of the *provveditori alle legne*. I would like to return briefly to the moment in 1454 when the Senate handed responsibility for the fuel supply to the firewood merchant Pietro Valier in the hopes that his knowledge of the trade would allow him to locate new sources of combustible material swiftly. In that instance, the Senate assigned Valier a budget of 1,000 ducats per annum and the political backing of the Ducal Palace, but little in the way of real institutional support. The Senate expected that the budget would cover all of his personal expenses in addition to payments to any agents or assistants he hired to help him discharge his duties. He could not ask for the assistance of Arsenal *proti*, citizen secretaries, or any other individuals in the Republic's service. He had to assemble and supervise his own collection of subordinates. Moreover, he did not have access to any sources of stored information or knowledge about mainland forests. There were no land registers, maps, or cadastral forest surveys for him to consult. The Republic's chancery did not possess any letters or reports by former officials for him to read. In short, Valier relied solely on his own experience in the trade as he set out to remedy the Republic's difficulties with the fuel supply. When the Senate elevated his successor Giorgio Venier to the new office of *provveditore alle legne* four years later, a bureaucracy had been created, but in terms of expertise the situation remained essentially unaltered. The sum total of the new firewood bureaucracy's knowledge was stored in the head of the individual patrician officeholder. Valier and Venier were not just the embodiment of everything the state knew about fuel and forests, they were the sole possessors of that knowledge.

Valier and Venier exemplify what the Venetians referred to as the *optime informati*, or "best informed men." These were individuals with personal experience in a matter of recognized importance. To use a modern term, they were experts.[4] Élisabeth Crouzet-Pavan has identified Marco Cornaro, whose 1442 treatise on the lagoon was discussed at length in chapter 2, as the prototypical *optimus informatus*, stressing his central role in the urban expansion of Venice in the first half of the fifteenth century.[5] But the importance of men such as Cornaro went well beyond the problems of water management and canal construction. In the fifteenth and early sixteenth centuries, the Republic relied heavily on *optime informati* to advise the Republic on issues ranging from diplomatic relations with the Porte to the design of industrial machines.[6] Their expertise was individual, particular, idiosyncratic, and above all empirical. No two *optime informati* possessed a common body of knowledge, because no two experts ever shared an identical set of experiences. Giorgio Venier and Pietro Valier probably had very different ideas about where the best sources of firewood were located and who the most reliable suppliers were. Yet in the eyes of the Senate they were equally qualified to manage the firewood supply because they both possessed personal, practical experience in the trade. In the short term, the differences of opinion that resulted from such idiosyncratic knowledge had few consequences, so long as the officeholder succeeded in his appointed task. As Venetian patricians, Venier's and Valier's loyalty to the Republic and its institutions mattered more than whether they agreed with each other about the details of where to find fuel.

Despite the effectiveness of individual *optime informati*, relying on individual knowledge regarding a vitally important problem—such as the management of the firewood supply—was untenable as a long-term administrative strategy. For bureaucratic knowledge to be truly useful it had to be both uniform and transferable; otherwise the state would always find itself beholden to its *optime informati* rather than the other way around. With respect to the firewood supply, the Senate recognized this problem from the outset and quickly moved to remedy the situation. In 1468, when it added a second patrician *provveditore* to the magistracy, the Senate deliberately staggered the terms of office of the firewood managers so that "the new officeholder might acquire the appropriate knowledge and information from the old."[7] In other words, the Republic's leaders wanted to ensure that the empirical expertise of men like Venier and Valier could be passed on to subsequent generations of *provveditori alle legne*, not all of whom would be former firewood merchants already privy to the secrets of the trade. Over the course of the sixteenth century, this transition away from individualized knowledge towards corporate knowledge would result in dramatic changes in both institutional organization and bureaucratic expertise.

By 1602, when Giovanni Garzoni departed Venice to conduct the third comprehensive cadastral survey of mainland oak forests, the Venetian forest bureaucracy had been completely transformed. Garzoni set out from the lagoon with an impressive retinue in tow. His state-supplied entourage included a large number of subordinate experts, each of whom had a specific and well-defined role to play in the survey. His secretaries took care of his correspondence, drew up legal documents, assisted at trials, recorded the results of the surveys in large bound registers, and compared the assembled data with records housed in local chanceries. They also mediated between the opinionated Garzoni and his sometimes testy superiors in the Council of Ten. The Arsenal *proti* and *sottoproti* did most of the actual work of measuring and counting trees and evaluating their suitability as Arsenal material. They also advised Garzoni on the harvest and transportation of timber and on other technical matters involving wood. In addition, Garzoni had at least one land surveyor with him on the expedition, whose task it was to survey the *boschi pubblici* and record their perimeters while the *proti* counted oak. As topographical maps became an important component in the process of tracking and regulating public forests during the second half of the seventeenth century, survey expeditions would come to include several cartographers who worked in conjunction with the surveyors to map the most important reserves. Garzoni also had an armed escort consisting of four men charged with protecting him from retribution by disaffected landowners and other local residents unhappy with his actions. Finally, at each stop on his tour Garzoni hired local labor to assist his team in placing identifiable stone survey markers and to help with other tasks related to the production of recognizable and measureable boundaries around state and community forests. At any one time, Garzoni would have been surrounded by at least a dozen assistants of various descriptions, and if one includes servants, the expedition probably numbered close to twenty-five men.

The difference between Garzoni's survey mission and the travels of fifteenth-century *provveditori alle legne* such as Venier and Valier went far beyond expedition size. As the sophistication of his letters to the Ten shows, Garzoni was undoubtedly an expert on forests, but the nature of his expertise differed significantly from that of his predecessors. Unlike the *optime informati* of an earlier era, *provveditori sopra boschi* such as Garzoni did not pretend to possess an intimate personal knowledge of every aspect of the timber supply system. Having served as *provveditori all'arsenale*, they were all acquainted with the importance of timber and understood at least the rudiments of the issues involved in timber acquisition, transportation, and quality—although they probably did not understand much more beyond this basic knowledge than any other Venetian patrician involved in politics. Yet in their correspondence with the Ducal Palace, they invariably showed the same nuanced grasp of forest management as Giovanni Garzoni. More importantly, the *provveditori sopra boschi* agreed to a man about the shortcomings of Venice's forest management regime. Their knowledge was no longer idiosyncratic. Rather, it had become almost entirely consistent and uniform. Individual *provveditori* might differ in terms of which factors they wished to emphasize in their reports—for some it was the greed of landowners, for others the need for more rigorous thinning or stricter accountability during the harvest—but they drew from a shared set of ideas about how best to confront the challenges they faced. By the turn of the seventeenth century Venetian forestry officials had concluded that the only way to guarantee future yields was through the active management of mainland forests. By embracing this type of managerial approach, the forest bureaucracy rejected the passive conservation program that the Republic had adopted in the fifteenth and early sixteenth centuries. One crucial factor was that, despite their apparent lack of deep personal experience with forests, the *provveditori sopra boschi* did not hesitate to assert strong claims to technical knowledge about forest landscapes. They consistently pointed out that they had observed the forests in person and that their advice was grounded in empirical experience. Indeed, as the last chapter showed, Garzoni was willing to stake his reputation—at least rhetorically—on the quality of the advice he was offering to the Council of Ten when he pointed out that earlier surveys had counted oak indiscriminately instead of distinguishing between Arsenal-grade material and scrap, saying "I am certain of this, as I am certain that I am rendering faithful service to the Republic and jealously guarding its interests by pointing it out to you."[8]

These confident and authoritative claims to an empirical knowledge of forests and a shared perspective on forest management draw attention to how successful the Venetians had been at creating a new kind of bureaucratic expertise over the course of the sixteenth and seventeenth centuries. The *provveditori sopra boschi*'s expertise was no longer that of the *optime informati*. They had not spent years purchasing timber or negotiating leases on community forests. They did not claim to possess unique personal knowledge that no one else could offer the state. Instead, their claims were grounded in the practical knowledge of others. This knowledge was impersonal, in the sense that every patrician who held the office enjoyed access to it. But it was also empirical, in the sense that it was a product of the combined individual experiences of hundreds of Arsenal *proti*, forest guardians, lumberjacks, cartographers, land surveyors, and patrician officeholders. In other words, when a *provveditore sopra boschi* appeared before the Council of Ten, he was the public face of the collective empirical knowledge of a vast network of mostly anonymous individuals whose first-hand experiences and observations had been amassed and stored for future use by Venice's forest bureaucracy. All concerned understood the fact that the *provveditori sopra boschi* were the official conduits for the empirical expertise of others, and the patrician officeholders did not attempt to take personal credit by disguising the contributions of their subordinates. In a few cases they even mentioned the *proti* and other assistants by name, or attached addenda written by the *proti* to their own reports. For example, in 1548 the Council of Ten dispatched two former *provveditori all'arsenale* named Bernardino Vettori and Francesco Duodo to locate prospective beech reserves on the mainland and in Istria. When Vettori and Duodo presented their findings to the Ten, they not only named the three master oarmakers who had accompanied them on their expedition, but they also attached a separate report penned by the three men, Alessio di Mathio, Luca di Nicolò, and Marco di Zuane, to the text of their speech before the Council.[9] The fact that the oarmakers' report contained far greater detail —including precise yield estimates for the Cansiglio forest—than the patricians' more formal presentation underscores the degree to which the expertise possessed by the *provveditori* was a product of the aggregated empirical knowledge of their underlings. Vettori and Duodo furnished the political capital necessary to make a compelling case before the Republic's most powerful body, but without Alessio, Luca, and Marco's knowledge as a foundation, their oration meant little. That the patrician *provveditore sopra boschi* so often needed to defer to his subordinates' superior knowledge is yet another reason why former *provveditori all'arsenale* made ideal *provveditori sopra boschi*, as they were already accustomed to leaning on the technical expertise of the shipyard's master craftsmen.

Far from being a cause for embarrassment, it was the very fact that the forest bureaucracy's knowledge was the product of the first-hand experiences of innumerable men of humble birth that made it trustworthy in the eyes of the Council of Ten and the Senate. In contrast to northern European states, which continued to rely on the self-professed expertise of men from outside the circles of government well into the eighteenth century, the Venetians valued the local bureaucratic expertise of men such as Giovanni Garzoni and Alvise Gritti. This preference was most pronounced in fields requiring technical mastery, such as forest and water management. While other states relied on aristocratic natural philosophers like Thomas Digges, or foreign experts such as the famous Dutch *dykmeister* Cornelius Vermuyden, to manage harbors and major land-reclamation projects, the Venetians relied exclusively on the empirical knowledge of homegrown experts whose knowledge was produced and sanctioned by the Republic, rather than by an outside institution such as England's Royal Society.[10] Furthermore, while northern states preferred their experts to be well-born (or at least be able to socialize with the well-bred), the Republic's leaders willingly and openly relied on citizens and craftsmen as much as they did on gentlemen of their own class. Indeed, in contrast to the aristocratic knowledge being produced by northern European institutions, Venetian bureaucratic expertise had a decidedly republican flavor.[11] The Venetians were by no means egalitarian—only the patrician officeholder could mount the rostrum in the Ducal Palace to deliver reports and receive applause—but to a far greater extent than other early modern states, Venice actively sought to take advantage of the technical skills and knowledge of artisans and skilled craftsmen. At the very least, the fact that they heavily privileged empirical knowledge made the Venetians more willing to recognize publicly the contributions of men such as Alessio di Mathio, Luca di Nicolò, and Marco di Zuane. Cornelius Vermuyden and his ilk undoubtedly relied just as heavily on craft experts as their Venetian counterparts. They merely sought to disguise that dependence as much as possible to protect their prestige and social status and bolster their claims to personal genius. The Venetian patricians who held the office of *provveditore sopra boschi* did not have to concern themselves with the possibility of losing social status through their association with vulgar craftsmen, as they were dealing with like-minded peers serving in a republican system where the collective nature of bureaucratic knowledge was seen as a source of strength. Nor did they have to fear being exposed as less knowledgeable than some other competing expert, for their claim to expertise was seen as impersonal and therefore immune to assault from outside the Republic's ruling institutions.

Even so, the degree to which the Venetians achieved consensus within the forest bureaucracy remains remarkable. After all, experts can and do disagree. And in seventeenth- and eighteenth-century Europe numerous rifts did develop between craft specialists and aristocratic experts, and between proponents of the new science and defenders of traditional forms of knowledge.[12] Yet in Venice, violent disagreements among bureaucratic experts remained rare. The Council of Ten often rejected specific pieces of advice from the forest bureaucracy, but the Republic's leaders never impugned the personal expertise of the *provveditori* and their subordinates. Nor did *provveditori sopra boschi* attack one another, or seek to undermine each other's individual credibility. As suggested here, this implicit consensus was partly a function of the fact that their expertise was a product of the Republic's institutions and therefore sanctioned by the state, which meant that to undermine the claims of one *provveditore sopra boschi* was to undermine them all. But the corporate basis of Venetian expertise constitutes an insufficient explanation for Venetian unanimity, as it is easy to imagine that individual *provveditori* might receive conflicting advice from their subordinates and therefore present contradictory findings to their superiors in the Ducal Palace. This sometimes happened in the sixteenth century, before the *provveditori sopra boschi* had become firmly established as the most important magistracy in Venice's forest bureaucracy. For example, as will be discussed presently, Giovanni Garzoni—operating on the advice of his *proti*—decided on an idiosyncratic classification system for his 1602 cadastral survey. But as the magistracy's collective knowledge became more firmly entrenched in the seventeenth century, such incidents became far less frequent, and the forest bureaucracy achieved a remarkable degree of consensus concerning the central problems of forest management.

Two technologies aimed at preserving and reproducing the knowledge generated by the forest bureaucracy helped to define and shape the boundaries of this emerging expert consensus concerning forest management. The comprehensive cadastral surveys of oak allowed the *provveditori sopra boschi* to envision what specific mainland forests had looked like twenty, forty, even a hundred years in the past and thus make critical judgments about the efficacy of the Republic's conservation efforts and the effects of local practices of forest exploitation. Topographical and narrative maps of the *boschi pubblici* gave bureaucrats a different view of the history of mainland forests and allowed them to track deforestation across the decades by charting changes in the boundaries of important stands. Together, these two technologies eventually allowed the *provveditori sopra boschi* and the Council of Ten to decide where and when to harvest timber with an eye towards preserving forest resources for future use. In addition, the quantitative surveys and maps helped create a common source of information on which the *provveditori sopra boschi* could base their proposals for reforming state and local practices. Most importantly, these two technologies helped to generate consensus within Venice's forest bureaucracy by creating a single, precise, historical narrative about what had happened to mainland forests beginning in 1569—the year of the first comprehensive cadastral survey. Indeed, one way that the *provveditori sopra boschi* attempted to use the maps and surveys was as a natural history of *terraferma* oak forests presented in actuarial terms. For Venetian patricians—especially the Republic's leaders—the belief that the narrative was grounded in a presumptively accurate empirical account of changes in mainland forest cover that had been generated by the collective efforts of republican institutions endowed it with its power and authority. In other words, both the narrative's empiricism and its inherent republicanism made it more trustworthy than a similar account presented by an outside expert such as Digges or Vermuyden would have been. For the bureaucracy, the narrative offered the key to creating a consensus about forest management, because it offered a single coherent account of almost everything that had happened to mainland oak forests since 1569. And once the *provveditori sopra boschi* and their subordinates agreed on exactly what had changed in the forest and why, they were far more likely to agree on what needed to be done to ensure the preservation of regional forest cover for future use.[13]

The Cadastral Surveys and the Preservation of Collective Knowledge

The Senate assigned the first comprehensive cadastral survey of mainland oak forests to the patrician Nicolò Surian in May of 1565.[14] Four years later, in the autumn of 1569, Surian delivered the results of his survey to the Ducal Palace in the form of seven enormous folio volumes containing an astonishing array of quantitative data about oak trees throughout the *terraferma*.[15] Over the course of four years, Surian had visited nearly every important jurisdiction on the mainland with the exception of the district of Brescia. Starting in the district of Vicenza in the west, working his way through the lower and middle Piave regions, and ending in the Friuli in the east, Surian and his team counted each and every oak tree they saw, including saplings and low-grade growth of insufficient quality for use in shipbuilding, and marked them all with a seal designating them as Arsenal property. Surian was clearly guilty of excessive zeal. The terms of his commission had been simply to "report on the number and condition of oak in the *Serenissima*'s dominions," but he had gone far beyond that.[16] He had not limited his efforts to forests. Rather, he set out to count every single living oak on the mainland, including those in windbreaks and in village squares. Surian's devotion to his task established a clear precedent for all the *provveditori sopra boschi* who would follow in his footsteps. Anything less than a complete account of standing oak trees became unacceptable after 1569.

But the standard set by Surian and his team went far beyond simply counting every oak tree in sight. Together with his *proti* and secretaries, Surian had created a new taxonomy for oak that would serve as the model for all subsequent cadastral surveys. His survey recorded the trees by size, quality, and location. Each page of the registers contained counts for individual forests or for sections of forest. At the top of each folio, the secretaries identified the jurisdiction in which forests stood by *podestaria*, territory, and locale (the nearest village or town). The heading of each entry recorded the ownership of the land on which the trees grew. In the case of community forests and *boschi pubblici*, the secretaries also recorded an estimate of the perimeter of the stand in question expressed in *perteghe*—a measure of length that varied between 1.56 meters and 2.086 meters, depending on locale. Underneath the heading, as many as fifteen rows of information were devoted to oak trees. The survey divided Arsenal oak by girth. Up to nine of the rows recorded every oak with a circumference between one and five feet, listed in half-foot increments. Larger exemplars were simply included in the five-foot row. Smaller growth was broken down into the categories of seedlings and saplings. A separate row was devoted to *stortami*—the crooked timbers that supplied the critical knees and rib sections of the hull. Finally, a row was assigned to *tolpi*—lower-quality poles that were unsuitable for naval construction but ideal for use as structural piles in breakwaters and other lagoon infrastructure. The secretaries who prepared the registers recorded all the data on the left-hand folios, leaving the right folios blank. In theory, every time the Arsenal requisitioned oak from a specific forest, one of the secretaries of the Council of Ten was supposed to note the details of the requisition on the blank folio opposite the page on which the data for the forest in question had been recorded. In practice this rarely happened. A comprehensive review of all the registers stored in the Archivio di Stato in Venice reveals that there were perhaps a dozen such notations in all.

Despite the clear emphasis on quantification, some qualitative information crept into the registers. The secretaries who prepared the schedules often added brief notes concerning particular forests. These notes constitute a record of the *proti*'s observations about factors that they thought merited attention but did not fit under any of the quantitative rubrics. The issues that the *proti* sought to include in this miscellaneous row ranged from the soil quality and terrain characteristics of the forest in question to its propensity to flood (a major threat to oak forests, which require well-drained soil), and the density of growth in the stand. In later surveys, the *proti* employed such notations to observe discrepancies between what they had seen and the information contained in older *catastici*. And in the eighteenth century, the *proti* also asked the secretaries to record any maintenance they had performed in the stand while surveying it. These notes open an invaluable window onto the collection and collation of the survey data, because they offer some of the only descriptive accounts of what the surveyors thought about what they had seen. More importantly, these notations represent one of the few records left by the hundreds of anonymous *proti* who performed most of the actual survey work, and therefore constitute the best evidence for the involvement of craft experts in the production of one of the most important forms of bureaucratic knowledge regarding forests.

All subsequent *catastici* followed Surian's template. The most common addition to Surian's model was the expansion of the number of rows devoted to Arsenal oak. For example, the 1741 *Catastico Tron*—which surveyed forests in the Friuli—counted poles up to nine feet in circumference in half-foot increments. In part this reflected a growing interest in the data. It also reflects important changes in naval technology. Extremely large poles were unsuitable for building the galleys that made up the backbone of the Venetian fleet in the sixteenth century. But the two- and three-deck heavy frigates turned out by the Arsenal in the late seventeenth and eighteenth centuries required much larger planking that could only come from poles of correspondingly greater girth, and the *provveditori sopra boschi* altered their taxonomic system in response to the need for much larger and more mature poles. In his 1602 survey of the lower Piave and Friuli forests Giovanni Garzoni also added a row recording the distance from the forest in question to the nearest navigable waterway expressed in miles—an innovation that made its way into nearly every subsequent *catastico*. All these taxonomic refinements reflect not only changing demand, but also the escalating specificity of the data being collected by the survey teams. The more the *provveditori sopra boschi* learned about mainland oak forests, the more they desired to know. And while they did not subject these data to the same modes of analysis as nineteenth- and twentieth-century statisticians, they clearly believed that numbers represented an important tool for producing useful knowledge about the natural world.

The *Catastico Surian* represented a watershed moment in the development of Venice's forestry regime. After 1569, the Republic's leaders displayed a marked preference for quantitative data over the kinds of qualitative descriptions that had characterized forest surveys dating back to Marco Cornaro's 1442 treatise. The decision to conduct such an exhaustive quantitative survey must have been Surian's, for nowhere in his commission did the Senate demand that he count every single oak tree he encountered—regardless of size, quality, or location—much less invent a complex taxonomy to interpret the exhaustive data he and his team had assembled. Indeed, at the same time that Surian and his staff were counting and marking trees in the district of Vicenza, another former *patrone all'arsenale* named Antonio Moro was conducting a similar survey in Istria under identical orders from the Senate.[17] Yet in spite of the fact that both men received the same instructions, Moro's survey looked quite different from Surian's. Moro and his chief assistant, an Arsenal *proto* named Piero Lando, visited the most important oak forests on the peninsula, including the Montona reserve. Like Surian, they had their subordinates mark the best poles with an official seal and keep track of the trees they had seen. But they returned to Venice with only a gross count of Istrian oak. They made no effort to distinguish between mature and immature growth, much less to break the trees down into fifteen separate categories accounting for both girth and quality. Clearly the Senate's instruction to "report on the number and condition of oak in the *Serenissima*'s dominions" could be interpreted in very different ways. For Surian it meant establishing a precisely elaborated, systematic rendering of every oak tree, large and small, while for Moro and Lando it meant offering a descriptive account of what they had seen, with a few gross and presumably rough counts appended.

The crucial differences between these two approaches to surveying underscore the degree to which Surian's survey represented a wholly new way of engaging with forest landscapes. The *Catastico Surian* offered the

Senate and the Council of Ten a complete inventory of oak in the coastal plain of the *terraferma*, along with a few marginal notes containing descriptive information. The *Catastico Lando*, as it became known, consisted almost entirely of descriptive accounts, including a considerable amount of demographic information—something that Surian clearly saw as immaterial, as he made no effort to collect such data.[18] Lando's report contained estimates of the human population, the number of hearths, and the number of working carts and wagons in each district he and Moro had visited. They had also counted the number of livestock on the peninsula. Lando's reports reveal that there were approximately seven large domesticated animals for every adult male in Istria, a ratio that only increased when "alien animals are brought across the border to pasture in our forests."[19] Clearly Lando and Moro thought that such information was critical, especially in light of the long-standing proscriptions against pasturing livestock in forests. Likewise, they were interested in the demographic data because of the clear relationship between population density and pressure on forest resources, and because the size of the available labor pool affected how much timber the Arsenal could expect to extract from the Montona and other Istrian forests in a given year. They counted the number of wagons and carts for the same reason, because such vehicles determined how much timber could be moved from the forest to the embarcadero on the River Quieto. Lando and Moro had obeyed the Senate's injunction to pay attention to numbers, but they had concentrated on those figures that affected the efficiency of the harvest, rather than trying to convey a precise measure of the available oak. Moreover, for Lando and Moro these data revealed but a single aspect of a complex problem, the full extent of which could only be conveyed through descriptive accounts of what they had seen. By contrast, for Surian the numbers took center stage, both as the primary concern of his survey and as the key to understanding mainland forest landscapes. Surian's focus on quantification to the exclusion of qualitative descriptions emerged in part from the conditions he encountered on his tour. In the densely inhabited districts of the lower Piave, population statistics had little relevance. For Surian the problem was not the labor supply or the number of available vehicles—both of which were relatively plentiful—but the oak supply, and his decision to focus exclusively on trees reflects a recognition of some of the limits of qualitative descriptions of forest landscapes as a management tool.

Moro and Lando were heirs to a long tradition of Venetian surveys that focused on lively chronicles of trees and terrain, but Surian's strikingly novel survey technique determined that the future of Venetian forest management would be based on numbers, not words. Descriptions would always be welcomed, especially as part of the formal presentation that every *provveditore sopra boschi* gave upon his return to Venice. But the Republic's forest bureaucracy increasingly placed its trust in the numbers and not in language, no matter how evocative, in large part because its members saw the numbers as both more precise and more empirical than personal accounts. To see how influential the quantitative data became, one need only examine the manifold fashions in which Venetian officials put them to use. The *provveditori sopra boschi* used the data contained in the surveys in three significant ways: to track changes in the total number of oak in the Republic's territory, to track changes in the density of specific stands, and to monitor the area covered by oak forests.

The traditional descriptive surveys had also attempted to monitor such changes, but viewed from the perspective of the Republic's institutions—especially its courts—the numbers produced powerful empirical evidence of alterations in mainland forests that could be used to enforce existing laws in ways that mere descriptions could not. By comparing the gross counts in two or more surveys, Venetian officials could track both the overall supply of oak and the composition of individual forests across several decades. What individual officials made of the numbers depended on the specific position they occupied within the Republic's complex institutional framework. Legislators in the Ducal Palace tended to see the numbers in extremely simplistic terms. They were most interested in the gross counts, because they believed that these offered the most general picture of the health of mainland forests without the distraction of local context. For their part, the *provveditori sopra boschi* were far more interested in monitoring highly specific local changes in identifiable forests than they were in the gross counts. For example, in 1684 Alvise Gritti used the most recent survey of the Montello—the *Catastico Canal*—as a benchmark to estimate how many poles the Arsenal had removed from the reserve in recent seasons, how many re-mained standing in the Republic's most important *bosco pubblico*, and how much material had gone missing. In other words, Gritti sought to track not only the progress of harvested poles out of the forest and down-stream to the lagoon, but also to monitor changes in the number and approximate distribution of oak trees in the reserve. In addition, the *provveditori sopra boschi* paid close attention to the perimeter surveys—especially with respect to Arsenal reserves. By comparing new surveys with the data stored in the older *catastici*, they tried to keep track of any changes in the total area of important forests. For example, in 1604 Giovanni Garzoni brought a case against "Friulian nobles who have erad-icated four or five *campi* worth of forest."[20] The perimeter estimates stored in the 1586 *Catastico Giustinian* supplied the key piece of evi-dence in the case. By comparing that information with the surveys con-ducted by his own team of *proti*, Garzoni was not only able to demon-strate that illegal clearance had taken place, he was also able to offer a presumptively accurate estimate of how much forest had been abusively cut down. Although, without the testimony of eyewitnesses, he could not state with precision exactly when the crime had taken place, he was among the first Venetian officials to mount a successful prosecution with-out recourse to an informant. In this regard, the cadastral surveys fur-nished officials with a new and powerful weapon with which to pursue lawbreakers. Even more importantly, the empirical basis and presump-tive accuracy of Garzoni's estimate of the area of missing forest meant that the conviction was more likely to survive the inevitable appeals to higher courts in Venice. Lastly, because punitive fines were based on the surface area that had been clear-cut, specific data concerning how much forest had once stood on a particular piece of land allowed him to make the most of his opportunity to assess heavy penalties against the local elites he so despised.

For the *provveditori sopra boschi*, the data stored in the cadastral sur-veys told a story about changes in mainland forests. With each successive survey, the story acquired new detail, depth, and sophistication. The *provveditori* initially interpreted the data in much the same way as the legislators—through the lens of the longstanding Venetian narrative about the decline of forest resources. By the turn of the seventeenth cen-tury, however, they began to see the information stored in the *catastici* in a new light, because they had finally accumulated sufficient knowledge to see some of the shortcomings of the traditional story. As noted in the last chapter, Giovanni Garzoni repeatedly emphasized that he took the 1586 *Catastico Giustinian* with him everywhere he went, using it as a benchmark for evaluating the new data being assembled by his own survey team. As his surveyors gathered and compiled more and more valuable data, Garzoni began to identify an increasing number of what he considered to be crucial flaws in the Republic's program of forest management. In February of 1603, for example, Garzoni wrote to the Ten concerning his recent inspection of the *bosco pubblico di Morgan*: "Based on the *Catastico Giustinian* I expected to find 36,000 oak, but instead found a mere 28,238 living trees, 1,311 dead trees, and 1,230 half-dead and miserable oak."[21] Garzoni attributed the discrepancy to a combination of bad record-keeping and poor maintenance in the stand. He argued strenuously that the Morgan reserve needed "to be cleared of bent and stunted growth, which is the main reason so many plants are withering."[22] The letter vividly illustrates some of the ways in which the new techniques of data collection pioneered by Surian in 1569 allowed later *provveditori sopra boschi* like Garzoni to create powerful new narratives about what was happening in mainland forests. For the Council of Ten a shortfall of nearly 8,000 trees simply confirmed the traditional view of forest resources as constantly dwindling, while for Garzoni, the same cadastral data told a story about a bureaucratic failure to properly manage critical oak resources. At the same time as the Council of Ten girded itself for still more austere conservation measures, Garzoni advised cutting down even more trees to create room for high-quality oak to reach useful maturity.

As his team continued to collect data in the region's oak forests, Garzoni continued to compare what they had found with the information stored in the *Catastico Giustinian*. The more discrepancies he discovered, the more convinced he became that the traditional approach to forest management, based on negative proscriptions and absolute bans, was partly to blame for the condition of many *boschi pubblici*. In April 1603 he returned even more forcefully to the issue of immature growth in state reserves. Garzoni argued that the Republic needed to be far more selective about applying the Arsenal *bollo* to oak trees under five feet in diameter.[23] Many such trees were branded, he argued, but few ever realized their potential as shipbuilding material. By reserving only the trees of the highest quality, Garzoni contended, the Arsenal would protect its own interests while at the same time making more material available for local use. Once again Garzoni, after consulting the cadastral data, concluded that higher yields could be achieved by harvesting more trees than could ever be achieved by traditional proscriptions.

Garzoni was reluctant to base his argument solely on the numbers, so he peppered his letters with references to the preservation of republican liberty and the protection of the public interest that were carefully calculated to appeal to his audience in the Ducal Palace. Yet a close examination of the data in the three cadastral surveys that had been conducted to date reveals exactly why Garzoni came to believe that the traditional story about declining forests had led the forest bureaucracy astray. Despite the shortfalls in individual stands, such as the Morgan reserve, Garzoni's team had counted far more Arsenal-grade oak in the district's ten *boschi pubblici* than either of his two predecessors, Giustinian and Surian—82,270, to be precise (see figure 5.1). Thus the gross counts supplied some cause for optimism. At the same time, less than half of this total—29,818 trees—consisted of Arsenal-ready poles, with the remainder still too immature for use in naval construction. In his April 1603 letter, Garzoni explained why the preponderance of immature poles offered cause for concern. As he patiently explained to his superiors in Venice, only a fraction of the remaining 52,452 poles would ever achieve the necessary size and quality for use as Arsenal material. Better to cut them down, he contended, than to leave them standing and allow them to choke out the best trees. He concluded his letter by pointing out that the lower-quality material could still be used as piles in the breakwaters and other lagoon infrastructure, or distributed to local communities that would then be less likely to poach good timber from the state reserves. Rather than constructing the kind of simple narrative of decline or progress favored by legislators, Garzoni sought to use the new knowledge embedded in the surveys to tell a far more nuanced story about why the *boschi pubblici* looked the way they did in 1602 and how the state should act to ensure that they would generate greater yields in the future.

To a sophisticated reader such as Garzoni, the data on community and private property told an even more complex tale. His survey revealed that the forty-two community forests in the district actually held nearly five times as many Arsenal-grade oak trees—389,408—as the *boschi*

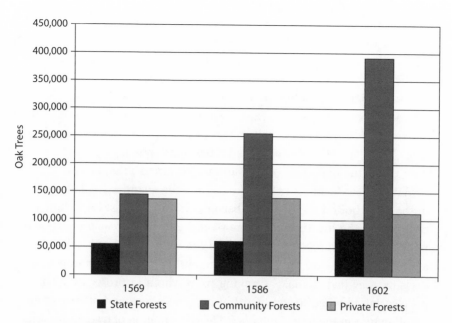

FIGURE 5.1 Oak supply
Total number of oak trees in the *boschi pubblici*, community forests, and privately owned forests in the district of Treviso, as recorded in the first three *catastici*.
SOURCE: ASV, *Provveditori ai Boschi*, B. 128, 134, and 141.

pubblici, despite the fact that villagers and other local residents enjoyed significant access rights in those forests. Just as in the case of the Arsenal reserves, Garzoni's total represented a marked increase over the previous two cadastral surveys. As was established in the last chapter, Garzoni tirelessly defended more humble rural residents against the traditional accusation that their actions contributed directly to the disappearance of critical forest resources. In fact, the cadastral data suggested that, contrary to conventional wisdom in Venice, community forests offered a relatively safe haven for the best oak to reach maturity as Arsenal-grade timber. Interpreted this way, the data fully supported Garzoni's argument that rural communities were the Republic's allies in the struggle to preserve precious resources. Moreover, the 318 private and institutional forests in the district contained 27,991 fewer oak trees than they had in 1568. More importantly, a mere 38,089 of these poles were Arsenal grade, a decrease of 20,767 with respect to the *Catastico Giustinian*. The fact that the number of oak trees in privately owned stands was in decline at the same time as the number in community and state forests was on the rise must have provided Garzoni with a powerful confirmation for his oft-repeated contention that landowning elites posed a greater danger to forest resources than rural communities. After thirty-four years and three cadastral surveys, the *provveditori sopra boschi* moved to challenge Venetian orthodoxy concerning the threat posed by peasant communities to the Republic's conservation efforts in mainland forests.

Within a century of the *Catastico Surian*, the quantitative data stored in the large bound registers had become the single most important repository for the institutional memory of the forest bureaucracy. By the middle of the seventeenth century, the *provveditori sopra boschi* relied almost exclusively on the cadastral surveys for nearly every important decision they had to make—ranging from whom to prosecute for illegal clearing to when to conduct thinning operations and other routine maintenance in the *boschi pubblici*. The combination of tree counts and perimeter surveys allowed officials to reconstruct the history of specific forests in considerable detail and then put that history to work for them in the courts or during the harvest.

The Cadastral Surveys as Natural Historical Narrative

By the end of the seventeenth century, individual *provveditori* possessed enough information to see nearly 150 years into the past of nearly every *bosco pubblico* and community forest on the mainland. And what they saw told a powerful story about the Republic's efforts to secure and conserve critical forest resources. For example, in 1726 Antonio Nani's *catastico* revealed that the total area covered by *boschi pubblici* in the district of Treviso had nearly doubled since the *Catastico Garzoni* in 1602—from approximately 241 hectares to approximately 441 hectares.[24] The significant increase in the total forested area of the *boschi pubblici* offered a lucid demonstration of just how effective Venice's forestry regime had been at both preserving and expanding the system of *boschi pubblici*, even in one of the most densely populated areas of the *terraferma*. Nonetheless, legislators in the Ducal Palace voiced their dismay at the discovery that the total number of Arsenal-ready oak trees in those stands had declined to slightly less than half that reported by Garzoni in a 1604 letter—13,403 as compared to 29,818. For an informed reader like Nani, however, the dramatic decline in the density of oak in the *boschi pubblici* revealed a more ambiguous situation. On the one hand, Nani remained keenly aware that in 1726 the Republic was only six years removed from nearly forty years of uninterrupted war with the Ottoman Empire, and he hypothesized that the low densities in the stands were likely the natural result of sustained wartime production in the Arsenal. On the other hand, as Garzoni had pointed out more than a century earlier, high counts could often be misleading, because not every oak tree would mature into an Arsenal-grade pole. Indeed, the eighteenth-century forest bureaucracy had begun to incorporate the practice of selective thinning into the cadastral surveys. For example, the *proti*'s marginal notations in the *Catastico Nani* record frequent instances of the aggressive removal of low-quality growth from state and community stands. In that context, the lower stand densities of 1726 would have suggested to Nani that he was viewing a healthier set of forests for producing Arsenal-grade oak than the ones that Garzoni had visited in 1602.

From Nani's perspective, the condition of community forests told a similarly positive story, but for different reasons. The proportion of Arsenal-ready oak in community forests was nearly identical to that found in the Arsenal reserves—46,288 in 1602 versus 21,541 in 1726—again a decline of slightly more than half. However, the total area covered by community forests had shrunk considerably since 1602—from approximately 2,364 hectares in 1602 to approximately 1,250 hectares in 1726—a painful reminder of the fact that the fiscal strain of the recent wars had forced the Republic to sell vast areas of *beni comuni* to balance the public ledgers.[25] The fact that the sale of public land had not resulted in a precipitous decline in the number of Arsenal-ready oak in community forests provides a clear indication of the increasing institutional power of the forest bureaucracy. Indeed, the survival of these oak trees suggests that for the most part, only marginal lands that did not contain valuable forest resources had gone on the block. Looking back at the changes that had taken place in the state and community forests of the Trevigiano since the *Catastico Garzoni*, Antonio Nani could see that despite the alterations in the total wooded area, the forest bureaucracy had succeeded in preserving many healthy oak forests. Therefore, the story that Nani could tell about both community and state forests was an overwhelmingly positive one that served as a confirmation of the forest management schemes that the *provveditori sopra boschi* had tirelessly promoted throughout the seventeenth century.

The history contained in the *catastici* looked quite different for the private and the institutional lands. Over the course of the seventeenth century, tracking and measuring private and institutional forests had proven far more challenging than those on public lands, because the Republic's interest in conservation so often came into conflict the owners' interest in profit. As private and institutional landowners sought to derive greater returns from their property, they repeatedly engaged in surreptitious clearing for cropland. The first step usually involved the intentional eradication of oak trees, because forests with no oak were not included in the cadastral survey. And once a forest had dropped out of the surveys, the owners could clear-cut it with impunity in order to convert the land to more remunerative uses. As Nani pointed out during his appearance before the Senate, "the owners of private forests have made every effort to ensure that softwoods dominate at the expense of oak, a practice that does not represent an innovation of our own time."[26] The *catastici* bore silent witness to the steady disappearance of oak from private forests. In 1602 Garzoni counted 318 distinct pieces of privately owned forest in the lower Piave, while Nani found only 53 in 1726. In addition, in Nani's survey those 53 stands covered a mere 170 hectares and contained a scant 15,940 Arsenal-ready oak trees, whereas Garzoni had counted 34,089 on nearly 3,000 hectares. The narrative concerning private and institutional forests contained in the *catastici* was one of abject failure on the part of the Republic's institutions. In fact, in the light of the *Catastico Nani*, Garzoni's dire predictions about the fate of oak on private property appear prophetic. Nani promised to investigate what had happened to the thousands of missing *campi*, but he was pessimistic that anything would come of it. "At the distance of more than a century," he lamented, "I cannot hope for a profitable conclusion."[27] Indeed, in some areas he was the first *provveditore sopra boschi* to pass through since 1663, and in a later letter he pointed out that "the silence of 63 years is far too great for there to be any hope that the public interest in these private forests might once again be renewed."[28] Nani was particularly fond of using metaphors of speech when referring to the data in the *catastici*. Nani depicted the registers as "holding their silence" or "recounting the events," suggesting that he thought they were telling a story and that he knew how to hear it. Nani believed that this ability to listen to and interpret the tales contained in the surveys was exclusive to *provveditori sopra boschi* and distinguished them from other officials in the forest bureaucracy. Unfortunately, he was also forced to acknowledge that the stories that the numbers had told him included significant lacunae, especially when it came to private and institutional property.

The challenges facing Nani and his survey teams as they tried to reconstruct the fate of the Trevigiano's privately owned forests in the seventeenth century underscore the degree to which the cadastral data represented a problematic repository of knowledge. As Nani admitted in his correspondence with officials in the Ducal Palace, the records for private and institutional property were far from complete. But the gaps in the data were not simply a product of irregular inspections. From the information contained in the registers, it is apparent that the survey teams spent far more time examining state and community forests than they did private and institutional lands. This disparity in effort is most evident in the perimeter surveys. The *proti* established and recorded the perimeters of community forests and *boschi pubblici* in exacting detail. The registers include both an estimate of the total length of the perimeter and a pace-by-pace account of the perimeter itself, with references to recognizable local landmarks. By contrast, for private and institutional forests the registers offered only an estimate of the total length of the perimeter, with no references to local landmarks or other contextual information that would have made it possible for later survey teams to reconstruct either their predecessors' itinerary or the exact location of the forest in question. Faced with such an imbalanced record, the *provveditori sopra boschi* came to the natural conclusion that community and state forests were far better preserved than their private and institutional counterparts. This is not to say that Garzoni's concerns about private and institutional landowners were ill-founded. Given the opportunity, many landowners were pleased to convert forests to more profitable uses. Yet the very fact that the *provveditori sopra boschi* and their survey teams focused so much effort on tracking and monitoring oak trees growing on common lands, and so little on trees standing on private property, made it possible for private and institutional forests to disappear from the record without a trace. And the more the forest bureaucracy came to rely on the natural historical narratives embedded in the surveys, the more the *provveditori sopra boschi* came to believe that oak had all but disappeared from privately controlled lands, leading them to focus even more of their efforts on the conservation of public forests. In this sense, the survey techniques and the stories that the *provveditori sopra boschi* told themselves about what was happening in mainland forests were mutually reinforcing.

Antonio Nani's final report to the Senate, delivered on 30 November 1726, reflects many of the ambiguities of the cadastral data. While Nani expressed considerable confidence in the tale that the surveys told about the *boschi pubblici* and community forests, he remained uneasy about the gaps between surveys, and especially about the problems with the data on private and institutional forests. Like every *provveditore sopra boschi* before him, Nani acknowledged that his own knowledge of the forests of the lower Piave region was almost entirely a product of the collective efforts of his predecessors and their subordinate experts rather than of his own personal expertise. "I relied almost entirely on the writings of the now deceased Leonardo Mocenigo [who had inspected much of the same territory in 1704] . . . and drew comparisons between my *catastico* and those of Zuane Capello in 1620 and Querini in 1663," he told the senators.[29] Just as Garzoni had carried Giustinian's survey everywhere he went at the dawn of the seventeenth century, so now Nani travelled with Garzoni's registers, which furnished his team with their initial benchmark for evaluating long-term changes in the region's forests. Nani was, in every respect, the perfect Venetian bureaucratic expert, drawing his knowledge from the painstaking and collective empirical work of his predecessors rather than from abstract theories of forest management. But instead of treating his reliance on the knowledge stored in the surveys as a source of authority, as so many of his predecessors had, he expressed serious misgivings about some of the more evident gaps in the data, which he argued had prevented him from "distinguishing between ancient usurpations that would be impossible to correct and newer crimes that could still be righted."[30] In other words, while it was possible to argue—as Garzoni had—that the surveys revealed the locations where illegal clear-cutting had occurred, Nani believed that without the knowledge of when the alleged crimes had taken place, the history lost much of its power, because it provided the defendants in cases involving illegal clearance with legitimate grounds to appeal their convictions.

Nani did not limit his critique of the cadastral survey data to the obvious gaps in the record. He also expressed regret concerning the degree to which the mediated experience of the data had completely supplanted personal experience in the administration of mainland forests. Nani recognized that the *catastici* remained a powerful and useful tool for the *provveditori sopra boschi*, but he also argued that "they should not be allowed to substitute for first-hand experience."[31] In essence, he advanced the claim that Venice's forest bureaucrats had become so dependent on the cadastral data for their understanding of mainland forests that they had all but forgotten about the virtues of getting their boots dirty walking around the real thing. The dearth of personal experience not only meant that individual officials lacked the requisite empirical expertise, but, according to Nani, it also undermined the effectiveness of the cadastral surveys themselves. To combat creeping ignorance, Nani suggested that the *provveditori* and local officials alike get their noses out of the virtual forests of the registers and go see the physical forests of the *terraferma*. He emphasized his point by noting that his *proti* "had found oak stands that did not appear in earlier surveys, and that local forest guardians did not even realize existed."[32] In keeping with this line of reasoning, he did not spare his own *catastico* from criticism. He complained with some bitterness that the Senate's time constraints had prevented him from personally visiting every single forest that his *proti* had surveyed. And without the certainty that only a physical inspection could offer, he felt compelled to conclude that "there may be yet more privately owned stands that wound up being omitted from my registers."[33] Nani had no doubt that greedy landowners had cleared significant areas of forestland in the lower Piave during the seventeenth century, but he was equally convinced that some of the missing forests were only missing on paper.

Nani offered a third criticism of the cadastral data. He pointed out that even if one accepted the counts as an accurate measure of how many oak trees stood in a particular forest, there was still a great deal of crucial contextual information missing from the record. The raw number of trees in a stand said nothing about how they were distributed on the ground, whether they were growing straight and tall on flat terrain or curved and gnarled on steep hillsides, and whether the soil offered the necessary drainage to nurture healthy durmast oak. For the *provveditori sopra boschi*, there were two reasons why this shortcoming in the data represented only a relatively minor problem. First, because Nani and his colleagues were consulting the original registers, they could read the marginal notations left by the *proti*, which contained precisely this kind of critical contextual information. Second, because every *provveditore sopra boschi* would have the opportunity to visit at least the *boschi pubblici* and community forests in his territory, he would be able to see for himself how things stood on the ground. What concerned Nani was that the decision-makers in the Ducal Palace saw neither the forests nor the marginalia in the registers, and therefore had developed a distorted understanding of what mainland forests really looked like. "It may come as a shock to your excellencies," he intoned from the rostrum, "but there are very few forests that are not composed of a mix of softwoods and oak."[34] He proceeded to argue that the legislators' ignorance on this score had led them to impose any number of misguided policies—from overly strict bans on *boschi pubblici* to the overly permissive distribution of licenses to harvest on private lands. In other words, Nani was arguing that until legislators learned to read the history of mainland forests that was contained in the registers in the same way as the *provveditori sopra boschi*, the Republic's forestry policies would always fail to meet their objective of conserving valuable oak.

There was also a fourth reason to be skeptical of the numbers contained in the registers. While each *catastico*, taken in isolation, had been designed to collect uniform sets of empirical data about oak trees, a careful examination of the registers reveals significant variations in the data-collection techniques and the classification schemes employed by individual *provveditori*. Nani did not mention this in his report, so it is impossible to say with absolute certainty whether he recognized the differences between his own survey and those of his predecessors, especially the 1602 *Catastico Garzoni* that he employed as his main benchmark. As we have seen, Garzoni—acting on the advice of his *proti*—became convinced that his two predecessors had wielded the Arsenal *bollo* with too much abandon, double-marking trees that would never mature into naval-quality oak. As a consequence, Garzoni decided to alter the basic taxonomy of his survey. Surian and Giustinian had rated all oak trees above three feet in circumference as Arsenal-grade, a practice that, Garzoni argued, had led to overgrown stands and a lack of adequate space for the best poles to mature. Therefore, Garzoni rated only five-foot poles as Arsenal grade, instructing his *proti* to single-mark many of the three- and four-foot poles as *tolpi*, freeing them up for use by the *savi ed esecutori alle acque* as replacement piles for the system of breakwaters and levees that protected the lagoon from winter storm surges. But Garzoni's successor, Fabio Canal, returned to the earlier system of double-marking all poles over three feet in circumference. Garzoni's decision to employ a unique taxonomy meant that the totals he reported to the Council of Ten at the conclusion of his tour had not been calculated on the same basis as those of his predecessors, rendering the kinds of gross comparisons favored by legislators meaningless. Thus, despite efforts to create a uniform empirical measure of mainland oak trees, each *catastico* remained something of an idiosyncratic exercise, heavily dependent on the personal interests of the patrician in charge and the advice he received from his subordinates. An informed reader such as Nani could correct for the differences between particular surveys, but as he pointed out with regard to variations in stand density and composition, the importance of such distinctions would probably come as a surprise to the gentlemen in the Ducal Palace.

Nani's critique of the cadastral data offers strong and convincing evidence of the way in which, by the end of the seventeenth century, Venetian officials at all levels of the state had come to treat the statistical data contained in the registers as the most meaningful empirical measure of mainland forests. His report before the Senate also illustrates the powerful new role that the *provveditori sopra boschi* had carved out for themselves as the only fully informed experts on forests. As Nani pointed out to the assembled senators, they were in a poor position to construct a meaningful history out of the numbers, because they lacked the contextual knowledge necessary to make sense of the data. Likewise, the *proti* were too close to the ground to construct a coherent narrative about changes in mainland forests. They counted the trees and recorded the crucial contextual information in the margins of the registers, but they lacked the broader understanding of the history of the forests that was needed to turn that contextual information into knowledge. Only the *provveditori sopra boschi* were in a position to interpret faithfully the significance of the ever-growing mountain of statistical data, because only they possessed both an intimate familiarity with the registers and a personal acquaintance with the physical forest landscape. The transformation of the bureaucracy was complete. The cadastral surveys had finally made experts out of the *provveditori sopra boschi*. Unlike Garzoni, who had been careful to acknowledge the contributions of his subordinates, Nani was staking a claim to authority that no one else but another *provveditore sopra boschi* could share. Fittingly, at the end of his speech Nani deliberately chose a military metaphor to describe his service as *provveditore*, saying that he saw his "duties as *provveditore sopra boschi* as akin to my military service in the recent wars."[35] By comparing service in the forest bureaucracy to service in battle, Nani echoed the traditional rhetorical device in which forests represented one of the cornerstones of republican liberty. However, the metaphor also effectively distilled his arguments concerning the *provveditori sopra boschi's* special brand of expertise. Like a general, Nani had marshaled his troops and led them to victory in the battle against deforestation. And, like a general, he believed that he possessed a unique and privileged view of the field of conflict—in this case mainland forests—that neither his subordinates on the front lines nor his masters back in the Ducal Palace could share. This metaphor speaks volumes about Nani, but it also suggests that by the eighteenth century, the *provveditori sopra boschi* viewed themselves as the only fully fluent interpreters of the quantitative language in which the surveys were encoded. The scores of experts who performed the hard labor involved in producing the survey data stored their first-hand experiences in the registers, but only the *provveditori sopra boschi* enjoyed complete and unfettered access to those experiences. In this sense the cadastral surveys had further reinforced the role of the *provveditori* as the embodiment of the collective knowledge of the timber bureaucracy by creating a language for speaking about the history and health of mainland forests that belonged to them alone.

Topographical Maps and the Reproduction of Knowledge

If Nani could claim a privileged perspective on the quantitative data stored in the *catastici*, the survey teams collected and reproduced information in forms that were harder for the *provveditori sopra boschi* to monopolize. By the second half of the seventeenth century, topographical maps—in the sense of maps based on a land survey and drawn to scale— had become a key component of every *catastico*.[36] Unlike the collection of elaborate quantitative data—which was largely an exclusive practice of the *provveditori sopra boschi*—many other seventeenth-century Venetian bureaucracies also employed elaborate cartographic representations as an instrument of power. The *provveditori sopra beni comunali* and *provveditori sopra beni inculti* produced scores of pictorial and topographical maps of commons and unused lands throughout the *terraferma*; the *savi ed esecutori alle acque* created several different types of charts and maps of the harbor and the larger lagoon; and still other magistracies mapped mainland fortifications, important mainland towns, and, of course, Venice itself.[37] The Venetians did not use a single uniform cartographic technology or style. The types of maps produced by the Republic's institutions ranged instead from traditional pictorial renderings that paid little attention to scale and accuracy, to chorographic bird's-eye city views, to the kinds of survey-based topographical maps more commonly associated with administrative mapping in seventeenth- and eighteenth-century Europe. Officials selected the type of map to use in a given situation based in part on whether the image was intended as an aesthetic production or a practical one—although these two categories frequently overlapped. For example, many pictorial maps and bird's-eye views were never intended as accurate representations of a city or a piece of land, but rather were meant to create a sense of place and provide decoration for official reports. Many of the renderings of common lands produced by the *provveditori sopra beni comunali* were pictorial maps of this sort, offering a somewhat impressionistic depiction of mainland commons. By contrast, hydrographic charts of the lagoon—especially those that showed the deeper channels that led into the main *bacino* in front of the Ducal Palace—were clearly intended to function as accurate representations of space that could be put to multiple uses—including navigation and the maintenance of the lagoon's infrastructure.[38]

The forest bureaucracy alone produced a wide range of maps, from bird's-eye views of important *boschi pubblici* used to embellish official reports to the painstakingly surveyed topographical maps that accompanied the cadastral surveys in the later seventeenth and eighteenth centuries.[39] These representations served two related purposes. Like the *catastici* to which most of them were attached, the maps recorded a history of individual *boschi pubblici*. The drawings usually contained fairly accurate information about the perimeters of state forests, information that the *provveditori sopra boschi* could exploit to identify quite minute changes to the contours of the *boschi pubblici*. From the point of view of the forest bureaucracy, these maps also supplied the *provveditori* with a particularly effective weapon to wield in the struggle to protect public forest resources from encroachment by individuals and institutions that did not share the Republic's concern for protecting and preserving critical resources. For the first time, the maps furnished officials outside of the forest bureaucracy with a far more vivid and immediate sense of mainland forest landscapes than the quantitative data could. At least in theory, the maps allowed legislators to see these landscapes through the eyes of the *provveditori sopra boschi*. Furthermore, because the drawings were easier for courts and legislators to interpret than the raw numbers, they were more likely to withstand legal challenges than the data contained in the cadastral registers alone. Thus the forestry maps comprised both a metaphorical and a practical instrument of state power. They constituted an obvious symbolic representation of the Republic's political reach, but, even more importantly, they supplied officials with a powerful tool with which to monitor specific forests and prosecute lawbreakers. The maps also played a crucial role in the production and reproduction of technical knowledge about forests within the bureaucracy itself. Again, because these renderings appeared to be easier to interpret than the numbers, they offered each new generation of *provveditori sopra boschi* an easy entry into the secret history of mainland forests stored in the *catastici*. Many of the maps duplicated and contextualized some of the information in the surveys, making it easier for new officials to interpret the quantitative data properly. In fact, the surveyors who produced the topographical maps of the *boschi pubblici* clearly intended them to be used in conjunction with the registers containing the quantitative data. In other words, the forest bureaucracy designed the maps and the numbers to function in tandem as an instrument of institutional memory.

The earliest Venetian surveys of mainland forests did not include pictorial or topographical maps of any sort. Traditional narrative surveys, such as Marco Cornaro's 1442 firewood inspection and the 1566 *Catastico Lando*, largely relied on written explanations of what the surveyors had seen rather than cartographic representations. Still, in many cases the descriptions contained in such traditional surveys functioned in much the same way as a map would have. Many of these narratives included a detailed *iter* that would have made it possible for an individual who was familiar with the area in question to replicate the original surveyor's itinerary. Cornaro included just such an *iter* in his 1442 treatise (see chapter 2). Nicolò Surian employed a similar narrative mapping technique in his 1569 *catastico*. He and his *proti* recorded a very precise *iter* of the perimeter of every *bosco pubblico* that they surveyed. Like Cornaro's 1442 *iter*, Surian's perimeter surveys made it possible for Giovanni Garzoni to retrace Surian's steps in the state forests with considerable precision thirty-three years later. Thus while Surian's survey represented a dramatic break from the tradition of narrative surveys, he did preserve at least one customary technology employed by his predecessors. Like the tree-by-tree counts, the step-by-step description of forest perimeters offered Surian an opportunity for empirical precision that even the best topographical maps of the time could not match. And, like nearly every feature of Surian's survey, the technique of narrative mapping was preserved in every subsequent *catastico* until the fall of the Republic.

The narrative maps were remarkable for their precision. Unlike Cornaro's 1442 *iter*, which assumed a significant amount of tacit knowledge of the network of inland canals that surrounded the lagoon, the *provveditori sopra boschi* and their *proti* made no assumptions of prior knowledge. Each leg of the *iter* started either from a recognizable—and presumably permanent—feature of the landscape or a stone survey marker placed there by the survey team. From there the *iter* walked the reader from marker to marker along the forest's perimeter until he returned once again to the point of departure. The surveyors recorded the distance and bearing between each marker and usually described the terrain along each leg in painstaking detail. A typical *iter* occupied at least half a folio page in the large survey registers, and for the more extensive *boschi pubblici*, the narrative map of the perimeter ran for several pages and include as many as two hundred individual legs (see figure 5.8). Because of the time it took to conduct the surveys on which such detailed narratives were based, the *provveditori sopra boschi* only performed them for the *boschi pubblici* and the largest and most important community stands. Nevertheless, despite the lack of cartographic representations in the earliest *catastici*—including Garzoni's 1602 survey—Surian and his immediate successors left behind astonishingly accurate narrative maps of the most important forests in the Arsenal's growing patrimony.

While the *provveditori sopra boschi* eschewed topographical and pictorial maps in favor of the more empirical narrative mapping techniques until the middle of the seventeenth century, other Venetian bureaucracies had already begun regularly employing topographical maps in land surveys in the mid-sixteenth century (see figure 5.2). In particular, the *provveditori sopra beni inculti*—the office in charge of cataloging and surveying unused land on the *terraferma*—kept a permanent staff of cartographers on hand to create the elaborate topographical maps that constituted the centerpiece of its surveys.[40] As legislators in the Ducal Palace became more familiar with topographical survey maps, they began to expect to see them as part of any land survey. Thus in September of 1609, when news reached Venice that the Brentella—one of the tributaries of the Piave that bordered the Montello reserve—had broken its banks and settled into a new course, the Senate decided that in addition to forcing villagers in the affected area to restore the stream to its bed, it would also commission survey maps of each of the thirteen principal sections of the reserve.[41] One of the *provveditori sopra beni inculti*'s cartographers, a man named Vincenzo di Anzolo, travelled to the Montello and drew topographical maps of each of the thirteen discreet sections of the reserve (see figure 5.3). The resulting representations combined sophisticated topographical mapping techniques with pictorial renderings of relief and of the oak trees in the reserve, creating a sense of place and space that was missing from most sixteenth-century maps.

Vincenzo di Anzolo made the drawings *ex novo*, without referring to the painstakingly prepared narrative maps and surveys of the reserve that Giovanni Garzoni's *proti* had produced only seven years earlier. This omission was due in part to the fact that the Republic's institutions only shared information when they habitually acted in concert—as in the case of the *provveditori sopra boschi* and the *provveditori e patroni all'arsenale*. No such relationship existed between the *provveditori*

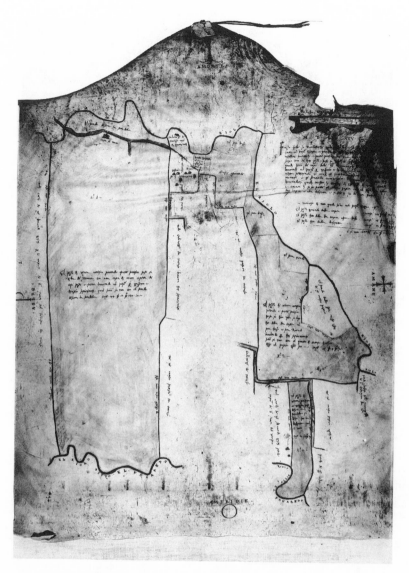

FIGURE 5.2 A 1570 map of monastic property near Treviso

The map is drawn to scale (in *perteghe trevigiane*) and partially depicts streams and roads where they bound the property in question. However, it shows no relief or other terrain. Instead, the contents of the fields in question are simply written in narrative form in the bounded areas. The total area of each field is given in the upper right. This is one of the earliest examples in the Venetian archives of a sophisticated survey map drawn to scale. Its existence shows that Surian's decision to forego topographical maps in favor of descriptive mapping for his 1569 *catastico* was due to conscious choice rather than a lack of access to skilled cartographers.

SOURCE: Archivio di Stato di Venezia, Atto di Concessione n. 51/2008.

FIGURE 5.3 A mixed map of the section of the Montello near the village of Giavera del Montello—one of the thirteen communities surrounding the reserve Like the 1570 map, this 1610 topographical map is drawn to scale (in *perteghe trevigiane*) and includes the main road on the southern side of the stand. The map is oriented to the north. Unlike the earlier map, however, this cartographer uses pictorial representations of hills, trees, and the large, low-lying meadow in the middle of the stand. He also distinguishes between heavily wooded areas and the more sparsely wooded section adjoining the buildings on the edge of the

continued on facing page

sopra boschi and the *provveditori sopra beni inculti*, even though to some extent the two bureaucracies shared a common preoccupation with the pernicious effects of deforestation. Instead, the *provveditori sopra beni inculti* shared information with the *savi ed esecutori alle acque*, who worried that erosion on unmanaged land was contributing to siltation in the lagoon. As a consequence, when the Senate chose not to appoint a *provveditore sopra boschi* to supervise the production of the new maps, the *Catastico Garzoni* languished unused on its shelf in the chancery while Vincenzo di Anzolo travelled abroad to survey the Montello. More importantly, the Senate's decision to send a cartographer from the *beni inculti* to conduct a survey that should have been the province of the *boschi* suggests the degree to which legislators had come to believe in the importance of topographical maps as the best source of presumptively accurate information about the *terraferma*. Thus the fact that the forest bureaucracy had traditionally eschewed topographical maps meant that the Senate felt compelled to entrust the new Montello survey to a bureaucracy that shared its own growing interest in cartographic representations of landscape. Undoubtedly, even if Vincenzo di Anzolo knew of the existence of the *Catastico Garzoni*, he might not have seen it as relevant to his own efforts, written as it was in a radically different mapping idiom from the cartographic language he was ac-

---

reserve. The buildings on the edge of the forest are drawn to scale, while Giavera is simply a blank space to the south of the main road. The space to the north of the town but outside the reserve is identified as "arable [land] belonging to the *Padri Certosini*." A mill belonging to the same monastery is to the west of the village. The northernmost buildings belong to the state and were the official residence for the local *capitano del bosco* (forest watchman). Thus the map combines elements of pictorial and topographical maps to provide both an impressionistic sense of place and a rendering of the southern boundaries of the stand. The topographical elements—the roads and buildings—are displayed in a horizontal projection, while the hills and trees are shown in the three-quarter view of bird's-eye images. The surveyor signed his name and title—Vincenzo di Anzoli, Perito—in the lower right-hand corner. In the description of the map above his signature, he further identifies himself as a *"perito* for the *provveditori sopra beni inculti."*
SOURCE: ASV, *Provveditori sopra Boschi*, R. 171, ds. 1. Archivio di Stato di Venezia, Atto di Concessione n. 51/2008.

customed to using. Certainly the fact that two important institutions employed such disparate survey techniques underscores the degree to which early modern bureaucracies often possessed unique cultures of knowledge and produced and packaged information in a profoundly idiosyncratic fashion, even within a small and relatively organized state such as Venice. For a man such as Vincenzo di Anzolo, who represented an institution accustomed to the use of topographical maps as the main technology for conducting land surveys and communicating their results, the narrative maps—with their emphasis on empirical precision—must have appeared fussy in their obsessive attention to small details and perhaps even a little quaint in their reliance on language over image.

While a narrative map like Garzoni's and a topographical map like di Anzolo's purported to describe the same piece of land, they communicated very different things to their respective audiences. The narrative maps offered later surveyors a precise account of the contours of a particular forest at a specific moment in time. In this regard, they were like the quantitative data—accurate and empirical, but ultimately only useful to individuals possessing both a basic understanding of forest management and personal first-hand knowledge of the forests in question. The narrative maps constituted a useful and keenly honed tool for the *provveditori sopra boschi* and their *proti*, because they allowed them to make fine-grained determinations about how specific *boschi pubblici* had changed since the last cadastral survey. In other words, these narratives faithfully and accurately reproduced the collective knowledge of one survey team and transmitted it intact to the next expedition and the *provveditore sopra boschi* who led it. Yet the bewildering details about survey markers, pace counts, bearings, and local terrain features conveyed little sense of the forest itself, or of the larger context within which it stood, to legislators and jurists in the Ducal Palace. The information was precise, to be sure, but without actually visiting the area, the reader could gain only limited insight into exactly where the forest was situated, the terrain it occupied, and what surrounded its carefully surveyed perimeter.

In stark contrast to the narrative maps, topographical maps were long on context and correspondingly short on the kind of details that would have been useful for surveyors and Arsenal *proti* attempting to determine whether significant changes had taken place within a given reserve since the last *catastico*. For example, looking at Vincenzo di Anzolo's rendering of the Giavera section of the Montello (figure 5.3), one gains an immediate sense of where the forest is located with respect to the village, the number and type of buildings in the area, and an impressionistic sense of topographical relief in the forest—all of which made the image far easier for legislators who had never travelled to the Montello to interpret than the detailed descriptions stored in the *provveditori sopra boschi's* cadastral registers. However, despite the fact that the map is drawn to scale, it would have been impossible for a group of *proti* at twenty or even a hundred years' remove to reproduce di Anzolo's survey with more than approximate accuracy. Only the sections of the perimeter that bordered on the roads are recorded with any precision. In fact, the bird's-eye view rendering of the hills actually overlaps with the northern boundary of the stand, making the map useless as a means of storing and reproducing the kind of detailed information about boundaries that the *provveditori sopra boschi* required to conduct their tree counts. Lastly, while the carefully rendered trees on the map must have given the viewer a dramatic sense of place, they also conveyed the false impression that the forest contained evenly spaced oak trees of similar age, girth, and height. And as Antonio Nani would make clear a century later when he pointed out to the Senate that "there are very few forests that are not composed of a mix of softwoods and oak," such drawings had indeed misled legislators into thinking that mainland oak forests were composed of even-aged, single-species stands.[42] As a consequence the two types of maps presented the reader with very different types of information. The narrative maps offered the kind of empirical precision demanded by surveyors, but which was of little interest to legislators, who would have encountered considerable difficulty in interpreting the information. Topographical maps of the sort favored by the *provveditori sopra beni inculti* offered legislators an easily legible and undeniably vivid picture of the appearance and location of the most important *boschi pubblici*, but they lacked most of the critical detail demanded by the *provveditori sopra boschi* and their subordinates.

Even after the Senate commissioned di Anzolo's topographical maps of the Montello in 1610, the *provveditori sopra boschi* remained reluctant to adopt the technology as part of the cadastral surveys. The next significant image of an important *bosco pubblico* was not a topographical map at all, but rather the full-color bird's-eye view of the enormous Cansiglio forest near Belluno that constitutes the centerpiece of Andrea Badoer's 1638 *catastico* of the mammoth beech reserve (figure 5.4).[43] The image itself is striking, and it was intended to emphasize dramatically the reserve's location on a high plateau that towers above the coastal plain to the south and the Piave valley to the north and west. The lion of Saint Mark, conspicuously placed at the center of the reserve, clearly symbolizes both the Republic's power over of the forest and the fact that the *catastico* itself was an instrument of that power. The twin compasses at the bottom indicate that the map's author was a surveyor and not an artist, and the bars bracketed by the compasses imply that it was drawn to scale—which it clearly was not. Even the placards showing the name and relative location of the Cansiglio's seventeen coupes furnish only an approximation of their actual position within the reserve and would have been useless as a means of orienting oneself within the forest. In nearly every respect the image looks like a mere adornment for the survey, and it appears to contain a good deal less useful information than the topographical maps of the Montello drawn by Vincenzo di Anzolo.

A closer examination of the 1638 *catastico* reveals that this chorography of the Cansiglio supplied a visual key to a wealth of technical information that the *provveditori sopra boschi* prized far more than di Anzolo's more accurate topographical maps. By adopting a cartographic idiom in which the *provveditori sopra boschi* had expressed limited interest up to that point, Badoer was able to show how maps could be used to bridge the gap between the highly local and empirical concerns of the forest bureaucracy and the more abstract understanding of legislators in the Ducal Palace. This attempt at what could be termed cartographic compromise structured the map's unusual composition. On the two folios immediately following the chorography, the information contained on the seventeen placards is reproduced in two different forms (figure 5.5). On the first folio Badoer recorded the seventeen coupes in tabular form. The table lists the coupes in the same numerical sequence as the placards on the large map, while the results of the tree counts appear in the three right-hand columns. Badoer divided the trees into three girth categories: saplings under a foot in circumference; more mature poles below six feet in circumference whose future quality could be fairly assessed; and fully grown poles over six feet in circumference, which was

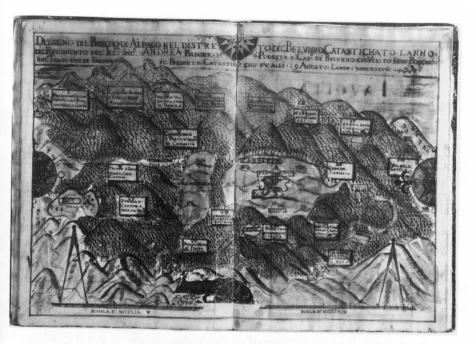

FIGURE 5.4 Andrea Badoer's 1638 map of the Cansiglio reserve near Belluno
The compasses on the scales (in miles) indicate that the map is the work of a
cartographer, even though it is a pictorial, bird's-eye view of the reserve and not
actually drawn to scale. The lion of Saint Mark in the center of the reserve leaves
no doubt as to the authority that lay behind the map or to its purpose. The
rectangular placards indicate the relative position of the reserve's seventeen
main coupes. The coupes are sequentially numbered, beginning with the coupe
that was used that year, which lay in the northwest corner of the reserve. The
map is oriented to the north.
SOURCE: ASV, *Provveditori ai Boschi*, B. 150 bis., ds. 21. Archivio di Stato di
Venezia, Atto di Concessione n. 51/2008.

the minimum girth for beech required by the Arsenal's sawyers. Badoer's
simple classifications show how counting and cataloging beech represented a far easier proposition than tracking oak, largely because the
only part of the ship made out of beech was the oars, while the shipwrights needed oak in several different shapes and sizes to construct the
hull, necessitating a far more nuanced taxonomic system. But Badoer
had done more than just order his craft experts to count the trees in the
reserve and enter the results in a register. By recording the counts by

coupe and placing the coupes in a deliberate and rationalized sequence, instead of simply recording the gross totals, Badoer had also successfully established a credible harvesting plan for the next seventeen years. For this reason, the real significance of the seventeen placards on the large map was revealed by the tabular arrangement of the quantitative data. The placards had not been placed there simply as adornments. They offered an artfully crafted visual cue to Badoer's carefully constructed plan for the Cansiglio. And Badoer had designed the cue specifically for uninformed legislators who preferred to look at maps rather than numbers. The quantitative data in the table were keyed back to the drawing, placing them in a context that was both more comfortable and more evocative for an audience that lacked familiarity with the basic problems of forest management. On the folio opposite the table containing the quantitative data, the seventeen coupes appear for a third and final time. In this instance, however, Badoer arranged the names in clockwise fashion on a wheel to show how, at the conclusion of his seventeen-year plan, the entire sequence of harvests would simply begin anew, presumably repeating itself ad infinitum—or at least until the fall of the Republic. The circular arrangement clearly reinforced the forest bureaucracy's belief that a properly conceived and executed management scheme could guarantee timber supplies in perpetuity, while at the same time subtly undermining the traditional view of forests—as finite and steadily dwindling—favored by legislators.

The fact that Badoer's map was primarily intended to reproduce a body of technical knowledge about the Cansiglio rather than to provide an accurate representation of space becomes even more apparent in the folios that follow the presentation of the survey data. Having established that the Cansiglio should be harvested on a seventeen-year cycle, Badoer proceeded to explain how to schedule the annual winter and fall harvests. On a page entitled "The rule that must be followed for the harvest," Badoer presented legislators with a working calendar illustrating the method employed by the *provveditori sopra boschi*, in cooperation with their subordinate craft experts, to schedule harvests (figure 5.6). The calendar consists of two rings. The outer ring displays the days of August, February, and September, arranged in sequence. The internal wheel, which is rigged to spin on the page, displays a crescent moon against a night sky with a pointing finger that bridges the gap between the two

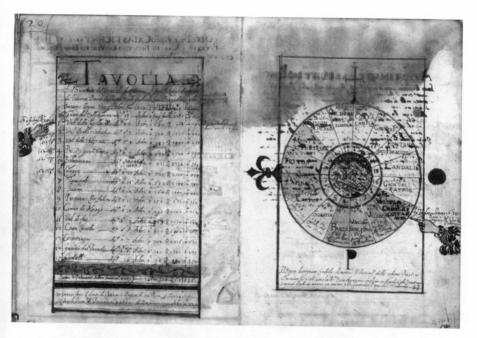

FIGURE 5.5 Andrea Badoer's list of the seventeen coupes of the Cansiglio reserve The coupes are listed in the same sequence as on the map in figure 5.4. On the left-hand folio the coupes are listed in the left-hand column, while the columns to the right of the names of the coupes contain the number of healthy beech trees, by girth, in each coupe. On the right-hand folio they are listed on a wheel that indicates both their geographic position within the reserve—the top of the wheel is north—and, by following the wheel clockwise, the order in which they are intended to be harvested. On both folios the hand points to the coupe Badoer harvested in 1638.

SOURCE: ASV, *Provveditori ai Boschi*, B. 150 bis., ds. 22. Archivio di Stato di Venezia, Atto di Concessione n. 51/2008.

wheels. In the accompanying text, Badoer explained that by spinning the pointer to the date of the last crescent moon in August or the first crescent moon in February and September, anyone could establish the season's harvest schedule, which the forest bureaucracy traditionally set to coincide with the crescent moon. Because the inner ring rotated, the calendar was not keyed to a specific year, but would work in perpetuity— just like the wheel with the names of the seventeen coupes. As with his presentation of the coupes, Badoer sought to use this calendar to allay

FIGURE 5.6 Andrea Badoer's perpetual calendar for scheduling the Cansiglio harvest

The internal wheel with the crescent moon and the hand spins, allowing the user to identify the exact date on which workers needed to be in the reserve in any given year. The top of the outside wheel shows all 28 days of February, while the left and right sides shows the days of August and September, respectively. The Venetian forest bureaucracy tried to schedule the harvest according to lunar phases. The first crescent moon in February, and either the last crescent moon in August or the first one in September—depending on when it fell in a particular year—marked the beginning of the winter and fall harvests, respectively.

SOURCE: ASV, *Provveditori ai Boschi*, B. 150 bis., ds. 18. Archivio di Stato di Venezia, Atto di Concessione n. 51/2008.

legislators' fears about the possible disappearance of timber resources and emphasize the forest bureaucracy's power to manage those resources over the long term.

Having firmly established the notion that the Cansiglio could and should be preserved and managed as a continually renewable resource, Badoer next contrived to offer legislators a crash course in evaluating timber. On two facing folios Badoer offered his readers four views of a beech tree (figure 5.7). The left-hand folio shows three beech trees growing side by side in the forest. The first pole illustrates the characteristics that the Arsenal *proti* prized in a beech: a straight, even grain and no small intermediate branches that would create knots along the length of the trunk. Such a tree, Badoer explained, would reliably produce six strong galley oars capable of years of service. The second pole, by contrast, has an uneven, curving grain. Although it, too, is free of small intermediate branches, Badoer pointed out that it was nonetheless entirely useless for manufacturing oars, because the curved grain would produce a weak oar that was unlikely to last even a single voyage. The third pole has a straight and even grain, but along one side it exhibits intermediate branches big enough to create hard knots in the wood that would make it impossible for the oarmaker to turn the oar. Badoer suggested that such a tree might produce only three or four sturdy oars, as opposed to the six yielded by the first tree. On the facing page, Badoer offered his readers a scale drawing of the bole of a beech tree. Badoer explained how to read the history of the tree in its rings and how important it was that the rings be evenly spaced. The drawing of the bole also shows how, once the pole reached the Arsenal, the sawyers would saw it radially into six wedges that the oarmakers would then turn into galley oars. With this guide to evaluating timber, Badoer sought to convey to legislators unfamiliar with forests that simply counting the trees in the reserve would never arm them with the knowledge they sought. His drawings stressed the fact that rating timber was an uncertain and complex business, and that only after crews had felled a tree would the *proti* be able to seek a definitive answer as to how many oars it might eventually produce. In addition, he wanted legislators to understand that the optimism expressed in his perpetual calendars was contingent on officials possessing a proper understanding of the intricate complexities of preserving large beech forests such as the Cansiglio. By using a visual

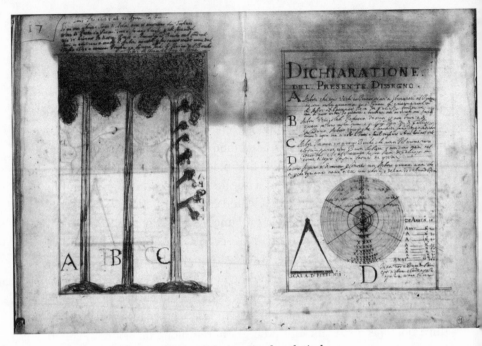

FIGURE 5.7 Andrea Badoer's guide to rating beech timber
The left-hand folio shows how to evaluate the suitability of a beech tree for oarmaking. Example A is an ideal pole with a straight, even grain that will produce strong, durable oars. Example B has a twisted grain and will produce weak oars. Example C has a straight grain, but the branches along one side of the trunk will create knots that make it impossible to turn oars. Therefore, a pole of this type will only yield three oars as opposed to the six yielded by example A. The right-hand folio shows how to read the bole of a felled beech tree. The importance of the even spacing of the rings is stressed. Also, note that the bole is divided into six sections, showing how the trunk was cut into wedges, each of which would then be turned to become an oar. The compass again indicates that the drawing is the work of a *proto* and not an artist.
SOURCE: ASV, *Provveditori sopra Boschi*, B. 150 bis., ds. 19. Archivio di Stato di Venezia, Atto di Concessione n. 51/2008.

idiom with which legislators were comfortable, Badoer sought to persuade them to abandon their simplistic ideas about forests and see the Cansiglio through the eyes of the *provveditori sopra boschi* and their craft experts. In this regard, Badoer's *catastico* represents an attempt to present the intricate collective expertise of the forest bureaucracy in a more accessible language than the complex quantitative idiom employed by Giovanni Garzoni and others in their cadastral surveys of oak forests. Badoer clearly hoped that by studying his *catastico*, members of the Council of Ten and other important legislative bodies could learn to read landscapes like surveyors, timber like an Arsenal *proto*, and numbers like a *provveditore sopra boschi*. Badoer's map and accompanying illustrations encompassed all the varied forms of craft and technical expertise embodied by the patrician *provveditori*.

In the second half of the seventeenth century, the *provveditori sopra boschi* definitively adopted topographical maps as a core component of the *catastici*. Cartographers became regular members of the *provveditore's* retinue, working in concert with the land surveyors to produce carefully rendered scale drawings of the *boschi pubblici*. For the Republic's forest bureaucracy, topographical maps clearly represented an extension of the traditional narrative maps it had long employed as a means of tracking the perimeter of important forests. The topographical maps produced by the forest bureaucracy's cartographers looked similar to the images of the Montello drawn by Vincenzo di Anzolo in 1610, but they had far more in common with Andrea Badoer's 1638 chorography of the Cansiglio. Like Badoer's drawing and his manual, the later topographic maps were clearly intended to reproduce the collective knowledge generated by the survey teams that performed the *catastici* in a form that would be more palatable to legislators in the Ducal Palace. Consequently, these cartographers emphasized aspects of the reserves that di Anzolo had largely ignored in his 1610 renderings. In particular, the *provveditori sopra boschi's* maps paid close attention to the perimeters of the reserves and took careful note of who owned the land outside the boundaries of the forests. Moreover, unlike di Anzolo's images—which were created *ex novo* and made no reference to other surveys—the forest bureaucracy's cartographers produced maps that were specifically designed to function in tandem with the narrative *iters* that formed the core of the cadastral surveys of the *boschi pubblici*. In this regard, the new topographical maps and the old descriptive maps were mutually constitutive, and helped the *provveditori sopra boschi* produce even more detailed and sophisticated histories of the Republic's forest patrimony.

Seen through the lens of the topographical and narrative maps, Antonio Nani's 1726 *catastico* represented the culmination of the development of the oak surveys. Nani and his team plotted every *bosco pubblico* in the district of Treviso twice. His land surveyors produced traditional narrative maps of every reserve, while his cartographers made carefully rendered topographical maps to match. The narrative maps contained the now-familiar accounts of survey markers, terrain features, pace counts, and bearings that would make it possible for later surveyors to reproduce the *iter* exactly. The topographical maps placed the forests in a recognizable local context that made it possible for someone unfamiliar with the area to picture the landscape. More importantly, the topographical maps created a visual record of the narrative maps. They also helped make sense of some of the complicated information contained in the survey registers by showing where the *boschi pubblici* stood in relation to other property and woodlands that appeared elsewhere in the survey. Nani's chart of the *Bosco di San Marco* near the town of Pordenone shows exactly how the new topographical maps were meant to enhance the narrative maps, rather than to replace them (figure 5.8). Several features in the drawing were keyed to the narrative maps and other information stored in the registers. The most obvious is the large hand at the center top that points to the position of the first survey marker in the descriptive map. Starting from that marker, anyone could theoretically walk each of the 175 individual legs of the perimeter, using both the narrative and the topographical maps. The image was also explicitly linked to the quantitative data in the register. In the top left-hand corner, Nani's cartographer recorded the gross results of the tree counts in three simple categories: *tolpi*, *stortami*, and Arsenal-ready oak. These totals conveyed significantly less information than the far more sophisticated taxonomy in the registers, but they permitted legislators and other individuals who lacked facility with the quantitative data to form a rough idea of how much oak timber the reserve contained at the time of the survey. Finally, around the edges of the forest, the cartographer carefully noted the identities of the landowners who controlled the property abutting the reserve. From this information it is possible to see that the reserve was bounded almost entirely by private forests along its southern border. Additionally, by cross-referencing the names on the map with the names recorded in the registers, it would have been possible to gain a sense of how some of the area's private forests stood in relation to the *bosco pubblico*. And while

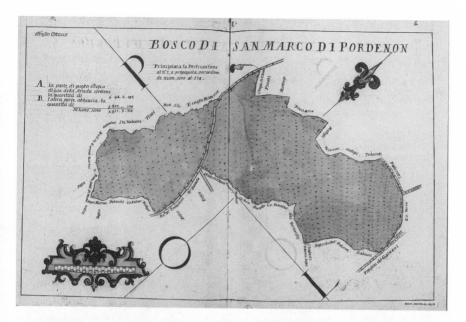

FIGURE 5.8 A topographical survey map from the 1726 *Catastico Nani* showing a *bosco pubblico* near Pordenone

Gone are the aesthetic flourishes of seventeenth-century survey maps. The simple plat shows the precise boundaries of the forest. As with earlier maps, where the perimeter is bounded by roads and streams, the features appear on the map. In addition, the map indicates the ownership and type of property on the other side of the boundary for each of the 174 discreet sections of the perimeter. The finger at the top of the map points to the first survey marker described in the narrative map contained in the *catastico* register, showing that the two maps were intended to work in tandem. On the left side, the map contains the gross counts of oak on either side of the road that bisects the reserve. The map is drawn to scale (in *perteghe trevigiane*) using triangulation. SOURCE: ASV, *Provveditori sopra Boschi*, Reg. 162, ds. 8. Archivio di Stato di Venezia, Atto di Concessione n. 51/2008.

legislators might not have immediately discerned why understanding the spatial arrangement of forests mattered, to an experienced and informed forestry official like Nani, the new topographical maps functioned as an index to the undifferentiated mass of virtual forests in the registers. As I have suggested, Nani was obsessed with reconstructing the history of private forests in the district, and it is no coincidence that his cartographers produced maps that deliberately emphasized the spatial relationships between private and public forests.

The depiction of individual trees is the only significant similarity between the topographical maps in the *Catastico Nani* and Vincenzo di Anzolo's 1610 drawings of the Montello. Legislators could be forgiven if, after viewing Nani's maps, they walked away with the idea that *boschi pubblici* such as the *Bosco di San Marco di Pordenone* contained evenly distributed oak trees. After all, Nani's cartographer had chosen to represent the trees in the reserve with a series of carefully placed dots. This failure might appear strange in light of Nani's admonishments that what legislators liked to think of as oak forests were in reality mixed deciduous forests containing pockets of durmast oak. However, Nani was clearly most interested in establishing a precise census of privately owned forests, and the maps in his *catastico*, with their careful record of private ownership along the perimeter of the *boschi pubblici*, accurately reflect that concern. It would be up to Nani's successors and their subordinate experts to place more emphasis on stand composition in their surveys.

The Senate entrusted the next survey of the lower Piave to Carlo Gradenigo in 1747, and Gradenigo and his subordinate experts responded to the lacunae in Nani's maps by attempting to generate more accurate representations of the actual distribution of oak in individual forests.[44] The marginal notes left in the registers by Gradenigo's *proti* reflect the *provveditore's* concern with issues of stand density and distribution. Not only did the *proti* report that they performed thinning operations in nearly every forest they had visited—irrespective of whether the forests were state, community, or private property—but they were also careful to note whether the oak trees stood in clusters or were more dispersed. The topographical maps of the *boschi pubblici* that accompanied the *catastico* also clearly reveal the acute interest of Gradenigo and his craft experts in the distribution of oak within individual stands. For example, the image of a state reserve near Cornuda depicts with considerable accuracy the actual placement of these trees in the forest through the simple device of arranging the dots representing oak to reflect their uneven distribution inside the reserve (figure 5.9). If Nani's maps had the potential to mislead legislators about where oak appeared in the mainland forests, Gradenigo's renderings leave little doubt as to the fact that even carefully managed *terraferma* landscapes such as the

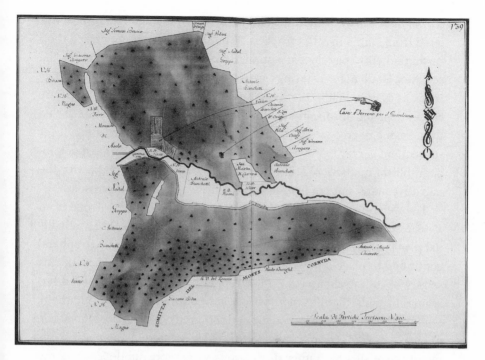

FIGURE 5.9 Topographical survey map of a *bosco pubblico* in the district of
Treviso from the 1747 *Catastico Gradenigo*

The map is drawn to scale in *perteghe trevigiane*. Like the 1726 map from the
Catastico Nani (fig. 5.8), this map is a simple plat. The hand points to the
capitano del bosco's house and fields. Note the detailed references to the
properties that adjoined the reserve. This survey map is not keyed to the
catastico's descriptive map in the same way as the 1726 map, but individual legs of
the descriptive map are clearly rendered on the topographical map, and the
surveyors placed markers and ended legs at each successive property line. The
cartographer employed the horizontal hashmarks to indicate the property lines
outside the reserve, and he recorded the names of the owners as well. He also
distributed the dots representing the oak trees unevenly, in an attempt to provide
a sense of both the location and the relative density of oak trees in the reserve.
SOURCE: ASV, *Provveditori sopra Boschi*, Reg. 164, ds. 57. Archivio di Stato di
Venezia, Atto di Concessione n. 51/2008.

boschi pubblici were anything but uniform. Gradenigo's maps also differed from Nani's in other respects. While both *provveditori* asked their cartographers to pay close attention to who owned the land adjoining the reserves, Gradenigo's drawings are not as carefully keyed to the narrative maps as Nani's. While the individual legs of the descriptive maps are clearly depicted, the location of the first survey marker is not emphasized to the same degree as it is on Nani's map, making it more difficult for subsequent survey teams to reproduce precisely his *iter*. Gradenigo's topographical maps were still intended to work in conjunction with the narrative maps, but not in exactly the same way as his predecessor's.

The differences between Nani's 1726 map and Gradenigo's one from 1748 testify to the fact that even into the eighteenth century, individual *provveditori* and their subordinate experts (such as cartographers) continued to place a powerful personal stamp on the *catastici*. In this sense the cadastral surveys do not represent perfectly rationalized bureaucratic tools. Significant idiosyncrasies continued to creep into them. Some of the particularities constituted serious deviations from the norm, as in the case of Garzoni's decision to employ a different taxonomy in his quantitative surveys. Other distinctions were more subtle, such as the cartographer's decision to emphasize distribution heavily in the topographical maps that accompanied the *Catastico Gradenigo*. Nevertheless, in both cases it is clear that the collective knowledge contained in the surveys was at once a force for creating consensus within the forest bureaucracy and a reflection of the specific concerns both of the individual *provveditori* and of the *proti* whose skills and experience they represented before the Senate and Council of Ten. The *provveditori sopra boschi*'s expertise was very different from that of the fifteenth-century *optime informati*, but it was not nearly as uniform and rationalized as that of their eighteenth-century colleagues in northern European states is purported to have been.[45] Yet it is evident that the quantitative surveys and topographical maps constituted powerful legal and administrative instruments in the experienced hands of the *provveditori sopra boschi*, and that they established the basis for the development of new forest management techniques, such as regular thinning of low-quality growth in the *boschi pubblici*. Amazingly, Gradenigo's *proti* were able to thin nearly every stand they visited, in spite of legislators' continuing dread that every tree felled brought the Republic one step closer to the day when its timber reserves would run out. In this case, the actions of Gradenigo's subordinate experts demonstrate just how politically powerful—and self-confident about its collective expertise—Venice's forest bureaucracy had become by the middle of the eighteenth century. Despite the persistence of fears about the imminent disappearance of critical timber resources, the view of forests as being simultaneously fragile and manageable that was implicit in the *catastici*—and explicit in Andrea Badoer's 1638 map and manual—profoundly shaped Venetian ideas about the proper relationship between humans and the natural world.

CHAPTER SIX

Nature's Republic or Republican Nature?

Forests are no longer worthy of the name, but
have become mere wilderness.

THIS BOOK OPENED WITH Leonardo Mocenigo's 1704 appearance before the Senate, because his speech represented an ideal example of
the Venetian penchant for adopting the language of scarcity and impending destruction when speaking about forests in general and high-
quality timber in particular. The introduction argued that such rhetorical appeals have misled many historians into assuming that the Republic
had run out of viable sources of high-quality timber by the turn of the
eighteenth century. Indeed, one of the main goals of this book has been
to situate such political oratory firmly in the context of Venetian efforts
to establish effective forest management policies and practices throughout their territories and show how this rhetoric did not always constitute
an accurate account of the mainland landscape.

When Mocenigo delivered his speech, he had just returned to Venice
from a two-year tour of the *terraferma* and Istria under the auspices of an
extraordinary commission as the *inquisitore sopra boschi*. As the unusual
title suggests, the Senate had not sent Mocenigo to conduct a *catastico*.
Rather, his mandate had been that of any good inquisitor: to "reinvigorate
the laws governing forest use throughout the Republic's dominion."[1] Unlike the *provveditori sopra boschi*, he did not carry the *catastici* with
him on his journey, so he did not have access to the history of mainland
forests that they contained. Nor was he surrounded by craft experts whose
knowledge he could use to help him interpret the landscapes he was
seeing. Instead, Mocenigo took as his guide a long list of legal precedents
dating back to the 1476 laws governing community woodlands. Consequently, he viewed the forests very much as the legislators did—as static

entities in peril—rather than as the *provveditori sopra boschi* saw them—as dynamic landscapes that could be preserved and renewed through flexible and empirically grounded practices of forest exploitation. Mocenigo's embrace of the Senate's perspective was also the product of the terms of his commission. Dispatched to evaluate local compliance with the laws governing forest exploitation, he was almost compelled to file a pessimistic report. Measured only against the letter of the Republic's legislation, rather than against the crucial historical and technical context created by the *catastici*, the Venetian forestry regime appeared to be failing badly.

This chapter now returns to Mocenigo's oration in greater detail, because it offers an important insight into how 350 years of Venetian attempts to secure strategic forest resources and control forest landscapes had conditioned the way that most Venetian patricians thought about the relationship between human action and environmental change. In a striking passage near the beginning of his speech, Mocenigo endeavors to convey to his audience the degree to which he had been dismayed by what he had seen:

> Thus mature oak that nature had struggled entire centuries to nourish, and seedlings and saplings too, were either felled by the iron (which wrought equal destruction amongst the softwoods) or devastated by beasts set to pasture; with the result that the vast majority of forests are no longer worthy of the name, but have become mere wilderness, stripped of useful vegetation and hollow at their very core.[2]

Mocenigo's dramatic assertion that the many oak forests in Venetian territory had turned to wilderness may appear peculiar to the modern reader. The terms he used for "forest" and "wilderness" were *bosco* and *selva*, respectively. By now the term *bosco* (forest) and its plural *boschi* should be familiar. As for *selva*, the word would have been instantly recognizable to his audience as coming from the opening lines of Dante's *Divine Comedy*, in which the poet awakens to find himself lost in a dark, mysterious forest:

> *Nel mezzo del cammin di nostra vita*
> *Mi ritrovai per una selva oscura*
> In the middle of the journey of my life
> I came to myself in a dark wood

By employing the terms in opposition, Mocenigo was deliberately contrasting what he saw as two very different relationships between humans and mainland forests—the first a desirable state of affairs, the latter disastrous. But the *selva*, or wild forest, was not, as one might expect, Dante's dark, foreboding wood where wild beasts and demons roam free and humans easily stray from the path of righteousness—or perhaps fall prey to the more tangible threats posed by bandits and other barbarians. Nor was it an untouched, pristine Eden in which humans might live in harmony with the divine plan as their original forebears once did. Instead, it was a place where human activity was ubiquitous and unrestrained, where peasants and landowners alike wielded the iron axe with abandon and put their animals to pasture without regard for their destructive tendencies. In other words, what made a forest landscape wild in Mocenigo's view was the moral quality of the human interaction with it, not the absence of human influence. Greedy, unrestrained humans ruined nature by overexploiting it, thereby transforming it into wilderness. This definition of wilderness was, in many ways, the very opposite of the untouched or underexploited landscape that the more familiar uses of the term imply.[3]

The literal sense of Mocenigo's words is clear, but their larger significance demands additional analysis. The simplest way to read them would be as a bit of linguistic bravura on the part of a Venetian patrician eager to display erudition and wit before his peers in the Senate. But the image of wilderness as the place where humans roam free and behave badly constituted more than mere wordplay. It neatly tapped into a powerful set of Venetian stereotypes concerning the ignorance and selfishness of local residents in comparison to the wisdom and selfless foresight of the Republic's institutions, while at the same time expressing a larger sense—one might even be tempted to say an ecological vision—of the relationship between human actions and the integrity of the natural world. Mocenigo's choice of words achieved three interrelated goals. His use of an inventive turn of phrase grabbed the attention of the notoriously unruly audience in the Senate chamber. His employment of well-worn accusations of profligacy and lack of foresight on the part of Venice's mainland subjects established the need for the state to continue intervening in local practices of forest exploitation. Most importantly, his evocation of the potentially devastating and irreversible environmental consequences of unrestrained human activity played on deeply-rooted fears about the fragility of Venice's lagoon and the Republic's lack of access to foreign sources of critical natural resources. In so doing, Mocenigo gave voice to a particularly Venetian sense that the natural world required active protection from private interests that threatened to damage it, and that such safeguards could only come from republican institutions designed to protect the common good. This view stands in stark contrast to more familiar northern European ideas about nature as almost infinitely improvable through the application of virtuous private labor and capital investment informed by the mechanistic principles of the new philosophy.[4] As such, Mocenigo's play on words with the term "wilderness" reveals that Venetians held an unusual, even a unique view of the relationship between humans and the natural world. This claim requires further explanation, and this chapter will offer an account of just what the Venetians thought about nature and why.

In his speech, Mocenigo juxtaposed two categories of nature—forests and wilderness—in an apparently unfamiliar fashion. He did not consider the presence or absence of humanity as the crucial difference between the two categories of nature. He simply took it for granted that humans always exercised an influence on nature through their actions in the world. Instead, Mocenigo focused on variations in the moral content of people's actions. For Mocenigo, the key distinction between the moral nature of the *bosco* and the immoral nature of the *selva* hinged on whether or not private property owners and rural communities alike were willing to sacrifice self-interest in favor of the common interest of the *res publica*. By contrast, eighteenth-century Europeans north of the Alps tended to speak of the natural world in terms of the more commonplace and familiar Lockean categories of improved and unimproved nature in which the distinction hinged on the presence or absence of human activity. For Locke, the human presence—measured through labor and the accumulation of capital—transformed nature into virtuous property, while human absence left nature as part of the wild commons— free for the taking, but also inefficient and uncivilized.[5] In both the Venetian and the northern European cases, notions of moral economy underpinned the distinction between civilized nature and unruly wilderness. But the Venetians stressed a secular Renaissance republican morality of collective interest in which the community protected and allocated crucial resources, while northern Europeans tended to embrace a reformed Christian morality of improvement and divinely sanctioned rule over nature in which the pious, hard-working individual played the central role, transforming wild nature into private property and private property into capital.[6]

This chapter will analyze the emergence of Venetian discourses about the relationship between human action and nature and demonstrate how the development of a distinctive Venetian moral economy of nature was intimately bound up in efforts to manage the environment—both in the lagoon and upstream in mainland forests—understood through the lens of Renaissance conceptions of the *res publica*. These discourses concerning the need to preserve a particular version of nature for the public's benefit reached their fullest expression in the early eighteenth century, just as the Republic's demand for high-quality timber reached its historical peak. The chapter begins by highlighting the connections between discourse and demand. Rising demand exacerbated long-standing Venetian fears of timber scarcity amongst the patriciate, leading some members of the Republic's ruling elite to express their dread of catastrophic deforestation in novel ways. I will then argue that the Venetian moral economy of nature that emerged from these concerns offers an important exception to conventional scholarly accounts of the seventeenth- and eighteenth-century transition from an organic understanding of the natural world as a living entity possessing active agency to a mechanistic view of nature as inert matter subject to the managerial whims of its human masters. Unlike their northern European counterparts, Venetian forestry experts were able to merge a traditional view of nature with the idea that landscapes required human protection, thereby creating a unique form of managerial organicism that saw natural agency and human technology as complementary rather than antithetical.

Peak Demand and Peak Anxiety in Eighteenth-Century Venice

When Leonardo Mocenigo made his appearance before the Senate in 1704, he had every reason to be anxious about the future of the Republic's forest patrimony. The Republic had won a hard-fought naval war against the Ottomans a mere five years earlier, and most legislators recognized that a renewal of hostilities over control of the Peloponnese was both inevitable and imminent. In addition, since the end of the first war of Morea in 1699, a palpable sense of panic about the timber supply had dominated the corridors of the Ducal Palace. The Arsenal managers, in particular, had been scrambling to secure sufficient timber to prepare the worn-out fleet to defend Venice's new Peloponnesian possessions. In February 1701 they reported to the Senate that they were in the process of stripping recently decommissioned ships of every piece of useable hardware and timber so that they could refit eight first-rates for immediate redeployment in the southern Adriatic, where French warships had lately been spotted.[7] The presence of foreign warships in what the Venetians still called their gulf served as a powerful reminder of the multiple threats that the Republic faced in its efforts to survive in the era of national monarchies, as well as just how far it had slipped in the world. Such a blatant violation of Venetian sovereignty over the Adriatic would have been unimaginable at the height of the Republic's maritime power in the fifteenth century. In August of that same year, the Senate ordered the shipyard to establish a sufficient store of fully-seasoned oak to build a minimum of six additional first-rates in the event of a new military emergency.[8] But the combination of an unusually harsh winter and widespread peasant resistance to the additional *angarie* severely hampered efforts to harvest the nearly 5,000 large oak trees the Arsenal needed to meet the Senate's goal. Concerned about the evident difficulties with the acquisition of crucial oak timber, the Senate decided to commission Mocenigo as *inquisitore sopra boschi* in November of 1702. Mocenigo's orders required him to proceed onto the mainland "to discover the causes of the delays and to reinvigorate the existing laws governing forest exploitation wherever necessary."[9] Four months later, in March of 1703, and again in January of 1708, the Senate advised the *savi alle acque* "to seek private suppliers of *tolpi*, even foreigners if necessary, for the coming season."[10] The request was noteworthy, because of the number of wooden piles potentially involved. In 1701 and 1702 the *savi alle acque* had requisitioned a total of 50,000 *tolpi* to rebuild and maintain the littoral breakwaters that protected the lagoon from winter storm surges. Locating private suppliers capable of providing such large numbers of *tolpi* on such short notice was no small challenge and would have entailed enormous additional costs. In short, the Republic's leaders be-

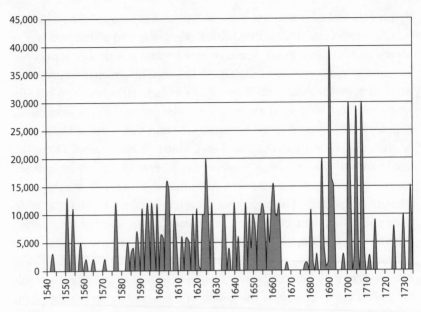

FIGURE 6.1 Licenses issued for piles used for the Lido breakwaters and levees
Requisitions for *tolpi* destined for the levees and breakwaters on the littoral
islands that protected the city from winter storm surges. The figures are of
necessity approximate, but the data allow for an accurate sense of the rising
demand for replacement piles in the last two decades of the seventeenth century
and the first two decades of the eighteenth century. After 1735 the demand
dropped to nothing, as the earth and timber breakwaters were gradually
replaced with Zendrini's famous stone breakwaters.
SOURCES: I drew the data from a number of different sources, including ASV,
Savi ed Esecutori alle Acque; ASV, *Senato Terra*; ASV, *Consiglio dei Dieci, Parti
Comuni*; and ASV, *Provveditori sopra Boschi*.

lieved that they were facing a crisis, and the tenor of Mocenigo's final
report clearly reflected that belief back at them in a thoughtful fashion.

The simultaneous rise in demand for both naval-grade and
construction-grade timber was hardly news in 1702. The need for *tolpi* to
maintain the lagoon's elaborate flood control infrastructure had reached
unprecedented levels beginning in the 1680s, when a series of particularly bad winters had destroyed large sections of the breakwaters that
protected the littoral islands from storm surges (see figure 6.1).[11] In the
three-year period between 1691 and 1693, the *savi alle acque* had re-

quested a total of over 71,000 replacement piles to rebuild the break-waters—in 1692 alone they asked for nearly 40,000. Even under normal circumstances, such a massive spike in demand would have placed a serious strain on the forest bureaucracy's financial and human resources. Throughout the sixteenth and seventeenth centuries, local *podestà* and *provveditori sopra boschi* complained of the difficulties of marshalling *angaria* labor. Their reports reveal that peasant workers and contractors often sought to slow the harvest down so as to compel Venetian officials to increase their pay. Beginning in the 1680s, with the median annual demand for *tolpi* roughly doubling, those challenges became even more acute. The forest managers were forced to supervise a greater number of simultaneous harvests spread out over a far wider area than ever before to meet the *savi alle acque*'s increasingly urgent need for construction timber. At the same time, changes in naval technology were also driving Arsenal demand to unprecedented heights. Building and maintaining the two-deck heavy frigates and other square-rigged ships that were becoming the mainstay of the fleet during this period required far greater quantities of oak than traditional galleys did. The Republic's need for the new vessels became especially acute during the during the first war of Morea, with the result that during the last two decades of the seventeenth century, the Arsenal requisitioned over 34,000 oak poles (see figure 6.2). With all these factors in mind, it comes as no surprise that the Republic was experiencing difficulties securing sufficient quantities of timber. And the Senate correctly recognized that labor shortages in timber-producing areas were contributing to the emerging crisis, which explains the 1703 and 1708 decisions to divert some of the demand for *tolpi* to foreign suppliers. The Senate used temporary measures of this sort to free up the limited pool of local labor to work exclusively on the Arsenal harvests. Still, despite a recognition of the role played by labor bottlenecks in the late seventeenth-century timber crisis, Venetian legislators could never quite shake the belief that shortages were ultimately symptoms of the permanent disappearance of mainland forests. It was this lurking fear that Leonardo Mocenigo confirmed when he reported that mainland residents had wielded their axes with abandon in every relevant district of the *terraferma*.

Previous scholars have attributed the late seventeenth-century timber shortages to failing supplies. Relying on Adolfo di Berenger's 1862 his-

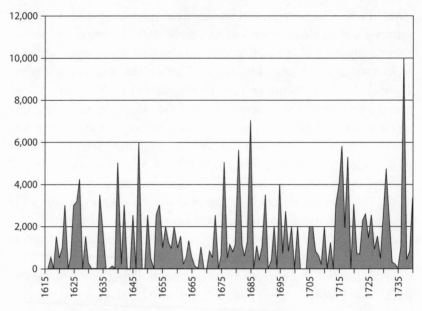

FIGURE 6.2 Arsenal oak licenses

Arsenal requisitions from 1615 to 1740. The data are approximate and do not
reflect actual deliveries to the shipyard, which in most cases fell far short of the
quantities requisitioned. Two trends, however, are clear. First, that demand
always peaked in the middle of and immediately following sustained periods of
war—note the spikes following the wars of Candia (1648–69), first Morea
(1684–99), and second Morea (1704–20)—as the shipyard struggled to
replenish its stocks of seasoned timber. Second, the shift from galleys to frigates
in the late seventeenth century drove average demand slightly higher. The spike
in 1735 is due to the need for private licenses in the wake of the *nave atta* reform
of that same year. Keep in mind, however, that almost all of those licenses
allowed the holders to take oak only in private and institutional forests, which
means that the strain on *boschi pubblici* remained fairly constant despite the
large number of new licenses being issued by the Senate.

SOURCES: I drew the data from several sources, including ASV, *Provveditori e
Patroni all'Arsenale*; ASV, *Provveditori sopra Boschi*; ASV, *Senato Terra*; ASV,
Senato Mar; and ASV, *Consiglio dei Dieci, Parti Comuni*.

tory of forests and on the traditional rhetoric of scarcity that permeated
the Senate's records, Frederic Lane concluded that by the turn of the
eighteenth century the Republic could no longer build enough ships
even to maintain control of the Adriatic.[12] While Lane was certainly

TABLE 6.1   Oak poles delivered to the Arsenal during the two wars of Morea
(1684–99; 1704–20)

Source	Quantity	Percentage
Montello	9,608	17
Montona	3,222	7
Carpeneda	500	1
Other lower Piave reserves	6,100	11
Friuli reserves	10,870	19
Private suppliers	25,200	45
Total	55,500	100

SOURCES: I compiled these data by combing through the *Filze* of the *Senato Mar* and *Senato Terra* series, the *Filze* of the *Consiglio dei Dieci, Parti Comuni*, and the records in the *Provveditori e Patroni all'Arsenale*, recording every mention of a delivery of Arsenal oak to the shipyard. The data are almost certainly incomplete, but they still provide a rough idea of the provenance of oak during the two wars. The lower Piave and Friuli reserves also include unspecified community forests. It is impossible to know where the private suppliers harvested the oak they brought to Venice, but over half of the total amount of timber used during the wars came from state and community forests.

correct that during the two wars of Morea a few timber merchants made vast fortunes, by my calculations less than half of the shipbuilding timber delivered to Venice between 1684 and 1720 came from private suppliers (see table 6.1). The remaining timber originated in a combination of community and state forests. Moreover, as chapter 5 shows, the data from Antonio Nani's 1726 *catastico* reveal that only six years after the conclusion of the second war of Morea, the mainland's *boschi pubblici* still contained vast quantities of durmast oak. Even if the toll taken by the war was evident in the relative scarcity of the largest, most mature growth, there was more than enough intermediate growth in 1726 to meet almost any conceivable emergency. The real concern, as Nani pointed out, was the apparent disappearance of vast areas of private and institutional woodlands during the eighty years since the onset of the War of Candia in 1648.[13]

In light of the *catastico* data, which demonstrate that there was no lack of timber in the mainland forest reserves, the causes of the shortages in the first decade of the eighteenth century must be sought elsewhere. A closer examination of the sources suggests that the most serious problems involved harvesting and transportation bottlenecks, which were caused by a combination of labor shortages on the mainland and a liquidity crisis in Venice. The two factors were obviously related. By the end of the seventeenth century the mainland peasantry—or in some cases private contractors who had purchased a quinquennial *condotta* monopoly for a particular district—had elevated work stoppages during the timber harvest to an art form. Every year during the February and late August harvest seasons, the Council of Ten, the *provveditori e patroni all'arsenale*, and the Senate all faced a flood of petitions from the *podestà* in timber-producing areas, seeking additional funds to pay off the financial demands of local labor. The *sussidio, carratada,* and other local taxes could not keep up with the cost of the *condotta,* because the workers and monopoly holders were both constantly renegotiating their terms. And with the Republic's treasury already straining to meet the costs of the war, there were few funds in Venice to help local authorities bridge the gap. Because of the limited window of opportunity for felling the timber and moving it out of the forest and down to the embarcaderos, even the poorest peasants possessed far more leverage than the most strong-willed Venetian *podestà.* Corporal punishment was all but useless as a weapon against malingerers, because by the time it could be imposed, the water levels in local rivers would already have dropped and the work crews disbanded. Consequently, Venetian officials were either forced to concede to the demands of labor and monopoly holders or allow harvested poles to sit unguarded for six months or more until the water levels rose enough to float them once more. A pair of letters preserved in the Arsenal's records expresses the dilemma concisely. The first, from the *provveditori all'arsenale* to the Senate in July 1703, pointed out that "the longer one defers the departure of harvested poles from the mainland towards our shores, the longer it will take to properly season them for public service. Consequently, you should reflect on the need to disburse money as needed and in a timely manner, as has been done in similar cases in the past."[14] The second, from the Senate to the *podestà* of Treviso in June of 1707, stressed that "the delays that the contractors create under various pretexts are unacceptable, and you must hold them to their agreements with the public authority . . . despite the favorable terms they have secured through these actions in the past."[15] Together, these two letters reveal how the Republic could not keep up with the higher prices and labor costs brought on by its own demand for high-quality timber.

Not every delay or cost overrun was the result of peasant resistance or greedy monopoly holders. Other factors, including a visible increase in erosion in upstream areas, also slowed the delivery of oak timber to the Arsenal. For example, in 1695 an accumulation of silt at the main embarcadero near Pordenone forced workers to move 227 oak logs several kilometers upstream to an alternate landing area, where the raftsmen could bind them together for eventual transportation to Venice.[16] The resulting operation took six months to complete and forced the *provveditori all'arsenale* to turn to the Senate with hat in hand for the necessary funds to pay for the additional labor involved. Even relatively small dramas of this sort could have significant repercussions for the timely delivery of Arsenal material, especially when several occurred simultaneously. In June of 1712, for example, the *provveditori all'arsenale* estimated that at least 2,600 felled oak poles—enough to build three first-rates—had been awaiting removal to embarcaderos along the Piave and Livenza rivers for at least six months, and in some cases far longer.[17] Likewise, an August 1706 harvest of "1,000 very large oak" from the Montello resulted in the delivery of only a quarter of that yield by the following April. And although the Arsenal managers declared that "the 250 poles we have received from the Montello harvest of last August are of the most perfect quality imaginable," it would be another year before the rest were successfully delivered.[18] Thus even when timber of the highest quality was both available and accessible, the forest bureaucracy still struggled to move it downstream to Venice in a timely fashion.

In the midst of a long and arduous war, delivery delays of even a single season—which amounted to approximately six months—had serious consequences. Every month that timber sat on the ground awaiting transportation left it vulnerable to pilfering at the hands of local residents and added to the already lengthy seasoning process that the oak timber had to undergo once it arrived in the shipyard. In some cases, military exigencies forced the shipyard to employ imperfectly seasoned timber with disastrous results. In May of 1705 major structural flaws were identified in three newly built first-rates, one of which—the *Tigre*—foundered and was lost.[19] Green timbers were blamed for the tragedy, which became the subject of a lengthy investigation.[20] In 1708, in response to the Arsenal managers' complaints about shortages of fully-seasoned timber in the yard, the Senate tried to lift a long-standing prohibition on the import of pre-seasoned and pre-cut timbers from foreign sources. But the measure was vehemently opposed by the shipyard's sawyers, who feared the resulting loss of work and pay.[21] Ultimately, the Senate agreed to give the sawyers a share of the import tariffs to make up for any income they would have to forfeit due to the purchase of pre-cut timbers. This apparently minor workplace conflict points to yet another way in which workers exerted significant influence over the flow of crucial timber resources into Venice and the Arsenal.

The combination of a markedly higher demand for piles to maintain the breakwaters and recurring problems with the *condotta* system for Arsenal timber sparked expressions of anxiety both from legislators and from officials such as Leonardo Mocenigo. Under ordinary circumstances, such a burdensome concatenation of unprecedented demand, rising labor costs, and a generalized fiscal crisis would have been cause for concern in the Ducal Palace. But the unfolding of the crisis at such a delicate and dangerous military and political juncture amplified traditional fears concerning the possibility of a catastrophic timber shortage into something closer to all-out panic. With the benefit of hindsight provided by the cadastral surveys, it is possible to see that the problems were not due to any real shortage of available oak in the state reserves— as so many have claimed—but rather were a product of the complex interaction of increasing demand, higher extraction and transportation costs, worker resistance to onerous *angarie*, and mild profiteering on the part of monopoly holders and private suppliers. However, in November 1704, as Mocenigo mounted the rostrum to address his colleagues in the Senate chamber, no one in the audience possessed a clear view of the many dimensions of the problem. As far as Venice's leaders were concerned, the state's need for timber resources was greater than it had ever been, and the Republic's carefully preserved forest patrimony was failing to meet those needs at a most inauspicious moment.

Institutional Reform and the *Res Publica* of Forests

Peak demand for high-quality timber at the turn of the eighteenth century supplies a crucial context for understanding both the content and tenor of Leonardo Mocenigo's 1704 report. But this context alone does not fully explain some of the most interesting features of the report—

especially his prescription for reforming the Republic's approach to managing its timber supply. Mocenigo's was not merely another voice being raised in alarm in the first decade of the new century. His report offers a remarkable vantage point from which to view the emergence of a coherent set of Venetian ideas about the relationship between human institutions and the natural world—especially regarding common resources such as timber.

Similar reports tend to survive only in manuscript form—either as transcripts of the formal oration produced by a chancery secretary or as the actual text that the patrician official carried with him to the rostrum and then surrendered to the secretaries for binding into the daily minutes of the Senate or the Council of Ten. Mocenigo's report is one of the few such documents produced by or for the forest bureaucracy that survives as a printed pamphlet. In and of itself, the creation of a printed pamphlet during this period is unexceptional. By the middle of the eighteenth century it had become quite common for the Senate to circulate printed copies of important decisions, both as a means of facilitating public dissemination of new legislation and of reinforcing existing laws that it believed were being ignored. Nevertheless, Mocenigo's pamphlet stands out for its relatively early date (as compared to similar productions) and for the fact that it contained not just a recapitulation of the most important forestry legislation, but the entire text of Mocenigo's oration before the Senate. Even a cursory glance at Mocenigo's pamphlet reveals that he had self-consciously produced a manual or handbook designed to help legislators understand what he considered the core issues involved in preserving the Republic's forest patrimony and improving the flow of critical forest resources into the lagoon. In this regard, the pamphlet represents Mocenigo's attempt to establish his bona fides as a bureaucratic expert who was privy to the secrets of good forest management, despite the fact that he had not enjoyed the guidance of either the *catastici* or the regular retinue of craft experts who normally participated in the production of the surveys. Indeed, the fact that Mocenigo lacked the support of the usual coterie of subordinate experts and yet still managed to write a speech that was recognizable as an expert production highlights the degree to which many of the forest bureaucracy's core ideas about the natural world had become part of the common political vocabulary by the beginning of the eighteenth century.

Mocenigo opened his report by lamenting at length the Republic's inability to enforce its own elaborate and long-standing legislation governing local practices of forest exploitation. He noted that in the past "the penalties have always been insufficiently harsh to dissuade individuals from destroying precious resources, and the rewards for reporting lawbreakers have likewise been insufficiently generous to persuade anyone to come forward and testify against wrongdoers."[22] He proceeded to argue that even when officials had endeavored to enforce the laws by applying the harshest possible penalties, "this only succeeded in altering the behavior of a few individuals without changing in any way their attitude towards common resources."[23] Mocenigo faulted lax local councils and village leaders who shirked their responsibility to enforce the laws, choosing instead to allow individuals to do as they pleased. And because "individuals had no objective in mind except excessive profit, they in turn ignored their responsibility to husband important public resources for the use of all."[24] So while Mocenigo firmly believed that the Republic's laws governing forest exploitation had failed to produce the landscapes that the Venetians had hoped for, he did not blame the laws, which he argued were mostly well-intentioned and properly conceived. Instead, Mocenigo blamed the sorry state of the Republic's legal regime on the Venetians' failure to convince mainland residents of the wisdom of preserving the most important resources for public use. In other words, the laws had failed in the face of the raw and unbridled greed of mainland elites—both private-property owners and village and town leaders.

In many ways, Mocenigo's decision to frame his analysis of the failure of the Republic's forestry legislation in terms of divergent public and private passions and interests represents one of the most traditional Venetian approaches to the problem. As chapter 3 noted in detail, the conviction that mainland residents cared only for personal profit, while the Venetians were the proper arbiters and guardians of the public good, helped to justify some of the earliest attempts to regulate local practices of forest exploitation—most notably the precedent-making 1471 Montello ban. Yet the wholesale condemnation of profit-taking in mainland forests that pervades nearly every page of Mocenigo's report marks a major shift in terms of both the tone and the content of Venetian critiques of mainland practices of forest exploitation. In 1471 the Senate had not attacked mainland residents' impulse to seek personal profit from forest resources; it had merely argued that they could easily "acquire those same resources elsewhere" and so did not need to enjoy unfettered access to the Montello.[25] By contrast, Mocenigo argued that "while owners of forestland enjoy property rights on those lands, those rights in no way contradict the just, direct, perpetual, absolute, and incontrovertible dominion of the Doge over all the seedlings and all the oak trees in our territories."[26] Not only was Mocenigo's claim concerning the extent of the Republic's sovereignty over forests of all descriptions incomparably greater than the Senate's 1471 claims with respect to the Montello, but he also placed far stricter limits on the rights of the Republic's subjects to pursue personal profit in forests containing even a single oak tree. In 1471 the Senate merely wished to restrict access to the best oak trees growing within the boundaries of the thirteen contiguous community stands that made up the Montello. In 1704 Mocenigo argued that the Republic had the incontestable right to restrict unilaterally the property rights of individuals, institutions, and communities in virtually any mainland forest containing oak of any quality. And in order to justify such expansive powers, Mocenigo had to argue that almost any profit-taking activity in such forests ran contrary to the public good and therefore should be subject to public regulation. That the Senate approved Mocenigo's report verbatim demonstrates the degree to which the Republic's claims to dominion over mainland forests had gone from a right —the traditional *diritto di riserva*—that had to be stated in carefully parsed language to a claim that could be asserted in the strongest possible terms, as if it were a simple and self-evident truth.

Mocenigo's sweeping claims concerning Venetian sovereignty over oak resources reveal the degree to which the development of the forest bureaucracy had enhanced the Republic's power over its mainland territories. In much the same way, his rhetoric about the important role that mainland communities needed to play in the enforcement of Venetian legislation highlights another crucial shift in the way that at least some Venetian patricians understood the problem of regulating access to mainland forest resources. As already seen, the 1471 Montello ban and the 1476 legislation governing community forests set the important precedent that forestry legislation should be proscriptive. To put it another way, from the very outset the Venetians had framed forestry legislation in terms of banning all those local practices that they believed impeded the state's access to critical forest resources, especially oak and beech timber. On the surface, Mocenigo's powerfully phrased accusations against mainland communities appear to reflect this traditional view that the Republic's needs and local needs were mutually exclusive. Yet a careful reading reveals that even the denizens of the Ducal Palace had developed a far more nuanced view of the constant tension between local practices and central necessities. In particular, the primary lesson that Mocenigo derived from past enforcement failures was that local communities needed to be assigned a far greater role in enforcing the existing forestry laws. By making village leaders one of the linchpins of the forestry regime, Mocenigo hoped to effect an ideological transformation that would lead local authorities to feel the same strong sense of collective responsibility for the public good as the members of the Senate and the Council of Ten. Only then would mainland residents take the preservation of forest resources as seriously as the Venetians did, thus guaranteeing the proper application of the laws.

To help foster this new sense of responsibility on the part of local councils and village leaders, Mocenigo proposed the creation of local forest bureaucracies modeled on already-existing Venetian institutions. Specifically, Mocenigo called for the appointment of two forest guardians in every mainland community. The guardians would serve for two years, and their responsibilities were to be modeled explicitly on those of the *capitani* of the *boschi pubblici* (who were appointed by the Arsenal managers), except that their authority would extend to every forest in their jurisdictions—including those standing on private and institutional property. The office could not be sold or rented out for profit, nor could it be refused on any grounds. And in a provision reminiscent of the fifteenth-century expansion of the *provveditori sopra il fatto delle legne*, Mocenigo specified that the term of office of each new pair of guardians overlap with that of the outgoing guardians by three months so that "the incoming officials might gain from the experience of their predecessors."[27] Finally, the legislation instructed each guardian to keep a *libretto*—or small account book—in which he would track the emergence of new growth in the forests under his watch and record the removal of every individual oak tree from them. The books were to be passed from guardian to guardian, thus preserving a running total of oak trees in every mainland jurisdiction. Interestingly, Mocenigo made no mention of the *catastico* registers on which the *libretti* were clearly modeled, so it is unclear whether he thought the information in the *libretti* could be used in conjunction with the registers to keep central authorities up-to-date on local changes in forest composition. Nevertheless, it is plain that he conceived of the system of local guardians as a Venetian forest bureaucracy in miniature—complete with its own appropriately simple and scaled-down set of quantitative tools to track changes in private, institutional, and community forests. As I will argue presently, Mocenigo hoped that the creation of a set of local institutions that mirrored the Venetian forest bureaucracy would effectively transform mainland residents' attitudes towards nature to match those of their Venetian rulers.

Mocenigo believed that the only way to guarantee widespread and uniform enforcement of Venetian forestry laws was to convince local authorities of the compatibility of their own interests with those of Venice. In other words, Mocenigo sought to persuade the leaders of mainland communities that they would benefit from embracing the Venetian definition of the public good. To be sure, Mocenigo's emphasis on creating a shared definition of the common good represented a significant change from the traditional Venetian conception of central and local interests in the forest as ultimately antithetical. However, it hewed closely to what had been one of the *provveditori sopra boschi*'s favorite themes in their correspondence with the Council of Ten since the early seventeenth century. Giovanni Garzoni and other representatives of the forest bureaucracy had steadfastly argued that the courts should treat peasants with lenience, in an effort to enlist their cooperation in bringing landowners and other elite scofflaws to justice. Garzoni reasoned that "the poor are not to blame for they act out of desperation, need, and ignorance, and there is little in their actions that is not forgivable."[28] In Garzoni's estimation, mainland elites posed the only meaningful threat to the integrity of *terraferma* forests, and the Republic's enforcement efforts should be directed solely at curbing abuses perpetrated by wealthy individuals and institutions. Garzoni and his fellow *provveditori sopra boschi* argued that in so doing, the Republic would gain the loyalty and cooperation of the peasantry, whose rightful portion of common resources was also threatened by local elites.

A careful reading of Mocenigo's report corroborates the idea that he shared the *provveditori sopra boschi*'s conviction that the most serious threat to the Republic's forest patrimony was the greed of already wealthy landowners. Where Mocenigo deviated from the forest bureaucracy's consensus view of the problem was in his emphasis on institutional forms and actions. Rather than practice leniency towards the peasantry to co-opt them in the struggle against landowning elites, Mocenigo argued that a "consistent and uniform application of the laws" was the only way to ensure that "councils and individuals feel equally accountable for the destruction of precious oak trees."[29] This was not to say that Mocenigo endorsed an unthinkingly punitive approach to enforcement. He explicitly noted that such efforts had always failed in the past. Instead, by creating a set of local institutions that deliberately mirrored the Republic's forest bureaucracy, Mocenigo believed that he could instill a sense of the common good in local elites that would likewise perfectly reflect Venetian ideas about the *res publica*. Mocenigo's faith in the power of institutions to shape people's political behavior mirrors one of the bedrock principles of Venetian republicanism. In most versions of the famous myth of Venice, the Venetians argued that it was the perfection of their institutions, not the virtue of the individual officeholder, that explained the Republic's remarkable longevity. So despite the fact that Venetian rule on the *terraferma* had long been premised on the idea that local institutions and traditions should be left intact, Mocenigo's report shows that the eighteenth-century Republic had become more aggressive in its efforts to create greater institutional and legal uniformity in its dominions. Similarly, Alfredo Viggiano has identified a parallel debate over institutional arrangements and republican ideology in Venice's Ionian island possessions in the second half of the century.[30] Of course, by focusing on village politics Mocenigo was operating on a much smaller stage than his colleagues in the *stato da mar*, but his ambition to transform the values that local councils attached to forest resources by, in effect, turning those councils into tiny versions of Venice was one that other eighteenth-century Venetians would have understood well.[31]

Mocenigo was not so naive as to imagine that the Republic could simply impose such a fundamental transformation by fiat. New institutions staffed by local experts trained in the Venetian tradition of localized empiricism would generate some of the necessary impetus, as would a more uniform application of the laws; but Mocenigo also argued that the new habits of mind he envisioned could only emerge through the introduction of regular and consistent practices of forest exploitation throughout the *terraferma*. For Mocenigo, this meant not only that the new forest guardians would have to be held accountable for their actions in defense of forests—he reserved the worst corporal penalties for guardians caught in dereliction of their duties—but that the Republic's institutions should behave much more consistently in their approach to forest management. In Mocenigo's view, the *provveditori e patroni all'arsenale* and the *provveditori sopra boschi* shared some of the blame for what he understood to be the sorry state of mainland forests, because they had not adhered to any kind of regular harvesting schedule or rotation. The Arsenal's traditional ad hoc approach to requisitioning oak had set a terrible example for local councils and village residents. After all, when years or even decades might pass between officially supervised harvests—to say nothing of cadastral surveys—it became extremely difficult to condemn mainland residents for thinking that forest resources were free for the taking. The Republic and its institutions had to set an example for local councils and the newly empowered local experts. That way local authorities would clearly comprehend exactly what was expected of them, both in terms of institutional forms and in terms of actual practices in local forests. Only then would local councils truly share the Senate's understanding of the *res publica* of forests. To achieve this congruence of interests, Mocenigo prescribed "a regular and inalterable *condotta* of oak for every forest in our territories."[32] He fervently hoped that by rationalizing the Arsenal's system for requisitioning and harvesting timber, the Republic could make responsible and rational foresters out of its mainland subjects.

Two decades later, in 1726, the *provveditore sopra boschi* Antonio Nani echoed Mocenigo's laments about the uneven official presence on the mainland when he argued that too much time had passed since the last *catastico* for him to successfully identify and restore illegally cleared forests on private lands.[33] Nani's analysis of the significant consequences of the gaps in the cadastral data certainly implied that Mocenigo's planned reforms had largely come to naught. Yet Nani failed to revisit Mocenigo's proposals, in large measure because he shared none of the latter's zeal for a uniform and clockwork *condotta* system. Nani undoubtedly hoped that more regular surveys would help fill in the gaps in the *catastico* data, thereby providing the *provveditori sopra boschi* with a more complete and reliable history of mainland forests. And Nani clearly believed that more comprehensive quantitative data would lead to better decisions about where and when to harvest oak on behalf of the Arsenal and the *savi alle acque*. But those decisions needed to be made anew every year, and on a case-by-case basis, taking into account both the specific needs of the moment, and the types of fine-grained local data that only the cadastral surveys could produce. In other words, where Mocenigo saw only chaos, Nani saw a system designed to account for the fact that state demand fluctuated significantly from year to year and that each forest was a unique entity requiring individualized treatment. A large reserve like the Montello might be able to withstand annual harvests, while other forests might only be exploitable once every three years, and still others once a decade. But the *provveditori sopra boschi* could only put themselves in a position to make such determinations if they enjoyed access to a complete and accurate history of each and every forest in the *terraferma*. A regular and uniform schedule of the sort proposed by Mocenigo violated the very premise on which the *provveditori sopra boschi* had built the Renaissance forestry regime—that an intimate empirical knowledge of local political, economic, and ecological contexts mattered more than a set of abstract and universal rules, however carefully conceived. What appeared rational to Mocenigo was profoundly irrational to Nani. So when Mocenigo called for "keeping count, strict count of the oak in every forest,"[34] he may have believed he was speaking the quantitative language of the *provveditori sopra boschi*, but he was actually laboring under a deep misapprehension about how the Republic's forest bureaucracy had long operated in practice.

The very different notions of instrumental rationality expressed by Antonio Nani and Leonardo Mocenigo italicize one of the truly distinctive features of Venice's Renaissance forestry regime—its careful attention to local context and detail. They also once again bring to the fore the persistent differences between the more generalized and abstract view of mainland forests held by officials in the Ducal Palace and the empiricism that had for so long informed the perspectives of members of the forest bureaucracy, such as Giovanni Garzoni and Antonio Nani. The tension between the schematic view of officials like Mocenigo and the complex view of *provveditori sopra boschi* such as Nani gradually worsened over the course of the eighteenth century, culminating in a complete overhaul of the forestry regime in 1792.[35] The 1792 reforms established two forestry districts—Piave and Friuli—each of which was further divided into two departments—upper and lower Piave, and east and west of the Tagliamento. The Collegio appointed a superintendent to run each department; and in a dramatic break with tradition, the superintendents were drawn from regional agrarian academies on the mainland instead of from Venetian institutions such as the Arsenal.[36] Each department was further divided into eight subdistricts—for a total of thirty-two subdistricts in all—that the superintendents were supposed to harvest on a rotating basis to lessen the impact of Arsenal demand on any single area or forest. In nearly every respect, the new *sopraintendenza forestale* appeared to be a perfect example of an institution founded on the kinds of scientific principles that undergirded most eighteenth-century forestry practices in northern Europe. Unfortunately, it is almost impossible to assess either the substance or the effects of the 1792 reforms, because the dissolution of the Republic at the hands of Napoleon only five years later terminated the experiment before it had been fully implemented. The decision to replace the Renaissance forest bureaucracy with a completely new set of enlightened institutions—modeled on what the Senate, in one letter to the Arsenal, called "the better governed nations of France, England and Holland"[37]—marked the dissolution of the institutions that had formed the basis of the Renaissance forestry regime.

The bureaucracy's and the legislature's conflicting views of what constituted a rational approach to forest management also underscore the shortcomings of a straightforwardly Weberian frame of analysis as a way of understanding early modern states in the seventeenth and eighteenth centuries. Seen from the perspective of comparable European institutions in the eighteenth century Mocenigo's version of rational forest management—with its emphasis on regularity, uniformity, and universality—is instantly recognizable. Seen in the same light, Nani's ideas appear unnecessarily complex and retrograde. Consequently it becomes possible to dismiss the eighteenth-century Republic as a stubborn holdover of a premodern form of state organization.[38] But such a view elides the fact that Nani's distinctively Venetian privileging of complexity and local context over uniformity and generalization underpinned a carefully considered forestry regime, one that employed a well-articulated form of instrumental rationality, both in terms of its objectives—to ensure the preservation and reproduction of key resources—and its reliance on sophisticated empirical and quantitative technologies. One might even argue that given our own renewed attention to local problems and ecological contexts, Nani's version of instrumental rationality appears decidedly more sophisticated than Mocenigo's—a distant forerunner of the now ubiquitous admonition to "think globally, act locally." Finally, even the 1792 reforms—for all their apparent enlightened rationality—still bore the unmistakable imprimatur of the Venetian preference for local context over standardization. The Venetians opted to employ the tree counts in the *catastici* as the basis for establishing the boundaries of the thirty-two subdistricts, in the hopes that each subdistrict would contain an equal number of oak trees. The result was a patchwork quilt of unevenly sized areas displaying highly irregular boundaries and requiring significant local knowledge to interpret. Northern European foresters preferred to divide forestry districts into equal areas, making them easier to survey and identify on a map. So even amidst the transition to an enlightened forestry regime, the Venetians clung to the notion that certain kinds of local context mattered more than creating standardized measures that were easier for bureaucrats and legislators alike to understand, monitor, and track. In this regard the Venetian forestry regime also offers an important challenge to the assumption—rooted in the work of Michel Foucault—that the modern bureaucratic state functioned primarily to institute procedures for standardized surveillance and knowledge production.

Beyond its implications for our understanding of early modern statecraft, Mocenigo's report illustrates another important dissonance between legislators' conceptions of the challenges of forest management and those of the *provveditori sopra boschi* and other members of the forest bureaucracy. Dispatched to see to the reinforcement of all the existing laws governing forest exploitation, Mocenigo understandably framed the problem of forest management as a question of law. If a solution to the problem of timber scarcity was to be found, Mocenigo reasoned that it would only be found in a system of just laws enforced by virtuous institutions. In contrast, Nani, Garzoni, and other *provveditori sopra boschi* saw the problem as a question of nature. In their view, the best approach involved preserving and reproducing a particular form of nature through empirically based practices of forest management. Nani and his fellow *provveditori sopra boschi* displayed little interest in either individual or institutional virtue, except insofar as they agreed with legislators that exemplary punishments should be meted out to the worst offenders. These competing approaches to forest management were not necessarily incompatible, except that the *provveditori sopra boschi* had clearly opted to ignore those laws that, in their estimation, hampered the forest bureaucracy's primary mission of preserving, replenishing, and requisitioning critical forest resources. To put it slightly differently, the *provveditori sopra boschi* believed that the question of whether or not the laws were just was merely a secondary consideration. They placed far greater emphasis on whether the laws produced acceptable practices of forest exploitation at the local level.

The most dramatic example of the tension between these two competing views of the law can be seen clearly in Mocenigo's treatment of the Council of Ten's 1531 reforestation statute mandating the replanting of oak on eight percent of all cleared land, regardless of who owned it.[39] The *provveditori sopra boschi* had traditionally paid little attention to the statute as written. The marginal notes in the *catastico* registers prove that the *proti* made every attempt to reseed the *boschi pubblici* with acorns, while virtually ignoring private and institutional forests.[40] And Giovanni Garzoni went so far as to confiscate those forests with the highest potential for regrowth and add them to the Republic's forest patrimony, even before commencing reforestation efforts.[41] Garzoni's actions illustrate how the *provveditori sopra boschi* only saw reforestation as a viable option in those forests over which they could exert direct control, and for the most part they were willing to forego what they thought of as fruitless efforts to force private and institutional landowners to overcome their selfish interest in personal profits in order to replant oak on behalf of the state. Conversely, Mocenigo placed enormous emphasis on the 1531 law, reflecting that "reason persuades us that with the passing of time and by taking full advantage of all the available seeds, the number of saplings will multiply, both from the acorns that fall and are collected and from the simple, spontaneous action of nature that makes the forests so fertile."[42] Once again, Mocenigo revealed his unshakable faith that an existing law, properly enforced, had the power to enhance the natural renewal of mainland forests. Furthermore, Mocenigo's presumption that the 1531 law could ultimately succeed was premised on the idealistic belief that institutions had the power to re-shape the values of mainland residents to match those of their Venetian rulers. Once that transformation was complete, Mocenigo seemed to have faith that even private landowners would gladly reseed their land with acorns for public benefit—a notion that a hardened cynic like Garzoni would surely have found laughable.

The marked contrast between Mocenigo and Garzoni accentuates the overarching contradiction that structured the Renaissance forestry regime. On the one hand, the Venetians' ongoing efforts to establish a set of laws capable of shaping local practices of forest exploitation reveals their faith in the power of republican institutions to generate useful compromises between individuals and groups driven by apparently conflicting passions and interests. On the other hand, the bureaucratic experts' deep commitment to empirical knowledge and locally calibrated approaches to forest management demonstrates how the Republic's officials often preferred to resolve tensions between different groups on a case-by-case basis, rather than waiting to see whether institutions really could transform the political and economic attitudes of the *Serenissima*'s mainland subjects. The *provveditori sopra boschi*—empirically minded bureaucratic experts who walked the halls of the Ducal Palace and spent years tromping through forest reserves—possessed a privileged perspective on this contradiction. But their powers as mediators between local conditions and central edicts remained limited. The *provveditori sopra boschi* could chide legislators over the latter's ignorance of mainland forests, but they could not always personally shape the laws that emanated from the Ducal Palace. Likewise, they could make any number of informal arrangements with local communities to undermine the power of property-owning elites, but they could not be present at every Arsenal harvest to ensure that those agreements were honored. Their real influence surfaced in their power to shape and frame Venetian ideas about the operation of the natural world.

The Venetial Moral Economy of Nature

If Mocenigo's perspective on the challenges that the Republic faced in its efforts to create a workable forest management program foregrounds the persistence of the gap separating the *provveditori sopra boschi*'s understanding of mainland forests from that of their superiors in the Ducal Palace, it also points to the existence of some important common discursive ground between the two groups. In particular, most Venetian patricians shared a set of deeply held beliefs about the relationship between humans and the rest of the natural world, one that emphasized nature's ultimate fragility in the face of humanity's destructive power. As we have already seen, the persistent fear that the Republic would eventually run out of the timber—and thereby lose its liberty—had always been closely connected to lurking anxieties about the power of even small peasant communities to damage the landscape in a permanent fashion. Mocenigo openly acknowledged that fear when he deplored the fact that rural residents armed only with axes and their flocks of domesticated animals had reduced mainland forests from resource-rich landscapes to "hollow" shells in no time at all. This destructiveness was especially appalling when measured against the centuries that "nature had struggled" to produce those same forests.[43] While Giovanni Garzoni, Antonio Nani, and other *provveditori sopra boschi* did not always share Mocenigo's bleak view of either the present or the future of the Republic's forest reserves, they clearly agreed that humans had the power to destroy important landscapes—or, as Garzoni put it in one of his frequent jeremiads against wealthy mainland residents, to "eradicate entire forests."[44]

Human destructiveness was not the only lens through which the Venetians viewed the relationship between humans and the natural world. If people could "eradicate entire forests" for personal gain, the converse was also true. They might plant trees for the common good, or survey, mark, and maintain the boundaries of the *boschi pubblici* to forestall the destruction of common resources. They might divide forests into coupes to prevent their depletion. They might even count every oak tree with an eye towards making informed decisions about where and when to harvest. The Venetians had built the Renaissance forestry regime on the conviction that forests and forest resources could be preserved through a concerted effort, one that was regulated and directed by the state. Ultimately, this was the forest bureaucracy's answer to legislators' fears of environmental disaster. Most Venetians concurred with the idea that, left to their own devices, people would surely destroy every last forest for personal gain. But the *provveditori sopra boschi* also believed that through the use of powerful tools—such as regular inspections, cadastral surveys, and maps—the state could coerce its subjects into working in concert with nature to produce forests capable of meeting all the most pressing common needs in perpetuity. A very early expression of this hope can be found in the fascinating report written by Alessio di Mathio, Luca di Nicolò, and Marco di Zuane—the three *proti* who first surveyed the Cansiglio reserve in 1548. Prominently displaying their craft knowledge, the three craftsmen assured the Council of Ten that "we can promise your excellencies that, properly managed, it will provide oars for your needs for many tens, no hundreds of years."[45] And it was with this same sense of guarded optimism that Leonardo Mocenigo proposed his institutional reforms in 1704. Just as Mocenigo and the *provveditori sopra boschi* agreed about the destructive capacities of men, they also agreed that through the collective efforts of all its subjects, the Republic had the power to put those same capacities to work in preserving crucial resources. Where they differed was on the question of what the best means for achieving this critical common goal should be.

The Venetian belief in humans' capacity to control the environment—for good as well as for ill—was not limited to the problem of forest management. As Élisabeth Crouzet-Pavan has observed, the long struggle to maintain what the Venetians believed was an ideal balance of silt-laden fresh water and tide-borne salt water in the lagoon had profoundly shaped Venetian ideas about themselves and about the unusual environment in which they lived well in advance of the conquest of the *terraferma* in the early fifteenth century.[46] Crouzet-Pavan concludes that the demands of building and maintaining a city in such a complex and perilous environment forced the Venetian patriciate to cooperate in social and political arenas in ways that their mainland counterparts in cities like Florence and Milan did not. From this perspective, the Republic's vaunted political and social cohesion and stability were, in large measure, the products of the demands that the city's difficult and distinctive geographical situation placed on both its common residents and its rulers. In essence, Crouzet-Pavan proposes that the Venetian lagoon produced Venetian republicanism. Or, to put it another way, Venice was very much nature's republic.[47]

It is only proper to view Wittvogelian arguments such as Crouzet-Pavan's with considerable skepticism. Geographical determinism always makes for good copy, but rarely withstands careful scrutiny. The lagoon did not make Venice a republic any more than the Lombard plain made Milan a despotism. Nevertheless, there can be little doubt that the demands of living in the lagoon indelibly marked the way that the Venetians chose to describe the relationship between human action and environmental change. The Venetians went to incredible effort and expense to reshape the lagoon to serve the needs of their city and its port. They moved the mouths of three major rivers, dredged incalculable quantities of sediment from the floor of the lagoon, converted it into landfill, and built a complex and costly system of breakwaters and levees to hold back the worst of the winter storm surges that threatened to wash away the barrier islands and inundate the city. In every respect the lagoon was the product of human toil on a vast scale. But the Venetians, looking back at it from the vantage point of the eighteenth century, amazingly did not view this herculean effort as having altered the lagoon's essential qualities and character. Instead, they saw themselves as having, in Cristoforo Sabbadino's famous formulation, "preserve[d] nature with art."[48] As Manfredo Tafuri astutely points out, Sabbadino's maxim presupposes a specific view of the relationship between technology and the natural world, one that was rooted in the principle that "it ought to stress the work of Nature, it should not change or disturb. It is first called upon to 'preserve,' and then to 'renew.'"[49] More specifically, Sabbadino's maxim reminded his fellow Venetians that the goal of every interaction with the natural world should be to preserve it in its ideal state.

The potent idea that the goal of human action should be to preserve and renew nature rather than alter and improve it found its fullest expression in the Republic's efforts to manage the lagoon. The Venetians well understood that left alone, the lagoon would eventually have silted up and become part of the mainland. They also knew that arresting that process would potentially incur the equally dangerous prospect of losing the barrier islands and being swallowed by the Adriatic. Consequently, they sought to establish and maintain a balance between the dueling forces of sea and land that would allow both the lagoon and the city to carry on in an approximation of their existing state. The allegorical frontispiece to Bernardo Trevisan's 1715 *Della laguna di Venezia* perfectly captures this idealized state of equipoise as eighteenth-century Venetians perceived it (figure 6.3). The engraving renders the elements of sea and earth as a pair of giant human figures wrestling for control of the lagoon under a banner that reads "element opposed to element." The Ducal Palace, Piazzetta, and Campanile loom in the background, in a position that emphasizes both the inherent vulnerability of the city to the immense forces of earth and water and its central and irreplaceable role as arbiter in the perpetual contest between the two dueling elements.

As Trevisan's image suggests, eighteenth-century Venetians believed they had preserved—and continued to preserve—the lagoon in the truest sense of the word. They neither sought to restore the lagoon to some mythical status quo ante, nor imagined that they could improve on that which God or nature had already wrought by further transforming it into some better form, one theoretically more suitable for human use and habitation. Instead, they strove to maintain the lagoon in the exact state it was in at the precise moment that it had achieved what the Venetians believed was a providential condition of natural perfection. In a quintessentially humanist move, the Venetian program for preserving the lagoon integrated, on a truly grand scale, the classical Aristotelian and Vitruvian ideal of *imitatio naturae* with the Christian belief in divine providence. In this fashion, the Venetians were able to offer an explanation for nature's apparent ability to offer such a perfect location for their city, while at the same time acknowledging that this ideal environment was ultimately transitory, fragile, and contingent on the ability of its human inhabitants to protect and preserve it. The development of a favorable natural order happened as a result of providence, but its preservation in that providential state depended almost entirely on properly directed human effort.[50] If that effort lagged, or became misdirected, then the providential state would be lost along with all the natural benefits that had accrued from it. According to this model, nature was at once powerful and fragile, and human communities possessed the ability either to preserve or to destroy it, but not to improve upon it in any meaningful way. In fact, throughout the early modern period, the Venetians staunchly resisted the sorts of profitable reclamation projects that northern European improvers so often embraced, precisely because large-scale reclamation around the lagoon's periphery threatened to upset the desired balance between sea and land by eliminating the marshy areas where crucial backwater accumulated during each tidal cycle.[51] Back-

OPPONESI ELEMENTO AD ELEMENTO

A.° Zucchi Sculp.

FIGURE 6.3 The allegorical frontispiece to Bernardo Trevisan's 1715 *Della laguna di Venezia*

The frontispiece shows female *terra* and male *mare* locked in an eternal struggle for control of the lagoon, with the city of Venice in the background. The image neatly summarizes the Venetian view of the goal of lagoon management, which was neither to restore the lagoon to some mythical status quo ante, nor to remake it into a totally new environment, but rather to preserve the delicate balance of elements in perpetuum, for the benefit of the city.

SOURCE: Image courtesy of the Bancroft Library, University of California at Berkeley. *Della laguna di Venezia*, trattato di Bernardo Trivisano [Trevisan]. Call number DG 674 .T7.

water served two important purposes in this context. By absorbing storm surges and the higher fall tides, backwater areas attenuated the city's famous flooding problem, thereby maintaining the proper balance of seawater. And by increasing the rate of flow at every ebb tide, backwater accumulation helped flush sediment from the harbor, thereby maintaining the proper balance of land. Thus Venetians clearly understood the tradeoffs between preserving marshland and pursuing profitable reclamation projects along the lagoon's periphery, and they consciously chose to regulate private interests in order to defend the Republic's clear and overriding interest in protecting the city and the harbor.

The view that the Republic should preserve and renew nature did not confine itself to the lagoon. Eighteenth-century Venetians saw their efforts to conserve valuable forest resources in a similar light. And the history of Venetian ideas about forest conservation closely parallels the history of Venetian ideas about preserving the lagoon. When the Venetians conquered the mainland in the fifteenth century, they brought with them the seeds of their belief that the ideal human relationship with the natural world involved preserving nature, not transforming it. From the very outset of the conquest, Venetian accounts of mainland landscapes stressed the need to maintain these environments in a proper state. Chapter 2 argued that their initial lack of familiarity with forests and other important features of the mainland environment led Venetian officials to focus their attention on rivers, streams, and irrigation canals. Writers such as the 1413 anonymous and the patrician Marco Cornaro often expressed their anxieties about the amount of sediment suspended in these bodies of water in terms of the Republic's need to take aggressive steps to reinforce the "natural order."[52] Of course, the order that Cornaro and others invoked was one that protected a well-established set of Venetian political and economic interests in the lagoon at the expense of mainland agricultural ones. Yet that should not necessarily be taken to mean that Cornaro and his fellow patricians were merely opportunistic conquerors looking for any justification to further the *Serenissima*'s territorial ambitions. There is no question that from the outset of the conquest, the Republic's leaders delightedly exploited uneasiness over the environmental effects of deforestation, erosion, and siltation as a powerful political lever with which to undermine the authority of entrenched mainland elites; but the uses to which those concerns were put in no way detracts from their sincerity. Centuries of living in a difficult and dangerous environment had taught the Venetians to distrust the appearance of any sudden change in the natural order. Thus, as they expanded their political and military control over the mainland, they seamlessly mapped their apprehensions about the waterscapes of the lagoon onto heretofore alien landscapes, especially forests.

The earliest official accounts of mainland landscapes tended to emphasize their susceptibility to degradation caused by human choices and practices. In 1442, for example, Marco Cornaro drew explicit parallels between the siltation that threatened to swallow the lagoon and the erosion in upstream areas that threatened to destroy valuable arable land. The fact that Cornaro was able to identify a clear causal relationship between upstream forest clearance, erosion, and downstream changes to Venice's local watershed helped him—and his audience—to see that mainland landscapes were linked to the lagoon and shared its vulnerabilities. Cornaro's experiences with the problem of maintaining the lagoon allowed him to recognize something of the region's ecological interconnectedness. By framing his account in terms of a set of risks with which his audience in the Ducal Palace was intimately acquainted, Cornaro argued convincingly that upstream environments were not only conjoined with the lagoon, but potentially just as fragile. If poorly executed water management schemes had the potential to upset the tenuous balance of elements in the lagoon in ways that might damage the *res publica*, then forests and rivers were also subject to destruction at the hands of thoughtless individuals and communities. As we have seen, this view of mainland forests as being easily destroyed not only framed the earliest Venetian interpretations of mainland landscapes, but proved to be a remarkably durable heuristic amongst Venice's ruling elite. The persistence of this vision of a fragile and disappearing landscape is demonstrated by the fact that Leonardo Mocenigo continued to employ it nearly three centuries later when he referred to forests being turned into wilderness with alarming and irreversible speed.

Yet as the striking frontispiece to Trevisan's treatise suggests, the declensional view of a fragile lagoon under assault by greedy landowners coexisted with an understanding of nature as an almost miraculous agent of divine providence. And once the Republic's officials gained greater familiarity with the alien forest landscapes of the *terraferma*, their conceptions of them were informed as much by this providential view of nature as by their anxieties about nature's vulnerability to human abuse. By the sixteenth century, members of the forest bureaucracy were just as likely to express wonder when they gazed upon mainland forests as they were to express dismay at their pitiable condition. It was that sense of amazement that permeated the 1548 report on the Cansiglio that Bernardino Vettori and Francesco Duodo presented to the Council of Ten. The two patricians described the future beech reserve as "vast and beautiful . . . greater and better than we could have ever imagined," and referred to the trees it contained as "most perfect in strength."[53] Even the more prosaic report filed by the three *proti* who had accompanied Vettori and Duodo referred to the forest as "a beautiful jewel."[54] While Duodo and Vettori clearly hoped that their florid prose would inspire the Council of Ten to take decisive political action, their language also reflected the enduring Venetian vision of a providential nature in need of human protection. As the three *proti* put it, "although we know that it will entail a great expense, we hope that out of reverence for God and your own goodwill, your excellencies will provide" for its preservation.[55] Like the lagoon, nature had brought the Cansiglio to a state of near perfection, and it was now up to the Venetians to keep it that way. The three *proti* saw preserving the Cansiglio both as an act of self-protection and an act of respectful devotion towards the beneficent creator of the natural processes that had created the beautiful jewel in the first place.

Even the normally hard-bitten and dour Giovanni Garzoni briefly interrupted his furious rhetorical assaults on greedy mainland elites to wax poetic concerning some of the landscapes he encountered in the district of Asolo. In a letter dated 7 June 1603, Garzoni described a series of forests that the Asolani themselves had banned in 1538 as "an earthly paradise," marveling at the "great supplies of oak I have encountered here."[56] Like Mocenigo a century later, Garzoni clearly saw these forests as almost miraculous creations of nature that could not be matched by any human effort. If anything, unrestrained human action could only destroy those landscapes. In fact, in his very next letter Garzoni returned to his more usual admonitory tone, complaining of his "fear for the future of these forests" and warning the Ten that without deliberate and concerted state intervention, "the Arsenal will have no timber and everything will fall into such disorder that it would be just as well to spare the expense of dispatching so many ministers to examine them."[57] Vacillating rapidly between wonder and worry, Garzoni's letters perfectly capture a relatively early version of what were emerging as the two primary Venetian discourses about nature. On the one hand, nature could create an "earthly paradise" capable of providing all the most important material underpinnings of the state. On the other hand, human actions could undo all that nature had wrought by "eradicating entire forests" unless the state moved forcefully to preserve the most important landscapes intact.

While both the 1548 Cansiglio report and Garzoni's 1603 letter to the Council of Ten clearly foreshadow a set of tropes that would find their fullest expression in eighteenth-century writings about forests, it is also important to note the ways in which they differ from later examples. Neither the 1548 Cansiglio report, nor Giovanni Garzoni's 1602 letters, made the kinds of expansive assertions about the public interest and state authority that Mocenigo would in 1704. Garzoni, in particular, consistently framed his claims fairly narrowly, expressing them in terms of the Arsenal's needs rather than the more abstract public interests favored by Mocenigo and other eighteenth-century commentators. To return to an earlier point, this limited conception of the problem reflects the fact that the *provveditori sopra boschi* held few illusions about the transformative power of the Republic's forestry legislation. Their approach tended towards the pragmatic. Garzoni was willing to compromise with the peasantry by allowing them to continue pilfering small quantities of timber from the public stockpile, so long as the overall goals of keeping the shipyard supplied and slowing the rate at which private and institutional landowners were clear-cutting forests on their property were met. In Garzoni's view, the relationship between resources and state sovereignty still remained somewhat limited, and the efforts of the forest bureaucracy correspondingly narrow. If the best forests could not be preserved for future use by the Arsenal, Garzoni reasoned, then it was better simply "to spare the expense" involved in the attempt. By contrast, in 1704 Mocenigo saw the state's claim over mainland forests as unlimited, or, as he put it in his oration, "just, direct, perpetual, absolute, and incontrovertible."[58] Where his view and Garzoni's overlapped was on the question of nature's inherent providence and inherent fragility. Thus Mocenigo stressed that "nature had struggled entire centuries" to produce the forest landscapes he had seen, while at the same time arguing that these miraculous natural artifacts could easily and irreversibly fall prey to selfish, misguided, and rapacious groups and individuals.

By the first half of the eighteenth century, it would become common for all manner of Venetian officials to inject the same rhetoric used by Mocenigo in 1704 into their descriptions of forest landscapes and their relationship to the public interest. For example, in 1715 the *capitano* of Raspo, Lauro Querini, reported the theft of nearly 400 oak poles from the *bosco pubblico di Briz* in Istria to the Council of Ten. In his letter, Querini blamed local landowners, who, he claimed "in a very brief time consumed such a substantial number of trees that nature had long struggled to produce for the public advantage."[59] In a 1720 letter to the Senate, the *podestà* of Belluno called the Cansiglio reserve "an enchanted place of prodigious marvelousness," and described the forest's fertility as "more miraculous than natural."[60] In the preamble to its commission of Antonio Nani as *provveditore sopra boschi* in April of 1725, the Senate declared that a new *catastico* was needed "in consideration of the weighty matter of forests, especially those that with their natural fertility have contributed so much to the construction of great armadas for the protection of liberty and the governance of states."[61] Then, in a 1726 letter to the Senate, Nani himself described the *bosco pubblico di Comagno* in the Friuli as "a place so fertile with oak, containing no mixture of softwoods in it, and placed almost artfully by nature, with one oak spaced the ideal distance from the next."[62] And in 1730 the *podestà* of Belluno, Zuane Venier, wrote to the Senate that he had "recently visited that precious reserve of Your Serenity, vast and full of trees well placed by nature and most useful for public needs."[63] All of these phrases closely echo the language in Mocenigo's 1704 pamphlet, stressing that "nature struggled for centuries" to produce landscapes of almost miraculous fertility—a provident nature indeed, but also a terrifyingly vulnerable one in the face of the collective and individual greed of human beings.

One interesting feature of these providential discourses about nature is the degree to which God disappears from seventeenth- and eighteenth-century formulations of the concept. While the three *proti* who inspected the Cansiglio reserve in 1548 felt comfortable explicitly naming the creator of the nature that required preservation, by the turn the seventeenth century Venetian writers had become noticeably reluctant to invoke God directly in their observations of the natural world. Garzoni's 1603 reference to the Asolo reserves as an "earthly paradise" clearly places the forests within an explicitly religious framework for thinking about nature, but nowhere in the letter does he actually name God. Likewise, the frequent eighteenth-century formulations of certain forests as "more miraculous than natural" bring the possibility of supernatural causation to mind without directly linking it to the Christian divinity. Thus the source of providence gradually appeared to shift from divine will to nature itself. This hesitation to refer to God is notable, especially in light of the Venetians' almost relentless invocation of divine will in fourteenth- and fifteenth-century accounts of the natural perfection of the lagoon, not to mention the prominent role of divine election in the several foundation myths that collectively underpinned the larger myth of Venice.[64] For Venetians, the shift, which straddled ancient and modern concepts, served a dual function: preserving a Renaissance humanist view of nature as being miraculous or magical, while at the same time avoiding the suspicion of heterodoxy that would inevitably be aroused by claims of special election in an era of violent confessional conflict between Catholics and Protestants. In other words, by omitting God from their descriptions of important forest landscapes, Venetian forestry officials were able to place nature at the center of their providential framework by employing phrases such as "miraculous" and "earthly paradise," which implied the agency of a Christian God while avoiding the language of special election that increasingly defined those on the other side of the confessional divide. Ultimately, the rhetoric of providential nature that was favored by Venetian forestry officials reflects the persistence—in Italy—of Renaissance ideas of an organic, mystical nature during a period when, as Keith Thomas has shown, Protestant Europe was often concerned with demystifying and desacralizing nature.[65]

Viewed in this context, the significance of Mocenigo's wordplay in juxtaposing forests and wilderness comes into sharper focus. Forests became wilderness when the state and local communities alike failed to treat them as both a public good and a fragile artifact of a provident nature. A true forest was a place where "natural fertility," under the constant and careful protection of state sovereignty, could "provide for all the most important public needs" while, at the same time, protecting Venice and its special form of republican liberty. A wilderness, by contrast, was a place where greedy humans had "consumed trees in such large numbers," or even "eradicated entire forests," placing the most pressing common needs at risk. In the same letter in which he praised the artfully spaced trees in the state reserve at Comagno, Antonio Nani decried local landowners who had deliberately damaged oak saplings on their property to prevent them from "reaching even the form of a *tolpo*," thereby eluding the scrutiny of the *provveditori sopra boschi* and other members of the forest bureaucracy.[66] In the minds of eighteenth-century Venetian officials, it was precisely such activities that reduced a forest to a wilderness. This view of the distinction between nature and wilderness underpinned a Venetian moral economy of nature in which preserving landscapes for the good of the *res publica* constituted the highest possible ideal and altering those same landscapes for personal profit constituted the worst possible crime. The fact that in spite of its evident power and fertility, nature was capable of achieving only a transitory condition of perfection without the protection of laws and institutions made it all the more important that the Republic intervene aggressively to safeguard and preserve crucial landscapes such as the lagoon and the best oak forests before ignorant local residents, selfish merchants, wealthy elites, and negligent institutions destroyed them forever. For Mocenigo and other eighteenth-century writers, the boundary between a well-preserved forest and a hollow wilderness was the same as the boundary between a state of republican liberty in which honors and resources were distributed equitably, and a state of tyranny in which a few monopolized wealth and power at the expense of the many.

Venetian Discourses in a European Context

The Venetians were not the only Europeans expressing concern over deforestation and its effects on the body politic in these centuries. In his famous 1662 treatise *Silva*, John Evelyn—the English natural philosopher and founding member of the Royal Society—expressed apparently congruous sentiments to those found in the reports of Giovanni Garzoni, Leonardo Mocenigo, Antonio Nani, and other Venetian forestry officials. Evelyn pointed to his fellow Englishmen's tendency "utterly to extirpate, demolish, and raze" what he referred to as the "wooden walls" of the kingdom—turns of phrase that are highly reminiscent of the language used by Venetian forestry officials and legislators dating back to the fourteenth century.[67] Similar reflections can be found in the writings of late seventeenth- and eighteenth-century writers in France and throughout German-speaking Europe.[68] Nevertheless, the Venetian version of a fragile nature requiring the state's constant protection for its preservation differs in at least two significant ways from the views of northern European legislators, foresters, and natural philosophers. By stressing the power of human beings to alter and manipulate nature in presumptively positive ways, northern European writers (especially Evelyn) usually tried to reconcile the individual's desire to extract the greatest profit from the land with the impulse to preserve resources. In other words, for Evelyn, the problem of nature was primarily an economic issue, whereas for the Venetians, it was an institutional or conservation one. In addition, almost all northern European thinkers saw expanding the extractive powers of the state into overseas colonies as the best and most logical way to resolve resource shortages closer to home.[69] The Venetians, by contrast, expressed very little enthusiasm for shifting their demand for timber to more distant sources, not even within the quasi-colonial context of Dalmatia and the Pelopponese.

Unlike the Venetian forestry experts, all of whom saw selfish interests as incompatible with forest conservation, Evelyn embraced a profit-driven approach to nature. As Carolyn Merchant observes, "Evelyn accepted the philosophy of self-interest and acquisitiveness, which he perceived to be of primary importance in society."[70] Consequently, rather than stress the need either to reform institutions—as Mocenigo did—or advise placing severe legal and practical limits on the profit-taking activities of merchants and wealthy elites—as Garzoni did—Evelyn recommended a broad-based program of land improvement and expansion through large-scale reclamation, canal construction, and enclosure projects. He also imagined that some of the newly created lands would be earmarked for afforestation, with the rest going to cropland and pasture. Evelyn placed special emphasis on planting what he deemed useful species of trees, especially fruit trees, not only because such species offered both an immediate reward in terms of a potentially profitable crop, but also because of their important aesthetic qualities—a reflection of his neo-Platonic inclinations. Continental writers who followed Evelyn, including Buffon and Duhamel de Monceau, also viewed forests through an economic lens, rather than a legal one. They conceived of the purpose of forest management as maximizing profit through the promotion of commercially valuable growth, not preserving landscapes in a condition that reflected a natural optimum. These authors shared a common view of forest management as a branch, or subset, of agriculture—what would become known as silviculture—rather than as a means of preserving specific landscapes and resources. As Richard Grove has argued, "Evelyn's *Silva* appealed specifically to a notion of forest science and economics rather than law or custom."[71] In other words, northern European foresters and natural philosophers envisioned a mode of forest management that transformed trees into a commodity with a measurable value, whereas the Venetians stressed both law and custom as important ways of approaching local practices of forest exploitation.

Perhaps the most important difference between Evelyn's arguments and those of Venetian forestry officials can be seen in the former's explicit identification of New England forests as the ideal solution to the want of timber in England. Not only did Evelyn imagine that New England would supply shipbuilding material, but he also urged the crown to force England's iron industry to relocate to the colonies, where presumably unlimited expanses of timber awaited conversion into high-quality charcoal capable of fueling its furnaces.[72] As Carolyn Merchant aptly puts it, "conservation at home was thus to be purchased at the expense of frontier expansion abroad."[73] A similar sense that foreign supplies of timber could solve the dilemmas of local deforestation can be found in the seventeenth-century expression "Amsterdam is standing on Norway," which referred to the fact that the Dutch fleet—and therefore the wealth of the United Provinces—was built almost entirely of Scandinavian timber secured through the Baltic trade.[74] Even Evelyn's recommendation that gentlemen should plant their property with trees "for some miles about" was closely connected to the colonial context—part of an imperial fantasy in which the English country gentleman could imagine himself at repose in a lush tropical paradise.[75] By contrast, the Venetians had few illusions about the possibility of either purchasing timber from foreign sources (like the Dutch) or transferring the extraction of critical resources to colonial sites (like the English). The Arsenal managers considered Dalmatian and Pelopponesian timber to be of lesser quality—especially taking the increased transportation costs into account—and limited their efforts there to the acquisition of *stortami* for the production of structural knees.[76] As for foreign sources, there were relatively few Austrian forests connected to the Venetian side of the Alpine watershed —most of them in the Duchy of Trent—which meant that foreign supplies were limited and prices correspondingly high. Both of these factors forced the Venetians back to their home territories in their search for ever-greater quantities of forest resources.

Because they were limited to their *terraferma* possessions, the Venetians developed a far different notion of conservation than their northern European counterparts. Evelyn, a great admirer of Francis Bacon, could afford to invoke his idol's motto, *plus ultra*. It must have seemed to Evelyn and his seventeenth- and eighteenth-century followers that there was always another forest over the next hill in the New World. Evelyn's conception of the forests themselves was also Baconian. As part of a mechanistic nature, forests obeyed a comprehensible set of universal rules and were subject to uniform methods of improvement and exploitation that lead inexorably towards social and economic progress.[77] Carolyn Merchant has famously dubbed this seventeenth-century demystification of the world "the death of nature." In her estimation, Europeans abandoned a traditional organic view of nature as being alive in favor of a new mechanistic understanding of nature as inanimate and malleable.

Yet in spite of the fact that the Venetians were no strangers to the new mechanistic philosophy that was dominating European thought by the turn of the eighteenth century, Mocenigo, Nani, and their peers maintained a decidedly Aristotelian and organic outlook on the natural world. Humanist appeals to a miraculous and organic nature, one possessing autonomous agency, continued to dominate the writings of Venice's forestry officials, but an Aristotelian logic was also powerfully at work in their conception of the world. Their mental and physical universe remained a clearly delimited plenum offering no real avenues for expansion. There were no new forests awaiting discovery and exploitation over the next hill, no frontier for the Venetians to "go beyond." What was true in 1548 when Bernardino Vettori and Francesco Duodo defined the Cansiglio as a "most perfect" product of nature's toil was still true in 1726 when Antonio Nani returned from his tour as *provveditore sopra boschi* and spoke of "forests planted to perfection by nature." If the Venetians were going to preserve their resource base, it would have to be through a concerted conservation effort aimed at making the most of whatever resources nature had already produced within their own territories. The Venetians were no less managerial than northern Europeans. Rather, they simply found a way to integrate a vitalist conception of nature with a state-directed effort at forest preservation, through a complex system of what could be termed "managerial organicism." Nature could not be allowed to die in Venice, because the Republic could not exist without it. This was the message contained in the allegorical frontispiece to Trevisan's treatise on the lagoon, but it could just as easily have described Venice's relationship to its forests. Venice could not endure without them, nor could they maintain their naturally produced state of perfection without the protection of the Republic and its just system of institutions and laws aimed at promoting the common good. Venice may not have been—as Crouzet-Pavan would have it—nature's Republic, but as Trevisan's treatise and the writings of scores of forestry officials clearly demonstrate, its ruling elite sought desperately to preserve a republican nature.

Conclusion

> Gavardo had rendered the forest into a skeleton
> by means of deliberate, open, and continuous
> removal of timber.

THIS BOOK HAS TOLD the story of how, beginning in the middle of the fourteenth century, the Republic of Venice initiated a series of centrally directed efforts to control critical forest resources in its extended hinterland in northeast Italy and Istria. What emerged over the course of 450 years was not only Europe's earliest fully articulated legal and institutional apparatus dedicated entirely to resource conservation, but also its most unusual. The Venetian forestry regime is remarkable for its early inception, in addition to its distinctive culture of knowledge production and its peculiar form of what I have called managerial organicism. The book analyzed the Venetian forestry regime from two main perspectives. Chapters 1, 3, and 4 focused primarily on the practical, legal, and institutional challenges that the Republic had to overcome in order to exert direct control over the most important forest resources in its territories. Those chapters paid close attention to the special form of administrative logic that resulted from the sometimes difficult interplay between laws conceived in the relative isolation of the Ducal Palace and real conditions on the ground in timber-producing parts of the *terra-ferma*. Chapters 2, 5, and 6 engaged the problem of how Venetian officials interpreted the forest landscapes that confronted them on their journeys throughout the mainland. These chapters placed significant emphasis on the complex interaction between the empirical technologies —quantitative surveys and various mapping techniques—that the Republic's bureaucratic experts employed and the political and cultural values that they brought to bear on their understanding of the operations of the natural world.

In the end, what made the Venetian forestry regime so distinctive was not merely its particular institutional arrangements, or even its aggressive legislative program aimed at regulating local practices of forest exploitation. Instead, the unique combination of a small territorial state forced to rely almost exclusively on domestic timber resources and a republican ideology that defined the public good in opposition to unfettered economic liberty drove the Venetians to develop a form of environmental management that stressed the need to preserve an explicitly organic nature. In other words, the fact that Venice was an insular Italian republic with limited access to foreign sources of timber helps explain both the Venetian rejection of many aspects of the new mechanism and their adoption of a highly empirical form of managerial organicism in place of the more familiar seventeenth- and eighteenth-century northern European approaches to controlling nature.

By way of conclusion I would like to return once again to a Venetian forest reserve—this time the Montona reserve in Istria—to examine the trial of an important member of Istrian society named Pietro Gavardo. In 1710, Gavardo stood accused of orchestrating an elaborate scheme to steal several thousand oak trees from the most important *bosco pubblico* on the peninsula, in order to convert them into charcoal for sale in Capo D'Istria and Pirano. Gavardo's crime, and the official reaction to it, offer an appropriate way to close this analysis of the Venetian forestry regime. His trial brings to the fore the three main themes in this volume: the immense legal and institutional challenges that the Republic faced in its attempts to regulate local practices of forest exploitation; the technologies that mediated the forest bureaucracy's understanding of woodland landscapes and aided it in its efforts to track and manage forest resources in state and community forests; and the Venetian view of nature as a fragile but fertile provider whose best works required attentive preservation by the state. In the story of Gavardo's crime and punishment we can see both the ideas about nature and the practices of forest management that made the Venetian forestry regime so distinctive.

The Three Trials of Pietro Gavardo

It all began with a brawl in the village of Raspo. On 12 February 1709, which was the last day of Carnival, a man named Paolo Clavich tried to force a pretty girl to dance with him. Unfortunately for Clavich, she was the daughter of a local dignitary named Zorzi Paulich. A commotion ensued in which Paulich and some of his henchmen confronted Clavich and ordered him to leave the festivities immediately. Cornered, Clavich "drew his scimitar and struck Iseppo Cicchietti in the head" before fleeing the scene.[1] The *capitano* at Raspo, a young patrician named Federico Calbo, convened a trial on 24 February in which he declared Clavich "an insolent troublemaker" and banished him from Venetian territory—a sentence later ratified by the Council of Ten.[2] But like so many bandits, Clavich did not leave, and in September he showed up at a local fair where Paulich was acting as one of the presiding figures. Clavich approached Paulich, "cursing and insulting him while brandishing a pistol." An armed guard overpowered Clavich, and he was taken to the local castle to await the arrival of Calbo from Raspo.[3] When Calbo appeared on the scene to take Clavich into custody, the prisoner offered to inform him of a great crime in exchange for leniency. Calbo agreed to listen, and Clavich proceeded to tell the *capitano* a story about Pietro Gavardo, one of the wealthiest residents of Capo D'Istria. According to Clavich, Gavardo had conspired with other local residents to steal great quantities of oak from the Montona reserve, which was part of Calbo's jurisdiction as *capitano* of Raspo. This was not the first time that such accusations had swirled around Gavardo. Calbo's predecessor had tried to bring similar charges against him but had failed, due to the absence of witnesses to the alleged conspiracy. Calbo decided to investigate. He opened an inquiry that would lead to more violence in Istria, scandal in the Arsenal, and a public trial for the crime of "stealing public resources for personal gain, and humiliating the public authority."[4]

In a letter to the Council of Ten dated 17 December 1709, Calbo reported on the results of the first phase of his inquiry into the "incomparably serious accusations against the person of Pietro Gavardo, gentleman of Capo D'Istria."[5] Calbo had been able to confirm that in 1706 Gavardo had purchased the monopoly on the Montona *condotta* in the area around the village of Toppolovari. The monopoly placed Gavardo in a position to organize the work crews who would enter the forest in the company of a *proto* sent from Venice to oversee the Arsenal harvest. By custom, Gavardo was obliged to hire peasants from Toppolovari to do the work at preestablished rates of pay—a fact that would prove to be part of his undoing. Crucially, the monopoly also included the right to buy low-grade oak trees that a *proto* or other Arsenal representative had marked for removal from the reserve as part of any selective thinning that occurred in conjunction with an Arsenal harvest. Gavardo had then bribed Domenico Nicheta, one of the Arsenal *proti* sent to oversee the 1706 harvest, to help his men cut the *bollo*, or seal, out of the trunks of at least 700 trees. After obliterating the *bolli*, Nicheta authorized the removal of the oak as inferior scrap material. In this way, Calbo reported, Gavardo had fraudulently secured several hundred high-quality oak trees at scrap prices. He then converted the lumber into top-grade charcoal, which he sold in a black-market transaction to Pietro Caldana, who owned a foundry in Pirano. When describing the damage that Gavardo's scheme had done to the section of the Montona in question, Calbo employed a decidedly organic metaphor, saying that "Gavardo had rendered the forest into a skeleton by means of deliberate, open, and continuous removal of timber."[6] Calbo also reported that Gavardo had kept local residents quiet through threats and intimidation, and that he had imported thugs from the Friuli to do the actual work of harvesting the trees from the reserve, breaking them into smaller pieces, and then setting up the charcoal pits. In this fashion, Gavardo could be confident that there would be no local witnesses to the physical destruction of the trees and their subsequent conversion into charcoal.

Calbo expressed his dismay both at the reported scale of the crime and at the discovery that Gavardo had successfully bribed or intimidated a number of public officials. The revelation that an Arsenal *proto*, the *capitano del bosco*, and several other public officials were "all completely corrupted by Gavardo, who gave them large sums of money" caused considerable stir in Venice.[7] Even more discouraging to Calbo was the discovery that his predecessor had attempted to mount two trials against Gavardo, to no avail. Gavardo managed to have the first trial transferred to the local civil court in Capo D'Istria, knowing full well "that this court was subject to all his arrogant opulence."[8] He derailed a second trial by again getting it transferred and then bribing or intimidating the few witnesses willing to come forward on behalf of the Republic's interests. "All the while," Calbo seethed, "he continued to remove trees from the forest."[9] Calbo concluded that he himself needed to make an effort to mount a third trial, and in light of the fact that many of Gavardo's *condotta* licenses—which recorded how many trees had been felled—turned out to have been either corrupted or forged, he decided to make the difficult journey to the Montona "to see for [himself] and discover the pure and singular truth concerning this matter."[10] What he found was far worse than anything he could have imagined. Calbo wrote that one of the *proti* who accompanied him on his trip described the area in which Gavardo had operated as having once been "one of the richest and most fertile forests that nourished the public need in this entire province."[11] What Calbo and the *proti* saw instead was a forest that had been "devastated over an area of many miles."[12] Calbo and his guides counted "more than 3,000 stumps, many of them quite recently cut."[13] Moving deeper into the forest, Calbo's party discovered the remnants of eighty-seven separate charcoal pits. Furthermore, Calbo realized to his distress that Gavardo's men had stripped the small and medium branches off of all the trees in the area surrounding the pits to make kindling for the burn chambers. In so doing, they had rendered even more good oak all but useless for the shipyard. Calbo returned from his inspection determined to prosecute Gavardo, "who is not only the most opulent and destructive citizen of Capo D'Istria, but also abused his position to gain the trust of many ministers."[14] He understood that Gavardo's status insulated him against ordinary court proceedings, because "his mere name is sufficient to render difficult and even vain my efforts to discover the whole truth."[15] Likewise, he confessed to the Ten that trying to get at Gavardo through his network of underlings was useless, since "witnesses either disappear, are threatened and subjected to blandishments, or are beaten until they change their stories."[16] Nevertheless, he asked the Council of Ten for permission to mount one last trial of the principal in the plot who, "by the most odious means has converted public capital into personal profit."[17]

The third trial of Pietro Gavardo took place in Capo D'Istria in April of 1710. As the presiding magistrate, Calbo was responsible for laying out the charges and the evidence in the case. He had assembled a devastating set of indictments against Gavardo, and his presentation of the evidence was calculated to place the accused in the worst possible light. Relying on the records that his predecessors had left behind, as well as the tree counts from recent harvests that the representatives of the Arsenal had deposited in the local chancery, Calbo was able to offer a detailed account of the conspiracy that had led to the devastation he had witnessed in the Montona the previous year. Calbo could produce not only the forged documents that Gavardo's men had used to harvest the trees illegally, but he was also able to reconstruct—in considerable detail—how Gavardo had filled the harvest crews with Friulian thugs and filed blatantly false *condotta* records. Had Gavardo used local labor, he would have had to bribe or intimidate even more people, Calbo contended. Indeed, evidence of Gavardo's plot had first surfaced through a 1706 lawsuit filed by some peasants residing in Toppolovari. The peasants had seen Gavardo's Friulian work crews entering the section of the Montona nearest to the village and, realizing that the work and resulting pay was rightfully theirs, "they rose up against the lack of faith displayed by Gavardo."[18]

Having explained the mechanics of Gavardo's operation, Calbo then proceeded to expose the true scale of the crime. One of the *proti* who assisted in the investigation took the stand and described the area in which Gavardo's men had operated as a place that "was formerly referred to by everyone with the distinguished title of 'garden among forests' and all agreed that no finer oak trees could be found anywhere else, nor any forest so fertile as this one."[19] Calbo closed his exposition with a lengthy and detailed imputation of Gavardo's character. In a tale reminiscent of the famous baptism scene in Francis Ford Coppola's film *The Godfather*, Calbo recounted how "on 2 April of this year, which was Holy Friday, Gavardo attended mass and took communion in the church. Upon leaving the church he heard that a new trial was being organized and immediately summoned Mattio Scherlich—whom he believed to be my informant—and personally beat him almost to death with a club."[20] According to Calbo, Gavardo also contrived to have other possible witnesses imprisoned elsewhere on false charges, so that they could not give evidence, and "ordered his men to tear the roof off the residence of a poor widow whom he suspected of having offered testimony against him."[21] Calbo closed by declaring that "in consideration of the many and various facts in the case, and for the many foul incidents involved, it is my considered judgment that he should be impaled."[22] Calbo believed that only a dramatic and painful punishment would dissuade others from follow-ing Gavardo's example and engaging in the "most serious and deplorable destruction of public resources."[23] The Montona was a singular and irre-placeable resource, and it required an equally singular level of protec-tion. From the Venetian perspective, this was frontier justice at its best.[24]

Finding Meaning in the Forest

Gavardo's trial provides a rich and dense picture of the unique challenges faced by Venetian officials in the sparsely populated border regions of the Republic's territories. It also offers a particularly vivid view of the net-works of violence and retribution that in many ways defined these fron-tier societies.[25] But for the purposes of this conclusion, I would like to focus on what the trial reveals about the three main themes of this book.

Throughout the volume, I have argued that while Venice's leaders were genuinely concerned about the risk of running out of timber, they also were eager to use that concern as a political lever in their perpetual struggle to establish and then reinforce the Republic's sovereignty over powerful local elites on the mainland and in Istria. Because the Venetian fears of resource depletion were clearly genuine—to the point of being almost visceral—I have resisted a purely instrumental interpretation of the political dimensions of the problem of securing adequate supplies of crucial timber resources. Nevertheless, it is undeniable that the steady and inexorable increase in state demand for Arsenal timber and con-struction material to maintain the lagoon infrastructure—not to men-tion private demand for industrial and domestic fuel—furnished the Republic with both the opportunity and the desperate need to reinforce its claims to sovereignty over critical landscapes and resources through-out the *terraferma* and Istria. Seen in this light, Gavardo's trial con-stitutes an obvious example of a Venetian administrator translating his sincere concern about the condition of an especially important public landscape into an opportunity to make a particularly vivid example out of a powerful member of the provincial elite. The late date of the trial also reveals the degree to which establishing the Republic's authority throughout its mainland possessions remained an incomplete and ongo-ing project well into the eighteenth century. In other words, the trial reveals both the seriousness of Venice's institutional commitment to forest preservation as well as the ways in which the Republic's institutions could employ that concern as an effective instrument of state power.

The trial also exposes some of the important limits of state power in Venice's peculiar republican system. As chapter 3 demonstrated, the Republic's courts offered local elites and peasants alike an opportunity to resist Venice's claims to authority over local practices of forest exploitation. In fact, independently of his use of violence and witness intimidation, Gavardo twice managed to avoid prosecution by manipulating the court system in his favor through more legitimate means. By arguing that the crime in question was a simple case of *spoglio*—or petty theft— Gavardo was able to get the case transferred to a local civil court where his social stature virtually guaranteed him an acquittal. It was only after Calbo discovered the actual extent of the crime that the state was able to retain jurisdiction over the case and successfully obtain the long-sought-after conviction. Thus, while Venetian officials were eager to use the laws governing local practices of forest exploitation as an instrument of state power, Venice's republican system made the job far more difficult than it might have been in the monarchical context of northern Europe. In other words, as this book has argued repeatedly, it is impossible to divorce Venice's efforts at resource control and preservation from the republican legal and political context in which those efforts took place.

Unfortunately for Gavardo, local elites were not the only members of provincial society with access to the Republic's courts. The testimony that led directly to the discovery of Gavardo's crimes came from a group of unhappy peasants and a violent outlaw, highlighting the complexity of the legal and institutional setting within which the forest bureaucracy operated. That the first accusations surfaced as part of a *supplica* (a formal legal petition) submitted by the peasants of Toppolovari, who were angry about their exclusion from an Arsenal harvest, reveals just how important the forest bureaucracy's presence had become—especially in relatively poor frontier regions such as Istria. As the peasants made clear in their petition, they looked forward to the arrival of the Arsenal *proti*, because it meant an opportunity to earn badly needed wages during a season when there was little remunerative work of any description available. And when the *proti* and the *condotta* holder—in this case Gavardo —did not hire them to work in the forest, they were determined enough to bring their grievances to court and informed enough to know that Gavardo should be the focus of their ire. So not only were the peasants well aware of what an Arsenal harvest meant to them in financial terms, they also knew where to turn for legal redress and how to phrase their accusations to produce the best chance of success. In this way it is possible to see the degree to which both Venice's forest bureaucracy and its courts were no mere abstractions. By the turn of the eighteenth century, the forest bureaucracy had become an integral part of rural life in the timber-producing regions of the Republic's territories. I can think of no better measure of how powerful and socially significant the institution was on the ground.[26]

The trial also brings to the fore a second important theme in the book: the creation, reproduction, and circulation of specialized knowledge about forests and forest landscapes. Beginning with the rudimentary accounts of "places full of trees" featured in early fifteenth-century descriptions of mainland forests, and culminating in the vast quantities of information produced by the fully articulated quantitative and cartographic technologies employed by the *provveditori sopra boschi*, this volume traced the development of a coherent Venetian understanding of crucial forest landscapes. Chapter 5 argued that this understanding was equally the product of the specific technologies that the Venetians developed to interpret the forests on the mainland and the Republic's privileging of a collective form of expertise that gave the *provveditori sopra boschi* and other members of the forest bureaucracy access to the craft knowledge of a whole host of subordinates—Arsenal *proti*, cartographers, and *agrimensori perticatori*, among others. Gavardo's trial reveals that a relatively young official, such as Calbo, could quickly acquire meaningful knowledge of an important forest landscape like the Montona. It also underscores the degree to which that knowledge was the product of Calbo's interactions with individual members of the forest bureaucracy and with the technologies of knowledge production that the *provveditori sopra boschi* routinely employed to construct meaningful narratives about changes that had occurred in mainland forests.

When Calbo finally decided to travel to the Montona to see for himself how matters stood on the ground, he was accompanied by a pair of Arsenal *proti* who acted as both guides to the reserve and as interpreters of the landscape. Calbo employed the words of his escorts to describe what the small inspection party saw in the forest. So when Calbo claimed that the area in question had been "one of the richest and most fertile forests that nourished the public need in this entire province," he was channeling the sentiments of a craft expert who possessed the kind of knowledge that the Venetians prized above all—first-hand experience of the specific landscape in question. But the two *proti* provided Calbo with far more than their empirical knowledge of the Montona. They also helped Calbo interpret the copies of the most recent quantitative surveys of the reserve, which he had retrieved from the local chancery prior to his departure. With the *proti's* assistance, Calbo was able to use these data to paint a damning picture of the scope and despicable nature of Gavardo's crime. Calbo and his assistants began by conducting a simple stump count to arrive at a useful approximation of just how many oak trees Gavardo had stolen—slightly over 3,000. Then, using the survey records they had brought with them as a benchmark, Calbo offered the Council of Ten a surprisingly precise count of how many poles remained—1,884 useful oak and 2,434 saplings of various sizes. Presumably on the advice of the *proti*, Calbo also placed special emphasis on the fact that scores of precious *stortami* had gone missing—although he was quick to point out that 436 remained intact. Calbo represented these counts to the Council of Ten as accurate assessments, not mere approximations. His claim to precision helped him drive home the severity of the case—if we accept the numbers drawn from the surveys, Gavardo had stolen well over half the Arsenal-grade oak that had once stood in that section of the reserve. At the same time, Calbo and the *proti* stressed the fact that the area still held enough good oak to make it worth recovering as part of the Republic's forest patrimony. The survival of a good number of *stortami* established yet another urgent justification for bringing Gavardo to justice as quickly as possible—lest he resume his destructive activities after the conclusion of Calbo's term of office.

By using the empirical knowledge embedded in the survey data and trusting the experiences of his craft experts, Calbo was able to build a compelling case against Gavardo. Without the assistance of the *proti* and the knowledge preserved in the surveys, it is hard to imagine Calbo being able to convince the Council of Ten to allow him to pursue such an aggressive prosecution of an important local figure. The case would probably once again have wound up in the local civil court, where Gavardo enjoyed de facto immunity. Seen in this light, Gavardo's trial offers a memorable example of the forest bureaucracy's craft expertise and quantitative technologies of knowledge production in action. And Calbo's enthusiastic embrace of the *proti*'s perspective on the case is an excellent illustration of the weight that officials at all levels of the state accorded to the forest bureaucracy's view of critical landscapes such as the Montona.

The third theme of this book was the emergence of a distinctive Venetian view of a provident nature in need of aggressive preservation on the part of the state. Chapter 6 argued that this mode of understanding the relationship between humans and the rest of the natural world constituted a peculiar fusion of a traditional organicist understanding of nature with the Venetian tendency to frame issues involving resource exploitation in an explicitly republican idiom of the common good. It also contrasted the Venetian view of the human role in preserving nature for the common benefit with the more famous Baconian expression of "power over nature," as well as with the Lockean imperative to transform nature into capital. This combination of a humanist-inspired view of a provident nature and a preservationist approach to vulnerable resources such as wood and water resulted in the uniquely Venetian approach to conservation that I termed managerial organicism. The Republic's commitment to this idea was on full display during Gavardo's trial—from the rhetoric deployed by Calbo and the Arsenal *proti* to the fact that the court chose to frame the charges in terms of the opposition between public good and private profit, rather than merely in terms of the simple theft of critical resources.

When Calbo wrote to the Council of Ten seeking permission to pursue a third trial against Gavardo, he must have realized that he was making an unusual request. Gavardo had successfully avoided prosecution twice before, and there was little hope that the *capitano* would be able to convince a sufficient number of witnesses to step forward to secure the conviction he so doggedly sought. There were almost certainly more promising ways for Calbo to spend in his time in office than attempting to punish an important local personage, whatever the severity of his crimes. But the depth of the disgust that Calbo expressed in his letters to the Ten and in his presentation of the evidence against Gavardo reveals just how serious he was about obtaining justice in this specific case and for these specific crimes. The story that Calbo told about Gavardo's actions on Good Friday was precisely calibrated to elicit revulsion in his audience. It also set up an implicit parallelism between Gavardo's insult to God and his insult to the Republic, one that made particular sense to a Venetian audience in the Ducal Palace that was highly attuned to the problem of preserving important resources. Gavardo's beating of the helpless Scherlich immediately after receiving communion on one of the holiest days in the Christian calendar was obviously an especially foul act of blasphemy. And Calbo singled out this particular crime as a way of suggesting that Gavardo's looting of one of the Republic's most important forest reserves should be seen in a similar light. In other words, by destroying public resources for private and dishonest gain, Gavardo had committed a premeditated crime against the divine will embodied in the fertility and productivity of a provident republican nature.

Calbo gave full voice to the *proti*'s assessment of the forest's former state of glory, when it "nourished the public need" and was a "garden among forests." Both expressions reflect the well-established providential view of nature favored by the Venetians. The use of the term garden evoked Eden, the earthly paradise where God's original plan for nature had found its fullest and most perfect expression. And the emphasis on nature's fertility and ability to nourish or nurture the common needs of the Republic and its subjects offers a paradigmatic example of the fusion of a humanist political discourse about republics and the common good with the Venetian belief in a divine providence that operated through the natural order. In this instance the state had failed to preserve that order properly, with the dire and perhaps irremediable consequence that the landscape had been reduced "to a skeleton." Like Leonardo Mocenigo's invocation of Dante in his wilderness wordplay, Calbo made use of a classical reference to dramatize his point. The image of a skeletal landscape derives from the most famous passage of Plato's *Critias*, in which the title character presents a lengthy comparison between the disaster that befell Atlantis and the pernicious effects of "a lack of husbandry" on the landscapes of Attica. Midway through his speech, Critias tells Socrates and Timaeus how the failure to tend to Attica's hillsides had resulted in a slow but irreversible process of erosion that had left behind an impoverished remnant of once rich lands: "And just as happens with small islands, what now remains compared with what then existed is like the skeleton of a sick man."[27] By his recourse to an august classical authority, Calbo was doing more than displaying his education and erudition for all to see. He was establishing a powerful parallelism between his own perspective as an eighteenth-century Venetian official charged with protecting a critical public landscape and Plato's ancient account of calamitous environmental change. The message was unmistakable. It was imperative to prosecute Gavardo for a third time, because if the Republic failed to stop those who committed crimes against nature, Venice, like Atlantis, could be erased permanently in a natural cataclysm—a just punishment for a supposedly virtuous Republic that failed to husband its most important public resources.

Calbo must have hoped his reference to the *Critias* and the mythical Atlantis would capture the attention of his superiors in the Council of Ten by emphasizing once again just how fragile works of nature were in the face of human greed. The reference also served as a potent reminder of Venice's literal and metaphorical insularity. Like the Athenians in Plato's dialogue, the Venetians needed to keep in mind the importance of preserving the plenum in an ideal state of variety and abundance, because without the protection that only proper husbandry could provide, even an apparently rich landscape was just as vulnerable to destruction as a small island. This warning held special meaning for the *Serenissima*, for there was no other place to go, no replacement resources for the Venetians to access. Their very survival as a small independent Republic with a limited resource base was predicated on adopting a deliberate and aggressive conservation strategy.

As I suggested at the outset of this volume, the fact that the closest parallel to the Venetian forestry regime of this period is to be found in Tokugawa Japan simply reinforces the point that insularity was one of the key prerequisites for the development of a conservation mentality in the early modern period. Certainly not all insular societies—Britain comes to mind—adopted the kinds of conservation regimes that the Venetians and Japanese did. But invariably, the insular societies that eschewed conservationist policies enjoyed access to plentiful alternatives to domestic resources through trade, colonial expansion, or some combination of the two. So it was not insularity in general, but rather a particular form of insularity, defined by a limited resource horizon, that had the potential to lead an early modern state to make specific claims to authority over landscapes and resources, with an eye towards preserving both. Such assertions were not always successful, but the fact that two such disparate political and social units as the Venetian Republic and the Tokugawa Shogunate both advanced similar claims to authority over natural resources during this period can help environmental historians to see past geographical divisions and make effective comparisons in a truly global context. Venice's claims were unique in terms of their republicanism and their emphasis on a providential nature; but in terms of defining a particular relationship between the state and the natural world, they were functionally parallel to the Tokugawa assertions of jurisdiction over forest landscapes. Most of all, both governments sought to achieve the same goal—to preserve critical landscapes and resources and thereby avert catastrophic changes to the environment. That the two regimes framed the state's claim to authority in quite disparate and culturally specific ways is only to be expected, but this should not distract us from the similarities in their efforts to preserve specific kinds of forest landscapes containing particular kinds of forest resources. Moreover, it is crucial to recognize some of the shared processes—proscriptive legislation, selective thinning, and attempts at reforestation—through which both states sought to achieve their respective goals.

If I may be permitted to editorialize at the end of a long discussion, I would suggest that the problem of island environments is perhaps more urgent and important today than it was when Calbo initiated his pursuit of Pietro Gavardo. With the growing recognition that the globe itself is a large and incomprehensibly complex island environment with no access to outside resources, it seems to me that the history of the Venetian forestry regime is worth revisiting. The Republic may not have always met its conservation aims. And some of its enforcement methods may appear unpalatable to modern sensibilities. But the existence of a recognizable and respectable public discourse about the need to preserve the natural world for the mutual benefits that can be derived from it for all of its inhabitants—rather than constantly altering it in an effort to extract as much wealth as possible from it—strikes me as a worthwhile *exemplum* to consider when discussing our own environmental predicaments in our own oligarchic republic.

Reports and Correspondence Cited in the Text

Date	Author	Office	Geographical Area	Cited in Chapters
1413	anonymous	none	unspecified	2, 3, 6
1442	Marco Cornaro	*provveditore alla giustizia vecchia*	Sile, Piave, Livenza	2, 3, 4, 5, 6
1471	Domenico Lion	Arsenal *proto*	Montello	3
1507–9	Ludovico Bon	secretary of the *provveditori alle legne*	Friuli, Istria	4
1514	Giacomo Querini	*provveditore all'arsenale*	Trevigiano, Friuli, Istria	4
1548	Bernardino Vettori and Francesco Duodo	*provveditori all'arsenale*	Cansiglio	3, 5, 6
1548	Alessio di Mathio, Luca di Nicolò, and Marco di Zuane	Arsenal *proti*	Cansiglio	3, 5, 6
1569	Antonio Moro and Piero Lando	*provveditore sopra boschi* and Arsenal *proto*	Istria	5
1585	Giacomo Giustinian	*provveditore sopra boschi*	Trevigiano, Friuli	4
1602–5	Giovanni Garzoni	*provveditore sopra boschi*	Piave, Friuli	4, 5, 6
1627	Giovanni Battista Briani	*capitano di Cadore*	Cadore	4
1638	Andrea Badoer	*provveditore sopra boschi*	Cansiglio	5
1656	Antonio Barbarigo	*capitano di Raspo*	Istria	4
1684	Alvise Gritti	*provveditore al Montello*	Montello	5
1704	Leonardo Mocenigo	*inquisitore sopra boschi*	Trevigiano and Friuli	Introduction, 6
1709	Federico Calbo	*capitano di Raspo*	Montona	Conclusion
1715	Lauro Querini	*capitano di Raspo*	Montona	6
1726	Antonio Nani	*provveditore sopra boschi*	Trevigiano	5, 6
1730	Zuane Venier	*podestà di Belluno*	Cansiglio	6
1734	Bertuccio Dolfin	*provveditore sopra boschi*	Piave	3
1741	Antonio Tron	*provveditore sopra boschi*	Friuli	5
1775	Simone Stratico	professor of physics, Padua	all oak forests	3

Cadastral Surveys Conducted by the *Provveditori sopra Boschi*

Year	*Patrician* Provveditore	*Areas Surveyed*
1569	Surian	Trevigiano, Friuli
1569	Lando (*proto*)	Istria
1586	Giustinian	Trevigiano, Friuli
1593	Venier	Vicentino
1588	Bembo	Padovano
1602	Garzoni	Trevigiano, Friuli
1627	Canal	Friuli
1638	Badoer	Cansiglio (beech)
1660	Querini	Friuli
1671	Molin	Asolo
1726	Nani	Trevigiano
1740	Mocenigo	Motta and Oderzo
1741	Tron	Friuli
1741	Contarini	Conegliano
1743	Mocenigo	Carnia (beech)
1747	Gradenigo	Trevigiano

Principal Magistracies and Institutions Composing the Firewood and Timber Bureaucracy

Magistracy	*Dates*	*Area of Responsibility*
provveditori sopra il fatto delle legne e boschi	1437–1441	firewood market
ad hoc firewood agent	1454–1458	firewood market
provveditori alle legne	1458–1792	firewood market
provveditori sopra boschi (ad hoc)	1569–1792	cadastral surveys, *boschi pubblici*
inquisitore sopra boschi (ad hoc)	1702–1704	review of mainland statutes
sopraintendenza forestale	1792–1797	all areas of forest management

Abbreviations

ACVB	Archivio Curiale Vescovile di Belluno
ASB	Archivio di Stato di Belluno
ASV	Archivio di Stato di Venezia
B.	*Busta* (folder or box containing unbound material)
BCB	Biblioteca Civica di Belluno
BNM	Biblioteca Nazionale Marciana (Venice)
c.	*carta* (folio)
ds.	*disegno* (drawing or map)
f.	*fascicolo* (folder)
Filza	*Filza* (unbound daily minutes of Council and Senate meetings)
MCC	Museo Civico Correr (Venice)
Ms.	*Manoscritto* (manuscript)
n.n.	*non numerato* (not numbered)
Reg.	*Registro* (bound volume)

Introduction

Epigraph. ASV, *Amministrazione Forestale Veneta*, B. 10, printed pamphlet, c. 4.

1. Quoted in Lane, *Venice*, 358.
2. Merchant, *Death of Nature*.
3. See Crosby, *Columbian Exchange*; Crosby, *Ecological Imperialism*; Cronon, *Changes in the Land*; Merchant, *Ecological Revolutions*; Grove, *Green Imperialism*; Dean, *With Broadax and Firebrand*; Marks, *Tigers, Rice, Silk, and Silt*; Marks, *Origins of the Modern World*; Walker, *Conquest of Ainu Lands*; Richards, *Unending Frontier*; and Warde, *Ecology, Economy, and State Formation*.
4. See Moore, "*Modern World-System* as Environmental History?"
5. The most explicit expositions of this view are in Merchant's *Death of Na-*

ture and her *Ecological Revolutions*, but the idea is implicit in the work of Alfred Crosby and others. In addition to Crosby's *Ecological Imperialism*, see his *Measure of Reality*.

6. Marks, *Origins of the Modern World*, 15–16.

7. Merchant, *Death of Nature*, 238.

8. Merchant, *Death of Nature*, 238.

9. Totman, *Green Archipelago*.

10. See, for example, Marks, *Tigers, Rice, Silk, and Silt*; Marks, *Origins of the Modern World*; and Richards, *Unending Frontier*. R. Bin Wong makes a similar argument about historical models of state development in *China Transformed*.

11. See Grubb, *Firstborn of Venice*; Ferraro, *Family and Public Life*; Muir, *Mad Blood Stirring*; Povolo, *L'intrigo dell'onore*; Viggiano, *Lo specchio della repubblica*; and McKee, *Uncommon Dominion*.

12. Examples of exceptions are Ciriacono, *Acque e agricoltura*; Viggiano, *Governanti e governati*; and Grubb, *Provincial Families*.

13. See, for example, Strayer, *Western Europe in the Middle Ages*; Anderson, *Lineages of the Absolutist State*; W. McNeill, *Pursuit of Power*; Tilly, *Coercion, Capital, and European States*; Ertman, *Birth of the Leviathan*; and Scott, *Seeing Like a State*.

Chapter One: Forest Exploitation before the Venetian Conquest

Epigraph. ASV, *Provveditori e Patroni all'Arsenale*, B. 5, c. 65.

1. Chinazzo, *Cronica de la guerra*, 208.

2. ACVB, *Lite con l'Arsenale per Dazio*, B. 10, c. 3.

3. ASV, *Avogaria di Comune, Civile*, B. 27, f. 8.

4. See Lane, *Venetian Ships and Shipbuilders*, 230–33.

5. See Vera, *Grazing Ecology and Forest History*. Vera argues that the European landscape was already composed of a patchwork of grassland and forest long before the advent of sedentary agriculture.

6. Williams, *Deforesting the Earth*, 193.

7. Lane, *Venice*, 378.

8. For more on Venetian industry, see Trivellato, *La fondamenta dei vetrai*; Molà, *Silk Industry*; R. Davis, *Shipbuilders*; and Caniato and dal Borgo, *Le arti edili*.

9. See Lane, *Venice*, 11–18; Crouzet-Pavan, *Sopra le acque salse*; Howard, *Architectural History of Venice*; and Zorzi, *Golden Age*.

10. An exact figure is impossible to establish. However, the records of the construction of the Salute reveal that in 1630 the Venetian Senate purchased at least 12,000 piles for the project from Habsburg sources on the Isonzo River:

ASV, *Senato Terra*, Filza 321 (26 October 1630). From this figure it is possible to extrapolate a rough estimate for the Renaissance urban core of somewhere in the range of 20,000,000 piles.

11. For more on the Tyrol trade, see Occhi, *Boschi e mercanti*; and Agnoletti, *Segherie e foreste*.

12. Most of the forests in the *Vicentino* stood too far from the river to exploit for timber and were used mainly for fuel. In the 1593 survey of the region, for example, there were only 108 forests containing any oak, and almost all of them were more than eight miles from the nearest useful river. See ASV, *Provveditori sopra Boschi*, B. 138.

13. See, for example ASV, *Provveditori e Patroni all'Arsenale*, B. 24, c. 93r; and ASV, *Provveditori e Patroni all'Arsenale*, B. 12, c. 99r–v.

14. See Nicoletti and Spada, *I carbonai*; and Borin, "I carboneri."

15. For a general history of the Arsenal, see Concina, *L'arsenale della repubblica*. On naval construction, see Lane, *Venetian Ships and Shipbuilders*; and Lane, *Venice*, especially chapters 10 and 11. On the division of labor, see R. Davis, *Shipbuilders*.

16. Lane, *Venetian Ships and Shipbuilders*, 9–16.

17. Great galleys had a working life of around thirteen years, while light galleys lasted as many as twenty (Lane, *Venetian Ships and Shipbuilders*, 126). See also Martin, *Art and Archaeology*, especially chapter 3.

18. The best brief history of the myth is found in Muir, *Civic Ritual*, 13–54. Other representative analyses include Crouzet-Pavan, *Venice Triumphant*; Kallendorf, *Virgil and the Myth of Venice*; Finlay, "The Myth of Venice"; and Schreiner, *Il mito di Venezia*. On the suppression of factions and the promotion of cooperation in Venice, see Finlay, *Politics in Renaissance Venice*; Queller, *Venetian Patriciate*; and Lane, *Venice*, 109–10.

19. See Crouzet-Pavan, *Sopra le acque salse*, 217–18; Crouzet-Pavan, *Venice Triumphant*, 18–33; and Crouzet-Pavan, "Toward an Ecological Understanding."

20. Epstein, *Genoa and the Genoese*, 11; Gatti, *Navi e cantieri*, 19–40, 54–74.

21. See ASV, *Provveditori sopra Boschi*, B. 131.

22. Keahey, *Venice Against the Sea*, 70–74; and Crouzet-Pavan, *Sopra le acque salse*, 343, 762.

23. Grubb, *Provincial Families*, 133–55; and Del Torre, *Venezia e la terraferma*, 143–50.

24. See Cammarosano, *Le campagne friulane*; and Bianco, *Le terre del Friuli*, 51–102.

25. Disputes over the control of forest and water resources often lay at the heart of factional violence in the Friuli, including the infamous 1527 massacre of

Della Torre followers by members of the rival Savorgnan faction in Udine. For more on Friulian violence and its relationship to vital natural resources, see Muir, *Mad Blood Stirring*, 78–90.

26. Ivetic, *Oltremare*, 10.

27. Ivetic, *Oltremare*, 40–43.

28. In the seventeenth century the Venetians invested heavily in efforts to clear the tributaries connecting the Montona forest to the Quieto, but the problems with corruption, pilfering of stocks, siltation in tributaries, and lack of labor were apparent from a much earlier date. Representative examples are ASV, *Amministrazione Forestale Veneta*, B. 7, f. Carnia e Territorio, c. n.n. (30 March 1487); ASV, *Provveditori e Patroni all'Arsenale*, B. 133, c. 13; ASV, *Capi del Consiglio dei Dieci, Lettere di Rettori*, B. 264, c. 7; and ASV, *Provveditori e Patroni all'Arsenale*, B. 9, c. 32v.

29. See Caniato, "Notizie di segherie"; and De Vecchi, "Segheria e fucine lungo." For more on water-driven mills in general, see Vergani, "Energia dall'acqua."

30. See Perco, *Zattere, zattieri e menadàs*.

31. See Caniato, "Il vescovo e il mercante."

32. Ciani, *Storia del popolo cadorino*, 10–11.

33. The Cadore also contained a good deal of summer pasture, but the scale of transhumance in the northeast was minor, especially compared to southern Italy, because the region's fledgling wool industry imported higher-quality Spanish wool rather than relying on inferior local varieties. See Perco, *La pastorizia transumante*; Andrea Mozzato, "Note e documenti"; and Mozzato, *La mariegola*. As a point of comparison with southern Italy, see Marino, *Pastoral Economics*.

34. See, for example, ASV, *Amministrazione Forestale Veneta*, B. 7, f. Carnia e Territorio, c. n.n. (30 March 1487); ASV, *Amministrazione Forestale Veneta*, B. 35, c. 48; ASV, *Provveditori e Patroni all'Arsenale*, B. 11, c. 90v–91r; and ASV, *Senato Mar*, Filza 554, c. n.n. (5 February 1666 m.v.).

35. For more on *angarie*, see Muir, *Mad Blood Stirring*, 32–48.

36. ASV, *Relazioni di Rettori in Terraferma*, B. 34. Fourteenth-century consumption was probably well below this number. Indeed, Pasqualigo was describing a recent surge. However, charcoal production was likely proportionally lower, too.

37. The damage done by livestock in forests is a common theme in the records. See, for example, ASV, *Provveditori alla Camera dei Confini*, B. 192, Processo contro l'Austria, c. 229–31; ASV, *Secreta, Materie Miste Notabili*, B. 131, c. n.n. (31 July 1608); and ASV, *Avogaria di Comune, Penale*, B. 335, c. 4.

38. For example, in the Friuli in 1569, there were 63,686 Arsenal-grade oak

trees in community forests versus 27,967 on feudal or private lands. Data are drawn from ASV, *Provveditori sopra Boschi*, B. 131.

39. ASV, *Provveditori e Patroni all'Arsenale*, B. 5, c. 65. See also Vergani, "Le materie prime." Cf. Lane, *Venetian Ships and Shipbuilders*, 217–18. Lane ranks larch above beech, mostly because he claims the oars were less important than the decking. This ranking makes sense in terms of the construction of the ship, but not in terms of timber consumption, which is why beech became a regulated species and larch did not.

40. ASV, *Provveditori all'Arsenale*, B. 5, c. 80–82.

41. Lane, *Venetian Ships and Shipbuilders*, 24.

42. Lane, *Venetian Ships and Shipbuilders*, 218.

43. During the second war of Morea, for example, a number of ships of the line foundered because they had been made with poorly seasoned timber. See ASV, *Provveditori e Patroni all'Arsenale*, B. 22, c. 1r–v.

44. For more on salt, see Hocquet, *Le sel et la fortune*. A similar study of the wheat trade remains a *desideratum* in the scholarship.

Chapter Two: The Venetian Discovery of Mainland Forests

Epigraph. BNM, *It IV, 590 (5398)*, c. 1.

1. See ASV, *Amministrazione Forestale Veneta*, B. 4, f. G, for a copy of the Senate's instructions to Cornaro and the others.

2. The manuscript copy is at BNM, *It IV, 590 (5398)*, and the treatise was eventually published under the title *Marco Cornaro* (ed. Pavanello, 1919). See also Appuhn, "Politics, Perception, and the Meaning of Landscape"; Crouzet-Pavan, "Toward an Ecological Understanding," 49–53; and Ciriacono, "Scrittori d'idraulica."

3. The age of political majority in Venice was 25. For the *cursus honorum*, see J. Davis, *Decline of the Venetian Nobility*. See also Finlay, *Politics in Renaissance Venice*, 181–95; and Queller, *Venetian Patriciate*, 133–71.

4. See *Dizionario biografico*, 254–55; cf. Crouzet-Pavan, *Sopra le acque salse*, 363.

5. Eventually the Senate created the *savii et esecutorii alle acque* to manage the lagoon. For more, see Rompiasio, *Metodo*. See also Crouzet-Pavan, *Sopra le acque salse*; Ciriacono, *Acque e agricoltura*; and Dorigo, *Venezia*.

6. *Dizionario biografico*, 254–55.

7. Cornaro, *Marco Cornaro*, 75–157.

8. See Lambert, *Making of the Dutch Landscape*; Danner, *Polder Pioneers*; and Ciriacono, *Acque e agricoltura*.

9. See Crouzet-Pavan, *Sopra le acque salse*.

10. See Crouzet-Pavan, "Toward an Ecological Understanding."

11. BNM, *It IV, 590 (5398)*, c. 1.

12. Cornaro, *Marco Cornaro*, 29.

13. BNM, *It IV, 590 (5398)*, c. 2.

14. BNM, *It IV, 590 (5398)*, c. 2.

15. BNM, *It IV, 590 (5398)*, c. 3.

16. The dangers posed to republican liberty by the passions—and, to a lesser extent, self-interest—were among the most common concerns of Renaissance political thought. See Pocock, *Machiavellian Moment*; Muir, "Sources of Civil Society"; Muir, "Republicanism in the Renaissance Republics?"; Brown, "De-Masking Renaissance Republicanism"; Jurdjevic, "Florentine Republican Moment"; and Hirshman, *Passions and Interests*.

17. Cornaro, *Marco Cornaro*, 46.

18. See BNM, *It VII, 395 (8648)*, c. 1–3. See also Cornaro, *Marco Cornaro*, 23.

19. Since Cornaro was born in 1412 and the anonymous tract is clearly dated 1413, it is obviously not his work. The *Dizionario biografico*'s mistaken attribution is due to the strong similarities between the ideas contained in the 1413 piece and those found in the 1442 work. Pavanello suggests that a transcription error is to blame, but he offers no alternative to the 1413 date. See Cornaro, *Marco Cornaro*, 23–24.

20. BNM, *It VII, 395 (8648)*, c. 3.

21. See Payne, *Architectural Treatise*; Guillaume, *Les traités d'architecture*; Grafton, *Leon Battista Alberti*; Alberti, *On the Art of Building*; and Filarete, *Trattato d'architettura*.

22. ASV, *Rason Vecchie*, B. 47, c. n.n. (15 June 1456).

23. BNM, *It IV, 590 (5398)*, c. 3.

24. BNM, *It IV, 590 (5398)*, c. 3.

25. Grubb, *Firstborn of Venice*, 7.

26. See Kohl, *Padua under the Carrara*, 318–36.

27. Grubb, *Firstborn of Venice*, 8.

28. Law, "Venetian Mainland State," 158. See also Law, "Venice and the Problem of Sovereignty"; and Law, *Venice and the Veneto*.

29. See Cozzi, "Politica, società, istituzioni," 15.

30. Cozzi, "La politica del diritto."

31. The Venetians had a common-law tradition, but most of their subject cities relied on Roman law. The difficulties inherent in administering territories with wildly different legal traditions eventually led to the creation of the *consultori in jure*, an office dedicated exclusively to reconciling mainland Roman-law traditions with Venetian common law. The magistracy was usually staffed by law docents from the University of Padua. For more, see Cozzi, "La politica del

diritto." For more on the *consultori in jure* and land rights, see Barzati, "Consultori in iure e feudalità." Even cities with Roman-law traditions, such as Florence, experienced problems reconciling different legal systems. See, for example, Black, "Constitutional Ambitions, Legal Realities."

32. See Hespanha, "Early Modern Law," 192; and Calvero, *Antidora.*

33. MCC, *Mss., Ms. 2252/7*, c. 1 con allegati. This folder contains both the orders and the documents relevant to several appeals. The appeals lasted until 1592, when the tax burden was shifted from property owners to the entire community through the creation of a collective *angaria* obligation.

34. Grubb, *Firstborn of Venice,* 114–15.

35. See, for example, ASV, *Senato Misti,* Reg. 60, c. 39, for a 1437 law specifying market quotas for firewood.

36. ASV, *Amministrazione Forestale Veneta,* B. 4, f. 4 F.

37. BCB, *Documenti Antichi, transcritti da Francesco Pellegrini,* 5:39.

38. BCB, *Documenti Antichi, transcritti da Francesco Pellegrini,* 5:145.

39. ASV, *Compilazione Leggi,* B. 102, c. 45.

40. ASV, *Senato Misti,* Reg. 60, c. 107; and ASV, *Amministrazione Forestale Veneta,* B. 7 (12 March 1438).

41. ASV, *Amministrazione Forestale Veneta,* B. 4, c. G (12 May 1438). One copy identifies the third *provveditore* as Andrea Corner rather than Andrea Gritti.

42. ASV, *Senato Misti,* Reg. 60, c. 153 (18 June 1438).

43. ASV, *Amministrazione Forestale Veneta,* B. 35, c. n.n.

44. ASV, *Amministrazione Forestale Veneta,* B. 4, c. G,; also B. 7 and B. 9.

45. BNM, *It IV, 590 (5398),* c. 1. Cf Berenger, *Saggio storico,* 12–13. See also Braunstein, "De la montagne à Venise."

46. ASV, *Amministrazione Forestale Veneta,* B. 7 and B. 9.

47. ASV, *Amministrazione Forestale Veneta,* B. 21.

48. ASV, *Amministrazione Forestale Veneta,* B. 7, Carnia e Territorio, contains a summary of the complaints along with the Senate's response.

49. See, for example, BNM, *It VII, 1895 (9087),* c. 22.

50. See, for example, ASV, *Amministrazione Forestale Veneta,* B. 20, f. Dazio Legne, c. n.n. (17 October 1532).

51. ASV, *Amministrazione Forestale Veneta,* B. 7, Carnia e Territorio; and B. 9, Comune di Brischia.

52. ASV, *Amministrazione Forestale Veneta,* B. 7, Carnia e Territorio (4 August 1458); and ASV, *Senato Terra,* Reg. 4, c. 81.

53. ASV, *Senato Terra,* Reg. 4, c. 154; and ASV, *Amministrazione Forestale Veneta,* B. 7, Carnia e Territorio (8 February 1463 m.v.).

54. ASV, *Senato Terra,* Reg. 6, c. 25 (21 June 1468).

55. Cornaro, *Marco Cornaro,* 46.

Chapter Three: Venetian Forestry Laws and the
Creation of Public Forest Reserves

Epigraph. Quote from the 1471 Senate decree establishing the Montello reserve. See ASV, *Senato Terra*, Reg. 6, c. 152v.

1. ASV, *Senato Terra*, Reg. 6, c. 152v.

2. ASV, *Senato Terra*, Reg. 6, c. 152v.

3. See, for example, ASV, *Provveditori e Patroni all'Arsenale*, B. 21, c. 62v.

4. Quoted in Ciani, *Storia del Popolo Cadorino*, 395.

5. ASV, *Amministrazione Forestale Veneta*, B. 4, f. G. Another copy can be found in ASV, *Provveditori sopra Beni Comunali*, B. 293, c. 209.

6. Berenger, *Saggio storico*. The *diritto di riserva* was similar to the French *droit de martellage*.

7. Today the forest is part of a national park called *La Somadida*.

8. Ciani, *Storia del popolo cadorino*, 11–13.

9. ASV, *Senato Terra*, Reg. 6, c. 152v.

10. ASV, *Senato Terra*, Reg. 6, c. 152v.

11. Grubb, *Firstborn of Venice*, 136–48; and Muir, "Republicanism in the Renaissance Republics?" 154–59.

12. See, for example, ASV, *Compilazione Leggi*, B. 102, c. 107; ASV, *Amministrazione Forestale Veneta*, B. 35, c. 33 and 36–39; ASV, *Consiglio dei Dieci, Parti Comuni*, Filza 76, c. 101; ASV, *Amministrazione Forestale Veneta*, B. 4, 19 August 1559; ASV, *Amministrazione Forestale Veneta*, B. 35, c. 9; ASV, *Amministrazione Forestale Veneta*, B. 69, c. 120; and ASV, *Compilazione Leggi*, B. 102, c. 498.

13. ASV, *Provveditori e Patroni all'Arsenale*, B. 28, c. 49v.

14. ASV, *Provveditori e Patroni all'Arsenale*, B. 28, c. 20r.

15. ASV, *Provveditori e Patroni all'Arsenale*, B. 28, c. 20r.

16. ASV, *Consiglio dei Dieci, Parti Miste*, Reg. 23, c. 70 and 76v; Reg. 24. c. 85v–86r and 176r; Reg. 28, c. 241r; and Reg. 30, c. 148v, 162r, and 169. Cf. Knapton, "Il Consiglio dei Dieci," 238.

17. See, for example, ASV, *Senato, Deliberazioni Costantinopoli*, Reg. 7, c. 166; ASV, *Documenti Turchi*, B. 7, c. 865; and ASV, *Capi del Consiglio dei Dieci, Lettere di Rettori*, B. 264, c. 5. See also Ortega, "Ottoman Muslims in the Venetian Republic"; and Wolff, *Venice and the Slavs*, 232–34.

18. Knapton, "Il Consiglio dei Dieci," 245–46.

19. ASV, *Consiglio dei Dieci, Parti Comuni*, Filza 20, c. 12; ASV, *Consiglio dei Dieci, Parti Comuni*, Filza 32, c. 212; ASV, *Capi del Consiglio dei Dieci, Lettere di Rettori*, B. 299, f. 7, *Provveditori e Patroni all'Arsenale*, B. 20, c. 76r–v; and *Provveditori e Patroni all'Arsenale*, B. 21, c. 9v, respectively.

20. The most complete set in the *Amministrazione Forestale Veneta* can be found in B. 35, c. 3. Cf. *Senato Terra*, Reg. 7 (7 January 1475 m.v.).

21. The use of coupes was common in community forests throughout Europe. See Young, *Royal Forests*; James, *History of English Forestry*; Price, "Medieval Land Surveying"; Birrell, "Common Rights in the Medieval Forest"; Rubner, *Untersuchung zur Forst-verfassung*; De Moor, Shaw-Taylor, and Warde, *Management of Common Land*; Warde, "Fear of Wood Shortage"; and Warde, *Ecology, Economy and State Formation*, 77.

22. See, for example, the 1535 Burgundian forestry laws in the Archives générales du royaume, Bruxelles, *Conseil des Finances*, B. 139, c. 2, allowing pigs to enter royal forests in August and September. For a German example, see Warde, *Ecology, Economy and State Formation*, 81–83.

23. BNM, *It IV, 338 (5344)*, c. 15.

24. BNM, *It IV, 338 (5344)*, c. 15. Stratico also proposed a system of progressive pruning aimed at replicating the same effect.

25. Grubb, *Provincial Families*, 137–42.

26. The most famous "improver" was the sixteenth-century Paduan writer Alvise Cornaro. For more on Cornaro, see Tafuri, *Venice and the Renaissance*, 137–58; Ciriacono, *Building on Water*, 110–15; Cozzi, "Storie e politica del dibattito veneziano"; and Appuhn, "Friend or Flood?"

27. Older, wealthier patricians would simply refuse minor offices and pay the fine. See Finlay, *Politics in Renaissance Venice*, 181–95; Queller, *Venetian Patriciate*, 133–71; and J. Davis, *Decline of the Venetian Nobility*.

28. Corazzol, *Cineografo di banditi*, 17 (my translation).

29. ASV, *Compilazione Leggi*, B. 81, c. 1 and B. 143, c. 10. Cf. Pitteri, "La politica veneziana," footnote 23.

30. ASV, *Avogaria di Comune, Civile*, B. 27, f. 8.

31. ASV, *Senato Terra*, Reg. 6, c. 152v.

32. ASV, *Consiglio dei Dieci, Parti Comuni*, Filza 11, c. 126.

33. See Caniato, "Il legname"; and Šebesta, "Struttura ed evoluzione della zattera."

34. I will cite only a sample of the vast literature on the Cambrai crisis. See Bouwsma, *Venice and the Defense of Republican Liberty*; Gilbert, "Venice in the Crisis"; Gilbert, *The Pope, His Banker, and Venice*; Muir, "Republicanism in the Renaissance Republics?"; Ventura, *Nobiltà e popolo*; Del Torre, *Venezia e la terraferma*; Mallett and Hale, *Military Organization*, 221–27; and Cozzi, "Politica, società, istituzioni," 83–98, who outlines a general history of the events.

35. In 1510 the Constantinople galleys resumed. However, the Flemish, English, Spanish, and North African galleys failed to sail and severely harmed the Venetian economy. See Cozzi, "Politica, società, istituzioni," 93.

36. See Finlay, "Fabius Maximus in Venice"; and Del Torre, *Venezia e la terraferma*, 11–13.

37. Knapton, "Il Consiglio dei Dieci," 250.

38. See, for example, ASV, *Amministrazione Forestale Veneta*, B. 29, f. Carradori, c. 3r–4r and passim. The folder contains dozens of petitions from boatmen, carters, and woodcutters involved in the firewood trade.

39. See Grubb, *Provincial Families*, 134–35, for a discussion of the difficulties involved in determining the scale of Venetian ownership of rural property.

40. On the *corpi territoriali* and the *estimi*, see Grubb, "L'economia rurale"; Zamperetti, "I sinedri dolosi"; and Knapton, "Il territorio vicentino."

41. Zamperetti, "I sinedri dolosi," 277–78; and Zamperetti, *I piccoli principi*. For an overview of rural institutions in Italy, see Chittolini, *La formazione dello stato*.

42. For more on the *Avogaria di Comune*, see Viggiano, *Governanti e governati*, 51–146.

43. ASV, *Avogaria di Comune, Civile*, B. 27, f. 8.

44. See, for example, Claudio Povolo, *L'intrigo dell'onore*.

45. Del Torre, *Venezia e la terraferma*, 143.

46. ASV, *Senato Terra*, Reg. 20, c. 37. Cf. Del Torre, *Venezia e la terraferma*, 145.

47. Sanuto, 53:293. Cf. Del Torre, *Venezia e la terraferma*, 146.

48. Sanuto, 45:353–54 and 357.

49. Sanuto, 45:381.

50. ASV, *Consiglio dei Dieci, Parti Comuni*, Reg. 4, c. 12v–13r; and Sanuto, 46:552. Cf. Del Torre, *Venezia e la terraferma*, 148.

51. Sanuto, 48:33.

52. Sanuto, 48:40.

53. Sanuto, 48:74. Cf. Del Torre, *Venezia e la terraferma*, 149.

54. ASV, *Consiglio dei Dieci, Parti Comuni*, Reg. 4, c. 126. Cf. Sanuto, 49:195.

55. See ASV, *Consiglio dei Dieci, Parti Comuni*, Reg. 4, c. 157v, for Giustinian's commission.

56. The first measure was passed on 15 December 1528 and is found in ASV, *Consiglio dei Dieci, Parti Comuni*, Reg. 4, 132v. For extensions of the rule, see ASV, *Consiglio dei Dieci, Parti Comuni*, Reg. 4, 141r, 145r, and 155r. Cf. Del Torre, *Venezia e la terraferma*, 150.

57. ASV, *Provveditori e Patroni all'Arsenale*, B. 14, c. 155.

58. Lanaro, *Centre of the Old World*, 34–44; Luzzato and Berengo, *Storia economica*; and Rapp, *Industry and Economic Decline*.

59. ASV, *Consiglio dei Dieci, Parti Comuni*, Filza 12, c. 157 (January 1530 m.v.).

60. ASV, *Consiglio dei Dieci, Parti Comuni*, Filza 12, c. 157 (January 1530 m.v.).

61. ASV, *Amministrazione Forestale Veneta*, B. 24, f. 2. Cf. Sanuto, 20:209.

62. ASV, *Consiglio dei Dieci, Parti Comuni*, Filza 11, c. 123.

63. ASV, *Consiglio dei Dieci, Parti Comuni*, Filza 12, c. 157.

64. ASV, *Consiglio dei Dieci, Parti Comuni*, Filza 11, c. 126.

65. ASV, *Consiglio dei Dieci, Parti Comuni*, Filza 11, c. 126.

66. ASV, *Consiglio dei Dieci, Parti Comuni*, Filza 12, c. 157.

67. ASV, *Consiglio dei Dieci, Parti Comuni*, Filza 12, c. 157.

68. ASV, *Consiglio dei Dieci, Parti Comuni*, Filza 12, c. 157.

69. ASV, *Consiglio dei Dieci, Parti Comuni*, Filza 12, c. 157.

70. ASV, *Consiglio dei Dieci, Parti Comuni*, Filza 12, c. 157.

71. See, for example, ASV, *Amministrazione Forestale Veneta*, B. 1, c. 51A–53A; ASV, *Provveditori sopra Boschi*, B. 137, c. 159–60; ASV, *Provveditori e Patroni all'Arsenale*, B. 23, c. 293v; and ASV, *Provveditori e Patroni all'Arsenale*, B. 28, c. 18v–22r.

72. ASV, *Amministrazione Forestale Veneta*, B. 4, f. G, c. n.n. (1 March 1524).

73. ASV, *Compilazione Leggi*, B. 102, c. 69.

74. For more on the problems caused by reclamation, see Appuhn, "Friend or Flood?"; Ciriacono, *Acque e agricoltura*; Crouzet-Pavan, *Sopra le acque salse*; Keahey, *Venice against the Sea*; Avanzi, *Il regime giuridico*; and Bevilacqua, "La conterminazione della laguna."

75. ASV, *Capi del Consiglio dei Dieci, Lettere di Rettori*, B. 299, f. 7 (12 March 1561) cites the 1557 decree and outlines the resistance encountered by the Arsenal manager Girolamo Contarini when he destroyed several charcoal pits near the Montello.

76. ASV, *Consiglio dei Dieci, Parti Comuni*, Filza 46, c. 127, allegato 1.

77. ASV, *Consiglio dei Dieci, Parti Comuni*, Filza 46, c. 127, allegato 1.

78. ASV, *Consiglio dei Dieci, Parti Comuni*, Filza 46, c. 127, allegato 1.

79. ASV, *Consiglio dei Dieci, Parti Comuni*, Filza 46, c. 127, allegato 1.

80. ASV, *Consiglio dei Dieci, Parti Comuni*, Filza 46, c. 127, allegato 2.

81. ASV, *Consiglio dei Dieci, Parti Comuni*, Filza 46, c. 127, allegato 2.

82. ASV, *Consiglio dei Dieci, Parti Comuni*, Filza 46, c. 127, allegato 2.

83. ASV, *Consiglio dei Dieci, Parti Comuni*, Filza 46, c. 127 (21 November 1548).

84. ASV, *Consiglio dei Dieci, Parti Comuni*, Filza 46, c. 127, allegato 2.

Chapter Four: The Venetian Forest Bureaucracy

Epigraph. ASV, *Capi del Consiglio dei Dieci, Lettere di Rettori*, B. 299 bis, f. 6, c. n.n. (4 November 1602).

1. For Garzoni's commission, see ASV, *Consiglio dei Dieci, Parti Comuni,* Filza 235, c. n.n. (28 November 1601). Elected in late 1601, he did not depart Venice until the spring of 1602.

2. ASV, *Amministrazione Forestale Veneta,* B. 7, Carnia e Territorio, (4 August 1458); and ASV, *Senato Terra,* Reg. 4, c. 81.

3. R. Davis, *Shipbuilders,* 49–50.

4. ASV, *Amministrazione Forestale Veneta,* B. 7, Carnia e Territorio, (8 March 1487).

5. ASV, *Senato Terra,* Reg. 6, c. 25 (21 June 1468).

6. ASV, *Senato Terra,* Reg. 6, c. 25 (21 June 1468).

7. Davis points out that the Arsenal managers' duties were also becoming exceptionally onerous in this period, due to the increasing specialization of production in the shipyard. See R. Davis, *Shipbuilders,* 50.

8. ASV, *Senato Terra,* Reg. 6, c. 152v.

9. For the political rhetoric of lagoon management, see Crouzet-Pavan, *Sopra le acque salse;* and Crouzet-Pavan, "Toward an Ecological Understanding,"

10. Grubb, *Firstborn of Venice,* 144–47 and 178–83. See also Knapton, *Venezia e la terraferma,* 237–60.

11. See ASV, *Amministrazione Forestale Veneta,* B. 9, f. Comune di Brischia, c. 6.

12. ASV, *Amministrazione Forestale Veneta,* B. 4, f. G, c. n.n. (14 June 1508); and ASV, *Amministrazione Forestale Veneta,* B. 7, f. Carnia e Territorio, c. n.n. (18 December 1508).

13. See Bianco and Amaseo, *1511, la "crudel zobia grassa";* Bianco, *Contadini, sbirri e contrabbandieri;* Bianco and Ambrosoli, *Comunità e questioni di confini;* Muir, *Mad Blood Stirring;* and Ivetic, *Oltremare.*

14. ASV, *Amministrazione Forestale Veneta,* B. 9, f. Comune di Brischia, c. n.n.

15. ASV, *Amministrazione Forestale Veneta,* B. 9, f. Comune di Brischia, c. 5 (1487 m.v.). See also ASV, *Amministrazione Forestale Veneta,* B. 7, f. Carnia e Territorio, c. n.n. and BNM, *It VII, 1895 (9087),* c. 17–18 for additional copies.

16. See BNM, *It VII, 1895 (9087),* c. 2, dated 1313, for a description of a *passo.*

17. BNM, *It VII, 1895 (9087),* c. 18.

18. BNM, *It VII, 1895 (9087),* c. 18; and Tassini, *Curiosità veneziane,* 478.

19. See, for example, Molà, *Communità dei lucchesi,* 73–86; and Shaw, *Justice of Venice.*

20. See Martini, *Manuale di metrologia.*

21. ASV, *Amministrazione Forestale Veneta,* B. 4, f. G, c. n.n. (28 February 1532 m.v.); and ASV, *Amministrazione Forestale Veneta,* B. 1, c. 46A.

22. See Dursteler, *Venetians in Constantinople*; Dursteler, "The Bailò in Constantinople"; Rothman, "Between Venice and Istanbul"; and Neff, "A Citizen in the Service."

23. The Cambrai crisis may account for the fact that no trace of Bon's formal report exists. In the face of far more pressing problems, the Council of Ten probably neglected to give the secretary an audience.

24. ASV, *Amministrazione Forestale Veneta*, B. 24, f. 2.

25. Andrea da Mosto's authoritative finding aid, *L'archivio di stato di Venezia: Indice generale storico, descrittivo, ed analitico*, which is still every scholar's first step in Venice's massive archive, reflects the cataloging error. Under the heading *"provveditori sopra boschi,"* da Mosto provides a detailed description and history of the *provveditori alle legne*, along with a brief account of the archive's holdings of documents that deal with forests. Restoring order to the archive by separating the records of the two offices will be an exceptionally difficult and time-consuming undertaking. Until then, scholars need to read with care, as individual *buste* inevitably contain a random assortment of documents produced by both the *provveditori alle legne* and the *provveditori sopra boschi*.

26. Berenger, *Saggio storico*. See also Appuhn, "Environmental Politics and State Power." I fell into the same trap, and it was only after several years of struggling with inconsistencies in the documents that I finally recognized that the two offices were distinct.

27. ASV, *Amministrazione Forestale Veneta*, B. 24, f. 2 (1 January 1514 m.v.).

28. ASV, *Amministrazione Forestale Veneta*, B. 24, f. 2 (1 January 1514 m.v.). Cf. Sanuto, 20:209 for a mention of Querini's letter.

29. ASV, *Amministrazione Forestale Veneta*, B. 24, f. 2 (1 January 1514 m.v.).

30. ASV, *Amministrazione Forestale Veneta*, B. 24, f. 2 (1 January 1514 m.v.). Cf. Sanuto, 20:227.

31. See Perco, *Zattere, zattieri e menadàs*.

32. ASV, *Provveditori e Patroni all'Arsenale*, B. 133, c. 6.

33. ASV, *Capi del Consiglio dei Dieci, Lettere di Rettori*, B. 299 bis, f. 6, c. n.n. (4 November 1602).

34. Corazzol, *Cineografo di banditi*, 15–52.

35. ASV, *Provveditori e Patroni all'Arsenale*, B. 133, c. 6. Corramexin pointed to his successful fulfillment of both Arsenal and firewood contracts as proof of his reliability.

36. R. Davis, *Shipbuilders*, 50.

37. ASV, *Consiglio dei Dieci, Parti Comuni*, Filza 32, c. 203.

38. ASV, *Amministrazione Forestale Veneta*, B. 7, f. Carnia e Territorio, c. n.n. (30 March 1487).

39. ASV, *Capi del Consiglio dei Dieci, Lettere di Rettori*, B. 264, c. 5 (16 February 1529 m.v.). *Morlacchi* was the Venetian term for the Slavic populations of Istria and Dalmatia.

40. See Del Torre, *Venezia e la terraferma*, 59–84.

41. For representative examples, see ASV, *Provveditori sopra Boschi*, B. 137, c. 161–65; ASV, *Capi del Consiglio dei Dieci, Lettere di Rettori*, B. 299, f. 7 (24 November 1588); ASV, *Provveditori e Patroni all'Arsenale*, B. 19, c. 6v; and ASV, *Provveditori e Patroni all'Arsenale*, B. 22, c. 179v–180v.

42. ASV, *Capi del Consiglio dei Dieci, Lettere di Rettori*, B. 264, c. 29v.

43. ASV, *Capi del Consiglio dei Dieci, Lettere di Rettori*, B. 264, c. 29v.

44. ASV, *Senato Mar*, Filza 554 (5 February 1666 m.v.).

45. ASV, *Senato Mar*, Filza 554 (5 February 1666 m.v.).

46. ASV, *Senato Mar*, Reg. 134, c. 459v–460r.

47. ASV, *Provveditori sopra Boschi*, B. 137, c. 164v.

48. See, for example, ASV, *Capi del Consiglio dei Dieci, Lettere di Rettori*, B. 299 bis, c. 6 and c. n.n. (20 April 1602).

49. ASV, *Amministrazione Forestale Veneta*, B. 35, c. 345.

50. ASV, *Capi del Consiglio dei Dieci, Lettere di Rettori*, B. 299 bis, f. 6, c. n.n. (4 November 1602).

51. ASV, *Capi del Consiglio dei Dieci, Lettere di Rettori*, B. 299 bis, f. 6, c. n.n. (4 November 1602).

52. ASV, *Consiglio dei Dieci, Parti Comuni*, Filza 101, c. n.n. con 2 allegati (29 January 1568); and ASV, *Provveditori e Patroni all'Arsenale*, B. 11, c. 52r, respectively.

53. ASV, *Senato Mar*, Reg. 134, c. 460r.

54. ASV, *Senato Mar*, Reg. 134, c. 460r.

55. ASV, *Amministrazione Forestale Veneta*, B. 10, f. B, c. n.n. (19 November 1704).

56. ASV, *Capi del Consiglio dei Dieci, Lettere di Rettori*, B. 270, c. 146–48; ASV, *Amministrazione Forestale Veneta*, B. 24, f. Primo, c. n.n. (13 October 1585); ASV, *Provveditori e Patroni all'Arsenale*, B. 14, c. 33r–v.; and ASV, *Provveditori sopra Beni Communali*, B. 293, f. 209, c. 16r–21v, respectively.

57. ASV, *Capi del Consiglio dei Dieci, Lettere di Rettori*, B. 299 bis, f. 6, c. n.n. (18 March 1603).

58. ASV, *Capi del Consiglio dei Dieci, Lettere di Rettori*, B. 299 bis, f. 6, c. n.n. (18 March 1603).

59. ASV, *Provveditori e Patroni all'Arsenale*, B. 11, c. 52r.

60. Rewards for anonymous tips represented a common practice in Venice, and courts had stringent rules for corroborating hearsay. Garzoni, for example,

refused to prosecute cases without at least two witnesses. For more, see Horodowich, *Language and Statecraft*.

61. See De Moor, Shaw-Taylor, and Warde, *Management of Common Land*.

62. ASV, *Capi del Consiglio dei Dieci, Lettere di Rettori*, B. 270, c. 147.

63. ASV, *Capi del Consiglio dei Dieci, Lettere di Rettori*, B. 270, c. 148.

64. ASV, *Capi del Consiglio dei Dieci, Lettere di Rettori*, B. 270, c. 148.

65. ASV, *Capi del Consiglio dei Dieci, Lettere di Rettori*, B. 270, c. 148.

66. ASV, *Provveditori sopra Beni Communali*, B. 293, f. 209, c. 16r.

67. ASV, *Provveditori sopra Beni Communali*, B. 293, f. 209, c. 16r.

68. ASV, *Provveditori sopra Beni Communali*, B. 293, f. 209, c. 16r.

69. ASV, *Provveditori sopra Beni Communali*, B. 293, f. 209, c. 16r.

70. ASV, *Provveditori sopra Beni Communali*, B. 293, f. 209, c. 16r.

71. ASV, *Provveditori sopra Beni Communali*, B. 293, f. 209, c. 16r.

72. ASV, *Provveditori sopra Beni Communali*, B. 293, f. 209, c. 17r–v.

73. See ASV, *Consiglio dei Dieci, Parti Comuni*, Filza 235, c. n.n. (28 November 1601) for the full text of Garzoni's commission. Note also that the Venetians referred to the cadastral surveys by the family name of the *provveditore sopra boschi* who supervised them. So the 1602–5 survey was officially known as the *Catastico Garzoni*.

74. See ASV, *Collegio, Notatorio*, B. 47, c. 127 for a copy of Giustinian's commission.

75. ASV, *Consiglio dei Dieci, Parti Comuni*, Filza 235, c. n.n. (28 November 1601).

76. ASV, *Capi del Consiglio dei Dieci, Lettere di Rettori*, B. 299 bis, f. 6, c. n.n. (16 September 1602).

77. ASV, *Provveditori e Patroni all'Arsenale*, B. 13, c. 115r–v.

78. ASV, *Capi del Consiglio dei Dieci, Lettere di Rettori*, B. 299 bis, f. 6, c. n.n. (18 January 1603 m.v.).

79. ASV, *Capi del Consiglio dei Dieci, Lettere di Rettori*, B. 299 bis, f. 6, c. n.n. (16 February 1603 m.v.).

80. ASV, *Capi del Consiglio dei Dieci, Lettere di Rettori*, B. 299 bis, f. 6, c. n.n. (30 March 1604).

81. ASV, *Capi del Consiglio dei Dieci, Lettere di Rettori*, B. 299 bis, f. 6, c. n.n. (1 June 1603).

82. ASV, *Capi del Consiglio dei Dieci, Lettere di Rettori*, B. 299 bis, f. 6, c. n.n. (20 April 1602).

83. ASV, *Capi del Consiglio dei Dieci, Lettere di Rettori*, B. 299 bis, f. 6, c. n.n. (4 November 1602).

84. ASV, *Capi del Consiglio dei Dieci, Lettere di Rettori*, B. 299 bis, f. 6, c. n.n. (8 March 1603).

85. ASV, *Capi del Consiglio dei Dieci, Lettere di Rettori*, B. 299 bis, f. 6, c. n.n. (18 March 1603).

86. ASV, *Capi del Consiglio dei Dieci, Lettere di Rettori*, B. 299 bis, f. 6, c. n.n. (7 September 1603).

87. ASV, *Capi del Consiglio dei Dieci, Lettere di Rettori*, B. 299 bis, f. 6, c. n.n. (18 January 1602 m.v.).

88. ASV, *Capi del Consiglio dei Dieci, Lettere di Rettori*, B. 299 bis, f. 6, c. n.n. (18 January 1602 m.v.).

89. ASV, *Capi del Consiglio dei Dieci, Lettere di Rettori*, B. 299 bis, f. 6, c. n.n. (18 January 1602 m.v.).

90. ASV, *Capi del Consiglio dei Dieci, Lettere di Rettori*, B. 299 bis, f. 6, c. n.n. (24 April 1603).

91. ASV, *Capi del Consiglio dei Dieci, Lettere di Rettori*, B. 299 bis, f. 6, c. n.n. (14 April 1603).

92. ASV, *Capi del Consiglio dei Dieci, Lettere di Rettori*, B. 299 bis, f. 6, c. n.n. (4 February 1602 m.v.).

93. ASV, *Capi del Consiglio dei Dieci, Lettere di Rettori*, B. 299 bis, f. 6, c. n.n. (24 April 1603).

94. ASV, *Capi del Consiglio dei Dieci, Lettere di Rettori*, B. 299 bis, f. 6, c. n.n. (3 December 1602).

95. ASV, *Capi del Consiglio dei Dieci, Lettere di Rettori*, B. 299 bis, f. 6, c. n.n. (4 February 1602 m.v.).

96. ASV, *Capi del Consiglio dei Dieci, Lettere di Rettori*, B. 299 bis, f. 6, c. n.n. (27 January 1602 m.v.).

97. ASV, *Capi del Consiglio dei Dieci, Lettere di Rettori*, B. 299 bis, f. 6, c. n.n. (14 April 1603).

98. ASV, *Capi del Consiglio dei Dieci, Lettere di Rettori*, B. 299 bis, f. 6, c. n.n. (14 April 1603).

99. ASV, *Capi del Consiglio dei Dieci, Lettere di Rettori*, B. 299 bis, f. 6, c. n.n. (22 August 1603).

100. ASV, *Capi del Consiglio dei Dieci, Lettere di Rettori*, B. 299 bis, f. 6, c. n.n. (22 February 1602 m.v.).

101. ASV, *Capi del Consiglio dei Dieci, Lettere di Rettori*, B. 299 bis, f. 6, c. n.n. (22 February 1602 m.v.).

Chapter Five: The Preservation and Reproduction of
Bureaucratic Knowledge

Epigraph. ASV, *Provveditori e Patroni all'Arsenale*, B. 11, c. 94r.

1. ASV, *Amministrazione Forestale Veneta*, B. 36, c. 127v (12 April 1684).

2. ASV, *Amministrazione Forestale Veneta*, B. 36, c. 122v (12 April 1684).

3. ASV, *Amministrazione Forestale Veneta*, B. 36, c. 125v (12 April 1684).

4. The *Oxford English Dictionary* gives 1825 as the earliest use of the term *expert*. Certainly experts, in the sense of individuals possessing a particular skill, existed prior to the coinage of the term, but early modern expertise differed considerably from its modern manifestations. One of the key challenges facing early modern states such as Venice was distinguishing the "real experts" possessing verifiable practical knowledge of technical problems from the charlatans seeking patronage based on flimsy invented claims of secret knowledge or techniques. See, for example, Ash, *Power, Knowledge, and Expertise*; Long, *Openness, Secrecy, Authorship*; Smith, *Body of the Artisan*; and Shapin, *Social History of Truth*.

5. Crouzet-Pavan, *Sopra le acque salse*.

6. See, for example, Berveglieri, *Inventori stranieri a Venezia*; Dursteler, *Venetians in Constantinople*; and Rothman, "Between Venice and Istanbul."

7. ASV, *Senato Terra*, Reg. 6, c. 25 (21 June 1468).

8. ASV, *Capi del Consiglio dei Dieci, Lettere di Rettori*, B. 299 bis, f. 6, c. n.n. (14 April 1603).

9. ASV, *Consiglio dei Dieci, Parti Comuni*, Filza 46, c. 127, allegato 1 and 2.

10. See Appuhn, "Friend or Flood?" In this instance an expert in water management from outside the Republic's bureaucracy presented the Senate with an alternative breakwater design. In the ensuing trial of the design, the traditional expertise of the Venetian *proti* triumphed decisively. For more on Thomas Digges and Dover Harbor, see Ash, *Power, Knowledge, and Expertise*, 55–86.

11. On gentlemanly knowledge, see Shapin, *Social History of Truth*, 42–125; Shapin, "A Scholar and a Gentleman"; and Shapin, "Trusting George Cheyne." On English technical experts, see Ash, *Power, Knowledge, and Expertise*, 19–54.

12. Golan, *Laws of Man*, 5–51.

13. For an example of dueling narratives, see Golan, *Laws of Man*, 27–34.

14. ASV, *Provveditori e Patroni all'Arsenale*, B. 11, c. 26v–27r.

15. The intact registers can be seen in ASV, *Provveditori ai Boschi*, B. 126–32. Each register contains the data for a single major district, or for two or three minor districts.

16. ASV, *Provveditori ai Boschi*, B. 126–32.

17. See ASV, *Provveditori e Patroni all'Arsenale*, B. 11, c. 23r for a copy of Moro's commission.

18. ASV, *Provveditori sopra Legne e Boschi*, B. II, f. 1. I cannot offer a defintive explanation for why the *Catastico Lando* is the only survey named after a *proto* instead of the patrician supervisor who held the commission to conduct it. It may be that while Moro gave the formal oration before the Senate, the descriptions contained in the volume he presented to his superiors are all written in Lando's voice. In contrast, the quantitative surveys named after patricians were impersonal and not written in the voice of any one individual.

19. ASV, *Provveditori sopra Legne e Boschi*, B. II, c. 1.

20. ASV, *Capi del Consiglio dei Dieci, Lettere di Rettori*, B. 299 bis, f. 6, c. n.n. (18 January 1603 m.v.).

21. ASV, *Capi del Consiglio dei Dieci, Lettere di Rettori*, B. 299 bis, f. 6, c. n.n. (4 February 1602 m.v.).

22. ASV, *Capi del Consiglio dei Dieci, Lettere di Rettori*, B. 299 bis, f. 6, c. n.n. (4 February 1602 m.v.).

23. ASV, *Capi del Consiglio dei Dieci, Lettere di Rettori*, B. 299 bis, f. 6, c. n.n. (24 April 1603).

24. These are my own estimates, based on the detailed perimeter surveys contained in the two surveys. See ASV, *Provveditori sopra Boschi*, Reg. 141 and 149.

25. My estimates are drawn from the same surveys cited in the above note. For the fiscal crises of the late seventeenth century and the consequent sale of common lands, see Berenger, *Saggio storico*, 48–54; Bianchetti, *Ville friulane*; and Perdezani, *Venezia e lo "stado de terraferma."*

26. ASV, *Provveditori e Patroni all'Arsenale*, B. 25, c. 66v.

27. ASV, *Provveditori e Patroni all'Arsenale*, B. 25, c. 39v.

28. ASV, *Provveditori e Patroni all'Arsenale*, B. 25, c. 59r.

29. ASV, *Provveditori e Patroni all'Arsenale*, B. 25, c. 58v–59r.

30. ASV, *Provveditori e Patroni all'Arsenale*, B. 25, c. 59r.

31. ASV, *Provveditori e Patroni all'Arsenale*, B. 25, c. 60r.

32. ASV, *Provveditori e Patroni all'Arsenale*, B. 25, c. 60r.

33. ASV, *Provveditori e Patroni all'Arsenale*, B. 25, c. 60r.

34. ASV, *Provveditori e Patroni all'Arsenale*, B. 25, c. 61r.

35. ASV, *Provveditori e Patroni all'Arsenale*, B. 25, c. 68r.

36. See Harvey, *History of Topographical Maps*, 153–68. Harvey distinguishes between pictorial maps and bird's-eye views of cities, both of which were drawn by artists, and topographical maps, which were drawn by surveyors. For

more on bird's-eye views, see Wilson, *World in Venice*. See also Schulz, "Jacopo de' Barbari's View of Venice"; and Howard, "Venice as a Dolphin."

37. See Casti, "State, Cartography, and Territory."

38. See Caniato, "L'organismo delicato"; and Bevilacqua, "Conterminazione della laguna."

39. See Marino, "Administrative Mapping." Marino points out that, compared to the rest of Europe, Italian states were relatively late to adopt topographical maps as an administrative tool. Casti, however, argues that Venice adopted administrative cartography a full two centuries before any other Italian state ("State, Cartography, and Territory," 877).

40. See Cosgrove, "Mapping New Worlds."

41. ASV, *Amministrazione Forestale Veneta*, B. 35, c. 105.

42. ASV, *Provveditori e Patroni all'Arsenale*, B. 25, c. 61r. See also Appuhn, "Inventing Nature."

43. The *catastico* can be seen in its entirety at ASV, *Provveditori ai Boschi*, B. 150 bis. See also Lazzarini, "Boschi a remi."

44. ASV, *Provveditori e Patroni all'Arsenale*, B. 95, c. n.n. (7 October 1747).

45. See, for example, Lowood, "The Calculating Forester"; and Merchant, *Death of Nature*, 236–52.

Chapter Six: Nature's Republic or Republican Nature?

Epigraph. ASV, *Amministrazione Forestale Veneta*, B. 10, f. B, printed pamphlet, c. 4.

1. ASV, *Amministrazione Forestale Veneta*, B. 10, f. B, printed pamphlet, c. 5.

2. ASV, *Amministrazione Forestale Veneta*, B. 10, f. B, printed pamphlet, c. 5.

3. See Cronon, "The Trouble with Wilderness"; Coates, *Nature*, 107 and passim; Evernden, *Social Creation of Nature*, 120; and Oelshlaeger, *Idea of Wilderness*.

4. See, for example, Merchant, *Death of Nature*; Thomas, *Man and the Natural World*; and Coates, *Nature*.

5. See Merchant, *Death of Nature*, 78; Merchant, *Reinventing Eden*, 147–53; Merchant, *Ecological Revolutions*, 100–103; Cronon, *Changes in the Land*, 78–79; and Grove, *Green Imperialism*, 483. For accounts of English views of forests as an impediment to progress as well as an object of veneration in the early modern period, see Thomas, *Man and the Natural World*, 192–223; Coates, *Nature*, 110–24; and, in a slightly broader European context, Harrison, *Forests*, 107–54.

6. For a good summary of the English view of humanity's rights and obliga-

tions to manipulate and improve nature, see Thomas, *Man and the Natural World*, 17–30. The connection between a reformed Christian morality and the power to improve nature was a commonplace trope, especially in Anglophone pamphlets and literature. Perhaps the most famous example of this discourse can be found in Daniel Defoe's *Robinson Crusoe*, in which the penitent castaway achieves an unmediated relationship with God through his efforts to transform the wild island into an improved agrarian landscape, complete with domesticated plants and animals. For more on the "robinsonnade" and its connections to English and French ideas about nature, see Grove, *Green Imperialism*, 225–49.

7. ASV, *Provveditori e Patroni all'Arsenale*, B. 20, c. 52v–53r. In this context, a "first-rate" does not mean a ship of the line, as it would for the Atlantic navies of this period. A Venetian first-rate was similar to a heavy frigate in the Atlantic context. For more on the seventeenth-century Venetian fleet, see Candiani, "Lo sviluppo dell'armata"; and Candiani, "Tiburzio Bailo," 677–706.

8. ASV, *Provveditori e Patroni all'Arsenale*, B. 20, c. 85v–86r.

9. ASV, *Provveditori e Patroni all'Arsenale*, B. 20, c. 141r–v.

10. See ASV, *Provveditori e Patroni all'Arsenale*, B. 20, c. 159v; and ASV, *Provveditori e Patroni all'Arsenale*, B. 21, c. 190r–v, respectively.

11. Appuhn, "Friend or Flood?"

12. Lane, *Venice*, 416–17; Lane, *Venetian Ships and Shipbuilders*, 233–4; and Berenger, *Saggio storico*.

13. ASV, *Provveditori e Patroni all'Arsenale*, B. 25, c. 55v–68v.

14. ASV, *Provveditori e Patroni all'Arsenale*, B. 20, c. 172v.

15. ASV, *Provveditori e Patroni all'Arsenale*, B. 21, c. 152v.

16. ASV, *Provveditori e Patroni all'Arsenale*, B. 19, c. 24v.

17. ASV, *Provveditori e Patroni all'Arsenale*, B. 22, c. 120r–v.

18. See ASV, *Provveditori e Patroni all'Arsenale*, B. 21, c. 111v–112v; and ASV, *Provveditori e Patroni all'Arsenale*, B. 21, c. 144v.

19. ASV, *Provveditori e Patroni all'Arsenale*, B. 21, c. 62v.

20. The final report on the incident blamed a combination of unseasoned timber and faulty construction techniques. See ASV, *Provveditori e Patroni all'Arsenale*, B. 22, c. 1r–v.

21. See ASV, *Provveditori e Patroni all'Arsenale*, B. 21, c. 213v–214r for the proposal and ASV, *Provveditori e Patroni all'Arsenale*, B. 21, c. 249r–v for the sawyers' objections. The sawyers were among the most valued and important members of the Arsenal's workforce, because the task of sawing seasoned logs into precisely fitted planking for the hull required incredible skill.

22. ASV, *Amministrazione Forestale Veneta*, B. 10, f. B, printed pamphlet, c. 40.

23. ASV, *Amministrazione Forestale Veneta*, B. 10, f. B, printed pamphlet, c. 41.

24. ASV, *Amministrazione Forestale Veneta*, B. 10, f. B, printed pamphlet, c. 41.

25. ASV, *Senato Terra*, Reg. 6, c. 152v.

26. ASV, *Amministrazione Forestale Veneta*, B. 10, f. B, printed pamphlet, c. 6.

27. ASV, *Amministrazione Forestale Veneta*, B. 10, f. B, printed pamphlet, c. 6.

28. ASV, *Capi del Consiglio dei Dieci, Lettere di Rettori*, B. 299 bis, f. 6, c. n.n. (20 April 1602).

29. ASV, *Amministrazione Forestale Veneta*, B. 10, f. B, printed pamphlet, c. 21–22.

30. Viggiano, *Lo specchio della repubblica*. The idea that the Republic's institutions created political balance and consensus was articulated in Venice even earlier and provided one of the central arguments of Gasparo Contarini's 1543 treatise *De magistratibus et republica venetorum*. For a detailed discussion of Contarini's political theory, see Gleason, *Gasparo Contarini*, 110–28; Bouwsma, *Venice and the Defense of Republican Liberty*, 144–61; and Pocock, *Machiavellian Moment*, 272–332.

31. See Wolff, *Venice and the Slavs*, 49–63, for his discussion of Francesco Grimani's 1755 agrarian reforms in Dalmatia. In a similar move to Mocenigo's, Grimani wished to convert the pastoral *morlacchi*—as the Venetians called the inhabitants of Dalmatia—into sedentary farmers, thereby transforming them into better Venetian subjects.

32. ASV, *Amministrazione Forestale Veneta*, B. 10, f. B, printed pamphlet, c. 5.

33. ASV, *Provveditori e Patroni all'Arsenale*, B. 25, c. 59r.

34. ASV, *Provveditori e Patroni all'Arsenale*, B. 25, c. 59r.

35. See Lazzarini, *Trasformazione di un bosco*; and Bianco and Lazzarini, *Forestali*. The full text of the reforms can be found in ASV, *Amministrazione Forestale Veneta*, B. 77, c. n.n. (5 May 1792).

36. On the agrarian academies, see Simonetto, *I lumi nelle campagne*. Simonetto traces the emergence of regional agrarian academies in the second half of the eighteenth century and shows their connection to Enlightenment ideals of scientific knowledge and good government. Simonetto emphasizes that the rhetoric of scientific knowledge often failed to match the actual activity in the academies, many of which simply provided a venue for local landowners to exercise their authority. Nevertheless, Simonetto argues, the academies managed to gen-

erate a significant amount of debate on agrarian science and the living conditions of the peasantry.

37. ASV, *Provveditori e Patroni all'Arsenale*, B. 26, c. 74v.

38. Appuhn, "Inventing Nature." Similar critiques of the Weberian model have been deployed by historians of Asia, who argue that the emphasis on a specific and ultimately peculiarly northern European form of instrumental rationality distracts us from other pathways of state development in the same period. See, for example, Wong, *China Transformed*. Wong argues that an emphasis on institutional processes distorts the way we understand state goals and state actions in China. I would argue that it also distorts our understanding of the Venetian Republic. See also Marks, *Origins of the Modern World*; Richards, *Unending Frontier*, 1–57; and Pomerantz, *Great Divergence*. For a critique of Weberian analyses of European forms of state development, see Adams, *Familial State*. Adams focuses on another European oddity, the Dutch Republic.

39. ASV, *Consiglio dei Dieci, Parti Comuni*, Filza 12, c. 157. I discussed this statute in detail in chapter 2.

40. See, for example, the marginal notes in the *Catastico Nani* and the *Catastico Gradenigo* in ASV, *Provveditori sopra Boschi*, Reg. 149 and 152, respectively. In both cases, the *proti* thinned and reseeded every *bosco pubblico* in the lower Piave region but made no effort to do the same in forests on private and institutional lands.

41. ASV, *Capi del Consiglio dei Dieci, Lettere di Rettori*, B. 299 bis, f. 6, c. n.n. (27 January 1602 m.v.).

42. ASV, *Amministrazione Forestale Veneta*, B. 10, f. B, printed pamphlet, c. 8.

43. ASV, *Amministrazione Forestale Veneta*, B. 10, f. B, printed pamphlet, c. 8.

44. ASV, *Capi del Consiglio dei Dieci, Lettere di Rettori*, B. 299 bis, f. 6, c. n.n. (4 November 1602).

45. ASV, *Consiglio dei Dieci, Parti Comuni*, Filza 46, c. 127, allegato 2.

46. See Crouzet-Pavan, *Sopra le acque salse*. For a concise summary of her argument in that much larger book, see Crouzet-Pavan, *Venice Triumphant*, 18–33; and Crouzet-Pavan, "Toward an Ecological Understanding." For a synopsis of the lagoon management projects that stretches into the eighteenth century, see Appuhn, "Friend or Flood?"; and for a longer history, see the excellent and accessible Keahey, *Venice against the Sea*.

47. I am deliberately invoking Cronon's *Nature's Metropolis* here, because the differences between Cronon's approach and Crouzet-Pavan's are instructive. Crouzet-Pavan sees the environment as shaping the development of the city and the ideology of its inhabitants, while Cronon sees the pull of urban markets in

Chicago and the emerging ideological dominance of capitalism as shaping the landscapes and environments of the entire upper Midwest and much of the plains.

48. Quoted in Tafuri, *Venice and the Renaissance*, 141.

49. Tafuri, *Venice and the Renaissance*, 141–42.

50. Providence played an important role in eighteenth-century European thought in general, not just in Venice. See, for example, Clark, "Providence, Predestination and Progress."

51. See Appuhn, "Friend or Flood?"; Cozzi, "Storie e politica del dibattito veneziano"; Tafuri, *Venice and the Renaissance*, 139–96; and Ciriacono, *Acque e agricoltura*.

52. BNM, *It VII, 395 (8648)*, c. 3.

53. ASV, *Consiglio dei Dieci, Parti Comuni*, Filza 46, c. 127, allegato 1.

54. ASV, *Consiglio dei Dieci, Parti Comuni*, Filza 46, c. 127, allegato 2.

55. ASV, *Consiglio dei Dieci, Parti Comuni*, Filza 46, c. 127, allegato 2.

56. ASV, *Amministrazione Forestale Veneta*, B. 1, c. 1B.

57. ASV, *Capi del Consiglio dei Dieci, Lettere di Rettori*, B. 299 bis, f. 6, c. n.n.

58. ASV, *Amministrazione Forestale Veneta*, B. 10, f. B, printed pamphlet, c. 6.

59. ASV, *Capi del Consiglio dei Dieci, Lettere di Rettori*, B. 271, c. 218.

60. ASV, *Provveditori e Patroni all'Arsenale*, B. 24, c. 44v–45v.

61. ASV, *Provveditori e Patroni all'Arsenale*, B. 24, c. 278v–280v.

62. ASV, *Provveditori e Patroni all'Arsenale*, B. 25, c. 36r–39v.

63. ASV, *Provveditori e Patroni all'Arsenale*, B. 26, c. 13v–14v.

64. See Muir, *Civic Ritual*; and Crouzet-Pavan, *Venice Triumphant*.

65. See Thomas, *Religion and the Decline of Magic*; and Thomas, *Man and the Natural World*.

66. ASV, *Provveditori e Patroni all'Arsenale*, B. 25, c. 36r–39v.

67. Evelyn, *Silva*, 1.

68. See, for example, Ellis, *The Timber Tree Improved*; the Comte de Buffon, "Sur la conservation et rétablissement des forêts"; Buffon, "Sur le culture et exploitation des forêts"; Duhamel de Monceau, *Des semis et plantations*; and Duhamel de Monceau, *Traité des arbres fruitiers*.

69. See Moore, "*Modern World-System* as Environmental History?" Moore makes the case for silver and sugar as the two main "commodity frontiers" in the early modern world-system. However, his analysis can also be used to describe the rapidly shifting production frontiers for high-quality timber.

70. Merchant, *Death of Nature*, 237. For more on economic thought in this period, see Appleby, *Economic Thought and Ideology*.

71. Grove, *Green Imperialism*, 58.

72. Evelyn, *Silva*, 567–77. See also Carroll, *Timber Economy*; and Cronon, *Changes in the Land*, 108–26.

73. Merchant, *Death of Nature*, 239.

74. Sögner, "Norwegian-Dutch Migrant Relations." Thanks to Jason Moore for pointing out this reference.

75. Grove, *Green Imperialism*, 41.

76. See, for example, ASV, *Senato Mar*, Filza 686 (3 June 1690); and ASV, *Provveditori e Patroni all'Arsenale*, B. 18, c. 8r–v. The Arsenal managers even complained about the low quality of the *stortami* coming from the Pelopponese, but, due to chronic shortages of crooked timbers, they were forced to accept them.

77. Merchant, *Death of Nature*, 236–8. Merchant calls Evelyn's view an example of "managerial conservation" and argues that it represents a "sell-out of organicism" in the way that it subordinates an older organicist view of nature to the demands of the mechanist philosophy of the seventeenth century.

Conclusion

Epigraph. ASV, *Capi del Consiglio dei Dieci, Lettere di Rettori*, B. 271, c. 175r.

1. ASV, *Capi del Consiglio dei Dieci, Lettere di Rettori*, B. 271, c. 172r.

2. ASV, *Capi del Consiglio dei Dieci, Lettere di Rettori*, B. 271, c. 172v.

3. ASV, *Capi del Consiglio dei Dieci, Lettere di Rettori*, B. 271, c. 174r.

4. ASV, *Capi del Consiglio dei Dieci, Lettere di Rettori*, B. 271, c. 175r.

5. ASV, *Capi del Consiglio dei Dieci, Lettere di Rettori*, B. 271, c. 175r.

6. ASV, *Capi del Consiglio dei Dieci, Lettere di Rettori*, B. 271, c. 175r.

7. ASV, *Capi del Consiglio dei Dieci, Lettere di Rettori*, B. 271, c. 177r.

8. ASV, *Capi del Consiglio dei Dieci, Lettere di Rettori*, B. 271, c. 177v.

9. ASV, *Capi del Consiglio dei Dieci, Lettere di Rettori*, B. 271, c. 175v.

10. ASV, *Capi del Consiglio dei Dieci, Lettere di Rettori*, B. 271, c. 175v.

11. ASV, *Capi del Consiglio dei Dieci, Lettere di Rettori*, B. 271, c. 175 (seconda pagina)r.

12. ASV, *Capi del Consiglio dei Dieci, Lettere di Rettori*, B. 271, c. 175 (seconda pagina)r.

13. ASV, *Capi del Consiglio dei Dieci, Lettere di Rettori*, B. 271, c. 175 (seconda pagina)v.

14. ASV, *Capi del Consiglio dei Dieci, Lettere di Rettori*, B. 271, c. 175 (terza pagina)r.

15. ASV, *Capi del Consiglio dei Dieci, Lettere di Rettori*, B. 271, c. 175 (terza pagina)r.

16. ASV, *Capi del Consiglio dei Dieci, Lettere di Rettori*, B. 271, c. 177.

17. ASV, *Capi del Consiglio dei Dieci, Lettere di Rettori*, B. 271, c. 175 (terza pagina)r.

18. ASV, *Capi del Consiglio dei Dieci, Lettere di Rettori*, B. 271, c. 177v.

19. ASV, *Capi del Consiglio dei Dieci, Lettere di Rettori*, B. 271, c. 177v.

20. ASV, *Capi del Consiglio dei Dieci, Lettere di Rettori*, B. 271, c. 180 (seconda pagina)r.

21. ASV, *Capi del Consiglio dei Dieci, Lettere di Rettori*, B. 271, c. 181 (seconda pagina)v.

22. ASV, *Capi del Consiglio dei Dieci, Lettere di Rettori*, B. 271, c. 181 (seconda pagina)v.

23. ASV, *Capi del Consiglio dei Dieci, Lettere di Rettori*, B. 271, c. 180v.

24. Because of the way the Venetians filed judicial records, I have been unable to locate the *raspa* file that would confirm the execution of the sentence. However, it is nice to imagine Gavardo, as Calbo did, "perforated at the gates of the city."

25. For more on the role of violence and retribution in the Venetian hinterland, see Muir, *Mad Blood Stirring*.

26. For a study of the complex relationship between village councils and central authorities in the Roman countryside, see Castiglione, *Patrons and Adversaries*.

27. Plato, *Critias*, 110c–111d. Cf. Glacken, *Traces on the Rhodian Shore*, 121. Glacken notes that the passage enjoyed great popularity in the late seventeenth and early eighteenth centuries, which fits with Calbo's use of the metaphor. The sudden interest in the *Critias* was in part inspired by widespread discussion of the fragility of tropical island environments. For more on the influence of tropical environments on European ideas about conservation, see Grove, *Green Imperialism*.

Arsenal. The Venetian ship-building complex.

capitano. A Venetian patrician elected by the Great Council to an eighteen-month term as military governor in a mainland district. In major towns the *capitano* served under a *podestà*. In rural districts, the *capitano* often served alone, holding both military and judicial authority.

capitano del bosco. An official elected by the Council of Ten or Senate to administer a state forest. The *capitano del bosco* was usually either a respected local resident, or an Arsenal craftsman able to judge the quality of timber.

Collegio. Elected by the Senate, the Collegio acted as a steering committee for the legislature.

contado. The rural jurisdiction of an urban center on the mainland.

Council of Ten. Elected by the Great Council, the Council of Ten acted as both a court and a legislative body in matters deemed to affect state security.

Doge. The Doge was the Venetian head of state, elected for life.

Great Council. The largest assembly in the Venetian government. All patrician males over the age of twenty-five were eligible. Not a legislative body per se, it did, however, elect most state officials and occasionally voted on legislation coming from the Senate.

podestà. The Venetian governor in a mainland district. Elected by the Great Council for a term of eighteen months, the *podestà*'s main responsibilities were to keep the peace and enforce the laws through the exercise of judicial authority.

proto. An expert with practical experience in a building trade—including naval construction, forest management, and water management. The term connoted empirical knowledge, including the capacity to judge the quality of primary materials and finished work.

provveditore. A patrician official elected to supervise a bureaucracy or manage an important task. There were many different offices that carried the title *provveditore*. The three most important *provveditori* mentioned herein are the *provveditori sopra boschi* (forest inspectors), the *provveditori alle legne* (firewood managers), and the *provveditori all'arsenale* (Arsenal managers).

Senate. The main legislative body of the Venetian government. The Senate included approximately 120 senators elected by the Great Council and at least 200 more officials who entered ex officio.

BIBLIOGRAPHY

Archives and Manuscript Collections

Venice

Archivio di Stato, Venezia
Biblioteca Nazionale Marciana
Museo Civico Correr

Belluno

Archivio Curiale Vescovile
Archivio di Stato, Belluno
Biblioteca Civica, Belluno

Published Primary Sources

Alberti, Leon Battista. *On the Art of Building in Ten Books.* Translated by Joseph Rykwert, Neil Leach, and Robert Tavenor. Cambridge, MA: MIT Press, 1988.

Chinazzo, Daniele di. *Cronica de la guerra da veniciani a zenovesi.* Monumenti storici, n.s., vol. 11. Venice: n.p., 1958.

Cornaro, Marco. *Marco Cornaro (1412-1464), scritture sulla laguna.* Edited by Giuseppe Pavanello. Venice: C. Ferrari, 1919.

Filarete, Antonio Averlino. *Trattato d'architettura.* 2 vols. Edited by Anna Maria Finoli and Liliana Grassi. Milan: Polifilo, 1972.

Pellegrini, Francesco. *Documenti antichi, transcritti da Francesco Pellegrini.* 4 vols. Belluno, Italy: Biblioteca civica di Belluno, 1991.

Rompiasio, Giulio. *Metodo in pratica di sommario o sia compilazione delle leggi, terminazioni & ordini appartenenti agl'illustrissimi & eccelentissimi collegio e magistrato alle acque.* Edited by Giovanni Caniato. Venice: Ministero per i beni culturali e ambientali, 1998.

Sanuto, Marino. *I diarii di Marino Sanuto.* 58 vols. Edited by R. Fulin et al. Venice: F. Visentini, 1879-1903.

Works Cited

Adams, Julia. *The Familial State: Ruling Families and Merchant Capitalism in Early Modern Europe*. Ithaca, NY: Cornell University Press, 2005.

Agnoletti, Mauro. *Segherie e foreste nel trentino: Dal medioevo ai giorni nostri*. San Michele all'Adige, Italy: Museo degli usi e costumi della gente trentina, 1998.

Anderson, Perry. *Lineages of the Absolutist State*. London: N.L.B., 1979.

Appleby, Joyce. *Economic Thought and Ideology in Seventeenth-Century England*. Princeton, NJ: Princeton University Press, 1978.

Appuhn, Karl. "Environmental Politics and State Power in Early Modern Venice, 1300–1650." Ph.D. diss., Northwestern University, 1999.

———. "Friend or Flood? The Dilemmas of Flood Control in Late Renaissance Venice." In *The Nature of Cities: New Approaches to Urban Environmental History*, edited by Andrew Isenberg, 79–102. Rochester, NY: University of Rochester Press, 2006.

———. "Inventing Nature: Forests, Forestry, and State Power in Renaissance Venice." *Journal of Modern History* 72 (2000): 861–89.

———. "Politics, Perception, and the Meaning of Landscape in Late Medieval Venice: Marco Cornaro's 1442 Inspection of Firewood Supplies." In *Inventing Medieval Landscapes: Senses of Place in the Latin West*, edited by John Howe and Michael Wolfe, 70–88. Gainesville: University Press of Florida, 2002.

Ash, Eric H. *Power, Knowledge, and Expertise in Elizabethan England*. Baltimore: Johns Hopkins University Press, 2004.

Avanzi, Silvano. *Il regime giuridico della laguna di Venezia: Dalla storia all'attualità*. Venice: Istituto veneto di scienze, lettere ed arti, 1993.

Barzati, Antonella. "Consultori in iure e feudalità nella prima metà del seicento: L'opera di Gasparo Lonigo." In Cozzi, *Stato, società e giustizia*, 2:121–52.

Berenger, Adolfo di. *Saggio storico della legislazione veneta forestale dal sec. VII al XIX*. Venice: Tipografia municipale di G. Longo, 1862.

Berveglieri, Roberto. *Inventori stranieri a Venezia, 1474–1788: Importazione di tecnologia e circolazione di tecnici artigiani inventori; Repertorio*. Venice: Istituto veneto di scienze, lettere ed arti, 1995.

Bevilacqua, Eugenia. "La conterminazione della laguna di Venezia attraverso i documenti cartografici." In *Conterminazione lagunare: Storia, ingegneria, politica e diritto nella laguna di Venezia*, 39–78. Venice: Istituto di scienze, lettere ed arti, 1992.

Bianchetti, Alma. *Ville friulane e beni comunali in età veneta*. Udine: Forum, 2004.

Bianco, Furio. *Contadini, sbirri e contrabbandieri nel Friuli del settecento*. Pordenone, Italy: Edizioni biblioteca del'immagine, 1990.

————. *Le terre del Friuli: La formazione dei paesaggi agrari in Friuli tra il XV e il XIX secolo.* Verona: Cierre, 1994.

Bianco, Furio, and Gregorio Amaseo. *1511, la "crudel zobia grassa": Rivolte contadine e faide nobiliari in Friuli tra '400 e '500.* Pordenone, Italy: Centro studi storici Menocchio, 1995.

Bianco, Furio, and Mauro Ambrosoli, eds. *Comunità e questioni di confini in Italia settentrionale: XVI–XIX sec.* Milan: FrancoAngeli, 2007.

Birrell, Jean. "Common Rights in the Medieval Forest: Disputes and Conflicts in the Thirteenth Century." *Past and Present* 117 (1987): 22–49.

Black, Jane. "Constitutional Ambitions, Legal Realities and the Florentine State." In *Florentine Tuscany: Structures and Practices of Power,* edited by William J. Connell and Andrea Zorzi, 48–64. Cambridge: Cambridge University Press, 2000.

Borin, Luciano. "I carboneri." *Quaderni del Lombardo-Veneto* (1986): 105–8.

Bouwsma, William J. *Venice and the Defense of Republican Liberty.* Berkeley and Los Angeles: University of California Press, 1968.

Braunstein, Philippe. "De la montagne à Venise: Les réseaux du bois au XVe siècle." *Mélanges de l'École Française de Rome* 100 (1988): 761–99.

Brown, Alison. "De-Masking Renaissance Republicanism." In *Renaissance Civic Humanism: Reappraisals and Reflections,* edited by James Hankins, 179–99. Cambridge: Cambridge University Press, 2000.

Buffon, Comte de. "Sur la conservation et le rétablissement des forêts." Article 3 in *Histoire naturelle, générale et particulière,* vol. 31 (supplément, tome 2). Paris: Imprimerie royale, 1775.

————. "Sur le culture et exploitation des forêts." Article 4 in *Histoire naturelle, générale et particulière,* vol. 31 (supplément, tome 2). Paris: Imprimerie royale, 1775.

Calvero, Bartolomé. *Antidora: Antropologia católica de la economia moderna.* Milan: Giuffrè, 1991.

Cammarosano, Paolo. *Le campagne friulane nel tardo medioevo: Un analisi dei registri di censi dei grandi fondiari.* Udine, Italy: Casamassima, 1985.

Candiani, Guido. "Lo sviluppo dell'armata grossa nell'emergenza marittima." *Storia di Venezia* (2003): 89–96.

————. "Tiburzio Bailo e i cannoni di Sarezzo: Politica navale e forniture militari nella repubblica di Venezia durante la prima guerra di Morea (1684–99)." *Società e Storia* (2003): 677–706.

Caniato, Giovanni, ed. *L'arte dei remèri: I 700 anni dello statuto dei costruttori di remi.* Verona: Cierre, 2007.

————. "Il legname: Approvigionamento e tutela." In *Arte degli squerarioli,* edited by Giovanni Caniato, 69–72. Venice: Stamperia di Venezia, 1985.

———. "Notizie di segherie e altri impianti nella podesteria di Belluno." In Caniato, *La via del fiume*, 155–64.

———. "L'organismo delicato: Il governo idraulico e ambientale." In *La laguna di Venezia*, edited by Giovanni Caniato, Eugenio Turri, and Michele Zanetti, 387–404. Verona: Cierre, 1995.

———. "Il vescovo e il mercante." In Caniato, *La via del fiume*, 275–86.

———. ed. *La via del fiume: Dalle Dolomiti a Venezia*. Verona: Cierre, 1993.

Caniato, Giovanni and Michela dal Borgo, eds. *Le arti edili a Venezia*. Rome: Edilstampa, 1990.

Carroll, Charles F. *The Timber Economy of Puritan New England*. Providence, RI: Brown University Press, 1973.

Casti, Emanuela. "State, Cartography, and Territory in Renaissance Veneto and Lombardy." In *The History of Cartography*, edited by David Woodward, 3:874–908. Chicago: University of Chicago Press, 2007.

Castiglione, Caroline. *Patrons and Adversaries: Nobles and Villagers in Italian Politics, 1640–1760*. Oxford: Oxford University Press, 2005.

Chittolini, Giorgio. *La formazione dello stato regionale e le istituzioni del contado, secoli XIV e XV*. Turin: Einaudi, 1979.

Ciani, Giuseppe. *Storia del popolo cadorino*. Padua: n.p., 1856.

Ciriacono, Salvatore. *Acque e agricoltura: Venezia, Olanda e la bonifica Europea in età moderna*. Milan: FrancoAngeli, 1994.

———. *Building on Water: Venice, Holland, and the Construction of the European Landscape in Early Modern Times*. Translated by Jeremy Scott. New York: Berghahn Books, 2006.

———. "Scrittori d'idraulica e politica delle acque." In *Storia della cultura veneta*, edited by Girolamo Arnaldi and Manlio Pastore Stocchi, 3:491–512. Vicenza, Italy: Pozza, 1981.

Clark, J. C. D. "Providence, Predestination and Progress; or, Did the Enlightenment Fail?" *Albion* 35, no. 4 (2004): 559–89.

Coates, Peter. *Nature: Western Attitudes since Ancient Times*. Berkeley and Los Angeles: University of California Press, 1998.

Concina, Ennio. *L'arsenale della repubblica di Venezia: Tecniche e istituzioni dal medioevo all'età moderna*. Milan: Electa, 1984.

Corazzol, Gigi. *Cineografo di banditi su sfondo di monti, Feltre 1634–1642*. Milan: Unicopli, 1997.

Cosgrove, Denis. "Mapping New Worlds: Culture and Cartography in Sixteenth-Century Venice." *Imago Mundi* 44 (1992): 65–89.

Cozzi, Gaetano. "La politica del diritto." In Cozzi, *Stato, società e giustizia* 1:17–152.

———. "Politica, società, istituzioni." In *La repubblica di Venezia nell'età moderna*, edited by Giuseppe Galasso, Gaetano Cozzi, Michael Knapton, and Giovanni Scarabello, 3–271. Vol. 12, tome 1 of *Storia d'Italia*, edited by Giuseppe Galasso. Turin: Einaudi, 1986.

——, ed. *Stato, società e giustizia nella repubblica veneta (secc. XV–XVIII)*. 2 vols. Rome: Jouvence, 1981–85.

——. "Storie e politica del dibattito veneziano sulla laguna." In *Conterminazione lagunare: Storia, ingegneria, politica e diritto nella laguna di Venezia; Atti del convegno di studio nel bicentenario della conterminazione lagunare, Venezia, 14–16 marzo 1991*, 15–38. Venice: Istituto veneto di scienze, lettere ed arti, 1992.

Cronon, William. *Changes in the Land: Indians, Colonists, and the Ecology of New England*. New York: Hill and Wang, 1983.

——. *Nature's Metropolis: Chicago and the Great West*. New York: Norton, 1991.

——. "The Trouble with Wilderness." In *Uncommon Ground: Toward Reinventing Nature*, edited by William Cronon, 69–90. New York: Norton, 1995.

Crosby, Alfred W. *The Columbian Exchange: The Biological and Cultural Consequences of 1492*. Westport, CT: Greenwood, 1972.

——. *Ecological Imperialism: The Biological Expansion of Europe, 900–1900*. Cambridge: Cambridge University Press, 1986.

——. *The Measure of Reality: Quantification and Western Society, 1250–1600*. Cambridge: Cambridge University Press, 1997.

Crouzet-Pavan, Élisabeth. *"Sopra le acque salse": Éspaces, pouvoir, et société à Venise, à la fin du moyen âge*. 2 vols. Rome: École française de Rome, 1992.

——. "Toward an Ecological Understanding of the Myth of Venice." In *Venice Reconsidered: The History and Civilization of an Italian City-State, 1297–1797*, edited by Dennis Romano and John Martin, 39–64. Baltimore: Johns Hopkins University Press, 2000.

——. *Venice Triumphant: The Horizons of a Myth*. Translated by Lydia Cochrane. Baltimore: Johns Hopkins University Press, 2002.

Danner, H. S. *Polder Pioneers: The Influence of Dutch Engineers on Water Management in Europe, 1600–2000*. Utrecht: Koninklijk Nederlands Aardrijkskundig Genootschap, 2005.

Davis, James. *The Decline of the Venetian Nobility as a Ruling Class*. Baltimore: Johns Hopkins University Press, 1962.

Davis, Robert C. *Shipbuilders of the Venetian Arsenal: Workers and Workplace in the Preindustrial City*. Baltimore: Johns Hopkins University Press, 1991.

De Moor, Martina, Leigh Shaw-Taylor, and Paul Warde, eds. *The Management of Common Land in North West Europe, c. 1500–1850*. Turnhout, Belgium: Brepols, 2002.

De Vecchi, Gianni. "Segherie e fucine lungo il basso cordevole." In Caniato, *La via del fiume*, 255–62.

Dean, Warren. *With Broadax and Firebrand: The Destruction of the Brazilian Atlantic Forest.* Berkeley and Los Angeles: University of California Press, 1995.

Del Torre, Giuseppe. *Venezia e la terraferma dopo la guerra di Cambrai: Fiscalità e amministrazione (1515–1530).* Milan: FrancoAngeli, 1986.

Dizionario biografico degli Italiani, vol. 59. Rome: Istituto della enciclopedia italiano, 1960.

Dorigo, Wladimir. *Venezia: Origini, fondamenti, ipotesi, metodi.* 2 vols. Milan: Electa, 1983.

Duhamel de Monceau, Henri Louis. *Des semis et plantations des arbres et de leur culture.* Paris: H. L. Guerin & L. F. Delatour, 1760.

———. *Traité des arbres fruitiers.* 2 vols. Paris: Saillant; Desaint, 1768.

Dursteler, Eric. "The Bailò in Constantinople: Crisis and Career in Venice's Early Modern Diplomatic Corps." *Mediterranean Historical Review* 16 (2001): 1–30.

———. *Venetians in Constantinople: Nation, Identity, and Coexistence in the Early Modern Mediterranean.* Baltimore: Johns Hopkins University Press, 2006.

Ellis, W. *The Timber Tree Improved, or the Best Practical Methods of Improving Different Lands with Proper Timber.* London: 1738.

Epstein, Stephen. *Genoa and the Genoese, 958–1528.* Chapel Hill: University of North Carolina Press, 1996.

Ertman, Thomas. *The Birth of the Leviathan: Building States and Regimes in Medieval and Early Modern Europe.* Cambridge: Cambridge University Press, 1997.

Evelyn, John. *Silva, or a Discourse of Forest Trees and the Propagation of Timber in His Majesty's Dominions.* York: printed by A. Ward for J. Dodsley, T. Cadell, J. Robson, and T. Durham, London, 1776.

Evernden, Neil. *The Social Creation of Nature.* Baltimore: Johns Hopkins University Press, 1992.

Ferraro, Joanne. *Family and Public Life in Brescia, 1580–1650: The Foundations of Power in the Venetian State.* Cambridge: Cambridge University Press, 1993.

Finlay, Robert. "Fabius Maximus in Venice: Doge Andrea Gritti, the War of Cambrai, and the Rise of Habsburg Hegemony, 1509–1530." *Renaissance Quarterly* 53 (2000): 988–1031.

———. "The Myth of Venice in Guicciardini's *History of Italy.*" In *Medieval and Renaissance Venice,* edited by Ellen E. Kittell and Thomas F. Madden, 294–326. Urbana: University of Illinois Press, 1999.

———. *Politics in Renaissance Venice.* New Brunswick, NJ: Rutgers University Press, 1980.

Gatti, Luciana. *Navi e cantieri della repubblica di Genova (secoli XVI–XVIII)*. Genoa: Brigati, 1999.

Gilbert, Felix. *The Pope, His Banker, and Venice*. Cambridge, MA: Harvard University Press, 1980.

——. "Venice in the Crisis of the League of Cambrai." In *Renaissance Venice*, edited by J.R. Hale, 274–92. London: Faber and Faber, 1973.

Glacken, Clarence J. *Traces on the Rhodian Shore: Nature and Culture in Western Thought, from Ancient Times to the End of the Eighteenth Century*. Berkeley and Los Angeles: University of California Press, 1967.

Gleason, Elizabeth. *Gasparo Contarini: Venice, Rome and Reform*. Berkeley and Los Angeles: University of California Press, 1993.

Golan, Tal. *Laws of Man and Laws of Nature: The History of Scientific Expert Testimony in England and America*. Cambridge, MA: Harvard University Press, 2004.

Grafton, Anthony. *Leon Battista Alberti: Master Builder of the Italian Renaissance*. New York: Hill and Wang, 2000.

Grove, Richard H. *Green Imperialism: Colonial Expansion, Tropical Edens and the Origins of Environmentalism, 1600–1860*. Cambridge: Cambridge University Press, 1995.

Grubb, James. "L'economia rurale e gli estimi del territorio di Vicenza (1519–1606)." *Annali Veneti: Società, Cultura, Istituzioni* 1 (1984): 97–109.

——. *Firstborn of Venice: Vicenza in the Early Renaissance State*. Baltimore: Johns Hopkins University Press, 1988.

——. *Provincial Families of the Renaissance: Private and Public Life in the Veneto*. Baltimore: Johns Hopkins University Press, 1996.

Guillaume, Jean, ed. *Les traités d'architecture de la Renaissance: Actes du colloque tenu a' Tours du 1er au 11 juillet 1981*. Paris: Picard, 1988.

Harrison, Robert Pogue. *Forests: The Shadow of Civilization*. Chicago: University of Chicago Press, 1992.

Harvey, P. D. A. *The History of Topographical Maps: Symbols, Pictures and Surveys*. London: Thames and Hudson, 1980.

Hespanha, António Manuel. "Early Modern Law and the Anthropological Imagination of Old European Culture." In *Early Modern History and the Social Sciences: Testing the Limits of Braudel's Mediterranean*, edited by John A. Marino, 191–204. Kirksville, MO: Truman State University Press, 2002.

Hirshman, Albert O. *The Passions and the Interests: Political Arguments for Capitalism before Its Triumph*. Princeton, NJ: Princeton University Press, 1977.

Hocquet, Jean-Claude. *Le sel et la fortune de Venise*. 2 vols. Villeneuve-d'Ascq, France: Publications de l'Université de Lille III, 1978.

Horodowich, Elizabeth. *Language and Statecraft in Early Modern Venice*. Cambridge: Cambridge University Press, 2008.

Howard, Deborah. *The Architectural History of Venice*. New York: Holmes and Meier, 1981.

———. "Venice as a Dolphin." *Artibus et Historiae* 35 (1997): 101–11.

Ivetic, Egidio. *Oltremare: L'Istria nell'ultimo dominio quattro*. Venice: Istituto veneto di scienze, lettere ed arti, 2000.

James, N. D. G. *A History of English Forestry*. Oxford: Blackwell, 1981.

Jurdjevic, Mark. "Virtue, Commerce, and the Enduring Florentine Republican Moment." *Journal of the History of Ideas* 62 (2001): 721–43.

Kallendorf, Craig. *Virgil and the Myth of Venice: Books and Readers in the Italian Renaissance*. Oxford: Oxford University Press, 1999.

Keahey, John. *Venice against the Sea: A City Besieged*. New York: St. Martin's Press, 2000.

Knapton, Michael. "Il Consiglio dei Dieci nel governo della terraferma." In *Atti del convegno Venezia e la terraferma attraverso le relazioni dei rettori, Trieste, 23–24 ottobre 1980*, edited by Amelio Tagliaferri. Milan: Giuffrè, 1981.

———. "Il territorio vicentino nello stato veneto del '500 e primo '600: Nuovi equilibri politici e fiscali." In *Dentro lo "stado italico": Venezia e la terraferma fra quattro e seicento*, edited by Giorgio Cracco and Michael Knapton, 33–116. Trent, Italy: Gruppo culturale civis, 1984.

———. *Venezia e la terraferma: Economia e società*. Bergamo: Comune di Bergamo, Assessorato alla cultura, 1989.

Kohl, Benjamin G. *Padua under the Carrara, 1318–1405*. Baltimore: Johns Hopkins University Press, 1998.

Lambert, Audrey M. *The Making of the Dutch Landscape: An Historical Geography of the Netherlands*. London: Seminar Press, 1971.

Lanaro, Paola. *At the Centre of the Old World: Trade and Manufacturing in Venice and on the Venetian Mainland (1400–1800)*. Toronto: Centre for Reformation and Renaissance Studies, 2006.

Lane, Frederic C. *Venetian Ships and Shipbuilders of the Renaissance*. 1934. Reprint, Baltimore: Johns Hopkins University Press, 1992.

———. *Venice, A Maritime Republic*. Baltimore: Johns Hopkins University Press, 1973.

Law, John E. "The Venetian Mainland State in the Fifteenth Century," *Transactions of the Royal Historical Society* 2 (1992): 153–74.

———. "Venice and the Problem of Sovereignty in the *Patria del Friuli*, 1421." In *Florence and Italy: Renaissance Studies in Honour of Nicolai Rubinstein*, edited by Peter Delam and Caroline Elam, 135–47. London: Committee for Medieval Studies, Westfield College, 1988.

———. *Venice and the Veneto in the Early Renaissance*. Aldershot, Hampshire, UK: Variorum, 2000.

Lazzarini, Antonio. "Boschi a remi (secoli XVII–XIX)." In Caniato, *L'arte dei remèri*, 127–38.

———. *La trasformazione di un bosco: Il Cansiglio, Venezia, e i nuovi usi del legno (secoli XVIII–XIX)*. Belluno, Italy: Istituto storico bellunese della resistenza e dell'età contemporanea, 2006.

Long, Pamela O. *Openness, Secrecy, Authorship: Technical Arts and the Culture of Knowledge from Antiquity to the Renaissance*. Baltimore: Johns Hopkins University Press, 2004.

Lowood, Henry E. "The Calculating Forester: Quantification, Cameral Science, and the Emergence of Scientific Forestry Management in Germany." In *The Quantifying Spirit of the Eighteenth Century*, edited by Tore Frangsmayr, J. L. Heilbron, and Robin E. Rider, 315–42. Berkeley and Los Angeles: University of California Press, 1990.

Luzzato, Gino, and Marino Berengo. *Storia economica di Venezia dall XI al XVI secolo*. 2nd ed. Venice: Marsilio, 1995.

Mallett, Michael E., and J. R. Hale. *The Military Organization of a Renaissance State: Venice c. 1400–1617*. Cambridge: Cambridge University Press, 1984.

Marino, John A. "Administrative Mapping in the Italian States." In *Monarchs, Ministers and Maps: The Emergence of Cartography as a Tool of Government in Early Modern Europe*, edited by David Buisseret, 5–25. Chicago: University of Chicago Press, 1992.

———. *Pastoral Economics in the Kingdom of Naples*. Baltimore: Johns Hopkins University Press, 1988.

Marks, Robert. *The Origins of the Modern World: A Global and Ecological Narrative*. Lanham, MD: Rowman and Littlefield, 2002.

———. *Tigers, Rice, Silk, and Silt: Environment and Economy in Late Imperial South China*. Cambridge: Cambridge University Press, 1998.

Martin, Lillian Ray. *The Art and Archaeology of Venetian Ships and Boats*. College Station: Texas A&M University Press, 2001.

Martini, Angelo. *Manuale di metrologia*. 1883. Reprint, Rome: E.R.A., 1976.

McKee, Sally. *Uncommon Dominion: Venetian Crete and the Myth of Ethnic Purity*. Philadelphia: University of Pennsylvania Press, 2000.

McNeill, William H. *The Pursuit of Power: Technology, Armed Force and Society since AD 1000*. Chicago: University of Chicago Press, 1984.

Merchant, Carolyn. *The Death of Nature: Women, Ecology and the Scientific Revolution*. San Francisco: Harper and Row, 1980.

———. *Ecological Revolutions: Nature, Gender, and Science in New England*. Chapel Hill: University of North Carolina Press, 1989.

———. *Reinventing Eden: The Fate of Nature in Western Culture*. New York: Routledge, 2004.

Molà, Luca. *La communità dei lucchesi a Venezia: Immigrazione e industria della seta nel tardo medioevo*. Venice: Istituto veneto di scienze, lettere ed arti, 1994.

———. *The Silk Industry of Renaissance Venice*. Baltimore: Johns Hopkins University Press, 2000.

Moore, Jason W. "*The Modern World-System* as Environmental History? Ecology and the Rise of Capitalism." *Theory and Society* 32 (2003): 307–77.

Mosto, Andrea da. *L'Archivio di stato di Venezia: Indice generale storico, descrittivo, ed analitico*. Rome: Biblioteca d'arte editrice, 1937.

Mozzato, Andrea. *La mariegola del'arte della lana di Venezia: 1244–1595*. Venice: Comitato editore, 2003.

———. "Note e documenti—il mercato dei panni di lana a Venezia nel primo ventennio del sec. XV." *Nuova Rivista Storica* 89 (2005): 165.

Muir, Edward. *Civic Ritual in Renaissance Venice*. Princeton, NJ: Princeton University Press, 1981.

———. *Mad Blood Stirring: Vendetta and Factions in Friuli during the Renaissance*. Baltimore: Johns Hopkins University Press, 1993.

———. "The Sources of Civil Society in Renaissance Italy." *Journal of Interdisciplinary History* 29 (1999): 379–406.

———. "Was There Republicanism in the Renaissance Republics? Venice after Agnadello." In *Venice Reconsidered: The History and Civilization of an Italian City-State, 1297–1797*, edited by Dennis Romano and John Martin, 137–67. Baltimore: Johns Hopkins University Press, 2000.

Neff, Mary. "A Citizen in the Service of the Patrician State: the Career of Zaccaria d'Freschi." *Studi Veneziani*, n.s., 5 (1981): 33–61.

Nicoletti, Gianmario, and Guido Spada. *I carbonai: Immagini di un mestiere scomparso*. Pordenone, Italy: Savioprint, 1988.

Occhi, Katia. *Boschi e mercanti: Traffici di legname tra la contea di Tirolo e la repubblica di Venezia (secoli XVI–XVII)*. Bologna: Mulino, 2006.

Oelshlaeger, Max. *The Idea of Wilderness: From Prehistory to the Age of Ecology*. New Haven, CT: Yale University Press, 1993.

Ortega, Stephen Santos. "Ottoman Muslims in the Venetian Republic from 1573 to 1645: Contacts, Connections, and Restrictions." Ph.D. diss., University of Manchester, 2002.

Payne, Alina. *The Architectural Treatise in the Italian Renaissance: Architectural Invention, Ornament, and Literary Culture*. Cambridge: Cambridge University Press, 1999.

Perco, Daniela. *La pastorizia transumante del Feltrino*. Feltre, Italy: Pilotto, 1982.

——, ed. *Zattere, zattieri e menadàs: La fluitazione del legname lungo il—Piave*. Castellavazzo, Italy: Centro per la storia della zattera, 1988.

Perdezani, Ivana. *Venezia e lo "stado de terraferma": Il governo delle communità nel territorio bergamasco (sec. XV–XVIII)*. Milan: Vita e pensiero, 1992.

Pitteri, Mauro. "La politica veneziana dei beni comunali (1496–1797)." *Studi Veneziani*, n.s., 10 (1985): 57–80.

Pocock, J. G. A. *The Machiavellian Moment: Florentine Political Thought and the Atlantic Republican Tradition*. Princeton, NJ: Princeton University Press, 1975.

Pomerantz, Kenneth. *The Great Divergence: China, Europe, and the Making of the Modern World Economy*. Princeton, NJ: Princeton University Press, 2001.

Povolo, Claudio. *L'intrigo dell'onore: Poteri e istituzioni nella repubblica di Venezia tra cinque e seicento*. Verona: Cierre, 1997.

Price, D. J. "Medieval Land Surveying and Topographical Maps." *Geographical Journal* 121 (1955): 1–10.

Queller, Donald. *The Venetian Patriciate: Reality versus Myth*. Urbana: University of Illinois Press, 1986.

Rapp, Richard. *Industry and Economic Decline in Seventeenth-Century Venice*. Cambridge, MA: Harvard University Press, 1976.

Richards, John F. *The Unending Frontier: An Environmental History of the Early Modern World*. Berkeley and Los Angeles: University of California Press, 2002.

Rothman, Ella-Natalie. "Between Venice and Istanbul: Trans-Imperial Subjects and Cultural Mediation in the Early Modern Mediterranean." Ph.D. diss., University of Michigan, 2006.

Rubner, Heinrich. *Untersuchung zur Forst-verfassung des Mittelalterlichen Frankreichs*. Wiesbaden, Germany: Steiner, 1965.

Schreiner, Peter. *Il mito di Venezia: Una città tra realtà e rappresentazione*. Rome: Edizioni di storia e letteratura, 2006.

Schulz, Juergen. "Jacopo de' Barbari's View of Venice: Map Making, City Views, and Moralized Geography before the Year 1500." *Art Bulletin* 60 (1978): 425–74.

Scott, James C. *Seeing Like a State: How Certain Schemes to Improve the Human Condition Have Failed*. New Haven, CT: Yale University Press, 1998.

Šebesta, Giuseppe. "Struttura ed evoluzione della zattera." In Caniato, *La via del fiume*, 183–208.

Shapin, Steven. "'A Scholar and a Gentleman: The Problematic Identity of the

Scientific Practitioner in Early Modern England." *History of Science* 29 (1991): 279–327.

———. *A Social History of Truth: Civility and Science in Seventeenth-Century England*. Chicago: University of Chicago Press, 1995.

———. "Trusting George Cheyne: Scientific Expertise, Common Sense, and Moral Authority in Early Eighteenth-Century Dietetic Medicine." *Bulletin of the History of Medicine* 77 (2003): 263–97.

Shaw, James E. *The Justice of Venice: Authorities and Liberties in the Urban Economy, 1550–1700*. Oxford: Oxford University Press, 2006.

Simonetto, Marcello. *I lumi nelle campagne: Accademie agrarie e agricoltura nella repubblica di Venezia, 1768–1797*. Treviso, Italy: Edizioni Canova, 2001.

Smith, Pamela H. *The Body of the Artisan: Art and Experience in the Scientific Revolution*. Chicago: University of Chicago Press, 2006.

Sögner, Solvi. "Norwegian-Dutch Migrant Relations in the Seventeenth Century." In *Dutch Light in the "Norwegian Night": Maritime Relations and Migration across the North Sea in Early Modern Times*, edited by Louis Sicking, Harry de Bles, and Erlend des Bouvrie, 43–56. Hilversum, Netherlands: Uitgeverj Verloren, 2004.

Strayer, Joseph. *Western Europe in the Middle Ages: A Short History*. 3rd ed. Princeton, NJ: Princeton University Press, 1974.

Tafuri, Manfredo. *Venice and the Renaissance*. Translated by Jessica Levine. Cambridge, MA: MIT Press, 1989.

Tassini, Giuseppe. *Curiosità veneziane*. 1887. Reprint, Venice: Filippi Editore, 1990.

Thomas, Keith. *Man and the Natural World: Changing Attitudes in England, 1500–1800*. Oxford: Oxford University Press, 1996.

———. *Religion and the Decline of Magic: Studies in Popular Belief in Sixteenth- and Seventeenth-Century England*. Oxford: Oxford University Press, 1997.

Tilly, Charles. *Coercion, Capital, and European States, AD 990–1990*. Cambridge, MA: Blackwell, 1990.

Totman, Conrad D. *The Green Archipelago: Forestry in Preindustrial Japan*. Berkeley and Los Angeles: University of California Press, 1989.

Trivellato, Francesca. *La fondamenta dei vetrai: Lavoro, tecnica, e mercato a Venezia tra sei e settecento*. Rome: Donzelli, 2000.

Ventura, Angelo. *Nobiltà e popolo nella società veneta del '400 e '500*. Milan: Unicopli, 1993.

Vera, F. W. M. *Grazing Ecology and Forest History*. New York: CABI, 2000.

Vergani, Raffaello. "Energia dall'acqua: Ruote idrauliche e mulini nel territorio montebellunese nei secoli XV–XVIII." *Studi Trevisani* 7 (1988): 73–103.

————. "Le materie prime." In *Temi: Il mare*, edited by Alberto Tenenti and Ugo Tucci, 285–312. Vol. 12 of *Storia di Venezia*. Rome: Istituto della enciclopedia italiana, 1991.

Viggiano, Alfredo. *Governanti e governati: Legittimità del potere ed esercizio del'autorità sovrana nello stato Veneto della prima età moderna*. Treviso, Italy: Fondazione Benetton, 1993.

————. *Lo specchio della repubblica: Venezia e il governo delle isole Ionie nel '700*. Verona: Cierre, 1998.

Walker, Brett. *The Conquest of Ainu Lands: Ecology and Culture in Japanese Expansion, 1590–1800*. Berkeley and Los Angeles: University of California Press, 2001.

Warde, Paul. *Ecology, Economy, and State Formation in Early Modern Germany*. Cambridge: Cambridge University Press, 2006.

————. "Fear of Wood Shortage and the Reality of the Woodland in Europe, c. 1450–1850." *History Workshop Journal* 62 (2006): 28–57.

Williams, Michael. *Deforesting the Earth: From Prehistory to Global Crisis*. Chicago: University of Chicago Press, 2002.

Wilson, Bronwen. *The World in Venice: Print, the City and Early Modern Identity*. Toronto: University of Toronto Press, 2005.

Wolff, Larry. *Venice and the Slavs: The Discovery of Dalmatia in the Age of Enlightenment*. Palo Alto, CA: Stanford University Press, 2001.

Wong, R. Bin. *China Transformed: Historical Change and the Limits of European Experience*. Ithaca, NY: Cornell University Press, 1997.

Young, Charles R. *The Royal Forests of Medieval England: The Middle Ages*. Philadelphia: University of Pennsylvania Press, 1979.

Zamperetti, Sergio. *I piccoli principi: Signorie locali, feudi e comunità soggette nello stato regionale dall'espansione territoriale ai primi decenni del '600*. Venice: Cardo, 1991.

————. "I sinedri dolosi." *Rivista Storica Italiana* 99 (1987): 269–320.

Zorzi, Alvise. *Venice: The Golden Age, 697–1797*. Translated by Nicoletta Simborowski and Simon Mackenzie. New York: Abbeville Press, 1983.

Further Reading

Agnoletti, Mauro, and S. Anderson. *Methods and Approaches in Forest History*. New York: CABI, 2000.

Anderson, Mark L., and Charles J. Taylor. *A History of Scottish Forestry*. London: Nelson, 1967.

Andreolli, Bruno, and Massimo Montanari, eds. *Il bosco nel medioevo*. Biblioteca di storia agraria medievale 4. Bologna: CLUEB, 1988.

Ashtor, Eliyahu. *Levant Trade in the Later Middle Ages*. Princeton, NJ: Princeton University Press, 1983.

Baron, Hans. *The Crisis of the Early Italian Renaissance*. Princeton, NJ: Princeton University Press, 1966.

Bassetto, Ivana Pastori. "La coltivazione e il commercio della canapa nella repubblica veneta." *Archivio Veneto* 141, no. 176 (1993): 5–65.

Bianco, Furio. "*Mihi vindictam*: Aristocratic Clans and Rural Communities in a Feud in Friuli in the Late Fifteenth and Early Sixteenth Centuries." In *Crime, Society and the Law in Renaissance Italy*, edited by Trevor Dean and K. J. P. Lowe, 249–73. Cambridge: Cambridge University Press, 1994.

———. *Nel bosco: Comunità alpine e risorse forestali nel Friuli in età moderna (secoli 15–20)*. Udine, Italy: Forum, 2001.

Borelli, Giorgio, Paola Lanaro, Francesco Vecchiato, Università di Padova, Sede distaccata di Verona, Istituto di storia economica e sociale, and Cattedra di storia delle istituzioni economiche e giuridiche venete, eds. *Il sistema fiscale veneto: Problemi e aspetti, XV–XVIII secolo; Atti della prima giornata di studio sulla terraferma veneta (Lazise, 29 marzo 1981)*. Verona: Libreria universitaria editrice, 1982.

Boserup, Ester. *The Conditions of Agricultural Growth: The Economics of Agrarian Change under Population Pressure*. Chicago: Aldine, 1966.

Bracewell, Catherine Wendy. *The Uskoks of Senj: Piracy, Banditry, and Holy War in the Sixteenth-Century Adriatic*. Ithaca, NY: Cornell University Press, 1992.

Braudel, Fernand. *The Mediterranean and the Mediterranean World in the Age of Philip II*. New York: Harper and Row, 1972.

Brotton, Jerry. *Trading Territories: Mapping the Early Modern World*. Ithaca, NY: Cornell University Press, 1998.

Buisseret, David, ed. *Monarchs, Ministers and Maps: The Emergence of Cartography as a Tool of Government in Early Modern Europe*. Chicago: University of Chicago Press, 1992.

Butlin, R. A., and R. A. Dodgshon. *An Historical Geography of Europe*. Oxford: Oxford University Press, 1998.

Butzer, Karl W. *Environment and Archeology: An Ecological Approach to Prehistory*. 2nd ed. London: Methuen, 1972.

Cacciamani, Giuseppe M. *L'antica foresta di Camaldoli*. Camaldoli, Italy: n.p., 1965.

Cacciavillani, Ivone. *La confinazione veneziana con gli imperiali*. Padua: Signum, 1991.

———. *Le leggi ecologiche veneziane*. Padua: Signum, 1990.

———. *Le leggi veneziane sul territorio, 1471–1789: Boschi, fiumi, bonifiche e irrigazioni*. Padua: Signum, 1984.

———. *La proprietá collettiva nella montagna veneta sotto la Serenissima.* Padua: Signum, 1988.

Cammarosano, Paolo, and Lellia Cracco Ruggini. *Il patriarcato di Aquileia: Uno stato nell'europa medievale.* 2nd ed. Udine, Italy: Casamassima, 2000.

Campbell, J. B. *The Writings of the Roman Land Surveyors: Introduction, Text, Translation and Commentary.* London: Society for the Promotion of Roman Studies, 2000.

Caniato, Giovanni, ed. *L'arte degli squerarioli.* Venice: Stamperia di Venezia, 1985.

Caniato, Giovanni, Eugenio Turri, and Michele Zanetti, eds. *La laguna di Venezia.* Verona: Cierre, 1995.

Caracciolo, Alberto. *L'ambiente come storia: Sondaggi e proposte di storiografia dell'ambiente.* Bologna: Mulino, 1988.

Chittolini, Giorgio. *La crisi degli ordinamenti comunali e le origini dello stato del rinascimento.* Bologna: Mulino, 1979.

———. *Origini dello stato: Processi di formazione statale in Italia fra medioevo ed età moderna.* Bologna: Mulino, 1994.

———. "The 'Private,' the 'Public,' the State." In *The Origins of the State in Italy, 1300-1600,* edited by Julius Kirshner. Chicago: University of Chicago Press, 1996.

———. "Un problema aperto: La crisi della proprietà ecclesiastica tra quattro e cinquecento." *Rivista Storica Italiana* 85 (1973): 352-93.

Cipolla, Carlo. *Before the Industrial Revolution: European Society and Economy, 1000-1700.* 3rd ed. New York: W. W. Norton, 1994.

———. "Une crise ignorée: Comment s'est perdue la propriété ecclésiastique dans l'Italie du Nord entre le XIe et le XVIe siècles." *Annales E.S.C.* 2 (1947): 317-27.

Ciriacono, Salvatore. *Land Drainage and Irrigation.* Studies in the History of Civil Engineering 3. Aldershot, Hampshire, UK: Ashgate, 1998.

Cochrane, Eric W. *The Late Italian Renaissance, 1525-1630.* London: Macmillan, 1970.

Cochrane, Eric W., and Julius Kirshner. *Italy 1530-1630.* New York: Longman, 1988.

Cozzi, Gaetano. "Authority and the Law in Renaissance Venice." In *Renaissance Venice,* edited by J. R. Hale, 293-345. London: Faber and Faber, 1973.

Cracco, Giorgio, and Michael Knapton, eds. *Dentro lo "stado italico": Venezia e la terraferma fra quattro e seicento.* Trent, Italy: Gruppo culturale civis, 1984.

Crouzet-Pavan, Élisabeth. *La mort lente de Torcello: Histoire d'une cité disparue.* Paris: Fayard, 1995.

Dal Borgo, Michela. "Acque, boschi, miniere: La gestione dei beni territoriali del Bellunese nell'ottica della repubblica di Venezia." *Protagonisti* 84 (2003): 77–91.

——. "Il Tagliamento: Un fiume della Serenissima (sec. 15–18)." In *I fiumi delle Venezie: Il Tagliamento*, edited by Luca Zentilini, 176–85. Venice, Lido: Supernova, 2004.

Delano-Smith, Catherine. *Western Mediterranean Europe: A Historical Geography of Italy, Spain, and Southern France since the Neolithic*. New York: Academic Press, 1979.

Doglioni, Lucio. *Notizie istoriche e geografiche della città di Belluno e sua provincia: Con dissertazioni due dell'antico stato e intorno al sito di Belluno*. Belluno, Italy: F. A. Tissi, 1816.

Doglioni, Virginio. *Belluno medioevale*. Belluno, Italy: Nuovi sentieri, 1978.

Fussell, George Edwin. *The Classical Tradition in West European Farming*. Newton Abbott, Devon, UK: David and Charles, 1972.

Georgelin, Jean. *Venise au siècle des lumières: Civilisations et sociétés*. Paris: Mouton, 1978.

Grafton, Anthony, and Nancy G. Siraisi. *Natural Particulars: Nature and the Disciplines in Renaissance Europe*. Cambridge MA: MIT Press, 1999.

Grove, A. T., and Oliver Rackham. *The Nature of Mediterranean Europe: An Ecological History*. New Haven, CT: Yale University Press, 2001.

Grubb, James. "Elite Citizens." In *Venice Reconsidered: The History and Civilization of an Italian City-State, 1297–1797*, edited by Dennis Romano and John Martin, 339–64. Baltimore: Johns Hopkins University Press, 2000.

——. "Memory and Identity: Why Venetians Didn't Keep *Ricordanze*." *Renaissance Studies* 8 (1994): 375–87.

——. "When Myths Lose Power: Four Decades of Venetian Historiography." *Journal of Modern History* 58 (1986): 43–94.

Ivetic, Egidio. *L'Istria moderna: Un introduzione ai secoli 16–18*. Trieste, Italy: Università popolare, 1999.

——. *La popolazione dell'Istria nell'età moderna: Lineamenti evolutivi*. Trieste, Italy: Università popolare, 1997.

Kain, Roger J. P., and Elizabeth Baigent. *The Cadastral Map in the Service of the State: A History of Property Mapping*. Chicago: University of Chicago Press, 1991.

Knapton, Michael. "L'Istria nel sei-settecento." *Archivio Storico Italiano* 162 (2004): 127–39.

——. "I lanifici veneti in età moderna." *Archivio Storico Italiano* 156 (1998): 745–55.

——. "Rural Religious Practice in the Sixteenth-Century Veneto: The Impact of Reform in the Valpolicella." *Renaissance Studies* 10 (1996): 343–57.

Kohl, Benjamin G. *Culture and Politics in Early Renaissance Padua.* Aldershot, Hampshire, UK: Variorum, 2001.

Kral, Friedrich. "Zur postglazialen Vegetationsgeschichte am Sudrand der Östalpen: II. Pollenanalytische Untersuchungen im nordlichen Friaul." *Botanische Jahrbuch* 103 (1982): 343–70.

Kuusela, Kullervo. *Forest Resources in Europe.* Cambridge: Cambridge University Press, 1994.

Lanaro, Paola. "Economic Space and Urban Policies." *Journal of Urban History* 30 (2003): 37.

———. *I mercati nella repubblica veneta: Economie cittadine e stato territoriale (secoli XV–XVIII).* Venice: Marsilio, 1999.

———. *Un'oligarchia urbana nel cinquecento veneto: Istituzioni, economia, società.* Turin: G. Giappichelli Editore, 1992.

———. *La pratica dello scambio: Sistemi di fiere, mercanti e città in Europa (1400–1700).* Venice: Marsilio, 2003.

Lanaro, Paola, Paola Marini, Gian Maria Varanini, Edoardo Demo, Università degli studi di Trento, Dipartimento di scienze filologiche e storiche, Verona (Italy), et al., eds. *Edilizia privata nella Verona rinascimentale: Convegno di studi, Verona, 24–26 settembre 1998.* Milan: Electa, 2000.

Latham, Bryan. *Timber, Its Development and Distribution: A Historical Survey.* London: George Harrap, 1957.

Law, John E., and Denys Hay. *Italy in the Age of the Renaissance: 1380–1530.* London: Longman, 1989.

Lazzarini, Antonio. *Diboscamento montano e politiche territoriali: Alpi e appennini dal settecento al duemila.* Milan: FrancoAngeli, 2002.

———. "Un progetto fallito: Il bosco del Cansiglio dopo la riforma veneziana del 1792." *Ricerche di Storia Sociale e Religiosa* 26 (1997): 75–106.

Lazzarini, Antonio, and Giovanni Luigi Fontana, eds. *Veneto e Lombardia tra rivoluzione giacobina ed età napoleonica: Economia, territorio, istituzioni.* Rome: Laterza, 1992.

Lewis, Michael Jonathan Taunton. *Surveying Instruments of Greece and Rome.* Cambridge: Cambridge University Press, 2001.

Litchfield, R. Burr. *Emergence of a Bureaucracy: The Florentine Patricians, 1530–1790.* Princeton, NJ: Princeton University Press, 1986.

Lo Basso, Luca. *Uomini da remo: Galee e galeotti del Mediterraneo in età moderna.* Milan: Selene, 2004.

Lowe, K. J. P., and Trevor Dean. *Crime, Society and the Law in Renaissance Italy.* Cambridge: Cambridge University Press, 1994.

Lowry, Martin. "The Reform of the Council of Ten, 1582–3: An Unsettled Problem?" *Studi Veneziani* 13 (1971): 275–310.

Marino, John A., ed. *Early Modern Italy, 1550–1796*. Oxford: Oxford University Press, 2002.

———. "On the Shores of Bohemia: Recovering Geography." In *Early Modern History and the Social Sciences: Testing the Limits of Braudel's Mediterranean*, edited by John A. Marino, 3–32. Kirksville, MO: Truman State University Press, 2002.

Mattingly, Garrett. *Renaissance Diplomacy*. Boston: Houghton Mifflin, 1955.

McNeill, John R. *The Mountains of the Mediterranean World: An Environmental History*. Cambridge: Cambridge University Press, 1992.

McNeill, William H. *Venice, the Hinge of Europe, 1081–1797*. Chicago: University of Chicago Press, 1974.

Moore, Jason W. "Capital, Territory, and Hegemony Over the *Longue Durée*." *Science and Society* 65 (2001): 476–85.

———. "Capitalism as World-Ecology: Braudel and Marx on Environmental History." *Organization and Environment* 16, no. 4 (Dec. 2003): 431–58.

———. "The Crisis of Feudalism: An Environmental History." *Organization and Environment* 15 (Sept. 2002): 296–317.

Mueller, Reinhold C., and Frederic C. Lane. *The Venetian Money Market: Banks, Panics, and the Public Debt, 1200–1500*. Baltimore: John Hopkins University Press, 1997.

Parker, Geoffrey, and Lesley M. Smith. *The General Crisis of the Seventeenth Century*. 2nd ed. New York: Routledge, 1997.

Pattaro, Giuseppe. *Il fiume Piave: Studio idrologico-storico*. Treviso, Italy: Camillo Pavan Editore, 1993.

Pieri, Piero. *Il rinascimento e la crisi militare italiana*. Turin: Einaudi, 1952.

Pitteri, Mauro. "Beni comunali nella terraferma veneta." *Annali Veneti* 1 (1984): 133–38.

———. *I mulini del Sile: Quinto, Santa Cristina al Tiveron e altri centri molitori attraverso la storia di un fiume*, 1988.

Pounds, Norman John Greville. *An Historical Geography of Europe*. Cambridge: Cambridge University Press, 1990.

Pullan, Brian S. *Crisis and Change in the Venetian Economy in the Sixteenth and Seventeenth Centuries*. London: Methuen, 1968.

———. *Rich and Poor in Renaissance Venice: The Social Institutions of a Catholic State, to 1620*. Cambridge, MA: Harvard University Press, 1971.

Pyne, Stephen J. *Vestal Fire: An Environmental History, Told through Fire, of Europe and Europe's Encounter with the World*. Seattle: University of Washington Press, 1997.

Romano, Dennis. *Patricians and Popolani: The Social Foundations of the Venetian Renaissance State*. Baltimore: Johns Hopkins University Press, 1986.

Ruggiero, Guido. *Violence in Early Renaissance Venice*. New Brunswick, NJ: Rutgers University Press, 1980.

Sahlins, Peter. *Boundaries: The Making of France and Spain in the Pyrenees*. Berkeley: University of California Press, 1989.

Schama, Simon. *Landscape and Memory*. New York: A.A. Knopf, 1995.

Schulz, Juergen. *La cartografia tra scienza e arte: Carte e cartografi nel rinascimento italiano*. Modena: F. C. Panini, 1990.

———. "Urbanism in Medieval Venice." In *City States in Classical Antiquity and Medieval Italy*, edited by Anthony Molho, Kurt Raaflaub, and Julia Emlen, 419–46. Stuttgart: F. Steiner, 1991.

Secco, Alberto. "Relazioni veneto-ottomane e politica delle costruzioni navali nell'arsenale di Venezia dalla pace di Passarowitz a quella di Aquisgrana (1718–1749)." *Navis* 3 (2006): 89–112.

Seligman, Avi Perevolotsky, and G. No'am. "Role of Grazing in Mediterranean Rangeland Ecosystems." *Bioscience* 12 (1998).

Sereni, Emilio. *History of the Italian Agricultural Landscape*. Translated by R. Burr Litchfield. Princeton, NJ: Princeton University Press, 1997.

Sievert, James. *The Origins of Nature Conservation in Italy*. Bern: Peter Lang, 2000.

Slicher van Bath, B. H. *The Agrarian History of Western Europe*. New York: St. Martin's Press, 1964.

Sorlin, Sverker, and Paul Warde. "The Problem of the Problem of Environmental History: A Re-Reading of the Field." *Environmental History* 12 (2007): 107–30.

Spada, Guido. *Il gran bosco da remi del Cansiglio nei provvedimenti della repubblica di Venezia*. Rome: Corpo forestale dello stato, 1995.

Stefinlongo, Giovanni Battista. *Pali e palificazioni della laguna di Venezia*. Sottomarina di Chioggia, Italy: Leggio, 1994.

Stella, Aldo. "La proprietà ecclesiastica nella repubblica di Venezia dal secolo XV al XVII." *Nuova Rivista Storica* 42 (1958): 50–77.

Stergulc, Fabio. "Foreste e boschi del Friuli dalla preistoria ai nostri giorni." In *Foreste, uomo, economia nel Friuli Venezia Giulia: Pubblicazione edita dal Museo friulano di storia naturale in occasione della mostra, dicembre 1986–dicembre 1987*, 147–68. Udine, Italy: Missio, 1987.

Stoddard, Charles Hatch, and Glenn M. Stoddard. *Essentials of Forestry Practice*. 4th ed. New York: Wiley, 1987.

Stumpo, Enrico. "Problemi di ricerca: Per la storia della proprietà ecclesiastica fra quattro e cinquecento." *Critica Storica* 1 (1976): 62–80.

Susmel, Lucio. "Artificio e naturalità degli attuali ecosistemi forestali." *Quaderni di San Giorgio* 34 (1973): 367–94.

Tenenti, Alberto. *Piracy and the Decline of Venice, 1580–1615*. Berkeley and Los Angeles: University of California Press, 1967.

———. *Venezia e il senso del mare: Storia di un prisma culturale dal XIII al XVIII secolo*. Milan: Guerini, 1999.

Tenenti, Alberto, and Ugo Tucci, eds. *Temi: Il mare*. Vol. 12 of *Storia di Venezia*. Rome: Istituto della enciclopedia italiana, 1991.

Thirgood, J. V. *Man and the Mediterranean Forest: A History of Resource Depletion*. New York: Academic Press, 1981.

Totman, Conrad D. *The Lumber Industry in Early Modern Japan*. Honolulu: University of Hawaii Press, 1995.

Tyrrell, Ian. *True Gardens of the Gods*. Berkeley and Los Angeles: University of California Press, 1999.

Ventrice, Pasquale. *La discussione sulle maree: Tra astronomia, meccanica e filosofia nella cultura veneto-padovana del cinquecento*. Venice: Istituto veneto di scienze, lettere ed arti, 1989.

Ventura, Angelo. "Il dominio di Venezia nel quattrocento." In *Florence and Venice: Comparisons and Relations*, edited by Sergio Bertelli, Nicolai Rubinstein, and Craig Hugh Smyth, 1:167–90. Florence: La nuova Italia, 1979.

Vernet, Jean-Louis. *L'homme et la forêt méditerranéenne*. Paris: Éditions Errance, 1997.

Warde, Paul. "Law, the 'Commune,' and the Distribution of Resources in Early Modern German State Formation." *Continuity and Change* 17 (2002): 183–211.

———. "Subsistence and Sales: The Peasant Economy of Wurttemberg in the Early Seventeenth Century." *Economic History Review* 59 (2006): 289–319.

White, K. D. *Roman Farming: Aspects of Greek and Roman Life*. Ithaca, NY: Cornell University Press, 1970.

White, Lynn. *Medieval Technology and Social Change*. Oxford: Oxford University Press, 1962.

Wickham, Chris. *The Mountains and the City: The Tuscan Apennines in the Early Middle Ages*. Oxford: Oxford University Press, 1988.

Williams, Michael. "Imperialism and Deforestation." In *Ecology and Empire: Environmental History of Settler Societies*, edited by Tom Griffiths and Libby Robin, 169–81. Seattle: University of Washington Press, 1997.

Zoccoletto, Giorgio. *I quattro fiumi: Sile, Zero, Dese, Marzenego*. Mestre, Italy: Centro studi storici, 2005.

Zupko, Ronald, and Robert Laures. *Straws in the Wind: Medieval Urban Environmental Law, the Case of Northern Italy*. Boulder, CO: Westview, 1996.

chestnut, location and distribution of, 32, 35, 39

Chioggia, war of, 16, 20

Clavich, Paolo, 291

Collegio: appointment of forest guardians, 162; and community property, 132; Marco Cornaro's appearance before, 65–68, 73–75, 87–89; knowledge of mainland, 57; and market restrictions, 89; *provveditori alle legne* and, 148, 165; regulation of firewood market, 154–56; and 1792 reform, 269

Comagno (forest), 282, 284

commons: tragedy of the, 177; wild, 251

community property. See *beni comunali; beni comuni*

condotta (five-year contract): effect on timber supply, 260; manipulation of, 169, 172, 258; proposed reform of, 267; social conflict over, 291, 293–94, 296; terms of, 164–65

Conegliano: as minor jurisdiction, 118, 159; as source of beech timber, 38

Convertite, Santa Maria delle, 193

coppice, 67, 150; as land management technique, 49; and Venetian timber shortages, 52

Coppo, Jacopo (*provveditore alle legne*), 91

Coppola, Francis Ford, 294

Cornaro, Alvise (Paduan nobleman), 313n. 26

Cornaro, Marco (*provveditore alla giustizia vecchia*): and Collegio, 74–75; commission of, 63–64, 86; descriptive mapping of forests, 209, 226–27; election of, 61; on environmental change, 138, 141, 147; and expertise, 157, 199; on natural order, 278; on public good, 106–7, 121; recommendations rejected, 77–80, 88; scope of survey, 92, 153–54; treatise of, 58–60, 64–74, 86–88

Cornua, Mattio (smuggler), trial of, 174–75, 177–78

Cornuda (forest), 244

corpi territoriali, 128

Corramexin, Bernardo (timber merchant), 164, 165

corvée. See *angarie*

Council of Ten: and Cansiglio ban, 142–43; and *condotta* contracts, 164; court cases, 121, 130–31, 291, 293, 298–99, 301; creation of state forests, 94–95, 97, 109–11, 124–29, 176–77; vs. forest bureaucracy, 96, 124, 152, 167–70, 173–74, 204; interference in firewood trade, 136–39; legislation passed by, 114, 119, 122, 135–36, 139–41, 149–50, 166; licenses issued by, 111, 189; vs. mainland elites, 151; petitions to, 83, 258; protection of community property, 132–35; protection of Montello, 108; reports to, 141–42, 144–46, 176, 181–82, 186–88, 190–97, 200, 201, 208–11, 223, 241, 246, 265, 274, 280–82; surveys commissioned by, 153–54, 158–63, 183–84, 203; and timber harvests, 166–67, 170–73, 205; timber requisitions, 207–8; *tolpi* requisitions, 150–51

coupe, 233–37; Cansiglio, 142–43; in community forests, 49–50, 112, 114–15; as conservation strategy, 50, 273; laws governing, 114–15, 122; in state forests, 104; surveys of, 154; and timber shortages, 120–21; variations in number and size of, 67; wartime abuse of, 128

degano, 161

Digges, Thomas, 203, 206

diritto di riserva: applied to individual trees, 187; as Cadore precedent, 101–3; Council of Ten use of, 109–11, 125–27, 129, 177; legal definition, 263; as Montello precedent, 103–7, 151; *provveditori sopra boschi* use of, 161

Dobiacco, 43, 101

Dolfin, Bertuccio (*provveditore sopra boschi*), 108

Duhamel de Monceau, 285–86

Duodo, Francesco (*provveditore all'arsenale*), Cansiglio report of, 141–43; and oarmakers' report, 203; rhetorical excess of, 280, 287

elm, 26, 32, 39; location and distribution of, 35, 41; in mixed stands, 67;

elm (*continued*)
theft of, 178; use in naval construction, 54
Emo, Leonardo (*provveditore sopra i denari*), 132–33
Evelyn, John, 284–87

Feltre, 118; and firewood trade, 125; as minor jurisdiction, 159
Filarete, 71
fines: on alienation of commons, 112; on clearing commons, 187–88, 191–93, 212; and firewood market, 81–82, 84, 87, 115, 121, 155–56; on illegal oak harvesting, 174–76; in lieu of taxes, 79; on lost oars, 52–53; and timber trade, 164; on violating Montello ban, 107
fir: demand for, 26; harvesting of, 168; location and distribution of, 34–36, 42–43; private suppliers of, 166; rhetoric concerning, 24; sources of, 28, 30, 32; state reserves of, 94, 100–103, 150; supply problems, 98; surplus of, 136, 138; surveys of, 160; transportation of, 43–45; uses in naval construction, 22, 54
fire, bans of: in agriculture, 112, 115, 124; in proximity of state forests, 140
firewood: in Belluno, 42; boatmen, taxes on, 88–90; in *boschi pubblici*, 146–47, 150; in Cansiglio, 143; consumption, 15, 33, 122; demand, 2, 6, 21–22, 26, 29–30, 48–49, 136; and expertise, 91–93, 149, 154–55, 198–200; in Feltre, 125; in Friuli, 40, 44, 153; in Isonzo region, 32; in Istria, 41, 169–70; legislation concerning, 54, 138; licenses to harvest, 105, 110–13; market for, 155–57; and market restrictions, 80–82, 100; merchant managers, 90–91, 148; in Piave region, 28, 38; political importance of, 123–24, 151–52, 163; pollarding for, 106; prices, 29, 52, 137; reserves, 94–95, 134; shortages, 24, 45, 83–84, 86, 90, 121; smuggling, 175; and supplier contracts, 163–65; suppliers, foreign, 7; and tax farmers, 82–83; theft of, 1;

transport, ease of, 30, 93, 123; warehouses, public, 97, 113, 152, 161
—harvesting: from community forests, 49–51, 96, 129, 133; finances, 127–28; planning, 104, 120; season for, 46–47
—surveys, 84–86; in Bon, 153–54, 157–59, 167; in Cornaro, 58–61, 63–70, 147, 227; in Mocenigo, 4
flooding, 67–68, 208, 278; infrastructure to control, 6–7, 150, 254–55
frigates, 2, 324n. 7; construction of, 208, 255, 259
Friuli: description of, 282; and firewood trade, 29, 52–53, 65, 124, 146, 153, 158, 163; and forest legislation, 138, 269; land tenure in, 39–40; *Luogotenente* of, 171–72, 179–80; pastoralism in, 50; population and economy of, 103–4, 292, 294; surveys of, 34, 133, 144, 162, 182–86, 206, 208, 212; and timber trade, 27, 34–35, 41, 44, 92–93, 164; Venetian conquest of, 16, 76
Fuliero, ZuanBattista, trial of, 175

galleys, 18, 30–31, 53; construction of, 54, 104, 116, 208, 255; oars for, 22, 52–53, 239; service in, as punishment, 112, 173–74; for state convoys, 125–26; and timber towing, 34, 36–37, 40
Garzoni, Francesco (*provveditore al comune*), 58–59, 63
Garzoni, Francesco (*provveditore sopra il fatto delle legne e boschi*), 83
Garzoni, Giovanni (*provveditore sopra boschi*): and *bollo*, 189–90; commission of, 183; and expertise, 182, 184–86, 200–202, 222–24, 268, 270–73; and forest guardians, 162; and forests in Piave region, 164; leniency towards peasant timber thieves, 174, 175–76, 212; letters of, 144–47, 181–82, 196–97; moral rhetoric of, 280–81, 283–85; and narrative maps, 227–28, 231–32; recommendations rejected, 190–94; and reform of timber licensing, 188–89; and timber theft, 173–74, 176, 185–88, 265. See also *Catastico Garzoni*
Gavardo, Pietro, trial of, 290–302